EX LIBRIS

RELIGION AND CULTURE SERIES

Joseph Husslein, S.J., Ph.D., General Editor

CHRISTIAN LIFE AND WORSHIP

I am the Vine; you are the Branches.

CHRISTIAN LIFE
AND
WORSHIP

REV. GERALD ELLARD, S.J., Ph.D.

PROFESSOR OF LITURGY
ST. LOUIS UNIVERSITY SCHOOL OF DIVINITY

Illustrations by
ADÉ DE BETHUNE

THE BRUCE PUBLISHING COMPANY
MILWAUKEE

Imprimi potest: P. A. BROOKS, Praepositus Provincialis, Prov. Missourianae, S.J.
Nihil obstat: H. B. RIES, Censor librorum
Imprimatur: ✠ SAMUEL A. STRITCH, Archiepiscopus Milwaukiensis

November 20, 1939

Revised and Enlarged
(Sixth Printing — 1946)

TO THE CATHOLIC COLLEGIANS OF AMERICA

MEN AND WOMEN

OF IDEALS, AND ARDOR, AND TRAINING

FOR LEADERSHIP,

INTO WHOSE HANDS THE CAUSE OF CHRIST

IN AMERICA PASSES,

THIS BOOK IS AFFECTIONATELY

DEDICATED

30484

PREFACE BY THE GENERAL EDITOR

THE modern Liturgical Movement dates its inception from the Pontificate of Pope Pius X. Drawing vitality from the liturgical interest and the liturgical devotion fostered by the Holy See, it rapidly developed and spread throughout the world. Its growth has been particularly rich and manifold in various parts of Europe.

In the United States it sprang up more slowly, but proved to be contemporary with another movement hardly less significant, the agitation for a more vital and dynamic presentation of religion in schools and colleges.

That these two movements should have greatly influenced each other is not surprising. As an immediate result the distinctive characteristic of the American Liturgical Movement came to be the strong appeal made by it to the student body. School after school, college after college opened wide its doors to give it welcome, and liturgical courses were inaugurated in the college Religion departments.

One thing only was still wanting, a suitable text, which under the circumstances was imperatively needed. This has now been supplied in an adequate manner. Author and publisher have vied with each other in contributing their best efforts to make of this volume a worthy offering to so high a cause. Presumably it is the first general textbook for collegiate use that has appeared in this field, and should, therefore, mark a new era in liturgical studies within our colleges.

But its utility is not to be restricted to the classroom only. The need of just such a book is too universal and has been too widely felt. The present volume is well adapted for popular as well as academic use. While scholarly in substance it is written in a truly popular vein, serving for inspiration and edification no less than for solid instruction, and making easily intelligible the general fundamental truth of Christ's Mystic Body and all the rich significance of the Church's liturgy. In addition, the reader will here come into direct touch with the Church's ritual for the various Sacraments, the entire Ordinary of the Mass, and even one complete canonical hour from the Breviary. All these are given in excellent English renditions, with copious and most informative annotations.

Of particular interest, too, in this volume, are the numerous citations gathered from monuments and documents of the early Church, the frequently recurring patristic testimonies, and the carefully chosen illustrations giving ocular demonstration of the Church's unity throughout the ages, her catholicity and apostolicity, no less than her unfailing holiness.

The author, it may here be noted, has for years stood in intimate contact with the Liturgical Movement both in Europe and America. In the latter country his liturgical activities began with the inception of the Movement there. He has served as associate editor of the *Orate Fratres* since the date of its first issue, in 1926, and has contributed articles to the leading clerical reviews.

In particular, however, he spent the years from 1927 to 1931 at the various European centers where progress along these lines had been most advanced, devoting his time to the study of liturgy and the Liturgical Movement. As a teacher, lecturer, and writer he has steadily sought to convey to others a true sense of the beauty and significance of the Church's corporate worship. Strictures that in time past have justly been leveled against extreme views and extravagant practices that have come to be connected in the minds of many with the Liturgical Movement, will find no application in the present volume. The best of things are open to abuses. We need but mention the most sacred of all mysteries, the Eucharist itself. Correction must come through inculcation of true ideals.

Fundamental in the present study is the concept of the Mystic Body, whereof Christ is the Head and we are the members, and where every single unit is vitalized and energized by the life-giving streams of the divine Blood flowing to us through the channels of the Sacraments, and making, as St. Paul says, the life of Jesus manifest in our very bodies. "It is no longer I that live; it is Christ that liveth in me," we too, may exclaim with the Apostle, as the living Christ more and more possesses us and we are filled "unto all the fullness of God," made partakers of His divine nature.

These, indeed, are truths than which nothing can be more sublime. And nothing can better reward us than bravely to wrestle with them, as Jacob with the Angel, until we, too, shall master them and they shall bless our lives.

But what in a special manner has been emphasized by the author is the profound social character of all this doctrine. Incorporated into the Mystic Body of Christ, we are at the same time, and as a necessary consequence, made "concorporeal" with one another. Such is the exquisite expression first used by St. Cyril of Alexandria and later effectively applied by St. Thomas. How can Christians who have once grasped this wonderful truth fail to love one another, to do good to one another, to serve for the love of Christ even those who as yet are only potential members of the Mystic Body!

Another fundamental fact is next dwelt upon. Man realizes in his very nature an impulse for worship. Not satisfied with internal acts alone, it seeks outward expression, and that in a manner also which is public and social. Most fully to comply with this the Church has given us her own beautiful and majestic liturgy, which marvelously answers the cravings of mind and heart for corporate worship.

Let me state briefly what in substance is the author's own summary of this subject, whose treatment naturally constitutes the major portion of his book.

In glorious review we here behold the Church's hierarchical priesthood; the inexhaustible wealth of her ceremonial; the almost limitless application of nature and art to divine worship; her sevenfold Sacramental system; her one Sacrifice, incessantly offered over all the earth, on uncounted altars, as the mystic and unbloody repetition of the Sacrifice itself of the Cross; her vast hosts of the Blessed, "the endless procession of Christ-in-His-brethren walking before us," with the Queen of all the Saints in garments embroidered with variety; and at the head of all, the sceptered Christ, King of kings and Lord of lords, with Heart meek and humble, and filled with love for us, Christ who is "all in all."

What a wonderful study, then, Catholicism presents when seen from the viewpoint of Christ's Mystic Body; what a sublime wealth it unfolds of public and corporate worship! And all this the author has set forth in clear-cut language, with an enthusiasm that is contagious, and a richness of illustration that is equally attractive and convincing.

To the student in the classroom, and to the reader in the larger school of life the volume is heartily recommended.

JOSEPH HUSSLEIN, S.J., PH.D.,

General Editor, Religion and Culture Series

Feast of St. Ignatius, 1933
St. Louis, Missouri

AUTHOR'S FOREWORD

THE truths, whereby it is intended that all men should attain salvation, and come to the knowledge that alone can make them happy, were entrusted by Christ to His Church with the bidding, "Keep the deposit." In preserving this faith safe and undiminished, the Church knows how, in every age and in the presence of the most diverse world conditions, to set out her precious doctrines in the manner best calculated, then and there, to win favor and credence. Everywhere and always she has been able to inspire men even to sell all things in order to purchase this pearl of great price. The Church is ever ready to meet the needs of the day, as one of her great sons phrased it, by teaching after a new manner, yet without ever teaching new things.

With each year it becomes increasingly clear that in our age the "new manner" in which Catholicism is being presented, both to its own adherents and to the world at large, is through her social organization and mission. As in course of time an outmoded social order collapses, the Church prays to be allowed to rebuild it on the Christian principles of justice and charity. Thus the multiple social relationships of Christians to one another and to non-Christians are being studied from every angle, and inculcated with every means modern civilization furnishes for the spread of truth. Now, the doctrine most capable of supplying a complete synthesis of the social implications of Christianity is that of "the Mystical Body of Christ." It is thus coming about that this very doctrine is at the present moment fast attracting the special attention of Catholics in their religious thinking.

Again, the corporate worship of the Church, not as a body of incidental knowledge, but as a living system of social sanctification, furnishes in turn the ideal presentation of the Mystical Body. In a masterful analysis of "Catholicism in the Nineteenth Century and at the Beginning of the Twentieth," an English author finds that all the special manifestations of Catholicism at present "fall under a general heading; namely, the corporate activity of the Church as the Mystical Body and renovator of society." In speaking of our Eucharistic worship, he goes on:

> Moreover, all that has been said so far about the social mission of the Church reaches its apogee here. The visible unity of the Church is manifested and defined in the liturgy of the Redemptive sacrifice, the social unity in Communion and the theological interpretation of this corporate life in the doctrine of the Mystical Body and sanctifying grace. . . .
>
> The whole trend of the prayer and behavior of the Church [nowadays] is dictated by the image called up by Christ of the vine and the vine-branches, toward that unit of the Head with the members, which has always been the secret of the Church, but is now being increasingly realized and manifested.[1]

Keeping pace with this growing realization of recent years, our educational curricula, from elementary grades to the universities and seminaries, are rapidly undergoing revision to include formal study of the *Mystical Body as mirrored in corporate worship*. Moreover, in that happiest token of a cultural growth among us, adult education, the subject of worship plays an ever increasing part in the work of study clubs, lecture groups, evidence guilds, round-table discussions, radio broadcasts, and the like. This widespread study of the liturgy does not aim, as do so many similar movements, at keeping abreast of an interesting, modern, intellectual development: it has the deep spiritual purpose of enabling one to share more intelligently and more fruitfully in the service of corporate worship in which our lives are necessarily lived.

But here is a striking fact, illustrative of the basic oneness of the whole Catholic life. While studying and reducing to practice the social implications of corporate *worship*, we find we thus possess ourselves of the key to so many modern problems of corporate *work*. Press reports constantly testify that numerous local, regional, or national Catholic organizations, formed to wrestle with the most varied problems, social or economic, literary or artistic, all find in this study of the liturgy the source of their proper motivation, the solution in large measure of their several problems. The masterful historical syntheses of Christopher Dawson have made clear, how in the past "every culture is a religion culture": this development of our own day furnishes an example that *our* culture is a religion culture, and that the integrating element of culture is cult.

---

[1] M. C. D'Arcy, *The Life of the Church* (New York: Sheed & Ward, 1932), pp. 320–22.

Thus while studying the liturgy in order to worship God more perfectly, we find we have come to know at close range, and find our places in, and play our several personal roles in, the Mystical Body at Prayer. In this light it is then possible to function as members "knit and compacted" into the same Body at external work, for which the modern name is Catholic Action. These ideas are set out with cameo sharpness in the epigrammatic words of our Supreme Pontiff: "What our age needs is communal prayer," and "The first element of Catholic Action is prayer." This study of the Mystical Body is the special apprehension of Catholicism proper to the twentieth century.

That this book may be a more serviceable tool for study-club groups, evidence guilds, and similar organizations, it will be found to contain abundant supplementary material. Besides a select bibliography, there will be found short reading lists in every chapter. Also certain allied subjects for discussion or further private reading along the lines of the chapter topics are there suggested. Lastly, the chapters themselves are terminated by some bit of documentation from original sources. In selecting these, as will be seen at a glance, the author's preferences have run steadily to the precious heirlooms of primitive Christianity. Several reasons have guided the writer here. There is, first, the universal and unfailing charm evoked by everything connected with the Church of the Apostles and the Martyrs. Again, the temper of the Christian life, resulting from the widespread consciousness of the social mission of the Church — the ideal aimed at in this book — finds its finest exemplar in the lives of the first Christian centuries. Lastly, if any group of men, then surely, as Cardinal Newman said, "the primitive Christians are to be trusted as witnesses of the genius of the Gospel system."

It will be noted that the New Testament quotations are cited, throughout, from the new and superior Westminster Version, now for the most part in print. Thus, passages long familiar in the Douay wordings are here found couched in somewhat different terms; but the superior intelligibility and the freshness of the Westminster renderings are ample warrants for adopting the newer translation. Longer citations are, as a rule, here broken into sense-lines, the advantages of which arrangement are so patent as to need no explanation.

The final and pleasant task remains of acknowledging assistance received while preparing the materials for this book. Almost every page has benefited by the discriminating touch of a brother, G. Augustine Ellard, S.J., Professor of Mystical Theology in St. Louis University. Permission to reproduce copyrighted matter was unstintingly given by many authors and publishers of America and Europe, as the frequent acknowledgments throughout the book will testify.

No small gratification was experienced when the publication of this book under the Religion and Culture aegis was arranged. That initial satisfaction, I am happy to state, has constantly increased, thanks to the wholehearted cooperation of the General Editor and the personnel of The Bruce Publishing Company. Their efforts enhance the value of the work.

May it find a warm welcome, and may it have its own share in forming Christ in the Christian of today!

GERALD ELLARD, S.J., PH.D.

The Presentation of Our Lady, 1933,
St. Mary's College, St. Marys, Kansas

PREFACE TO THE REVISED EDITION

SO CORDIAL was the welcome accorded this book seven years ago that its many known deficiencies have been a matter of acute embarrassment to me ever since. Minor inaccuracies and other blemishes were removed in successive printings, but the publication of this revision, long planned, has by force of circumstances been deferred to the present. Doubtless the delay has excellently served its purpose, for I saw the margins of my own classroom copy of the book gradually acquire scores of notations, many of them elaborated by the book's friends far and near. In particular the late scholar and apostle, August F. Schinner, D.D., sometime bishop of Spokane, spared himself no trouble to enhance the value of this work. By a happy inspiration, too, teachers across the country sent me the written criticisms and impressions of their classes. Most pupils and many teachers found the opening chapters of the first edition unmanageable, and these have been entirely recast now with a view of obviating the former difficulties. Apart from that, the changes introduced in revision have scarcely modified the original outlines. We trust they will be found to make for greater clarity and a more cogent documentation. In this connection one might note that in the former edition source readings were chosen almost exclusively from primitive Christian times: some students felt that documentation in a similar strain and running through the centuries right down to our own times would provide a stronger brief. Lastly, it was felt good in this edition to take more direct cognizance of the current American scene in the matters of active participation in corporate worship and the motivation of Catholic Action. The publisher is fortunate in having secured the services of Miss Bethune whose talent has lovingly translated the message of the script into noble and graphic beauty. The exacting tasks of seeing this through the press have been greatly lightened for me by the labors of Reverend Gilbert C. Peterson, S.J.

No book that has the things of God for its theme can be in any sense finished or complete, for, as the son of Sirach said long since,

> We shall say much and yet shall want words,
> but the sum of all our words is
> He is ALL.

Such as it is, may He deign to use it to His greater glory, and to the manifesting in America of an ensign for peoples near and far!

GERALD ELLARD, S.J., PH.D.

St. Marys, Kansas
The Manifestation (Epiphany)
of our Lord, January 6, 1940

CONTENTS

PREFACE BY THE GENERAL EDITOR vii

AUTHOR'S FOREWORD xi

PREFACE TO THE REVISED EDITION xv

CHAPTER

    I. ADULT CATHOLICISM AND A SECRET 1

        The limitations of childhood or adolescent knowledge of Catholicism are measured in terms of the special messages, which, by divine guidance, constituted the revelations most characteristic of St. Paul and St. John. The Church may be regarded as a Super-Sacrament.

    II. CATHOLICISM IS CHRIST BEING FULFILLED . . . 13

        The concept of the Church as the Mystical Body of Christ, one of St. Paul's favorite doctrines, is seen to be a teaching for which the Gospels furnished the content, and the Greco-Roman civilization, the metaphor of the head and members.

    III. GOD-LIFE SHARED WITH MAN 28

        What grace is, and how it works: the participation in the divine life a created super-life, with its own super-faculties, enabling the Christian to perform supernatural actions, and destined to culminate in the divine beatitude.

    IV. A LITURGIST FITTED TO OUR NEEDS 41

        The worship of God by Christians, unlike that of all other groups, is not direct, but through Christ, the one Liturgist, as Mediator between God and men, and to whose perfect homage all Christians are associated by becoming sharers in Christ's Priesthood.

    V. THE SOUL NATURALLY LITURGICAL 55

        Analysis of man's impulse to worship socially: an elemental law of being exercised in spontaneous and fairly uniform fashion, especially as regards the place of sacrifice in worship.

    VI. "THE SOUL NATURALLY CHRISTIAN" 67

        How Catholicism through the sacramentals, sacraments, and sacrifice preserved and elevated everything belonging to the

CHAPTER

native religious impulse of man, uniting all in a complete system of worship, wherein sanctifying processes are always linked to sense-objects.

VII. "COMMUNIONISM" AND THE BOND OF WORSHIP . 79

That the extraordinary social solidarity of the early Christians was based upon their conscious sharing with one another in the Eucharist is shown by apostolic and apologetic writings, by prayers, customs, and the like.

VIII. THE SACRIFICIAL CALENDAR 93

The dogmatic and moral purpose, the origin and development of feasts and feast-cycles.

IX. THE SETTING OF THE SACRIFICE 109

The significance of the altar as a representative of God: How the history of the altar mirrors successive stages of Eucharistic piety: Sacred vessels and vestments now in use.

X. HIGH MASS WITH ST. GREGORY THE GREAT . . . 124

The prominence of the corporate and sacrificial characteristics of Christian worship in the Roman manner, as illustrated by quotations from the extant ordinal of about Gregory's time.

XI. SACRIFICIAL-MINDEDNESS LARGELY LOST — AND FOUND 137

How the frequentation or abstention from Communion reacted on the popular sacrificial consciousness throughout the Church's history: present recovery of older points of view.

XII. HEIRS OF THE SYNAGOGUE 153

The Ante-Mass, or Mass of the Catechumens, seen to be the synagogue rites of Israel slightly modified and enlarged: rites Christ shared in every Sabbath.

XIII. THE MYSTERY OF FAITH 173

Historical development, dogmatic and liturgical exposition of the Offertory and Canon of the Roman Mass: offering of sacrifice as the highest function of the Christian life.

XIV. TABLE-GUESTS OF GOD 194

Communion as a natural complement of sacrifice in general, and Christian Sacrifice in particular: token of God's acceptance of the Gift; God's Gift-in-Return, and channel of Christ-life.

XV. THE MASS: NEW TIMES, NEW MODES 211

How public worship now fosters active, instead of merely passive, participation by the laity. The use of the missal, the spread of

CHAPTER

the Dialogue Mass, and the restoration of plainsong as typical phases of this change.

XVI. PRAYING WITH CHRIST 228
The worship of corporate prayer, in its origin, growth, and content; and its supreme social importance as the homage of Christ with and in His members.

COMPLINE FOR SUNDAYS 237
Text in English Translation of Compline for Sundays.

XVII. A CHRISTIAN BECAUSE CHRIST-ED 246
The incorporation into Christ a second "birth," a creative act, illustrated in teaching by rites of old catechumenate, and rites of present-day baptism.

THE RITE OF BAPTISM 253
Text in English translation of Baptismal Rites, with brief commentary.

XVIII. "RADIOACTIVE" CATHOLICS 265
The nature and abiding effects, importance and attendant circumstances of confirmation, the sacrament of Christian manhood.

THE RITE OF CONFIRMATION 273
Text in English translation of Confirmation Rites, with brief commentary.

XIX. OUR SUPERSUBSTANTIAL BREAD — EMMANUEL . 280
Holy Eucharist as a sacrament, with an interpretative study of the "uses" of this sacrament in the light of the history of Eucharistic adoration.

THE RITE OF HOLY EUCHARIST ADMINISTERED AS VIATICUM 288
Text in English translation of the Rites of Holy Eucharist administered as Viaticum.

XX. THE FATHER OF THE PRODIGAL 293
The dogmatic teaching concerning penance in the light of its historical variations in administration: social aspects of reparatory satisfaction.

THE RITE OF SACRAMENTAL ABSOLUTION 305
Text in English translation of the Rites of Sacramental Absolution, with brief commentary.

Chapter

XXI. A MYSTICAL BODY IN MINIATURE 309
The dignity of Christian wedlock in the light of St. Paul's teach-
ing that this is the same kind of union as between Christ and the
Church.

THE MARRIAGE RITE AS WITH THE NUPTIAL MASS 315
Text in English translation of the Marriage Ritual, with brief
commentary.

XXII. OTHER CHRISTS 323
The exalted prerogatives of those in holy orders; historical and
ritual commentary on certain striking features of the Ordination
Rites.

XXIII. THE HAND OF THE HEALER 336
Nature and effects of Extreme Unction; selected medieval usages
connected with this sacrament.

THE RITE OF LAST ANOINTING 343
Text in English translation of the Rite of Extreme Unction, with
brief commentary.

XXIV. FROM LIFE TO LARGER LIFE 353
The abundant consolations of the Church's rites for the departed,
as contrasted with the pagan attitude toward death: selections
from the Rites of Burial as illustrating the true sorrow of bereavement coupled with a firm belief in the life of bliss beyond.

EXTRACTS FROM THE RITES OF CHRISTIAN BURIAL . 361
Text in English translation of characteristic portions of the Rites
of Burial.

XXV. EMANCIPATING AND ENLISTING CREATION . . . 367
The rationale of all sacramentals, personal blessings, blessings of
homes, personal objects of home, and office; the function of
sacramentals in general as aids to sanctity, and the background
of the ideal Christian life.

XXVI. CHRISTOCRACY THROUGH LITURGY 379
View of the entire Church as a vast body in which the Christ-
germ is being reproduced in each individual: mutual interdepend-
ence of Christians "in growing into Christ"; Liturgy, the Mystical
Body at prayer, Catholic Action, the Mystical Body at work.

XXVII. IN RETROSPECT 391
Synthetic evaluation and co-ordination of the leading ideas of the
course: permanent gains, new bonds with Christ, new sense of

CHAPTER

fellowship with, and sense of responsibility toward, other Christians: the unifying concepts of Christ-life and Christ-work: nobility and dignity of working for Christ as "Christocrats."

SELECT BIBLIOGRAPHY 402

INDEX 407

PASSAGES OF HOLY WRIT 417

CHRISTIAN LIFE AND WORSHIP

CHRISTIAN LIFE AND WORSHIP

Chapter I

ADULT CATHOLICISM AND A SECRET

With milk I fed you,
not with solid food,
for you were not yet strong enough (I Cor. iii,2).

OST of us had as little to do with our becoming Catholics as with our being born into a given family, or holding citizenship in our nation. Early in our reasoning years we simply learned of these existing relationships. Just as naturally as we were taught to cherish parents and family in a unique manner, or to foster patriotism for our native land, so with equal spontaneity we grew into an attachment for Catholicism, as the dwelling place, so to speak, of God among men. In our earliest years we were grounded in its basic teachings, and this preliminary training was yearly expanded, somewhat like the annual rings of a tree's growth, in that each embodied the previous circuit and widened it ever so little all around. At adolescence we had learned, as we thought, all there was to know about the truths of faith, and had been inducted into the practice of its ordinary acts proper to our years. We were urged to hold steadfast to those teachings, and to be faithful to the practices learned. That is the training suitable to childhood. Like so much early training, it was largely a matter of storing the memory with truths that would only slowly and gradually take real root in the understanding, and so be a sufficient aid to the will. It is no one's fault that this childhood apprehension of religion, like childhood apprehension of anything else, is not deep: it is measured to the growing child. It is not meant to be the complete, but merely the preliminary part of one's religious education. The process of further education is, of course, largely a matter of using the known data in new associations and rela-

1

tionships. Higher mathematics studied in maturity can never dispense with the multiplication tables learned by rote in childhood, but in the matter of new associations goes far beyond any use of those tables possible to childhood. There is likewise what we may justly call the Catholicism studied in maturity, or, simply, adult Catholicism, which in corresponding fashion exceeds the shallows of the immature mind. Unfortunately few Catholics attain this mature understanding of their religion, because, in proportion to the full membership of the Church, so very few have the opportunity, as adults, to pursue this study in systematic, organized fashion. It is generally conceded that little systematic knowledge on the adult level is acquired by listening to sermons, even for a lifetime. For, to the majority of their hearers the preachers on Sundays could always say with St. Paul:

> We have much to say,
> and it is difficult to expound it . . .
> For whereas by this time ye ought to be teachers,
> ye still need someone to teach you
> the simplest elements of the oracles of God,
> and ye have become such that ye need milk,
> and not solid food.

Heb. v,11–14

But as collegians we are in the singularly privileged position of being able to

> pass over the initial teachings concerning Christ,
> and press on to their full development.

Heb, vi,1

What the Apostle in the same context calls the strong meat of fully developed doctrine can now enlarge the adolescent's apperception of revealed Truth:

> When I was a child,
> I spoke as a child,
> I felt as a child,
> I thought as a child,
> now that I am become man,
> I have made an end of childish ways.

I Cor. xiii,11,12

Elements of Christianity. It is not easy to characterize briefly and accurately this "elementary Catholicism" as distinguished from

> the breadth and length and height and depth

which St. Paul challenged his adult converts to explore. Perhaps it can be done by saying that the former is like a fair knowledge of Catholicism derived exclusively from the *Gospels* of *Matthew, Mark,* and *Luke* and the latter to a knowledge of Catholicism as mirrored also in *The Acts of the Apostles,* the *Epistles,* and *St. John's Gospel.* The first three Gospels, written roughly around the year 50, may be called a triple transcript of the preaching in which the *simplest elements* about Christ are given the chief emphasis. They show a Teacher, who speaks with authority from God, announcing truths of a future Church; they show a Saviour of tenderness and matchless sympathy for men, who died on a cross for man's salvation and the remission of our sins. *The Acts of the Apostles* picture Catholicism springing into existence in Pentecostal fire and spreading through that Circle of Lands on the shores of the Mediterranean, which the ancients called their universe. The *Epistles* of the New Testament, unlike the *Gospels of Matthew, Mark,* and *Luke,* are not the first elements of Christianity, but are addressed to those who have heard the Gospels. They are subsequent teachings and applications of Christianity. They came only when the elements, called milk by the Apostle, had prepared their hearers for a maturer presentation of the Good Tidings. Taking the full content of the former revelations for granted, they pass on to an *inner penetration* of the Sermon on the Mount, the Parables, and the Kingdom. Nothing in the early records is ever in least degree contravened or cast aside, but a luxuriant unfolding of inner verities replaces external features and detached historical facts. Those Gospels are a doorway, and St. Paul leads us over the threshold into the house of God on earth.

An Apostle's Great Secret. There is in St. Paul an inner, deeper knowledge of Catholicism, as we said, of which the more superficial Catholic may have scarcely an inkling. To neophytes, who were just a little wearied of their first elements, and longed for further knowledge, he could write:

> Among the [spiritually] *mature*
> we do speak of a wisdom . . .
> *the* wisdom of God [embodied] in a *mystery* . . .
> [Heretofore] I could not speak to you as spiritual men,
> but . . . as babes in Christ . . .

Heb. v,12

I Cor. ii,6

I Cor. iii,1

To quote Saint Paul
is to requote Jesus Christ.

(Saint John Chrysostom)

Here and elsewhere St. Paul speaks of a great "secret" entrusted to him. By divine guidance he emphatically preached to the growing churches a doctrine which was *not* emphasized in Matthew, Mark, and Luke. But Paul's secret shared the fate of so many secrets, in that it speedily became public. Indeed, his secret was not intended to be held back longer; as it was, the world had waited centuries for it:

> To establish you in *my* gospel,
> and in the preaching about Jesus Christ,
> in accordance with *His revelation of that mystery*
> *which in ages past was kept secret,*
> but now hath been made manifest. Rom. xvi,25,26

This passage in *Colossians* gives a summary formulation of the content of the secret:

> Now I rejoice in my sufferings on your behalf,
> and make up in my flesh
> what is lacking to the sufferings of Christ,
> on behalf of *His Body, which is the Church,*
> whereof I am become a minister.
> Such [is indeed] the command of God
> given me in *your* regard,
> to utter the *full* word of God *touching the mystery*
> which hath been hidden from former ages and generations,
> but it hath now been made manifest to His saints . . .
> to whom God hath willed to make known
> what is the wealth of the glory
> of this *mystery*
> for the *Gentiles,*
> which is Christ [*dwelling*] in you. Col. i,24–28

The "secret," the new "Gospel," the new "revelation," is that Christ dwells in the members of His Church, vivifying it into a living body. In brief, *Christ dwells in us.*

Secret Becomes Sacrament and Mystery. When translators rendered St. Paul's *Letters* into Latin, they sometimes put "sacrament" for his secret, and sometimes "mystery." Each term brings out a part of his meaning; together they lay bare the secret, on which, as he reminds us, his special emphasis was laid by divine guidance. If we substitute these two words in the passage from *Colossians* given just above, St. Paul's thought is this: *Christ dwells within His Church making us a living body, and this is a great mystery, and this is a great sacrament.* Any Catholic, asked to define "mystery," would answer readily enough that it is a truth of revelation partly understandable by man, but in part beyond our limited comprehension. We still subscribe to the definition quoted by Father Gruden from St. John Chrysostom, enunciated fifteen hundred years ago: "We call a mystery that of which one aspect is seen and the other aspect is believed."[1] "Sacrament," too, has a meaning every child knows by heart: a visible sign, instituted by Christ, to give [invisible] grace. The seven Sacraments have in current usage so exclusively appropriated that word to themselves that it is now not applied to anything else. But St. Paul called the Church a sacrament. Surely the Church, which contains all the Sacraments, may very justly and accurately be called a sort of Super-Sacrament. No reality on earth more eminently fulfills the definition of being a visible sign, instituted by Christ, to confer grace. Well, then, to sum up: The Catholic Church is revealed to us as a living body, and this is a "mystery": That is, one aspect of the Church is seen, the other unseen; one aspect is understood; the other remains mysterious. And Catholicism is revealed to us as a "sacrament," a divinely instituted sign of invisible grace. With the mention of grace we come closer to the full measure of adult Catholicism.

In Epis. I ad Cor. Hom. VII

Eph. v,32

Life and Light and St. John. When the nascent Catholic Church had assimilated with divine help, and over a period of about forty years,

> things hard to understand [naturally],
> as our beloved brother Paul . . . hath written to you,
> in virtue of the wisdom given him,

II Pet. iii,16

the time was ripe for the final revealed formulation, that of St. John's *Gospel,* written that *our joy might be full!*

I John i,4

---

[1] J. C. Gruden, *The Mystical Christ* (St. Louis: Herder, 1936), p. 59.

That which was from the beginning . . .
that which we beheld,
and our hands handled,
in regard of the WORD of LIFE:　　　　　　I John i,1–3
In Him was LIFE,
and the LIFE was the LIGHT of men . . .
Of His fulness we have all received,
and grace on grace.　　　　　　　　　　John i,4–16

Life, light, and grace in Christ: St. John portrays on one and the same canvas the first elements of the earlier Gospels, that is, the Christ of history, and the fuller developments of St. Paul, that is, the Christ of "mystery," where everything is dominated by the indwelling within us of the LIFE of God:

The glory which Thou hast given Me,
I have given them,
that they may be one,
as We are one,
I in them,
and Thou in Me,
that they may be perfected in unity . . .
in order that *the love*
wherewith Thou hast loved Me,
may be in them,
and I in them.　　　　　　　　　　　John xvii,23–26

This love, wherewith the Father loved the Son, is, as we shall see, the Person of the Holy Ghost. If St. Paul stresses chiefly that the Church is the Body of Christ, St. John further discloses that within that Body Catholics have in some way a share in God-life. These two doctrines are the hallmarks of adult Catholicism. Collegiate study of religion can begin in no better way than by a first grappling with them.

Christ of History, Christ of Mystery. All Catholics are taught to say the *Apostles' Creed* daily, but the "catechism" Catholic, as we may call him, repeats the statements of the *Creed* about Christ without going beyond the synoptists' history, or penetrating into the mystery. His birth, passion, death, resurrection, ascension into heaven, and future coming as Judge, state this Catholic's faith in Christ's redeeming function. To the mature Catholic, Christ is all that and besides is the Word Incarnate extended to the whole Catholic Church, making this a living, mysterious body, in which He lives, and grows, and attains fulfillment. Besides being King and Lord, Divine Exemplar, Christ is within us, sanctifying us and uniting us to the Father through the working of the Holy Spirit. Listen to St. Augustine, and see how the great Bishop of Hippo expands the *first elements* of the Creed:

Heb. vi,1

> Our Lord Jesus Christ is as one whole perfect Man, both Head and Body: We acknowledge the Head in that Man, who was born of the Virgin Mary, suffered under Pontius Pilate, was buried, arose from the dead, ascended into Heaven, sitteth at the right hand of the Father, whence we wait His coming as Judge of the living and the dead. This is the Head of the Church . . . Christ's Body, of which Christ is the Head.

In Ps. XC, Serm. II

Few have phrased this central doctrine of adult Catholicism as felicitously as Father D'Arcy in the words:

> The heart of the Christian mystery is this, that the Christ, who was both God and man, has determined to extend His life from the terrain of Galilee and Jerusalem to the ends of the earth, and His span of days from thirty odd years to the end of time; and He is to bear the same relation, as far as that is possible, to human individuals which His divine nature bore to His own body and soul. There is one fundamental difference, of course; His own soul and body had no human personality, whereas we, no matter how close we live in the divine life, remain persons, able to say: "no longer I but Thou!"[2]

I Cor. iii,23 **Ye Are Christ's.** We are Catholics. How did we become so? The answers given to that question might be an index of our understanding of adult Catholicism. One might conceivably compare becoming a Catholic with joining a club, or fraternity, or social grouping. That is simplicity itself: Some idea is proposed, accepted, this acceptance signified in simple fashion, as a payment, or signature, and the matter is accomplished. But in becoming a Catholic, one does not accept, one *is accepted*:

---

[2]M. C. D'Arcy, *The Life of the Church* (New York: Sheed and Ward, 1933), p. 19.

Ye have not chosen Me,
but I have chosen you.   John xv,16

Another might suggest that becoming a Catholic is like becoming a naturalized citizen, which is a much more difficult matter. St. Paul calls his converts newly enfranchised citizens:

Ye were at that time Christless . . .
But now ye are no longer strangers and foreigners,
but ye are fellow-citizens of the saints.   Eph. ii,13,19

The context of this quotation might possibly suggest yet another answer, that being accepted as a Catholic is like being named to membership in what we call the official family of the President:

Ye are . . . members of the household of God.   Eph. ii,19

Even so, membership in some capacity in a large official household is far from the same as being *adopted* legally and socially into the President's family circle. Well, every Catholic knows that our Baptism effects in us a *sonship of adoption*. In brief, one who has studied adult Catholicism, Eph. i,5 would be inclined to say: "One does not 'join' Catholicism: *Christ takes hold of a man and implants him into Himself*, and he is then a Catholic. Henceforth he lives in permanent, personal, *vital* relationship with Christ." Baptism is a rite, as we shall see, whereby man is embodied into Christ. Once baptized into Christ's Body, his life is supposed to be a I Cor. xii,13 *constant growing into* Christ:

Thus we shall be no longer children . . .
Rather we shall hold the truth in charity,
and *grow in all things into Him*
Who is the Head, Christ.   Eph. iv,14,15
Unto the building up of the Body of Christ,
till we all attain . . .
to the full knowledge of the Son of God,
to the perfect man,
the full measure of the stature of Christ.   Eph. iv,12,13

This corporate Catholicism of maturity will be studied in this book, but not so much directly, as by the indirect avenue leading through the acts of corporate worship.

Summary. Much deeper than in the "catechism" religion of childhood and adolescence, the Catholic Church is revealed to the mature mind as a mysterious Super-Sacrament, as it were, which Holy Writ calls a body, the soul of which is the Holy Spirit.

First-Century Source Material

(From "Letter of Pope Clement I" to the Church of Corinth on the occasion of schism in about the year 90.)

The great cannot exist without the small, nor the small without the great; there is a certain mixture among them all, and herein lies the advantage. Let us take our body; the head is nothing without the feet, likewise the feet are nothing without the head; the smallest members of our body are necessary and valuable to the whole body, but all work together and are united in a common subjection to preserve the whole body (xxxvii).

. . . Why are there strife and passion and divisions and schisms and war among you? Or have we not one God, and one Christ and one Spirit of grace poured out upon us? And is there not one calling in Christ? Why do you divide and tear asunder the members of Christ, and raise up strife against our own body, and reach such a pitch of madness as to forget that we are members one of another? . . . Your schism has turned aside many, and has cast many into discouragement, many to doubt, all of us to grief; and your sedition continues (xlvi).

Eph. iv,4–6

Take up the *Epistle* of the blessed Paul the Apostle. What did he first write to you at the beginning of his preaching? With true inspiration he charged you concerning himself and Cephas and Apollos, because even then you had made yourselves partisans. But that partisanship entailed less guilt upon you; for you were partisans of Apostles of high reputation, and of a man approved by them. But now consider who they are who have perverted you, and have lessened the respect due to your famous love for the brethren. It is a shameful report, beloved, extremely shameful, and unworthy of your training in Christ, that on account of one or two persons the steadfast and ancient church of the Corinthians is being disloyal to the presbyters . . . (xlvii).

Let him who has love for Christ, perform the commandments of Christ.

Who is able to explain the bond of the love of God? Who is sufficient to tell the greatness of its beauty? The height to which love lifts us is not to be expressed. Love unites us to God. "Love covereth a multitude of sins." Love beareth all things, is long suffering in all things. There is I Cor. xiii,4–7
nothing base, nothing haughty in love; love admits no schism, love makes no sedition, love does all things in concord. In love were all the elect of God made perfect. Without love is nothing well pleasing to God. In love did the Master receive us; for the sake of the love which He had toward us did Jesus Christ our Lord give His Blood by the will of God for us, and His Flesh for our flesh, and His life for our lives . . . (xlviii).

Topics for Further Discussion:

In the first three Gospels the word *Christ* (literally "anointed" and used as the equivalent of the Hebrew *Messiah*) is an adjective denoting a title, while in St. Paul and in St. John's Gospel it is used as a proper name. In the light of what we have said, do you see any significance in this fact?

The miracle of the loaves and the fishes is the only incident of the Public Life recorded in the first three Gospels (Matt. xvi, Mark vi, Luke ix) and *repeated* by St. John (vi). Try to assign a good reason for this singular fact.

In this chapter we have used the word *sacrament* in a wide sense: find three Postcommunion Prayers in your missal in which the word is used in the same broad sense.

St. Ambrose wrote a treatise with the title, *The Sacrament of the Incarnation of the Lord:* in what sense does he use the word *sacrament?*

A famous Cardinal, Berulle, once wrote, "Christ is Himself the major Sacrament." What does he mean by this?

Readings:

K. Adam, *The Son of God* (New York: Sheed and Ward, 1934), "The Sources for the Life of Jesus," pp. 49–86; "The Mental Stature of Jesus," pp. 87–133; "The Interior Life of Jesus," pp. 134–156.

R. H. Benson, *Christ in the Church* (St. Louis: Herder, 1913), "Introductory," pp. 3–34.

M. C. D'Arcy, ed., *The Life of the Church* (New York: Sheed and Ward, 1932), "The Faith of the Disciples," pp. 63–92.

R. Guardini, *The Church and the Catholic* (New York: Sheed and Ward, 1935), "The Awakening of the Church in the Soul," pp. 11–31.

C. Lattey, *The Atonement, Papers Read at the Summer School of Catholic Studies, Cambridge, 1931* (New York: Sheed and Ward, 1932), "In St. Paul's Epistles," pp. 47–81.

W. J. McGarry, *Paul and the Crucified* (New York: America Press, 1939), "We Preach Christ Crucified," pp. 29–69.

E. Mersch–J. R. Kelly, *The Whole Christ* (Milwaukee: Bruce, 1938), "St. John — Jesus Our Life," pp. 165–181; "St. John — Our Divine Life," pp. 182–195.

E. Mersch–D. F. Ryan, *Morality and the Mystical Body* (New York: Kenedy, 1939), "Religion, Christianity, Catholicism," pp. 3–18; "Christianity," pp. 19–37; "Catholicism," pp. 38–60.

E. I. Watkin, *The Catholic Centre* (New York: Sheed and Ward, 1939), "Liturgy, the Expression of the Catholic Centre," pp. 1–26.

Chapter II

CATHOLICISM IS CHRIST BEING FULFILLED

Unto the building up
of the body of Christ (Eph. iv,12).

WHEN God pitched His tent among men in the Person of His Son, as St. John phrased it in Greek, He proceeded to John i,14 make the great revelation spoken of in the preceding pages, and to establish, as the channel of salvation, an imperishable society Matt. xvi,18 which He called a Church. Recruits to this society, after freely accepting the revelation whole and entire, would be inducted by baptismal rites. Matt. xxviii,20 This society was often styled a kingdom, the kingdom of God in mankind, as in the Old Testament the Jewish people were called God's Kingdom. Another common metaphor of the Ancient Dispensation found more sparing use by Christ, that wherein the new union of God and man was likened to marriage. That the society would perforce live among Matt. ix,15 enemies was pictured in terms of a field sown by Christ with wheat and oversown with enemy cockle. That the original sowing would nevertheless Matt. xiii enjoy a vast, natural development was foretold by the comparison of a mustard seed, smallest of seeds, growing into a great tree. That from Matt. xiii small beginnings the new society would enliven and vitalize mankind as a whole was predicted in the figure of a handful of leaven fermenting the entire mass. That in some real manner Christ, even after His ascent Matt. xiii,33 into heaven, would abide within His kingdom all days was promised in several connections; as, that He would be with His teachers; would be Matt. xxviii,20 with even two or three gathered in His Name; that *He* would be fed and Matt. xviii,20 clothed and comforted in His needy brethren. Not Christ alone, but also Matt. xxv,40 the Holy Spirit, the Paraclete, whom the Father would send at Christ's behest, was to abide with the Church permanently and bring to its mind all those things once said by Christ Himself. On the occasion on which John xiv,26 He instituted the Holy Eucharist, at least, Christ used language that

13

Saul, Saul, why dost thou persecute Me?

clearly indicated an identity of life and of fruitfulness between Himself
and His disciples:

> I am the Vine,
>> ye the branches;
> he that abideth in Me,
>> and I in him,
> the same beareth much fruit.

John xv,5

To establish this society Christ died and rose from the dead. Thus, taken *John x,11–18*
comprehensively, Christ founded a visible society wherein man is taken
possession of by the Father, in Christ, through the instrumentality of
the Holy Ghost. To the fiercely separatist Jew, the revelation of Christ
could, and to some extent did at first, appear to sanction and promote
separatism, of salvation for the Jew and not for the Gentile.

An Apostle for the Gentiles. Among the most hostile opponents
of the new Way, as Catholicism was first called, was Saul, Pharisee
among Pharisees. At home and abroad he harried Christians in utter
fury. Once, while on such an errand, on the highroad to Damascus, at
midday, he saw a light brighter than the sun, whereat he and his associates fell to the ground. He tells the story:

> I heard a voice saying to me in the Hebrew tongue,
> "Saul, Saul, why dost thou persecute Me?
> It is hard for thee to kick against the goad."
And I said: "Who art Thou, Lord?"
> And the Lord said: "I am Jesus, Whom thou dost persecute.
> But arise, and stand upon thy feet;
> for to this purpose have I appeared to thee,
>> that I should appoint thee minister and witness
>>> both of what thou hast seen
>>> and to what thou shalt yet see of Me,
> delivering thee from the people and from the gentiles,
>> unto whom I am sending thee,
>>> to open their eyes,
>> that they should turn from darkness to light
>> and from the power of Satan unto God,
>> thus to receive forgiveness of their sins,
> and a portion with those sanctified by faith in Me."

Acts xxvi,14–18

Saul (the future Paul) rose up, a Pharisee turned inside out, as has been
said, the Apostle of the Gentiles.

Gal. i,11   **"The Gospel Preached by Me."** Years later, when the time came to fulfill what was specifically *his* mission to the Gentiles, that is, both to bring them into the Church, and to win acceptance for them from the separatist Jewish Christians, Paul showed how well he had studied his problem. What he had seen in the dazzling light near Damascus was the supreme fact of Jesus of Nazareth claiming identification with His persecuted Church; what he was to see in subsequent revelations in Arabia, whither he had retired, was the full content of the Christian revelation.

The gospel preached by me
is no gospel of man,
nor did I receive or learn it from man,
but by revelation from Jesus Christ.

Gal. i,11,12

In dealing with the Gentiles, Paul knew and used the metaphors of the
I Cor. vi,9   Kingdom, of marriage, of the sown field, of the leaven in the dough,
Eph. v,23
I Cor. iii,9   but his preference was all for expressions which emphasized an identity
I Cor. v,7   of life between Christ and Christian, as when he spoke of the Roman
Rom. xi,24   converts as fruitful because engrafted into Christ. In framing his message to the Greco-Romans, Paul would speak in terms of their culture as clearly as he could. Thus, no one of the Hellenic world would be ignorant of the famous fable of Aesop:

THE STOMACH AND THE MEMBERS

One fine day it occurred to the members of the body that they were doing all the work, while the stomach was getting all the food. So they held a meeting, and after a long discussion, decided to strike, until the stomach should take its proper share of the work. So for a day or two, the hands refused to take the food, the mouth refused to receive it, and the teeth had no work to do. But after a day or two the members began to find that they themselves were not in a very active condition: the hands could hardly move, and the mouth was all parched and dry, while the legs were unable to support the rest. So thus they found that even the stomach in its dull, quiet way was doing necessary work for the body, and that all must work together or the body will
Aesop's Fables   go to pieces.[1]

Every Roman citizen would know how the telling of that very fable

---

[1]*The Harvard Classics, XVII, Folk-Lore and Fable* (New York: Collier & Son, 1909), p. 22.

*" Clearly she is the Mother
of the members of Christ
which we are."
(Pius X quoting Saint Augustine)*

had eased a serious crisis in Roman history, when the plebs had seceded to the Sacred Mount. Xenophon, among the Greeks, had applied the analogue, Cicero among the Latins. Besides, applying the fable to the citizens and the State was merely a figurative way of expressing what Plato had taught in his *Republic*, that the State is but a man magnified.

Livy, ii,32
Xenophon, *Mem.* II, iii,18
Cicero, *De Offic.*, III, v,22
Plato, *Republic*

Although the Church is a far higher kind of society than the State, St. Paul found here apt data for casting the ancient analogue into a formulation of Catholicism. As a result, in simple, graphic terms the sublime mystery of the Christian man possessed and vitalized by the Father, in Christ, through the Holy Ghost, glows forever enshrined in the Inspired Gal. iii,20 Writing in terms of the head and members. The Hellenes of Galatia, Col. iii,11 of Colossae, of Ephesus, of Philippi, of Corinth, of Rome were taught Eph. ii,13 by Paul that the Catholic Church is a Person, a vast collective person-Phil. i,21 Rom. xii,4 I Cor. xii,12 ality, the Head of which is Christ, the body of which complements Christ by giving Him Catholics as members.

> He [the Father] hath subjected all things
> beneath His [Christ's] feet,
> and hath given Him for supreme Head to the Church,
> which is His body,
Eph. i,22,23 the fulness of Him Who is wholly fulfilled in all.

I Cor. xii,27 **"Ye Are the Body of Christ."** Before further analysis of the thought of the Apostle, it will help not a little to study his phraseology, so to speak, in his most detailed exposition of this concept. It will be noted that he improves the occasion to inculcate contentment with one's station in the Church:

> For as the body is one
> and hath many members,
> and all the members of the body,
> many as they are,
> form one body,
> so also [it is with] Christ.

> For in one Spirit
> all we, whether Jews or Greeks,
> whether slaves or free,
> were baptized into one body:
> and we were all given to drink of one Spirit.

> Now the body is not one member, but many.

> If the foot say,
> "Because I am not a hand, I am not of the body,"
> not for all that doth it cease to be of the body.

And if the ear say,
"Because I am not an eye, I am not of the body,"
not for all that doth it cease to be of the body.

If the body were all eye,
where would be the sense of hearing?
If it were all hearing,
where would be the sense of smell?

As it is, God hath set each several member of the body
according as He willed.

And if they were all a single member,
where would be the body?

But, as it is, there are many members,
yet one single body.

And the eye cannot say to the hand,
"I have no need of thee";
or again the head to the feet,
"I have no need of thee."

Nay, much rather, those members of the body
which seem to be weaker
are [still] necessary,
and those which we deem less honorable in the body,
we surround with special honor.

[Yea], God hath so compounded the body
as to give special honor where it is lacking,
that there may be no schism in the body,
but that the members may have common care for each other.

And if one member suffereth,
all the members suffer therewith;

if a member be honored,
all the members rejoice therewith.

Now ye are [together] the body of Christ,
and severally His members.   I Cor. xii,12–27

"An Ensign to the Nations." In a world in which the false religions Isa. v,26
of paganism and the transitional one of Judaism were everywhere met
with, Paul explained what we call the marks of Catholicism, its oneness,

universality, sanctity, and apostolic succession, by insisting on distinct phases of the doctrine of the body of Christ. How eloquently he argues that common incorporation into Christ through the Holy Ghost necessarily argues oneness in the body!

> [Be] careful to keep the unity of the Spirit
> in the bond of peace:
> one body
> and one Spirit,
> as ye are called in one hope, that of your calling;
> one Lord,
> one faith,
> one baptism:
> one God and Father of all,
> Who is above all,
> and throughout all,
> and in all.

Eph. iv,3–6

Gal. iii,28 Elsewhere he can say emphatically: "Ye are all one person in Christ Jesus." International, raceless, classless universality as conceived by St. Paul would strike us as more immediately comparable to modern situations if we used current racial, national, and proletarian names in his quotation:

> [In Christ] there is not gentile and Jew,
> circumcision and uncircumcision,
> barbarian, Scythian, slave, freeman,
> but Christ is all and in all.

Col. iii,11

Sanctity in the Christian life is of Christ, who

> loved the Church and gave Himself up for her sake
> that He might sanctify her . . .
> that He might present her to Himself
> a glorious Church . . . holy and without blemish.

Eph. v,25,26

If, in speaking of apostolicity, St. Paul feels that he must use the figure of the foundation rock employed by Christ, it will be noted how his thought, unashamed of mixed metaphors, reverts at once to the congenial concepts of incorporation and growth:

Matt. xvi,18

> Ye are built upon the foundation of the apostles and prophets:
> Christ Jesus is the corner-stone.

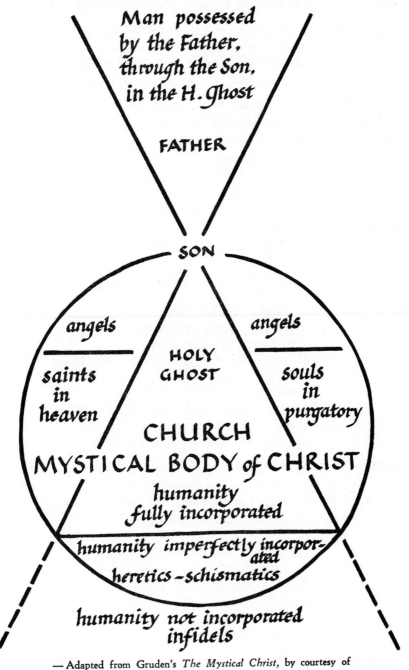

Man possessed
by the Father,
through the Son,
in the H. Ghost

FATHER

SON

angels   angels

HOLY
GHOST

saints
in
heaven

souls
in
purgatory

CHURCH
MYSTICAL BODY of CHRIST
humanity
fully incorporated

humanity imperfectly incorporated
heretics - schismatics

humanity not incorporated
infidels

— Adapted from Gruden's *The Mystical Christ,* by courtesy of
B. Herder Book Company.

In Him every building is duly fitted together
and groweth into a temple holy in the Lord;
in Him ye also are being built together
unto a spiritual dwelling-place of God.

Eph. ii,20–22

Head, Members, Spirit. Whatever be the aspect of the Church he wished to discuss, Paul adjusted his thought to the Church as a living body. That, too, as we shall see in another connection, was the starting point of all his moral exhortation. Here we turn to a brief examination of the principal parts of that body, its head, its constituent members, and its soul. The excellence of Christ's Person and work are often extolled in the New Testament, but perhaps nowhere so luminously as in the lines:

He is the Image of the unseen God,
First-Born before every creature.
For in Him were created all things
in Heaven and on earth,
things seen and things unseen,
whether thrones or dominations
or principalities or powers —
all creation is through Him and unto Him,
And Himself is prior to all,
and in Him all things hold together.
He again is the Head of the body, the Church . . .
For in Him it hath pleased the Father
that all fulness should dwell.

Col. i,15–19

Christ's functions, so to speak, as Head of the Church, are not merely owing to the pre-eminence of his humanity united with the Person of the Word. Much rather they are owing to His continual vital influx on His members. Life, union, cohesion, growth — all these derive from the Head:

Let no one cheat you of your prize . . .
and not holding fast to the Head.
For from this the whole body,
nourished and knit together
by means of the joints and the ligaments,
doth grow with a growth that is of God.

Col. ii,18,19

This lifegiving holding to the Head, this union, takes place through the intervention of the Holy Spirit, who is the soul, the informing principle, the living bond, between Christ and Catholics. By that Spirit we were engrafted into the living body, the Church, at baptism; once rooted in Him, to use another Pauline term, we received the vivifying draught of the Spirit in Confirmation. At Christ's behest the Spirit of the Living God dwells within us as in a temple: `Col. ii,7` `I Cor. xii,13`

> Your body is the temple of the Holy Spirit
> Who is within you,
> Whom you have from God. `I Cor. vi,19`

The indwelling Spirit is not idle; rather

> *we live in the Spirit;*
> by the Spirit let us walk. `II Cor. xiii,3`

This walking in the fellowship of the Spirit effects our transformation into Godlikeness:

> We . . . reflecting as in a mirror the glory of the Lord,
> are transformed into His very image from glory to glory
> as through the Lord, the [Holy] Spirit. `I Cor. iii,18`

"Christ Is All and In All." No one can read the New Testament and not see how, for St. Paul, the living union of Catholics with Christ the Redeemer was the central doctrine of Christianity. In trying to explain this joint living with the dying and risen Saviour, he enriched the Greek language with a full score of words, unfortunately untranslatable into English save by the weakening use of prepositional phrases. "To live with Him," "to be brought to life with," "to be united with His life," "to share His form," "to be built together with," "to be joint heir with," "to be comparticipant with," "to be concorporate with" — these and similar expressions are the Apostle's formulas of Catholicism, to be supplemented more than one hundred and fifty times by the shorter equivalent "in Christ." `Col. iii,11` `Rom. vi,8` `Col. ii,13` `Rom. vi,11` `Phil. iii,21` `Eph. ii,22` `Rom. viii,17` `Eph. iii,6`

Mystic Body and Mystery. The doctrine of the Catholic Church sketched from the New Testament in the preceding pages is called that of the mystic body, or mystical body, of Christ. By "mystic" we here mean "mysterious," because, like so much else in Catholicism, the reality is supernatural and spiritual, exceeding verification by the senses. This reality belongs, moreover, to God's great Mystery, withheld from the ancient Jews and made known in Christ, that redemption should be

No Father before Augustine,
no Theologian after him
has treated this mystical unity
so profoundly.   (Karl Adam)

catholic in scope, making the Gentiles *coheirs* and *concorporate* and *comparticipant,* the fullness of Him, who is wholly fulfilled in all.   Eph. i,23

Summary. Catholicism is a living society, which St. Paul presents in the familiar analogy of the head and members of a body. The risen Christ is the Head of the body, the Spirit of Love, its informing life; into it we are embodied at baptism, to grow as adults

> *unto the full knowledge* of the Son of God,
>   to the perfect *man,*
> the full measure of the stature of Christ.   Eph. iv,13

Second-Century Source Material

(In his great work, FALSE WISDOM UNMASKED AND REFUTED, *St. Irenaeus is argu-ing against Gnostics [the "Wise"], who held that nothing corporeal is holy or can be saved.)*

He [Christ] recapitulated in Himself the long history of men, sum-ming up and giving us salvation, in order that we might receive **again** in Christ Jesus that which we had long lost in Adam . . . (III, 18, 1). Those who say that He was only a man, the son of Joseph, remain **and** die in the slavery of the first disobedience; they are not united to **the** Word of God the Father, nor do they receive freedom from the Son, according to His words:

> If the Son shall make you free,
>   you shall be free indeed.   John viii,36

But since they know not the Emmanuel born of the Virgin, they are deprived of His gift, which is eternal life . . . (III, 19, 1).

Some do not receive the gift of adoption, because they sneer at **the** pure Incarnation and birth of the Word of God. They rob man of his ascent to God and remain ungrateful to the Word of God who became incarnate for their sakes. For this is why the Word of God is man, **and** this is why the Son of God became the Son of Man, that man might possess the Word, receive adoption, and become the son of God. . . .

God willed to be born, to be with us, to descend into the lower **regions** of the earth in order to find the lost sheep that is His own creature; **He** willed to ascend into heaven, to present to the Father this man that **He** had found, and to offer in Himself the first-fruits of man's resurrection. As the Head is risen from the dead, so the rest of the body of **every** man will rise again when the penalty of disobedience shall have been paid. This body will be united again by joints and sinews; it will be strengthened by a divine growth, and every member will have his own proper place in the body. There are many mansions in the Father's house, since there are many members in the body (III, 19, 3).

Topics for Further Discussion:

St. Paul appeals to the doctrine of the mystical body as motive in inculcating many moral virtues, as:

a) Fellowship in the Holy Eucharist (I Cor. x,14–22);
b) Fraternal "memberly" union (Eph. iv,4; Col. iii,15);
c) Love of husbands for wives (Eph. v,22–32);
d) Contentment with inferior lot (I Cor. xii,4–11);
e) Commiseration with others' suffering (I Cor. xii,26);
f) Rejoicing in good fortune of others (I Cor. xii,26);
g) Truthfulness (Eph. iv,25);
h) Modesty of demeanor (Rom. xii,4–11);
i) Chastity (I Cor. vi,15–19);
j) Supernatural equality of sexes (Gal. iii,28);
k) Union of Gentile and Jew (Eph. ii,19; Gal. iii,28);
l) Union of peoples of all races (Col. iii,9–11);
m) Union of all social classes (Gal. iii,28; Col. iii,9–11).

Pope Pius XI has appealed to this doctrine in his encyclicals: On His Accession, 1922; On St. Josaphat, 1923; On Kingship of Christ, 1925; On Church Unity, 1928; On Reparation to Sacred Heart, 1928; On Christian Education of Youth, 1929; On St. Augustine, 1930; On Marriage, 1930; On Centenary of Ephesus, 1931; On Reconstruction of Social Order, 1931; On Prayer During the Depression, 1932; On the Priesthood, 1936; (Address) To Spanish Refugees, 1936; On Atheistic Communism, 1937; (Apostolic Letter) Church Affairs in Mexico, 1937.

Readings:

K. Adam, *The Spirit of Catholicism* (New York: Macmillan, 1929), "The Church, the Body of Christ," pp. 31–45.
———— *St. Augustine* (New York: Sheed and Ward, 1932), pp. 39–56.
Father Cuthbert, *God and the Supernatural* (New York: Longmans, Green, 1920); E. I. Watkin, "The Church as the Mystical Body of Christ," pp. 235–276.
J. Duperray, *Christ in the Christian Life* (New York: Longmans, Green, 1927), "Incorporation in Christ," pp. 1–47.
A. Goodier, *The Inner Life of the Catholic* (New York: Longmans, Green, 1933), "Life in Jesus Christ," pp. 43–75.
C. Grimaud–J. F. Newcomb, *One Only Christ* (New York: Benziger, 1939), " 'Our' Union with the Head," pp. 39–55.
J. C. Gruden, *The Mystical Christ* (St. Louis: Herder, 1936), "The Mystical Body of Christ," pp. 27–63.
R. Guardini, *The Church and the Catholic* (New York: Sheed and Ward, 1935), "The Fellowship of the Liturgy," pp. 141–149.
F. C. Kolbe, *The Four Mysteries of the Faith* (New York: Longmans, Green,

1926), "The Third Mystery as the Mystical Body," etc., pp. 77–82; 89–103.

D. A. Lord, *Our Part in the Mystical Body* (St. Louis: Queen's Work, 1935), "The Astounding Truth," pp. 13–34; "The Sublime Figure," pp. 66–76.

C. Marmion, *Christ, the Life of the Soul* (St. Louis: Herder, 1923), "The Church the Mystical Body of Christ," pp. 85–98.

W. J. McGarry, *Paul and the Crucified* (New York: America Press, 1939), "The Mystical Body of Christ," pp. 208–256.

E. Mersch–D. F. Ryan, *Morality and the Mystical Body* (New York: Kenedy, 1939), "The Mystical Body and Contemporary Humanity," pp. 161–178.

E. Myers, *The Mystical Body of Christ*, TF,[2] 19.

M. Perkins, *Speaking of How to Pray* (New York: Sheed & Ward, 1944), "The Church Which Is His Body," pp. 48–65.

R. Plus, *God within Us* (New York: Kenedy, 1924), "Grace and Our Possible Relations with God within Us," pp. 74–122.

H. Pope, *The Church, Papers Read at the Summer School of Catholic Studies*, ed. C. Lattey (St. Louis: Herder, 1928), "The Mystical Body of Christ," pp. 57–90.

F. Prat, *The Theology of St. Paul* (London: Burns, Oates and Washbourne, 1926–27), I, "The Church, the Mystical Body of Christ," pp. 300–308; II, "The Mystical Body, Foundation of Morality," pp. 285–288.

F. J. Sheed, *A Map of Life* (New York: Sheed and Ward, 1933), "The Mystical Body of Christ," pp. 58–68.

A. Tanquerey, *The Spiritual Life* (Tournai: Desclée, 1930), "Jesus the Head of a Mystical Body," etc., pp. 75–99.

---

[2] *The Treasury of the Faith* Series is indicated by TF.

Chapter III

GOD-LIFE SHARED WITH MAN

In Him dwelleth all the fulness
of the Godhead corporally:
and ye are filled [therewith]
in Him Who is the Head (Col. ii,9,10).

THERE are insects, science assures us, whose life span is but a single day. It makes us marvel that birth, growth, the complicated processes of reproduction, senescence, and, after an allotted period, death itself could all be crowded into the space of twenty-four hours. In comparison to the length and more especially to the *depth* of man's mortal existence that of such an insect seems as nothing. Man's life as compared to God's is even at greater disadvantage than the insect's beside man's. For the insect and the man are both in the range of the finite, and both *can* be measured in the same terms. St. Bonaventure says that such is the reality of God's Being that ours by comparison is nothing. But man's *natural* life is not, and never was, the whole story. Man was created in God's image and likeness precisely with a view *to being lifted up by the grant of a share in God's own life itself.* Man's natural life is intended to serve only as the foundation, the substratum, of a second and incomparably higher *kind* of life, to be planted thereon by an act of God. We are accustomed to call the former, familiar living of man *natural* inasmuch as it corresponds to man's created *nature;* but because the second kind of life, the "superimposed life," the sharing in God-life, *altogether exceeds the capacities of any creature,* we are accustomed to call it *grace* (Latin for *gift*), as if one would say simply THE GIFT. Now, the words, *gift* or *grace,* do not directly suggest *life,* dynamic being and acting and growing with God-life, and so there is need of studying the supernatural reality we call grace in its primary meaning of God-life, rather than in its secondary characteristic of *something gratuitously conferred.* And as soon as we speak of grace in terms of *life,* we

28

find we are back in the mystic body system, too. It was in terms of this body that the Fathers of the Council of Trent defined the acquisition and functioning of grace:

> . . . Jesus Christ Himself as the Head [imparting life] to the members, and as the Vine [vivifying] the branches, ceaselessly communicates a life-force to those justified [i.e., to those who are in the state of grace], and this life-force always precedes, accompanies and follows their good works, and without it these could in no way be pleasing to God or worthy of merit. . . .

Eph. iv,15

John xv,5

Sess. vi

God-Life at the Source. The Ancient of Days from eternity called Himself, "I am who am." He is the uncreated, self-subsistent Spirit, whose Wisdom, Power, and Goodness knew no imaginable limitations. Such are God's perfections, too, that He, the one God, has a triple Personality. The Father has the Divine Nature; the Son has the same Nature, and likewise the Holy Spirit, but the *manner* in which each Divine Person has it is different, unique, and incommunicable. Contemplating the unfathomable depth of His own essence, the Father by an infinite act of the divine intelligence, knows Himself, expresses Himself to Himself, and thereby begets in intellectual generation a spotless Image of His Majesty. This Image is the Son, the Second Person of the Holy Trinity. With unspeakable and everlasting affection the Father regards the Beloved Son, and with no less affection the Son rejoices in the Father. From this never ceasing flow of love and love-for-love springs, as it were, a divine Fire, a Divine Love impersonate, and this is the Third Person of the Holy Trinity, whom we call the Holy Spirit (*Spiritus* = the *Breath* of the Father and the Son). Though we have no way of phrasing it which does not imply a difference in time or inferiority in perfection, we know that these incomparable processions of Godhead within God do not militate against perfect equality among the Three Divine Persons. These mutual and eternal relations of the Three Divine Persons to each other constitute the *life,* and the all-joyous *living,* and ineffable bliss of the Triune God. Infinite, pregnant Truth is ceaselessly contemplated, and beatifying Beauty enjoyed without cessation. "O happy Three-in-one," cries the Church in wondering adoration.

Dan. vii,9

God-Life Overflowing. God was perfectly sufficient for His own boundless bliss, but *love feels that it must give* and give of itself. As if compelled by love God *had* to create: "There remains nothing for God,"

De Pot. q. ix, a.9 says St. Thomas, "than that external activity which we call creation." So God made creatures, on whom He might heap benefactions, to whom He might give of His perfections and of His own beatitude. Highest were the angels, noble spirits of intellect and will, who radiate outward from Divinity through nine grades of created being. "A little less than *Ps. viii,6* the angels" God made man, who shares intelligence and free will with the celestial spirits, but is nonetheless immersed in corporeal nature. Man thus links in himself the immortal world of the spiritual and the mortal one of the flesh. Below man are the myriad forms of non-rational animal life and non-sentient vegetative life, and inorganic being devoid of life. These lower realms do not concern us here. Both angels and men are so made *naturally* that they can be made over, "built upon," *supernaturally:* Their finite nature and highest endowments were such that they could be raised or elevated by God Himself and made capable of sharing God-life, at least in its divine operations. To understand this elevation we must realize that there is question not merely of sharing *a* knowledge or *a* love of God, but of participating in *God's way of knowing, God's way of loving;* even, of sharing God's *act* of knowing, and God's *act* of loving. Thus, to characterize God's *kind* of knowledge, as compared with ours, it is enough for our present purpose to recall that, while we *derive* knowledge through sense pictures of objects, etc., God contemplates infinite Truth without any *medium of knowledge*. That *way* of knowing is natural only to God, not natural to any creatable nature. Now, in elevating man, or angel, to that condition wherein he is able to share *that* Act of knowing with Himself, God must divinize, or deify, the created nature at least to some extent. Thus, if in daily life we met a speaking *Mickey Mouse* we should know that, along with the rational function of speech, it had received enough rational nature on which to ground that function. So, St. Peter did not hesitate to say that we may

II Pet. i,4   become partakers of the divine nature.

St. John used the same argument, that sharing an Act proper only to God, argues in us a certain sharing in God-nature as well:

We shall be like to Him
I John iii,2   *because* we shall see Him as He is.

Old Adam — New Adam. This great GIFT of a new, supernatural

life was given as a *seed capable of developing* into the intimate sharing
of God's highest activity in heaven, God's generative knowing, God's
vital union in love. It was entrusted to our race in Adam, who was to
hand it on to his progeny, even as he transmitted our physical or natural
life. But everyone knows the sequel of Adam's fall, and our sad losses
therein. His recreancy cost us heavily, for he lost for us as well as for
himself the nice poise and balance of the various elements of human
nature, lost his freedom from sickness and pain, his bodily immortality,
and, worse than all else, lost the humanly irretrievable germ of God-life.
Man after Adam sank into savagery, barbarism, idolatry, and was called
by St. Augustine "a mass of sin." To restore the God-life, there was
need of a new Adam. God's answer is the Incarnation.

Atonement and At-one-ment. The Word, by whom all things were
made, the well-beloved Son, who was full of grace, who possessed the
God-life in all its plenitude, wedded our nature to His own in a per-   John i,3
                                                                         John i,14
sonal union so close that thenceforth *He* existed *in two natures.* The   John i,16
humanity of Christ, body and soul, intellect and will, was indissolubly
assumed to the Second Person of the Holy Trinity:

> He is the Head of the body, the Church . . .
> > *in Him*
> > it hath pleased the Father
> > that all fulness should dwell
> > > and *through Him*
> > to reconcile all things to Himself.   Col. i,9,10

To that sacred humanity in which

> dwells the fulness of the Godhead corporally   Col. ii,9

God communicated the plenitude of deity, to ennoble it, to consecrate
it, to adorn it with the uncreated Life of God. This is called Christ's
personal endowment. Over and above that, the same humanity was filled
with the plenitude of created, communicable riches of grace needed to
make all men

> gracious in the Well-Beloved.   Eph. i,6

This is the fullness of Christ as Head of the Body, the Church. By His
redeeming death Christ merited *a share of that grace* for us, so that our
baptism into Him effects in us a *finite, created reproduction of the just-*

ness of God. St. Paul speaks in the first person, but he speaks for all who are *in Christ*:

Phil. iii,9
> my justness . . . which is . . . in Christ,
> that justness which cometh from God.

In the very next verse the Apostle speaks, in one of those Pauline words impossible of translation, of becoming of *one and the same nature* with Christ in His death. The Tridentine Fathers, who specified this justness as "the justice of God, not that whereby He is just Himself, but that whereby He maketh us just," follow the Apostle in affirming that this great GIFT is given to His members, by Christ, through the indwelling of the Holy Spirit:

Phil. iii,10

Sess. vii

> Know ye not that your bodies are members of Christ? . . .
> Know ye not that your body is the temple of the Holy Spirit
> Who is within you,
> Whom ye have from God?

I Cor. vi,15–20

Gal. vi,15 The *effects* of this *new* life of the *new* creature in Christ cannot be summarily described more graphically than by the Apostle:

> If, then, any man be in Christ,
> he is a *new creature:*
> the former things have passed away:
> behold, I make all things *new.*

II Cor. v,17

Eph. iii,8 **"Unsearchable Riches."** Our yearnings and dreams for fullness of life, for a role commensurate with the talents and vital forces we feel surging within us — these rainbow dreams will never be realized during our mortal lives. The "flesh" is marked for its "crucifixion." By ineluctable destiny our talents, forces, and capacities will never in this life get their full chance *to live.* They are not created for so small a theater. Instead the task assigned us is to develop, even in the squirrel-cage smallness of everyday existence, that

Gal. v,24

I John iii,9
> seed of God abiding in [us].

John x,10 For out of that seed grows *the more abundant life,* wherein nothing less than

> the depth of the riches
> and of the wisdom
> and of the knowledge of God

Rom. xi,33

Christ dwells in us

THE BLESSED TRINITY
indwelling ~ elevating ~ energizing ~ divinizing man

	SUPER-NATURE	SUPER-FACULTIES	SUPER-ACTIVITY →	growing →	ASSIMIL-ATION	God-like
	Sanctifying grace	Faith Hope Charity	Prompt|Helping grace|ing grace		TO GOD →	HAPPINESS →
		Seven gifts of H.G.				

Supernatural Order — External Graces

| HUMAN NATURE | FACULTIES | ACTIVITY → |
| Soul | Intellect\|Will → | Stimu-\|Reac-lation\|tion → |

Natural Order — External Things

is to be the scope and field of our keen searching and our joy. Now, even our sluggard spirits are tireless in searching for truth: God beholds in His nature inexhaustible depths of clearest Truth. Our purblind wills cleave to whatever seems good to us: God enjoys from all eternity the serenest possession of endless goodness. The smallest, broken fragment of beauty, how it delights and ennobles and elevates man! How shall one picture God's fruition of limitless, all-embracing beauty? The enjoyment of this bliss is, so to speak, the lifework of God. Not less is the destiny given man in the mystic body. What if one's capacity to live the fullest life on earth go unrealized? The day-by-day growth in knowledge of God, and the loyal performance of daily duties, *internally fit us* for the fullest living of the God-life in Heaven.

> Filled with the knowledge of God's will
>   and all wisdom and spiritual insight.
> Thus may ye walk worthily of the Lord . . .
>   being fruitful in all good works
> and increasing in the full knowledge of God . . .
>   joyfully rendering thanks to the Father,
>   Who hath *fitted us*
>   for *our portion*
> of the inheritance of the saints in light.   Col. i,9–14

Two students, one of whom is only *naturally* alive, the other a Catholic *also supernaturally alive,* have a chemistry assignment to study under the common stimulus of a class quiz. But the student supernaturally alive has the additional stimulus of thereby serving God. For the first it is merely a matter of studying chemistry. In the case of the second the act of studying proceeds also from a vital principle *supernaturalized* by sanctifying grace, and is "stepped up" by special helping acts of God (actual graces), so that the very act by which chemistry is being assimilated, aids in the deepening and expanding of the God-life in the student. Any and every act performed in Christ, or "in grace," is a further divinization of the member of Christ, "since Jesus Christ Himself . . . Council of Trent ceaselessly imparts a life force," as was seen above.

A Difficulty. Before going on to survey the plane of the super-life, it is well to take cognizance of a *difficulty* which inevitably arises about taking this Scriptural language literally. In a Christian there is no visible manifestation of any vital change or transformation wrought within. The difference between him and an unbaptized person is not externally visible. But, if a living being must act, as is said, only in accord with its own *kind* of life, should there not be some external signs of this immeasurable elevation of nature? The complete answer to this difficulty must take account of two factors. First, that the supernatural life is *only embryonic* or latent in man *now,* to become fully operative at his "entrance" into heaven. Thus, the highest supernatural faculty, that of seeing God, is latent in us now, much the same as the gift of speech and other gifts are for a time latent or inoperative in young children. A more important phase of the problem, however, is the wholly *spiritual* nature of the realities here in question. The super-life and all that pertains to it is altogether spiritual, and completely escapes the senses. It is taken wholly on faith, just as the difference between a consecrated and a non-consecrated host. But mere inability to understand fully what one is or has in no way lessens the inheritance: a king's child has the presumptive rights and prerogatives of a king, though as yet he knows of them only imperfectly.

Life-Principle Superimposed. This chart will illustrate the *status* or *plane of the supernatural* life, with its own faculties, aspirations, and goal. Human nature, or the man-life, with all its faculties and powers remaining quite intact, receives by "being ingrafted into Christ" a super-nature, which permeates, and elevates, and assimilates human nature to the divine, without abolishing anything of it. The man-life is thus raised to heights and possibilities otherwise as far beyond it as the power of speech to a statue. Grace is often called a super-soul, a term quite intelligible in the light of what has been said. But it is more accurate to speak of this super-life as a real likeness of the life of God, produced by God within the human soul. Like every vital principle, it is a positive power, an operative force. It brings with it super-faculties, in virtue of which man is enabled to walk in what St. Paul calls newness of life.

Rom. xi,17–24

Super-Faculties in Act. The chief among these super-faculties, the infused virtues of *faith, hope,* and *charity,* harmoniously cooperate with man's intellect and will, so that *all combine* in the production of a supernatural act. This act is now evaluated by God in the light of the vital principle producing it, and since this is *principally* the Christ-life streaming through the Christian, the act takes on a worth and value as of Christ, or as of the Godhead itself. A supernatural act is an *act-in-Christ.* Thus the Christian, as a brilliant modern apologist has it, gains the value of Him with whom he is incorporate, and his actions, more than intertwined with Christ's, truly "Christ-ed," have Christ's value before God. Such is the Christian mystery. If a man be incorporate with Christ, God, looking down upon His Son, sees that man within Him; looking on the man, He sees Christ. When Christ praises God, I in Him am offering that praise; when Christ offers Himself to God, He offers me in Himself, I Him in myself, and myself in Him.[1]

Living Temples of God. Let us revert here to a circumstance but lightly touched upon above. There is with grace an *accompanying* phenomenon far more sublime than anything that has been said of grace itself. *Grace is always accompanied in the Christian soul by an intimate, personal presence of the three Divine Persons.*

> We will come to him,
> and make Our abode with him,   John xiv,23

said Christ in reference to the Christian. This indwelling of God in the soul, His being "at home" in the Christian, is usually attributed to the Person of the Holy Spirit, in His character of Sanctifier and Personal Love. Thus, the Holy Spirit is given to us, who makes of our bodies living temples, who helps us pray because we do not know how to pray as we ought, and, in a word, the Holy Spirit becomes for us a Paraclete, our Helper, our Comforter.   Eph. v,5 / I Cor. iii,16 / Rom. viii,26

Let us draw out the notion one step farther. If God is in us, then He acts in us. Now the *inner* life of God is the enjoyment, as we said, of the endless wonders of the All-Holy Trinity, and His *exterior* life is the governance of the universe. These two orders of action, taken together, make up the infinite, all-embracing Act of God. The Christian can assure himself that, as he is a permanent temple of the living God, so too does this infinite all-embracing Act go forward within him, through him, with him so that *his* every least action is caught up and associated with the very life of God. St. Paul spoke to the Athenians of a God in whom we move and live and are; with equal truth can the Christian speak of God who moves and lives and is in him. Even in this probation period the Christian enjoys unfathomable depths of *life*.   Acts xvii,28

Summary. Man was created with a view to a supernatural elevation by which he should share the divine life. After his fall, his sins may be

---

[1] C. C. Martindale, *The Faith of the Roman Church* (London: Methuen, 1927), p. 89.

forgiven, his super-nature restored, and his sharing by communication in God-life effected by contact with Christ in His mystic body. Christ pours the Holy Spirit upon His members, who, besides dwelling in them, effects in their souls a created reflection or reproduction of the God-life. This God-life within us is ordinarily called sanctifying grace. By Christian living this God-germ develops, and thereby fits man to enter more and more into and live by the life of God in heaven. There is no question, of course, of pantheism, or becoming God, for we retain our personalities and natures, though these are really "divinized" by cooption into God-life.

<blockquote>
It is no longer I that live,
but Christ that liveth in me.
</blockquote>

Gal. ii,20

Third-Century Source Material

(How Christians at Carthage reacted when some Numidian Christians were enslaved. A Letter of St. Cyprian.)

Cyprian to Januarius, Maximus, Proculus, Victor, Modianus, Nemesian, Nampulus, and Honoratus, Greeting:

With the greatest distress of spirit and not without tears have we read, dearest brothers, the letters which your solicitude has sent us about the captivity of our brothers and sisters. Who would not feel sorrow in such misfortunes, or who would not reckon the sorrow of his brother *his own* sorrow, since the Apostle saith:

<blockquote>
If one member suffereth,
all the members suffer therewith,
and if one member be honored,
all the members rejoice therewith,
</blockquote>

I Cor. xii,26

and in another place:

II Cor. xi,29

<blockquote>
Who is weak, and I am not weak?
</blockquote>

Hence to us here and now the captivity of our brethren must be reckoned our own captivity, and the sorrow of those in danger our own sorrow, since in our union we are only one body. Not alone love but even the duty of faith urges and impels us to redeem the members, the brethren. For the Apostle again saith:

I Cor. iii,16

<blockquote>
Know ye not that you are the temple of God,
and that the Spirit of God dwells in you?
</blockquote>

So that even if our love were not strong enough to rescue the brethren, we should in that case consider that it is the temples of God which are held captive. We dare not refuse, and, forgetful of sympathy, suffer it that temples of God be held in captivity, but with all the forces at our command must we strive and quickly bring it about that by our good offices we serve Christ our Judge and the Lord our God. For since the Apostle saith:

> All of you who were baptized into Christ,
> have put on Christ,   Gal. iii,27

we must see Christ in our captive brethren, and rescue Him from the danger of captivity who rescued us from the danger of death. . . .

All this has your letter made us consider and pierced us with sorrow. Therefore have all promptly and willingly gathered alms for our brethren. . . . For when the Lord says in His Gospel:

> I was sick and ye visited Me,   Matt. xxv,36

shall He now with much greater reward say to our almsgiving: "I was in prison and you have redeemed Me"? And as He elsewhere saith:

> I was in prison and ye came unto Me,   Matt. xxv,36

of how much more worth will it not be on the Last Day, when we shall receive our reward from the Lord, to hear Him say: "I was in the prison of captivity, lay chained and handcuffed among barbarians, and from that prison of slavery ye have bought Me My freedom."

And finally we thank you that you permit us to share your sorrow with you, and to have part in this good and necessary labor of love. . . . We hereby send you a hundred thousand sestercii [about $5,000], which were collected by the donations of our clergy and laity of our church, in which by God's mercy I am bishop. Apply this money there as your diligence suggests.

Lastly, we trust that in future no such misfortune overtake you, that our brethren, protected by God's power, be not again visited by such dangers. But if, for a testing of our faith and love something similar again befalls, do not delay in informing us by letter. Be assured that our church and the whole community here earnestly prays it may not happen, but if it does happen, know that we shall willingly raise alms. And that you may aid with your prayers our brothers and sisters, who have freely

contributed to this gift of love, I have subjoined the names of all. . . .
May you fare well ever in the Lord, and forget us not.

Topics for Further Discussion:

Entrance into heaven adds nothing fundamentally new to one's supernatural faculties, but merely releases the inhibitions now attaching to some of them.

It is not *natural,* but *supernatural,* for the angels to see God.

The super-life communicated to man is an incomparably higher kind of life than the natural life of an angel that has missed his destined supernaturalization.

The oldest extant Christian sermon (*II Clement*) embodies this idea: "Let us choose to belong to the Church of life, that we may be saved. You are not ignorant, I think, that the living Church is the body of Christ."

Why would the Church, in Newman's phrase, "rather save the soul of one single wild bandit of Calabria . . . than draw a hundred lines of railroad through the length of Italy"?

Readings:

E. Leen, *The Holy Ghost* (New York: Sheed and Ward, 1937), "Born of Water and the Holy Ghost," pp. 241–264.

D. A. Lord, *Our Part in the Mystical Body* (St. Louis: Queen's Work, 1935), "Bridging the Chasm," pp. 35–48; "How is This Done?" pp. 77–90.

C. C. Martindale, *Man and His Destiny,* TF, 9.

M. Perkins, *Speaking of How to Pray* (New York: Sheed & Ward, 1944), "In Whom We Have Redemption," pp. 36–47.

R. Plus, *In Christ Jesus* (New York: Benziger, 1923): "The Fact of Our Incorporation with Jesus Christ," pp. 1–11; "Jesus Makes Us Divine through His Spirit," pp. 36–42.

J. Pohle, "Grace, II, Sanctifying Grace," CE.[2]

F. J. Sheed, *A Map of Life* (New York: Sheed and Ward, 1933), "The Incarnation," pp. 45–57; "The Supernatural Life," pp. 121–131.

F. J. Sheen, *The Life of All Living* (New York: Century, 1929), "What is Life?" pp. 1–39.

A. Tanquerey, *The Spiritual Life* (Tournai: Desclée, 1930), "The Nature of the Christian Life," pp. 44–70.

E. Towers, *Sanctifying Grace,* TF, 16.

---

[2]The *Catholic Encyclopedia* is cited under this symbol.

Chapter IV

A LITURGIST FITTED TO OUR NEEDS

Now to crown what we have said:
such a High Priest we have . . .
at the right hand . . . of Majesty . . .
as Liturgist of the sanctuary (Heb. viii,1,2,
Greek).

NOT least among the doctrines to which adult Catholicism invites us to give the best study of which we are capable is that of the continuous role of Christ as Head of the Mystical Body. Among the new facts that emerge in this connection is that the New Testament in its original Greek speaks of Christ as a Liturgist, and of His work as a liturgy in which we have part. The word *liturgy* had not Heb. viii,2,6 won acceptance in our language when the older Scripture versions were made, and it is still usually rendered by a synonym in the English versions of the Inspired Writings. We here indicate some of the meanings of the word *liturgy* because it is a term so much to the fore at present, and well repays a little investigation. This is especially true of the Pauline meaning in which it has now become current. In classical Greek liturgy (λειτουργία) meant any public work or office or benefaction by an individual on behalf of the commonwealth, whether this was paying the chorus of a municipal opera, or furnishing the army with a span of horses. It was *something done by one from which the whole society profited.* Religion was conceived in such social terms by the ancients, that any act around the temples, down to the humble task of sweeping up, was a liturgy. Any act of worship of God profited the entire community, it was rightly conceived. When the Old Testament was rendered into Greek by the so-called Seventy Scholars, they chose the word *liturgy* to designate the services of the Jewish Temple. In the same sense the word greets us on the threshold of the New Testament, as when St. Luke wrote of Zachary that

41

Luke i,23

> when the days of his *liturgy* were completed,
> he departed to his home.

The first occasion we know of on which the term is applied to Christian worship happens to be that memorable for the ordination of SS. Paul and Barnabas:

> At Antioch,
> in the church which was there,
> as they were performing the *liturgy* to the Lord . . .
> the Holy Spirit said:
> "Set apart for Me Barnabas and Saul
> unto the work to which I have called them."

Acts xiii,2

But under the hand of St. Paul, who spoke with irresistible predilection in terms of our corporate union with Christ, the word takes on its truest Christian meaning. To the members Christ is the Head in worship as in all else beside, and so Christ in us and through us becomes *the* Worshiper, *the* Liturgist. We in Him and through Him worship along with Him, and so have part in His liturgy, whereof He is High Priest and Mediator. Let us add to an already long paragraph a somewhat full quotation of Paul's triumphant phrases on the matchless perfection of Christ's Priesthood:

> He, because He remaineth forever,
> hath an unchangeable priesthood,
> wherefore He can at all times save those
> who *approach God through Him.*
> Such was the High Priest fitted for our needs —
> holy, guileless, undefiled,
> set apart from sinners,
> and made higher than the heavens . . .
> one Who is *Son, forever perfect.* . . .

Heb. vii,24–28

> Now to crown what we have said:
> such a High Priest we have . . .
> Who hath His seat at the right hand
> of the throne of Majesty in heaven
> as Liturgist of the sanctuary,
> and of the true "tabernacle, which the Lord,"
> and not man, "hath set up" . . .
> He hath attained to a *liturgy*
> so much the more excellent,
> as the testament is better,
> whereof He is Mediator.

Heb. viii,1–6

Eternal High Priest. One of the most precious gifts we received from the hands of Pope Pius XI is the Encyclical Letter on the Priesthood, which deals in masterful fashion with the entire function of the priestly office in human society. By way of focusing attention on the very core and center of the entire doctrine, the great pope added a Mass in honor of Jesus Christ Eternal High Priest. If, instead of directing our attention to the Priesthood of Christ in such benign fashion, the pontiff had decreed that in Catholic usage the word *priest* would henceforth be limited exclusively to Christ, there would have been surprise and no small confusion. But such action would have had historic sanction, for scholars are unanimous in asserting that in primitive Christian literature the terms "priest," and "high priest," were in that way reserved to Christ as *the* Priest *par excellence*. But, nowadays, instead of restricting the title "priest," to Christ only, the Church is emphatically recalling that all Catholics in a true sense share the priestly character of their Head.

Religion Requires Priesthood. The very mention of priesthood calls up the cognate idea of public worship. Then, too, there arises the thought of sacrifice, which is both the highest office of worship and the chief function of the priest. Of these several concepts more detailed exposition will be found in subsequent chapters; rudimentary, rule-of-thumb definitions will answer present purposes. *Religion,* as one of the basic tendencies of human nature, is found among all peoples, throughout all ages of man's history. It is *man's recognition of his dependence* upon some superior Being. Man feels naturally constrained to give external and social expression to this feeling of submission, hence there arise at once organized and public acts of worship. Through the hands of persons designated to act for all, homage is paid the superior Being, be this by formal address, by extending the arms, lifting up the eyes, bowing the body to the ground, or by a hundred other actions suggestive of submission. Upon analysis, this recognition of dependence upon a superior Being carries with it the concept that one's very life is owing to Him. In consequence, man feels prompted to acknowledge this *complete* dependence upon God, who has given him all, even life, by giving something in return, by making God a Return-Gift which stands for man himself. This is sacrifice, and by universal consent, it is the foremost act of worship. To offer homage, and especially *the* homage of sacrifice, *priests* are chosen to act as society's representatives, the go-betweens, the ambassadors between man and God. Obviously society's first concern in selecting and accrediting a representative is to find one who is *sinless,* or at least as sinless as may be, lest he draw down wrath in place of benediction. Again, since *worship* involves recognizing the *relative worth* of Creator to creature, there is need of one with the closest approximation to a limitless knowledge of God. God is to be worshiped, King David sang,

Ps. cl,2   according to the multitude of His Greatness.

But our needs exceed our human capacities. Where could be found a son of Adam *either* sinless *or* possessed of anything like an adequate knowledge of God's Sovereignty or Sanctity, Loving-Kindness or Mercifulness? What mere man was at all capable of mediating between mankind and the Godhead?

Christ, the Bridge-Builder. The most important group of pagan priests of ancient Rome were called *pontifices,* literally bridge-builders. Whether this was, as Varro and Cicero and others believed, because these priests supervised the building of and kept in repair an important bridge across the Tiber, or for some other reason lost in the remoteness of history, no one knows for certain. But by whatever strange process it came about that the name *bridge-builder* was reserved for the highest rank of the priesthood, a name more expressive of the real nature of the priestly office could hardly be found. There is perhaps no better way to study the priestly character of the Redeemer, and the priestly character of the Christian body, than by focusing attention on Christ as One who builds a bridge between God and men.

But why is it necessary to speak of the priesthood, or of *Christ as a Priest?* Because the Fall was an act of *irreligion;* the supernatural order was lost by a deliberate refusal of homage, the homage of obedience, to God: hence, the Redemption will be in first instance an act of *religion;* the supernatural order will be recovered by a deliberate rendering of homage, the homage of obedience, to God. This was to be no private, personal undertaking, but the public act of an accredited representative of mankind. It was to be no inferior act of homage, but the highest possible expression of worship, the worship of sacrifice. This meant that a priest was necessary. The Redeemer was a Prophet and a King, but He *must* be pre-eminently a *Priest.*

Christ's Perfect Priesthood. The absolutely *unique perfection* of Christ's Priesthood becomes evident forthwith. None could really bridge the abyss between God and man but a Person who was God, equal to the Father from all eternity, and yet man, "tried in every way like ourselves, short of sin." Hence, in the very act of the Incarnation the *Heb. iv,15* Divinity anointed, as with the chrism of priestly ordination, the human flesh it assumed. Jesus, Son of Mary and Son of God, was therefore called the *Christ*, the *Anointed One*. He, the Head of mankind, came into the world to repair the primal refusal of worship. This He would do by offering the sacrificial gift that was hardest of all to make, the voluntary sacrifice of His own life. The Anointed One of God

> loved [you]
>   and delivered Himself up for you,
>   an offering and sacrifice of sweet savor to God. *Eph. v,2*

Clearly only a Person in whom Divinity and humanity meet and fuse into one can be a real Mediator. Listen to St. Augustine inculcate this in his preaching:

> Christ is the "Mediator between God and men," because He is God with the Father, and because He is man with men. Man is not a mediator with respect to the Divinity, God is not a mediator with respect to humanity. Behold the Mediator: the Divinity without the humanity [he repeats] is not the Mediator, nor is the humanity without the Divinity, but, between the Divinity alone and the humanity alone, the Mediator is the human Divinity and the Divine Humanity of Christ. *Serm. 47*

"Designated by God as High Priest." Before proceeding to the *Heb. v,10* analysis of Christ's priestly function, it will clear the ground to take a second cursory view of Christ's *qualifications* as a possible Mediator. Of the two requirements already mentioned, there is scarce need to recall His absolute sinlessness (did He not challenge His enemies to point to *any* sin in His life?), and His Wisdom incarnate. What St. Augustine *John viii,46* justly insists upon in the passage quoted is that Christ *unites in His Person the two natures* of which He was to be Mediator. St. Paul put it:

> It behooved Him
>   on account of Whom all things are,
>   and through Whom all things are,
>   when He was bringing many sons to glory . . .
>   it behooved Him to be made like unto "His brethren"
>   in all respects
> that He might become a merciful and faithful High Priest. *Heb. ii,10–18*

Of Christ's *vocation* (being called) to the priesthood the Apostle is no less clear and emphatic:

> None taketh to himself the honor,
> but one who hath been called by God, as was Aaron.
> So, too, Christ did not appoint Himself
> the honor of becoming High Priest,
> but He Who said to Him:
> "Thou art My Son . . ."
> as He elsewhere saith:
> Heb. v,4–6   "Thou art a Priest forever."

But let us see the Priest in act, in that act for which He was made High Priest, the offering of sacrifice:

> Every priest . . . is appointed
> as representative of men
> in the things that refer to God,
> Heb. v,1   that he may offer gifts and sacrifices for sin.

Christ's Perfect Sacrifice. Every Catholic knows how at the Last Supper Christ offered His life to the Father as a *sacrifice* and *sin-offering* for our redemption — and at the same time inaugurated a visible priesthood for the continuance of this new, this one *true*, sacrifice. The sacrificial offering made in the Cenacle was actually fulfilled later on the cross, when Christ voluntarily gave up His life. On the altar of the cross His Body was given for us; His Blood copiously ratified the new and eternal testament. The New Man as Priest had made His sacrifice.

But every sacrificial gift offered to God is made with the hope that God will accept it and even give some *sign* of His divine good pleasure. In Christ's sacrifice there could be no question but that the sacrifice would be most acceptable, since it had been agreed upon beforehand. But the divine good pleasure was wondrously shown to all mankind when God

> raised Jesus our Lord from the dead,
> who "was delivered up for our offenses,"
> Rom. iv,25   and rose again for our justification.

Apoc. v,12   This divine glorification of "the Lamb that was slain" was confirmed in a still more striking manner, if possible, when God lifted up our human nature in Christ to His eternal throne, and allowed Him to prove

GOD

IS WORSHIPED CONJOINTLY BY

CHRIST *(head)*

and the CHRISTIANS *(members)*

whose

ADORATION–THANKSGIVING–PETITION–REPARATION

is expressed in offices of

PRAYER : SANCTIFYING RITES : SACRIFICE

SACRAMENTS –SACRAMENTALS

– publicly –

by means of

speech – posture – symbols

in consecrated manner and setting

the efficacy of His sacrifice by sending thence the Pentecostal Spirit of Love upon His people, His brothers by adoption, purchased by His Blood, and incorporated into His Mystical Body.

He humbled Himself by obedience unto death,
yea, unto death upon a cross.
Wherefore God hath exalted Him above the highest,
and hath bestowed on Him THE NAME
Phil. ii,8,9   which is above every name.

In Him we have redemption through His blood,
the forgiveness of our transgressions. . . .
It was the purpose of His [the Father's] good pleasure —
a dispensation to be realized in the fulness of time —
Eph. i,8–10   to bring all things [as] to a Head in Christ.

Christ's Priesthood Perpetuated. But the final drama of Redemption was accomplished in a few hours: the sanctification of the whole race of Christians, *that* is a greater work of Christ, and that goes on and on, and will do so, as long as the world lasts. It will be found that this is no less a distinctly priestly work on Christ's part. For He came to act as Priest not only at the Redemption, or to show man how he was henceforth John iv,23 to worship God in spirit and in truth in the new dispensation, but *Christ as Head of the Mystical Body was to be henceforth and forever the High Priest of mankind, the one and only.*

He became
for all who obey Him
the Author of eternal salvation,
Heb. v,10   designated by God as High Priest: . . .
for this, then,
Heb. ix,15   is He the *Mediator* of the new testament.
[And just as] there is [but] one God,
[so there is] one Mediator also between God and man,
I Tim. ii,5   Himself man, Christ Jesus.

The entire process of Christian sanctification, which is called in Holy Eph. iv,12 Writ the building up of the [Mystical] Body of Christ, is thus a distinctly *sacerdotal function.* The vast structure of the world-wide Mystical Body, resting everywhere upon a priestly hierarchy of Pope and bishops and priests, is the divinely instituted sphere of Christ's priestly activity.

Priesthood

Confirmation

Baptism

Wherever we have Christians there also are to be found Christ's priestly representatives, His agents in the performance of priestly functions. As far as the work of sanctification is concerned, pontiff and bishops and priests are but so many visible expressions of the tireless, invisible work of the great Bridge-Builder "accomplishing the work God gave Him to do."

John xvii,4

That the words of the visible priests are the moral acts of Christ is illustrated by the forms "*I* baptize, *I* confirm, *I* absolve, this is *My* Body, *My* Blood." Christ and His minister are a moral unit, to their joint act Christ contributes the efficacy, the priest its visibility.

Christ's Priesthood Extended. There is another and very inspiriting phase of this subject; namely, *the priestly character of the Christian race*. From previous considerations we know that Christians are most intimately associated with, assimilated to, Christ. They are, so to speak, Christ-men; their lives are hid in Christ, they act in Him and through Him, and in them and through them Christ lives and acts. This being so, we should expect that Christ would associate the Christian with His chief prerogative — His priestly character. This is indeed what happens. St. Peter calls the general body of the Christians "a chosen race, a royal priesthood," and St. John twice praises Christ because He has made us priests of God.

I Pet. ii,9
Apoc. i,6; iv,10

Priesthood of the Laity. Of course, those initiated into Holy Orders are priests of Christ, but can it be true that *all Christians*, as such, men and women, are in some true sense *priests*? As will be further explained elsewhere, and particularly when dealing with baptism, it is a traditional tenet of the Catholic faith that every baptized person shares in the actual priesthood of Christ. Since the days of the religious rebellions of the sixteenth and seventeenth centuries, when this truth was distorted and exaggerated by heretics, Catholics have said little about this extremely ennobling doctrine of their faith. But now that the danger of misunderstanding is past, this truth is once more coming into its proper prominence. St. Irenaeus, a glorious martyr of Lyons (d. 202), says: "All the just have a priestly ordination." St. Chrysostom, the Mouth of Gold, echoes the same thought in the formula, "You were made a priest at baptism." St. Jerome calls baptism "the priesthood of the laity," and in his famous *City of God*, St. Augustine speaks as follows: "Just as we call all *Christians* because of the mystic chrism, so we call *all priests*, because they are *members of the one Priest*."

Adv. Haer. VIII,3
Hom. 3 in II Cor.
C. Lucif. IV

xx,10

Thus, in urging us to practice reparation to the Most Sacred Heart, Pope Pius XI adduces this priesthood of the laity as the objective basis for the value of *our* acts-in-Christ. The pontiff says in part (Douay):

The Apostle admonished us that "bearing about in our body the mortification of Jesus" and "buried together with Him by Baptism unto death," not only should we "crucify our flesh with the vices and concupiscences," "flying the corruption of that concupiscence which is in the world," but also that the "life of Jesus be made manifest in our bodies," and, having become partakers in His holy and eternal priesthood we should offer up "gifts and sacrifices for sins." For not only are they partakers in the mysteries of this priesthood, and in the duty of offering sacrifices and satisfaction to God, who have been appointed by Jesus Christ the High Priest as the ministers of such sacrifices, to offer God "a clean oblation in every place from the rising of the sun even to the going down," but *also those Christians called, and rightly so,* by the Prince of the Apostles, *"a chosen generation, a kingly priesthood,"* who are to offer "sacrifices for sin" not only for themselves but for all mankind, and *this in much the same way as every priest* and "high priest taken from among men is ordained for men in the things that appertain to God."[1]

*(Marginal references: II Cor. iv,10; Rom. vi,4; Gal. v,24; II Pet. i,4; II Cor. iv,10; Heb. v,1; Mal. i,10; I Pet. ii,9; Heb. v,1; Heb. v,1)*

Threefold "Character." As members of the one Priest, then, all Christians are with Him engaged in the priestly worship of God, and so are stamped with the seal of the priestly order. This is the sacramental seal imprinted at baptism (and at confirmation). St. Thomas Aquinas speaks of this common priesthood of the faithful in these terms:

Each of the faithful is deputed, to receive or to bestow on others, things pertaining to the worship of God. . . . Now the whole rite of the Christian religion is derived from Christ's Priesthood. Consequently it is clear that the sacramental character is specially the seal of Christ, to whose figure the faithful are likened by reason of their sacramental characters [of baptism and confirmation], which are nothing else than certain participations of Christ's Priesthood, flowing from Christ Himself.

(Marginal reference: S.T. III Q. lxiii, a.3)

Through this general priesthood of the laity we are all associated with the uniquely perfect priestly worship of God by the one High Priest. All real worship of God is "through Him," through Christ our Lord, as the concluding formula of our prayer never ceases to repeat. Ours is thus the precious opportunity to be

*(Marginal reference: Rom. xi,26)*

---

[1] Encyclical, *Reparation Due to the Sacred Heart*, May 8, 1928.

as living stones,
built up into a spiritual house,
to be a holy priesthood,
to offer spiritual sacrifices
I Pet. ii,5,6   well pleasing to God through Jesus Christ.

We are thus at all times enabled to share in the earth-wide, heaven-wide worship of God in the Person of the one true Priest, through whom earth and sky, men and angels, and all created things worship the uncreated God.

We called Christ a Bridge-Builder. Of similar content is a saying of Christ Himself, who one day spoke to Nathaniel of a great thing people were to witness, the great Ladder 'twixt earth and sky:

Ye shall see the heavens standing open,
and the angels of God ascending and descending
John i,51   upon the Son of Man.

This Ladder of the skies is the priestly mediation of Jesus Christ, who

can at all times save those
who approach God through Him,
Heb. vii,25   since He liveth to make intercession for them.

Summary. Since, in God's Providence, the irreligion of the Fall was to be atoned for by a perfect act of religious homage, a sacrifice, it was necessary that Christ be for mankind a Liturgist supreme. This office of His is eternal, and is now exercised through Christians associated in several degrees with Himself in the unique Priesthood of the New Law.

Fourth-Century Source Material

(The Saintly Mouth of Gold [Chrysostom] commenting on St. Paul's
II EPISTLE TO TIMOTHY.)

Knowest thou not what the priest is? He is a messenger of the Lord. Are they his own words that he speaks? If thou despisest him, thou despisest not him, but God that ordained him. But how does it appear, thou askest, that he is ordained of God? Nay, if thou suppose it otherwise, thy hope is rendered vain. For if God worketh nothing through his means, thou neither hast any Laver [of Baptism], nor art partaker of the Mysteries [of the Eucharist], nor of the benefit of blessings; thou art therefore not a Christian. What then, you say, does God ordain all, even the unworthy? God indeed doth not ordain all, but He worketh through all, though they be themselves unworthy, that the people may be saved. . . .

Why is he set over us? I beseech you, let us not speak ill of our teachers, nor call them to so strict an account, lest we bring evil upon ourselves. Let us examine ourselves, and we shall not speak ill of others. Let us reverence that day on which he enlightened [that is, baptized] us. He who has a father, whatever faults he has, conceals them all. For it is said,

> Glory not in the dishonor of thy father;
> for thy father's dishonor is no glory unto thee.
> And if his understanding fail,
> have patience with him.

Ecclus. iii,12,15

And if this be said of our natural fathers, how much more of our spiritual fathers. Reverence him, in that he every day ministers to thee, watches for thee, prays for thee, stands imploring God on thy behalf, offers supplications for thee, for thee is all his worship. Reverence all this, think of this, and approach him with pious respect. . . .

Is it the good life or the virtue of the priest that confers so much on thee? The gifts which God bestows are not such as to be the effects of the virtue of the priest. All is of grace. His part is but to open his mouth, while God worketh all. . . .

I am about to say what may appear strange, but be not astonished nor startled at it. The Offering [of the Eucharist] is the same, whether a common man, or Paul or Peter offer it. It is the same which Christ gave to His disciples, and which the priests now minister. This is nowise inferior to that, because it is not men that sanctify even this, but the Same who sanctifies the one sanctifies the other also. For all the words which God spake are the same which the priest now utters, so is the Offering the same, and the Baptism, that which He gave. Thus the whole is of faith. . . . And this is His body as well as that. And he who thinks the one inferior to the other, knows not that Christ even now is present, even now operates (Hom. II).

Topics for Further Discussion:

That in some ecclesiastical documents the Blessed Virgin is called a priest: the unique sense in which this is true of her, and the common sense in which it is true of every baptized woman.

The gross exaggeration of what Tertullian said as a heretic: "Are we not likewise priests and are we not doing all the priest does?" (*Exhor. Cast.* vii.)

Why Catholics ceased speaking of the priesthood of the laity at the time of the Reformation.

The differences in popular participation in our public worship which the spread of the consciousness of the priesthood of the laity will evoke.

Why the concept of the priesthood of the laity is well adapted to raise, and not lower, the laity's esteem of the clergy.

Readings:

K. Adam, *Christ Our Brother* (New York: Macmillan, 1931), "Christ's Redeeming Work," pp. 111–144.

M. C. D'Arcy, *Jesus Christ, Priest and Redeemer*, TF, 14.

—— *The Mass and the Redemption* (London: Burns, Oates & Washbourne, 1926), "The Sacrifice of the Mass," pp. 58–76.

G. Ellard, *Men at Work at Worship* (New York: Longmans, 1940), "A Perpendicular and Horizontal Union," pp. 69–82.

C. Grimaud–J. F. Newcomb, *One Only Christ* (New York: Benziger, 1939), "Priests with Christ," pp. 153–158.

J. A. Jungmann, *Liturgical Worship* (New York: Pustet, 1941), "In Whom the Liturgy Is Reposed," pp. 30–46.

C. Lattey, *The Atonement, Papers Read at the Summer School of Catholic Studies, Cambridge, 1926* (St. Louis, Herder, 1928), "The Principle of Solidarity," pp. 70–81.

D. A. Lord, *Our Part in the Mystical Body* (St. Louis: Queen's Work, 1935), "Royal Priests," pp. 138–147.

F. Prat, *The Theology of St. Paul* (London: Burns, Oates & Washbourne, 1927), II, "The Redeeming Mission," pp. 161–179.

J. Wilhelm, "Mediator, Christ as," CE.

Chapter V

THE SOUL NATURALLY LITURGICAL

*From one man He hath made
the whole human race
to dwell upon the entire face of the earth . . .
that they should seek God* (Acts xvii,26,27).

O NE of the great enigmas for the historians of the future will be
the fact that millions of men of our once Christian civilization
of the period, say, 1750–1930, sought happiness in *irreligion.*
However regrettable may be the continuous drifting farther from clear
beliefs to an indefinite theism, on through a still vaguer "religion of
nature," into positive disbelief, which was the singular misfortune of this
large group, *that* does not constitute the problem for the historian. Other
peoples have had Catholicity and have it no longer. But the ages to come
will ponder over the phenomenon, here met with for the first time in
human annals, of a widespread and deliberate attempt to build a culture
without the underlying foundation of a cult of some divinity, however
false. The most advanced civilizations and the least advanced, the records
of ancient Egypt, Persia, and Greece, those of Oriental Mohammedanism
of old or of Hinduism of today, all these are at one with the records of
the so-called primitives just emerging from savagery, in showing that
man everywhere knows *his nature demands a recognition of God.* The
soul of man is naturally liturgical; he must worship God, must even
worship Him socially, if he is to be true to himself. It makes one smile
now to read of how the ancient pagans railed at what they considered the
impiety of the early Christians, because these had, so they thought, no
public worship, and especially, no altar of sacrifice. "Why their mighty
effort to hide and shroud whatever it is they worship, since things honest
ever like the open day . . . ? Why have they *no altars, no temples, no
images?*" How those same ancient pagans would have scoffed, provided   *Octavius,* x,2
amazement did not render them speechless, had they been given a glimpse

55

of the irreligion of the modern "enlightened" and "emancipated" man. And, on his side, the religious "liberal" of the nineteenth and opening twentieth century looked down from immeasurable heights of sophistication on the natural reverence and pious folly of the ancients. Peter Wust trenchantly answers their charge:

> "They prayed to Zeus and Poseidon and to a multiplicity of gods, and that was folly." Of course it was folly; but the *actual prayer* itself was not folly. On the contrary, it was the ancients' supreme act of childlike wisdom. Their whole life was fashioned and hallowed to a liturgy, and from thence it derived its sheer greatness and its monumental quality, and that character of sacredness before which even today we still feel ourselves obliged to linger in reverence.[1]

Now that the world of cultless culture, built on sand and tumbled down by a crash in Wall Street, lies about us in ruins, the illusion of self-sufficiency, not to say, self-worship, has been dispelled. Modern man begins to realize that even for material well-being he needs God and the worship of God.

Modern Religiosity. But in the era just closed man's inborn hunger and thirst for God, and man's awful weariness of inescapable guilt, has fed itself on scraps and crumbs of information about religions, and speculation about "religious experiences." Witness the constantly recurring phenomenon of modern life, not only in America but elsewhere, that, when anyone has achieved eminence in any line of work, he is asked to expound his views on religion. Newspaper editors illustrate something similar in allotting the most conspicuous places in the papers to items concerning religion. Magazines constantly furnish their readers with articles on religion of the "Why-I-am-a ———" sort, since people who have but the faintest interest in other phases of cultural or social life, and no interest at all, it may be, in *living* a religion, avidly read minute accounts of the religions of even the most primitive savages. What the world's remotest barbarian thinks about religion seems to concern the whole world. Why is this, if not because the tendency which prompts religious worship is a vital bond making all men brothers? Religion is the business of life. A manual of Christian conduct of about the year 260 says in fact: "Pursue your trades therefore as a work of superfluity, for

---

[1] P. Wust, "The Crisis in the West," *Essays in Order* (New York: Macmillan, 1931), pp. 99, 100.

your sustenance, but *let your true work be religion.*" The modern capi- *Didas. Apos.* xiii
talist of America may actually realize as little as the pagan primitives
the reason of his interest in religion, but so long as he is a man, he has
a nature planned and built and fashioned for religion. Man is made *to
seek for God*. Less desirable and indeed erroneous manifestations of the
same basic tendency are shown in the widespread influence of superstition,
which is the first step toward the baleful realm of magic, or the attempt
to compel and control by spells preternatural or supernatural forces.
Newman was convinced that "they who are not superstitious without the
Gospel, will not be religious with it."

Man Made for God. Suppose we attempt a brief analysis of man's
religious impulse. On the one hand, the Creator could not fashion a race
of creatures *not destined to magnify His own glory;* on the other, this
Creator in His boundless goodness actually created man to share His
own life and beatitude. Things being so, God *had* to implant deep in
the very roots of man's nature a thirst unquenchable except at the Fountain of Life itself. "Thou hast made us, O Lord, for Thee," St. Augustine addresses God in a famous passage, "and our heart shall find no rest
until it rest in Thee." However incompletely man may know God, if he *Conf.* I
be true to the deepest impulse of nature, he will seek and grope for Him.
Man constantly tries to put himself into communication with the
Divinity.

Written in Human Heart. Because this tendency is universal among
men, it is not necessary in seeking a true and clear concept of religion
to open Holy Writ and read what God has revealed on the subject.
There, of course, one finds what might be called a religion let down
from heaven, the whole matter disclosed by Divine Wisdom Itself. But
as far as all the basic notions are concerned, one can turn to the history
of mankind, ancient or modern, civilized or savage, and find (with varying degrees of clarity and completion, to be sure), the same, single
religious sentiment incarnate from age to age *in the very heart of man.*
Man groping his way toward God possesses himself of exactly the same
fundamental religious notions as God was pleased to reveal to His
chosen people. St. Paul appealed to this very fact in addressing the
Romans:

> For when the Gentiles, who by nature have not the Law,
> fulfil the requirements of the Law,

these . . . are a law unto themselves,
> *showing as they do*
> *the demands of the Law to be written in their hearts;*
and an approving conscience beareth them out,

Rom. ii,14,15   amid the debate of thoughts that accuse or defend.

Creed, Code, Cult. A developed religion, then, whether directly revealed by God, or the fruit of man's own effort

> in discerning and contemplating
> in God's visible works
> His invisible attributes,

Rom. i,19   His everlasting power and divinity,

as St. Paul put it, embodies three elements, a *creed*, a *code*, and a *cult*. There is, first of all, a series of beliefs touching the divine origin of the world, and the divine origin and destiny of mankind. Moreover, these are beliefs, which, it is held, man is not at liberty to reject. The second element concerns conduct: Here it is agreed generally that certain norms of morality are imposed upon man with the sanction of the Deity. The third constituent deals with the regulation of communications between men and the Divinity. It consists in a system of rites and practices calculated to promote individual and social contact with the Deity. This is the elaborated and finished definition of religion. Let us look at this definition in the making, by quickly examining the psychological stages of its formation.

Dependence and Gratitude. When we analyze religious phenomena, we find these implications. At the bottom of all religious sentiment is man's explicit or implicit *recognition of his dependence* upon a Divinity. Whether this be in the full, clear light of the revelation of Sinai, "I am

Exod. xx,2   the Lord thy God," or in the sufficient, if indirect, light of deduction, man feels the selfsame urge:

> Come, let us bow down and fall prostrate . . .
> For He is the Lord our God,
> And we are people of His pasture,

Ps. xciv   the sheep of His hand.

Coincident with this recognition that the world and his own being are owing to God, man feels a prompting of *gratitude:* he says in substance

Ps. cv,1   "Let us praise the Lord *because He is good.*"

O Lord, our God,
   How wonderful is Thy Name
   In all the earth!
For Thy glory is exalted above the heavens. . . .

If I look on the heavens,
   The work of Thy hands,
   And on the moons and the stars which Thou hast made. . . .

What is man that Thou shouldst remember him?
   Or the son of man that Thou shouldst visit him?

[Yet] Thou hast placed him over the works
   of Thy hands,
All things hast Thou put beneath his feet.   Ps. viii

Love and Contrition. The very knowledge of God's goodness or lovableness shows man that his *happiness* will *consist* largely in having *God for his friend.* He is moved to adhere closely to God lest he cut himself off from this all-lovable Goodness. Logically man surrenders himself to God. To Him who gives him all, and who, he sees, is the source of his happiness, man gives himself in return. He feels that the closer he binds himself to God, the more liberal will God be in accepting him and treating him as a friend. Man therefore prays and proposes to remain ever acceptable to God.

I love the Lord,
   Because He hath heard my prayerful voice;

Because He hath bent to me His ear;
   I will cry out [unto Him] all my life long . . .

I will walk in God's pleasure
   In the land of the living.   Ps. cxiv

These relationships are those of a sinless creature with his Creator. But, alas! mankind inherits from Adam the heavy *consciousness of guilt.* Therefore his religion from the outset has necessarily included another note, the necessity of placating this good God now justly estranged by man's wrongdoing.

Out of the depths I cry to Thee, Lord!

If Thou, Lord, shouldst retain sin,
O Lord, who could stand?

My soul hopeth for the Lord
More than watchers for the morning.

For with the Lord is loving kindness
And plenteous redemption is with Him,

And He will ransom Israel
From all its sin.

Ps. cxxix

Need of Ceremonial. These fundamental religious concepts which we have been sketching — adoration, thanksgiving, petition, and propitiation — are in themselves *predominantly intellectual*. Theoretically speaking, a relationship based on them might be established between any single individual and the Divinity without enlisting the service of any bodily organs or operations. But "such is the nature of men," says the Council of Trent, "that, without external helps, he cannot easily be raised to the meditation of divine things." If men were all spirit, like the angels, and *if each lived in isolation apart*, they *could* so serve God. But, in the first place, man has his complex corporeal structure, so closely linked to his spiritual powers, that when he thinks, his *imagination,* his bodily *emotions,* and his nervous system, all to some extent come into play. The more intense his mental operations, the more necessary also it becomes for him to give *corporeal expression* to them in some way. Spontaneously and irresistibly, therefore, with the recognition of God's dominion over him, man feels urged to bow down, to kneel, to prostrate himself before this sovereign Lord. At the very sight of God's numberless gifts to him, arises a desire to make a gift in return:

Sess. xxii,c.5

How shall I make return to God,
For all His gifts to me?

Ps. cxv

(The answer to this question, which we will consider farther on, is: "I will offer Thee a sacrifice.") Similarly, there is the natural impulse to accompany a prayer of petition by raising the eyes toward heaven, by holding out our hands as if to receive divine favors, and by other gestures. The consciousness of guilt expresses itself in natural tokens of sorrow, such as beating the breast, which is the home, as it were, of the guilty heart. In this way man does not hesitate to employ any word or tone, any gesture or posture, fire or water, light or darkness, oil or incense, or any object about him as an aid in expressing his religious sentiment, just as in the political sphere citizens employ and honor a flag or other emblem to "personify" the country, and the like. On a moment's reflection it is seen how inextricably interwoven psychologically are creed and code and cult. Clearly, an inner, invisible worship is not enough for man.

Religion Essentially Social. Then there is another element of religion only hinted at thus far. Just as man is a compound of body and soul, and uses both to express himself suitably, so he is inevitably from birth until death a *unit in a social system*. He lives in constant and manifold relationships with his fellows, in the family, as well as in civic, political, and communal entities of numerous kinds. His instincts and impulses are social: the Emperor Marcus Aurelius phrased this thought in saying, "We are made for social action; to oppose one another is *Thoughts, ii,1* contrary to nature." *Religion*, therefore, *imposes* not only individual self-dedication to God, but *social self-dedication* to Him also. Families worship in common, communities worship in common; in other words, over and above the individual units, society, as society, worships God. How could *society* fulfill its obligation to worship *without* external rites?

Sacrifice, the Crown of Worship. Precisely because man is not a pure spirit, but a *corporeal* creature, we repeat, he feels obliged to express interior self-dedication to God by some outward gift given Him. This outward symbol is all the more necessary when worship is communal and not individual. Thus it came about that in almost all religions *sacrifice*, the public rendering of a gift to God, is considered the *highest, most perfect* expression of worship. The paramount importance of the idea of sacrifice demands that we have clear and exact notions about it. From its universality among men it has been argued that it belongs to the natural law itself. Thus St. Thomas says: "At all times and among all *S.T. ii, Q. lxxxv,* nations there has always been the offering of sacrifices. Now, that which *a.1* is observed by all is seemingly natural. Therefore the offering of sacrifice is of the natural law." The Council of Trent says pithily: "The nature of man *requires* sacrificial worship." *Sess. xxii,c.1*

Sacrifice is defined as *the public rendering to God through the hands of a priest of some visible gift that symbolizes a giving of one's self to Him*. It involves adoration of God as supreme Lord: it ought to include both thanksgiving for former favors and petitions for further ones; lastly,

*A pagan altar
made into the pedestal
         for a Christian altar*

when sin has intervened between God and man, the sacrificial gift likewise expresses an intention and attitude of reparation.

Food-Offerings, Blood-Offerings. Obviously any visible gift may
serve the purpose of sacrifice. But since *sacrifice is symbolic of complete
self-dedication,* foodstuffs, as the sustenance of life, have been the customary objects of oblation. Sheaves of freshly cut grain, flour, bread,
grapes, wine, all manner of food-offerings, have been laid upon the sacrificial altar. The bloody sacrifice, also so common, is directly connected
with the consciousness of guilt. "Without the *shedding of blood* there
is no pardon" was a commonplace among the ancients, *because* "the   Heb. ix,22
wages of sin is death." Guilt-laden mankind felt that only a vicarious   Rom. vi,23
blood-letting could adequately express his sentiments of contrition.

Altar, God's Agent. This formal gift-offering requires, of course,
that it be accepted by God, unless the whole process is to fail of its object.
From this fact arises in sacrificial ritual the importance of the altar,
considered as invested with God's holiness, a visible *representative of God,*
as it were, to receive in His place and stead the sacrificial gift.

Altar Becomes Banquet Table. But with the gift once offered on
the altar and accepted, is the sacrifice concluded? Strictly speaking, it is.
Yet, following upon their sacrifice, men have always sought some special
token of the divine acceptance, even some *divine largess* in return. This
has led to the sacrificial banquet. Man considers himself invited to sit
down as God's table-guest, and to partake of the (now sanctified) sacrificial food-offering. Here is the symbol of God's good pleasure in the
offering. In the sacrificial banquet the fruit of the sacrifice is gathered.

Christianity a Perfect Religion. Nothing has been said in this
analysis of worship that is specifically Christian, or even that applies
exclusively to the revealed religion of the Old Testament. Is Christianity
also a compound of creed and code and cult? Is it a religion of external
actions and rites? Is it essentially social and communal, like the imperfect
natural religions we have been studying? Has it that perfection of all
religions, public and sacrificial worship? There is among speculative
theologians a school of thought which maintains the proposition, that
even if man had committed no sin, Christ would nevertheless have been
born. One of the reasons alleged in support of this view is the claim that
only in a God-man as Priest can *perfect worship* be rendered to God.
The mediator must necessarily reach to both extremes, even as the bridge

must touch both shores if one is to pass over it. Without committing ourselves unreservedly to this hypothetical case, it will become clear in subsequent chapters that in the present order of things perfect worship of God is had, and had only, through

I Tim. ii,5   the one Mediator of God and men . . .
Col. i,18   the Head of the Body the Church . . .
Heb. vii,25   Jesus Christ always living to make intercession for us.

Summary. Since man was fashioned to find happiness in the enjoyment of God, his religious impulse, quite independently of "civilization," is spontaneous and fairly uniform. Dependence upon God the sovereign Lord, gratitude toward Him as the great Benefactor, love for Him as the Source of endless Goodness, and sorrow for having offended against a God so good — these are the basic concepts of religion. These convictions of a soul naturally liturgical naturally find expression in external and corporate worship, the highest form of which is called a sacrifice. Herein gifts as symbols of self-dedication are offered to God at the hands of a priest, and later received back from God with His blessings at a sacrificial meal. Christianity, because it has a God-Man as Priest, is the one perfect religion.

Fifth-Century Source Material
(St. Augustine on the Communism of the Mystic Body:
COMMENTARY OF PSALM CXXX,6.)

The eye seeth, and heareth not; the ear heareth, and seeth not; the hand worketh, but it neither heareth nor seeth; the foot walketh, but it heareth not, nor seeth, nor doth what the hand doth. But if there be health in one body, and the members contend not against one another, the ear seeth in the eye, the eye heareth in the ear; nor can it be objected to the ear that it seeth not, so as to say to it: You are nothing, you are inferior; can you see and discern colors, as the eye doth? For the ear answereth from the peace of the body and saith: I am where the eye is, I am in that body; in myself I see not, in that wherewith I exist I see. So when the ear saith, My eye seeth; the eye saith, My ear heareth; and eyes and ears say, Our hands work for us; the hands say, The eyes and the ears see and hear for us; the eyes and the ears and hands say, The feet walk for us; while all members do their work in one body, if there be health therein and the members be in concord, they rejoice, and rejoice with one another. But if there be any trouble in any member, they forsake not one another, but suffer with one another. . . . Thus, then, brethren, whosoever in the body of Christ cannot restore the dead to life, let him not seek this power, but let him seek that he may not be at discord in the body; just as there might be discord if the ear should seek to see. . . . When therefore a man who is progressing heareth this, as it were a calumny cast in his teeth by ignorant heathens, by men who know not what they speak of, in the sodality of the body of Christ let him answer and say: Thou who sayest, thou art not righteous because thou dost not work miracles, thou couldst also say to the ear, thou are not in the body, for thou seest not. You, he saith, should do that which Peter did. But Peter did it for me also, since I am in that body, wherein Peter wrought it. In him, from whom I am not divided, I can do what he can. In that I can do less, he suffereth together with me; and in that he can do more, I rejoice with him. The Lord Himself cried from on high on behalf of His body, "Saul, Saul, why dost thou persecute Me?" and no Acts ix,4 man was touching Him. But the head cried from Heaven for the body suffering on earth. — Quoted with permission from Przywara-Martindale, *An Augustine Synthesis*, New York: Sheed and Ward, 1936, pp. 255, 256.

Topics for Further Discussion:

The psychological impossibility of atheism or skepticism as a spontaneous attitude toward religion.

That false religions, because they are in some ways *false, cannot* provide a complete system of self-sanctification.

Strange aberrations of the impulse to offer sacrifice that come to light even in our times.

Your answer to one who says: "I worship God best in solitude, communing with nature."

Your answer to one who would say: "Paganism with all its hideous savagery is superior to Protestantism."

The desire to please God as voiced by a Persian pagan hymn:

How can I please Thee, Thou wise Lord? Full well I know that I am not good as it behooves me. This, I lament, O Lord. Vouchsafe me Thine aid as a friend to a friend. Teach me to merit bliss by a good heart. . . . O ye Spirits of wisdom and righteousness, your will will I accomplish. This is the resolve of my thought and my soul.

How an Egyptian pagan would like to stand at his final reckoning:

He must be able to say on the Day of Judgment in the presence of the Lord of truth: "Lo, I come before Thee. I have eschewed sin against Thee. I have not sinned against men, I have afflicted no man. . . . I have not cursed God, and have done nothing that is abominable in the sight of the heavenly ones. I have not slandered the servant to his lord, have suffered no man to hunger, have made no man to weep, have done no murder nor procured it to be done, have hurt no man, have not enlarged the corn measure, have done no deed of violence."

A Babylonian pagan's Act of Contrition:

(After a lengthy catalogue of sins was set before the penitent seeking quiet of conscience.) . . . In respect of all the evil whereby he hath disregarded his god and goddess. . . . It is searched out, it is seached out — now therefore may it be cancelled, Thou Judge, Shamash. Blot it out, O Marduk, compassionate Lord. Blot it out, Thou God of the sinner. Blot it out, Thou God of the evildoer.

A Roman pagan's treaty oath as sealed by sacrifice:

The Roman envoy to the inhabitants of Alba, as he slew the sacrificial victim: "If we are the first to violate with evil intent the treaty which we have publicly concluded, then, do Thou, Diespater, smite the Roman people as I now smite this sacrificial victim." — Quoted with permission from O. Karrer's *Religions of Mankind,* New York: Sheed and Ward, 1936.

Readings:

C. F. Aiken, "Religion," *CE.*

L. de Grandmaison, *Lectures on the History of Religions* (St. Louis: Herder, 1910), I, "The Study of Religion," pp. 1–28.

——— *Personal Religion* (New York: Sheed and Ward, 1929), "Piety," pp. 19–36.

C. C. Martindale, *Man and His Destiny,* TF, 9.

J. Pohle, "Sacrifice," *CE.*

A. D. Sertillanges, *The Church* (New York: Benziger, 1922), "Religious Feeling in General," pp. 1–6; "Necessity and Permanence of Religious Feeling," pp. 7–12; "Religious Feeling and Christianity," pp. 13–19; "Social Character of Religious Feeling," pp. 27–38; "Social Character of Christianity," pp. 39–44.

M. de la Taille, *The Mystery of Faith, an Outline* (New York: Sheed and Ward, 1930), "Sacrifice," pp. 3–10.

Chapter VI

"THE SOUL NATURALLY CHRISTIAN"

He that hath the Son,
hath the life;
he that hath not the Son of God,
hath not the life (I John v,11,12)

IN THE summer or autumn of the year 197, Tertullian of Carthage, then a rather recent convert from paganism, addressed to the provincial governors of the Roman Empire his *Defense of Christianity.* Referring in that work to certain words of a pagan judge, Tertullian used the expression: "Behold the testimony of a soul naturally Christian." *Apol.* xvii We see what store he set by his happy phrase since he wrote an appendix to his *Defense* merely to enlarge upon this thought. In his immediate context Tertullian really meant no more than that pagans, by spontaneous exclamations and ordinary modes of speech, often unconsciously betray a correct, *natural* knowledge of God, a belief in His unity and sanctity, and in the life of man with God beyond the grave. Suppose in borrowing Tertullian's words we broaden their original meaning and say: In God's present economy, every man is naturally Christian in the sense that only by becoming Christian can he begin to enjoy a full life. Only the elevating and transforming effects of grace fully release the possibilities of the human heart.

Catholicity Allows Full Homage. We do not in our turn intend here to launch upon a *Defense of Christianity.* Remaining well within the framework of our theme; namely, worship in its relationships to social life, we seek merely to indicate what Tertullian saw, what every instructed Catholic clearly recognizes, that the *sacramental* and *sacrificial system of the Church* puts perfect purpose and poise and order into the restless religious and liturgical yearning of the *nature of man* as we know him. It alone imparts the *supernatural life* in a complete system of sanctification, wherein all life's needs and aspirations are met so superabundantly. It alone allows an expression, perfect from every point of view, of man's humble homage; it alone brings to actual accomplishment man's longing to put himself into communication with, to unite himself with, God. Only Catholicity gives full play to the needs of bodily as well as spiritual homage, of corporate as well as individual homage, enabling society to enlist in its worship color and sound and fabric, lights and incense, oil and water, bread and wine.

"Spoils of Paganism?" A charge against Catholicity that never seems to grow outmoded, since it is still being repeated, after having done periodic service since early patristic times, is that she uses in her worship, besides an altar of sacrifice, lights, oil, processions, images, and other ceremonial objects very much like those used by pagan religions long ago. The external features of Catholic worship are thus said to be spoils of paganism. Well, that the false religions used these things does not mean that the things themselves are false. A true understanding of the nature of man dictated those expressions of man's true religious impulse. Christianity is not ashamed to use in the service of the true God the forms suited to man's nature, even though these were formerly used in paying divine homage to idols. To Faustus St. Augustine admits readily: "There can be no religion, true or false, without external ceremonial. . . . We *have* some things in common with the Gentiles, but our purpose is different." "Because we once worshiped idols, is that a reason," asks St. Jerome pointedly, "why we should not worship God, for fear of seeming to address Him with an honor like that which was paid to idols?" Moreover, so sure is the Church of Christ of her inherent power to sanctify all creation, that she stands ready to appropriate existing rites and customs. A classic instance is furnished by the example of St. Gregory the Wonder-Worker, who, on his appointment to the diocese of Pontus, found only seventeen Christians there. His biographer, St. Gregory of Nyssa, narrates and interprets with praise how he set about hallowing existing religious usages dear to the populace:

Contra Faustum,
xix,11; xx,23
Cf. Epis. 103, 18

C. Vigilant. viii

> After revisiting the country round about, he increased the devotion of the people everywhere by instituting festive meetings in honor of those who had fought for the faith. The bodies of the Martyrs were distributed in different places, and the people assembled and made merry, as the year came 'round, holding festival in their honor. This indeed was a proof of his great wisdom . . . for, perceiving that the childish and untrained populace were retained in their idolatrous error

Saint Gregory

by creature comforts, in order that what was of first importance should at any rate be secured to them, *viz.*, that they should *look to God in place of their vain rites*, he allowed them to be merry, jovial and gay at the monuments of the holy Martyrs, as if their behavior would in time undergo a spontaneous change into greater seriousness and strictness, since faith would lead them to it; *which has actually been the happy issue in that population.*

Vit. Thaum.
xxvii

That short passage might almost stand as a summary of *The History of Christ's Influence upon Creation:* Incorporation into the Mystical Body hallowed rational nature, while irrational nature is in some way sanctified by contact.

An Understanding of Mankind. The non-Catholic world often regards Catholicity as a gloomy system of superstition, based on fear and allied with magic, a sort of melancholia weighted with a sense of sin; in short, something quite at cross purposes with healthy human nature. The facts of the case are just the other way around. It is Christianity which has a sane and healthy, a bold and confident, a sympathizing and dignifying appreciation of our human nature and of the world we live in. Deeper, too, than all intellectual convictions, Christians have a new vital principle within them:

He that hath the Son,
hath the life;
he that hath not the Son of God,

I John v,11–12
hath not the life.

Spirit-World and Sense-World Wedded. Long had men thirsted to know the Living God. If He

had by many partial revelations
and in various ways
Heb. i,1
spoken of old to the Jews

still, to the vast majority of men, He was quite unknown. Then squarely and fully to satisfy this natural longing of men concerning Himself, God disclosed Himself to all mankind in the Person of His Son incarnate I Tim. vi,16 in human flesh. The Dweller in light inaccessible was made visible in the familiar lineaments of human nature. Heretofore the nature and attributes of God were capable of only the faintest comprehensions; now, as the Word of life, God dwelt among men so that

> their eyes could see,
> their ears hear,
> their hands handle Him.   I John i,1

Redemption was accomplished by *God-in-the-flesh;* in keeping with that dispensation, the Wisdom of God established a religion in which *things of the spirit* are constantly linked with *things of sense.* God will communicate His own absolutely spiritual life to man — but in a manner not wholly spiritual. God will catch up fallen humanity — but as by the cords of the New Adam, that is, by sensible, material objects and forms and symbols. This is one thing which makes Christianity so pre-eminently suited to human nature.

The New Birth. In His redeeming work Christ offered man the supernatural life. But He laid down as a condition of its bestowal a sensible rite, which He called a *new birth,* or *birth from above.* This new John iii,2 birth was to effect an interior renewal, the removal of original sin; to be, as it were, a birth into the grace-world. Therefore Christ chose that the new birth should be effected and exteriorly signified by washing with water or dipping into water. Thus man is *christened,* or made a sharer of the divine life through incorporation into Christ. The actuality is tremendously important; small wonder, then, that the rite becomes gradually invested with natural signs to express its importance. Christ means "Anointed," so the new member of Christ is actually anointed; the ablution removes all trace of sin from the soul, so the neophyte is robed in a white garment: the rebirth imparts a new and higher life within, so in the hands of the newly born is placed a bright and shining light.

The Strengthening Spirit. This new Christian,

> begotten anew,
> not from perishable,
> but from imperishable seed,   I Pet. i,23

can never be unbaptized, can never be de-Christianized. But he can *kill the divine life* within him by a deliberate violation of God's law in a serious matter. He carries his treasure in a vessel no stronger than a human will. Now the new life within must grow and unfold; hence, the human will must be *guarded* and *strengthened,* given a permanent *set* sufficient to meet all the dangers of the way. This spiritual effect will be achieved by giving the Christian a divine Helper, the Holy Spirit, with

His abundant gifts and graces. By anointing the body with oil the athletes of olden times sought to obtain litheness and suppleness for the Olympic and other games. Again, in the realm of spiritual things, the imposition of the hand of a sacred personage on the head of another signified the transferring of invisible force to such a one. These two sensible actions were, by Christ, made the external signs of the abiding communication of divine strength to the Christian in the Sacrament of Confirmation.

"Our Daily Bread." For the inner, *supernatural life* to unfold to its highest possibilities, and to recover the losses of everyday life, it must needs have *nourishment, sustenance*. Therefore, under the signs of bread and wine, received as food and drink, the Christian is enabled to unite himself immediately and most intimately with the Godhead dwelling in the Body and Blood of Christ.

> He that eateth My Flesh
>   and drinketh My Blood
> hath everlasting life,
> and I will raise him up on the last day.
>
> For My Flesh is food indeed,
> and My Blood is drink indeed.
>
> He that eateth My Flesh
>   and drinketh My Blood
> abideth in Me, and I in him.
>
> As the living Father hath sent Me,
>   and as I live of the Father,
>   so he that eateth Me,
>   he also shall live of Me.
>
> This is the bread that came down from heaven,
>   not as the fathers ate and died:
> he that eateth this bread shall live forever.

John vi,54–58

How this everyday sustenance of the supernatural within us is linked up with the natural impulse to sacrifice and to partake of a sacrificial banquet, needs no further explanation just now.

A Cordial of Bittersweet. In man's natural life come sicknesses, slight or grave, to be a passing inconvenience or to completely prostrate and paralyze him as the case may be. So the *life of God-within-us* can be lamed by slight strokes of malice, or killed outright by serious and deliberate sin. These contingencies are provided for in the *medicinal rites of penance,* to the healing of which are joined effectual comfort and strength. Here, too, the Catholic has always known what the modern research in mental hygiene now brings out so clearly, that from the purely natural point of view, the institution of confession answers a real and deep-seated need of human nature.

Social Obligations and Helps. Baptism admits one to Christianity; confirmation affords mature strength; Holy Eucharist keeps Christians as living, growing, functioning members of the Mystical Body. Penance is a medicine to counteract sin's poisons. There are other sacraments for other special crises in the full and normal supernatural life of the individual. The prompting *to marry* arises from the conviction that founding a family is a fuller, completer human existence. But the life of man and woman in marriage requires, for its success, mutual fidelity and a deep, never-failing love. Obligations so fearsome in their scope make marriage a grave step. Christian couples receive the supernatural helps needed to be faithful in these obligations because Christ has made their mutual promises a divinely instituted sacrament.

Troops of children to supply ever new members for the increase of the Mystical Body are assured by matrimony. Priests to effect the *spiritual parenthood* of sacramental administration in the same Mystical Body are guaranteed by the sacrament of holy orders. The priestly calling, if hedged by strict obligations, imparts tremendous powers. How much, therefore, in keeping with the far-reaching congruity of the whole sacramental system is all the stately ritual that surrounds the investing of the chosen candidate as deacon, priest, or bishop.

Strength at the Last. The hour of death, so universally dreaded, is in some ways the most serious crisis in human existence. Body and soul wrenched apart, the disembodied spirit is sent out into a world of which it has no sensible knowledge. Because this hour is the last wherein the use of human freedom can determine the weal or woe of the unending future, it becomes extremely critical for the Christian. This need was foreseen and provided for by Christ in the sacrament of the *last anointing.* As the symbol of this special sacramental *healing* and soothing *comfort* He appropriately chose *anointing with oil,* one of the commonest instruments of therapy in the ancient East.

Grace-World Well Planned. Such is the sacramental system, that series of sense-symbols, instituted to act as channels of the super-life circulating in the Mystical Body. By this system Catholics are, everywhere and always, both *living* a supernatural life and expressing their religious sentiment in a progressively *sanctifying worship of God.* The scheme is complete in *seven* sacraments: if there were but six, some human need would be unprovided for; if eight, there would be needless overlapping and duplication. *The Catechism of the Council of Trent,* in speaking of the number of the Sacraments, says:

> In order to exist, to preserve existence, and to contribute to his own and the public good, seven things seem necessary to man: To be born, to grow, to be nurtured, to be cured when sick, when weak to be strengthened; as far as regards the public welfare, to have magistrates invested with authority to govern, and to perpetuate himself and his species by legitimate offspring. Now, since it is quite clear that all these things are sufficiently analogous to that life by which the soul lives to God, we discover in them a reason to account for the number of the Sacraments.

II, I, *Q.* xv

The Crown of Sacrifice. Far reaching as these sacramental rites are, so completely in agreement and harmony with human nature, they would still, did they not include a sacrifice, fall far short of answering man's religious needs. To offer God gifts in a formal, social way, and as tokens of self-dedication is, after all, the *foremost expression of religion.* "Sacrifice," says St. Thomas, "expresses the right relation of the soul to God: the right relation of the soul to God implies man's recognition that all he has comes from God as from the first beginning, and man's direction of all to God as to the last end." A religious system without sacrifice would be inadequate and incomplete. But in Christianity, important as all other rites may be, they but radiate from the altar of the Christian Sacrifice.

S. T. I, II. *Q.* cii, *a.*3

In oft-repeated catechetical formulas all Catholics have heard such expressions as: the Mass is a real sacrifice; it is the renewal of the sacrifice of the cross; *the Priest* at Mass and the Victim are the same as on the cross; namely, Christ; the Mass is like the cross all over again, only in an unbloody manner; on the cross our Redemption was accomplished, in the Mass the fruits of it are applied, etc. But because we live in an atmosphere so thoroughly irreligious, the *concept of sacrificial worship* has lost its sharpness and clarity. Often in calling the Mass a sacrifice, one uses a conventional tag that conveys *no meaning* at all. To freshen this idea, let us ask two questions: What is meant by saying that *Christ's death* was a sacrifice? What is meant by saying that the Mass is the *Christian's sacrifice?*

Christ "Gave" Himself. Sacrifice, we remember, is the public rendering to God through the hands of a priest of some visible gift which symbolizes a giving of one's self to Him. Now the *Man-God, as representative* of the whole human race, and in accordance with an agreement arrived at in the august councils of the Holy Trinity, *offered* as gift *His own life's Blood* (to be shed by executioners into whose hands He voluntarily gave Himself). The offering was made at the Last Supper; the saving Blood was poured out upon the cross of Calvary. From creation onward this was the single sacrificial Gift wholly pleasing to God, and it effected mankind's Redemption, as we know. The Mass repeats as a perpetual memorial the offering of the supper room as consummated on the cross. In every Mass the peerless Gift, as slain, is presented once more to the Father, this Gift which is the Head of the Mystical Body, the Church. By reason of our incorporation, the Gift becomes ours, becomes, in a way, ourselves. St. Thomas has it: "As the Head and the members are, as it were, one mystical person, so the *satisfaction* of Christ *belongs to* all the faithful as to His members." In another passage he says more briefly: "The satisfaction of Christ has its effect in us as far as we are concorporated in Him."

Sup. Q. xiii,a.2

Q. xlix,a.3 ad3

We "Give" Christ and Ourselves. But have Christians no *personal gift* to offer at Mass by way of expressing their own internal sacrificial attitude of mind? If not, the great tomes of the Fathers, and the teachings of the Church for centuries are rendered meaningless. Meaningless, too, would be the canons of Church councils which anathematized such as wished to be present at Mass without contributing the sacrificial elements. The gift-offering of *bread and wine* (or their equivalent), *as symbol* and sign *of personal and social consecration* to the divine service, *that* is the individual Christian's part in the great sacrificial cycle. These petty, insignificant oblations of our bread and wine become in the divine dispensation changed into the one, great Gift, the Body and Blood of Christ; they are accepted by the Father in an odor of sweetness, and thus sanctified, they are returned to us as food at the supper table of the Lord, Holy Communion. At every Mass there must be self-immola-

Serm. 55,3   tion. St. Leo the Great speaks of "the oblation of our human nature";
St. Gregory the Great refers to the "necessity at Mass of imitating what
Dial. iv,59   we re-enact, and so making to God the sacrifice of our hearts." In the
same strain St. Cyril of Alexandria said: "In our sacrifices [of bread and
De Ador. in Spir. wine] we sacrifice our own souls in an image and offer them to God."
et Ver., I,11   Let St. Augustine's terse phrase close the patristic consensus: "[The
Church] being the body of Him, the Head, learns to offer herself through
De Civ. Dei, x,20   Him."

"Incredible Cogency of Mass." The truth outlined in the foregoing paragraphs is expressed with vigor and clarity in the lines here quoted:

> When a man is "in Christ," forthwith He and Christ are vitally united, and Christ offers Himself and His Christian in Himself, and the man offers Christ and himself in vital unity, and God, looking upon Mass, sees both His Son and those who are "in one" with Him. Hence you cannot but perceive the incredible cogency of Mass. It is a gift that God cannot resist: the priest, and the layman too, since there is solidarity between them, have omnipotence in their hands. Mass is an act — not a prayer recited, not a ceremony contemplated, but the supreme act of history unequaled in the world.[1]

Summary. As a composite of body and soul, man must use both in any satisfactory system of worship. Catholicity ideally meets this elemental demand, since it provides not only fullness of revelation in a God-man, but an entire system of worship on this "incarnational" plane, the constant union of sense-objects with sanctifying processes, a system which provides in sacramentals, sacraments, and Sacrifice the fullest possible satisfaction of the religious promptings of human nature.

Sixth-Century Source Material

*(St. Gregory the Great, who was one of the most influential popes the Church
has ever had, writes on the Mass and the Mystic Body.)*

At the beginning of this work [*Moralia*], in discussing the unity of head and body, we were careful to indicate in advance how close is its bond of love, since the Lord still suffers many things in His body, that is ourselves, and His body, the Church, is even now glorified in its Head; namely, the Lord, in Heaven. At this point the sufferings of that Head

---

[1] C. C. Martindale, *The Faith of the Roman Church* (London: Methuen, 1927), p. 115.

ought to be pointed out, so that it shall be clear how much He bears with in His body. For if our afflictions touched not our Head, He would in no wise cry out from Heaven on behalf of His agonizing members against the persecutor:

Saul, Saul, why dost thou persecute Me?   Acts ix,4

And if our pains were not His sufferings, Paul, converted and himself in torments, would never exclaim:

I . . . make up in my flesh
what is lacking to the sufferings of Christ. — Bk. III, ch. xii.   Col. i,24

*   *   *   *   *

We ought to immolate to God the daily sacrifice of our tears, the daily Offering of His flesh and blood. For this Offering peculiarly preserves the soul from eternal death and it renews for us in mysterious wise the death of the Sole-Begotten, who, although being risen from the dead, dieth no more, and death hath no more dominion over Him; yet, while   Rom. vi,9 in Himself He liveth immortal and incorruptible, for us He is immolated again in this mystery of the sacred Oblation. For it is His body that is there given, His flesh that is divided for the salvation of the people, His blood that is poured, no longer into the hands of unbelievers, but into the mouths of the faithful. For this let us ever estimate what this Sacrifice is for us, which for our absolution ever imitates the Passion of the Only-Begotten Son. For what one of the faithful can have any doubt that at the very hour of the Offering [Mass], at the word of the priest, the Heavens are opened, the choirs of angels are present at the Mystery of Jesus Christ, the lowest things are united to the highest, earthly things with the heavenly, and of the invisible and the visible there is made one?

But it is necessary that when we assist at the Sacrifice, we should by contrition of heart, sacrifice ourselves unto almighty God. For when we celebrate the mystery of our Lord's Passion, we ought to imitate what we do. Then it shall be a real sacrifice for us unto God, if we offer ourselves also to Him in Sacrifice. — *Dialogues,* ch. lvii, lix.

Topics for Further Discussion:

The myth, born of sixteenth-century polemics, of "primitive simplicity (barrenness) of Christian worship," in the sense that Christianity ever rejected cult acts because they appeal to the senses.

"It is only the Catholic Church that retains true worship," said Lactantius in the fourth century, and Pope Pius XI repeats his dictum with approval in the Encyclical on Promoting True Religious Unity (1928). What other religion has hallowed all the natural expressions of worship, a sacrificing priesthood, fixed ritual, hieratic use of music and art, nature symbols, and so forth?

The reasons for the widespread return at present to Catholic ritual and ceremonial by non-Catholic Christians and even by non-Christians.

"Mass — a solemn rite destined to take exclusive possession of mankind's religious consciousness." — *Walter Pater.*

How the Protestant endeavor to preserve Communion without sacrifice resulted in a tasteless "wafer," and an empty "cup," with no communicants.

The psychological necessity of confession as shown by the numberless "soul clinics," "psycho-therapy institutes," as well as the nonsacramental "confession" of some Protestant bodies.

Readings:

Father Cuthbert, *God and the Supernatural* (New York: Longmans, Green, 1920); C. C. Martindale, "The Sacramental System," pp. 277–305.

F. C. Kolbe, *The Four Mysteries of the Faith* (New York: Longmans, Green, 1926), "The Sacramental System," pp. 128–132.

C. C. Martindale, *The Sacramental System,* TF, 21.

A. D. Sertillanges, *The Church* (New York: Benziger, 1922), "The General Idea of the Sacraments," pp. 135–140; "The General Idea of the Sacramentals," pp. 187–192.

Chapter VII

"COMMUNIONISM" AND THE BOND OF WORSHIP

*They persevered in the teaching
of the Apostles,
and the fellowship,
the breaking of Bread and the prayers* (Acts ii,42).

WHEN Christ swallowed down death, that we might be the heirs of life everlasting — as the strong language of the Vulgate renders the original Greek — the Temple veil was rent from top to bottom, as a sign that the sacrificial worship of Israel was now fulfilled on the Cross. When the religion of Catholics was publicly inaugurated a few weeks later, new men, "Christ-men," suddenly appeared on the scene. Feeling themselves united to God by a Mediator, who was weak as themselves in human flesh but holy as God in the Spirit, this *new race*, as they called themselves and were called, was conspicuous for a sense of true manliness, of human dignity, liberty of spirit, a catholic, that is, a world-wide, all-embracing range of interest, and easy confidence of a triumphant future. But most of all they were marked off from Jew and Gentile alike by a sense of fellowship and mutual love. Their contemporaries charged many things against the Christ-men, but, as Tertullian sums up, "it is *mainly* the deeds of a love so noble that lead many to put a brand on us, '*See*,' they say, '*how they love one another*,' for they themselves are animated by a mutual hatred . . . and they are wroth with us, too, because we call each other brethren." Tert. *Apol.* xxxix
Again, a pagan could be quoted as saying: "They recognize each other by marks and signs, and love each other almost before they recognize." Min. Fel. *Oct.*ix
Thereby those pagans fulfilled to the letter prophetic words spoken by Christ, when He instituted the holy Eucharist:

> By this shall all know that ye are My disciples,
> if ye have love one for another.

John xiii,35

79

Glance back at the quotation from the *Acts* at the head of this paragraph, and note how St. Luke expands the "fellowship" with the appositional

Acts ii,42 phrases, "the breaking of Bread and the prayers." In his next little summation of expanding Catholicism, the Evangelist again signals out their mutual accord:

Acts iv,32 The multitude of believers were of one heart and soul.

When St. Paul came to speak of what we might call the effects of the Holy Eucharist, he used only that selfsame word of fellowship:

> The Cup of blessing, which we bless,
> is it not fellowship in the Blood of Christ?
>
> The Bread which we break,
> is it not *fellowship* in the Body of Christ?
>
> *We many are one bread, one body,*

I Cor. x,14–16 > *for we all partake of the one Bread.*

And lest a modern reader miss the *connection* between this *fellowship* and the bond that cemented it, the *Eucharistic Bread,* Pope Leo XIII took pains to point it out: "If in the record of the Church it is deservedly reckoned to the credit of its first ages that *the multitude of the believers*

Acts iv,32 *had but one heart and one soul,* there can be no doubt that this was due

Mir. Car. to their common meetings at the divine Table." This fellowship fostered by common feeding on the Eucharistic Bread illustrates in practice what the Fathers of the Council of Trent were to define as dogma fifteen hundred years later, when heresy had challenged it: "He [Christ] wished this Sacrament to be a symbol of that one *body* of which He is the Head, and to which we are all united as members . . . in order that

I Cor. i,10 all speak the same thing,

Sess. XIII, c.2 thus ending the divisions among you."

The new race of "Christ-ed" men found in the Eucharist the symbolical expression, and the actual nourishing of their distinctive fellowship one with another.

"A Love-Feast." The Sacrifice was instituted at the close of an elaborate, Jewish ritual supper, and it is *in a supper-setting* that we find it first mentioned in the *Acts.* The name "breaking the Bread" was already stereotyped when St. Luke wrote the *Acts.*

> Day by day they persevered
> with one accord in the temple,
> and breaking Bread at home,
> they took food with joyful simplicity of heart. Acts ii,46

This meal in common, of which we shall see St. Paul's picture below, was called *Agape,* a Love-Feast. One of the most charming features of dawning Christianity, it was, so to speak, too good to last. St. John Chrysostom calls it: "an occasion for practising charity, a means of alleviating poverty and of making wealth wiser, a grand spectacle of edification and a school of humility."

The *Acts* give only one clear picture of the Bread-Breaking. The scene is at Troas, not very far from Constantinople; the time, a Sunday evening of the spring of the year 57, "when we were assembled to break Bread." Paul was long a-preaching, so that a young man, Eutychus, Acts xx,7 began to nod, fell from his place on the window sill (it was the third story), and was picked up apparently dead. Paul went down, and after a bit assured them that Eutychus would revive. Then he returned to the assembly and "breaking Bread and tasting . . . so he departed." On Acts xx,11 this occasion, as far as one can judge, the Eucharist was not united with the Agape.

Abuses Rebuked by Paul. At Corinth, however, whither the Apostle was writing in the winter of 54–55, it was the custom to celebrate the Eucharistic Sacrifice in conjunction with the *Agape.* In the Apostle's absence disorders had crept in, disorders which grieved him sorely. The circle of the brethren was dividing into cliques; these groups, instead of sharing provisions with the community, consumed their own for themselves. Again, they did not wait for all to assemble; most serious of all, some so far forgot the sacred purpose of their common repast as to drink to excess. It is the rod of the pedagogue that Paul wields now:

> In the first place I hear
> that when you come together to church
> there are divisions among you,
> and in part I believe it.

> For there must even be factions among you,
> that those of tried virtue may become manifest
> among you.

When you meet together, then,
it is not possible to eat the Lord's Supper;
for at the repast each one taketh first his own supper,
and one is hungry and another drinketh overmuch.

Have you not homes in which to eat and drink?
Or do you despise the house of God,
and put to shame the needy?

What am I to say to you?
  Am I to praise you?
In this I praise you not.

For I have received from the Lord,
as I have also delivered to you,
  that the Lord Jesus
on the night wherein He was being betrayed,
took bread, and giving thanks
  brake and said,
"This is My Body which [is being given] on your behalf;
  this do ye in remembrance of Me."

In like manner after the supper
  He took the cup saying,
"This cup is the new covenant in My Blood;
this do ye, as often as ye drink [thereof],
  in remembrance of Me."

For as often as you eat this Bread
  and drink of the Cup,
you proclaim the death of the Lord,
  until He come.

So that whoever eateth the Bread
or drinketh of the Cup unworthily,
  shall be guilty of the Body and the Blood of the Lord.

But let a man prove himself,
and so let him eat of the Bread,
  and drink of the Cup;
for he that eateth and drinketh
without distinguishing the Body [from other food],
  eateth and drinketh judgment to himself. . . .

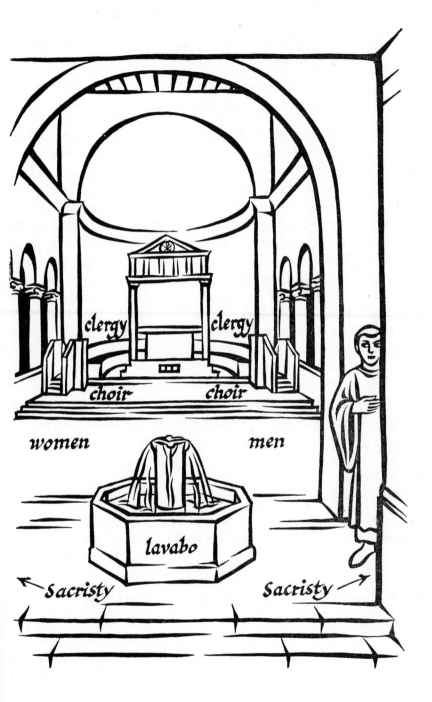

Wherefore, my brethren, when you come together for the repast,
wait for one another.

If one is hungry, let him eat at home,
lest you meet together [only] for judgment.

I Cor. xi,17–34   The rest I shall set in order when I come.

Communal-Fellowship in Eucharistic Body. The Agape and the celebration of the Eucharistic Mysteries, never inseparably united to each other, were destined to be permanently dissociated later on, and the former love-feast is scarcely recognizable in our annual or semiannnal parish dinners or parish picnics. But to recall that dual assembly of primitive usage is to glimpse the secret of the martyr's ardor, or the force behind the conquering apostolate, in brief, the transforming power of Christ-in-humanity. A miscellaneous group of all ages and social ranks, but with the poor and slaves in the majority, makes its way after nightfall to the designated meeting place, usually the spacious home of a "brother" of wealth. Mingling freely and at perfect ease, they converse together until a signal marks the entry of the clergy. The account of the Mass then following we give from the *Apology* of St. Justin, Martyr, which portrays the developments of about the year 160. The language is necessarily somewhat general, since Justin is writing for pagans, but for all that we can readily trace our Mass of today in these unadorned lines. Justin died for his "witness" not long after writing this.

Sunday.	On the day called Sunday, all who live in cities or in the country gather together
Single sacrifice.	to one place,
Scripture lessons.	and the *Memoirs of the Apostles* or the writings of the prophets are read, as long as time permits;
Sermon.	then, when the reader has ceased, he who presides gives a verbal instruction, and exhorts us to imitate these good examples.
Prayer in common.	Then we all rise together and pray,
Offering of gifts.	and . . . when our prayer is ended, bread and wine and water are brought, and he who presides in like manner offers Eucharistic prayers
Canon improvised.	and thanksgivings according to his ability, and the people assent saying, "Amen."

Communion to all.	And there is a distribution to each one, and a sharing in the Eucharistic Elements,
Even to absent.	and to those who are absent a portion is sent by the deacons.
Free-will offerings for needy.	And they who are well-to-do, and willing, give what each thinks fit; what is collected is deposited with the president [bishop] who succors the orphans and widows, and those who, through sickness or any other cause, are in want, and those who are in bonds, and the strangers sojourning among us, and in a word, takes care of all who are in need.
The Lord's Day.	Sunday is the day on which we all hold our common assembly, because it is the first day, on which God made the world; and Jesus Christ our Saviour on the same day rose from the dead.
Eucharistic Presence.	And this food is called by us the Eucharist. . . . Not as common bread and common drink do we receive these, but . . . we have been taught that this Food . . . is the Flesh and Blood of that Jesus who was made flesh.

The custom at Rome of emphasizing the unity of Christians in *communion* by sending to those who were absent, particles of the Holy Eucharist is also described for us in a letter of this period by St. Irenaeus, later martyred at Lyons, France, and others.

Fellowship in Mystic Body. The Eucharistic Mysteries concluded, or quite independently of them, as the case might be, the Agape took place. "As with God Himself," says Tertullian, "a peculiar respect is shown to the lowly," in that places of honor were given to the widows, the poor, and the dependent. With prayer the feast was commenced, and *Apol.* xxxix so it closed with prayer. Each in turn had the happy task of voicing the corporate prayer, either in recitation or in song, in the words of Holy Writ, or in improvisation. The meal was a natural occasion for the presentation of guests and pilgrims from other communities, for the interchange of news from far and near, rumors of impending persecution, for the writing of the letters to those engaged in enforced labor for conscience' sake, and so forth. At times there would be the saddening news of some strife among the brethren. When differences of note arose locally, the bishop heard both sides and rendered judgment. There is a charming injunction to a bishop to hold his court on Mondays, since that allowed the entire week, if it were needed, to reconcile the brethren, *before the Sunday Sacrifice*. The extreme judgment was what we call excommunication nowadays, and consisted "in the severance from us in prayer, in the assembly and in all sacred dealings." Alms were given of one's abundance, or of one's modest competence, or of one's dearth: alms for the support of the dependent, for the comfort of those in prison, for the decent burial of Catholic and non-Catholic dead. It was the view of one moralist that "fasting is better than prayer, but the giving of alms is better than both." What we might call a sociological feature of the assembly deserves note. This served regularly as an employment bureau for Catholics out of work, and there is even evidence that the Catholic community recognized the right of an unemployed coreligionist to secure a position from the brotherhood in his own locality.

Tert. Apol. xxxix

II Clem. xvi

Didache, xii, etc.

"Gathered from Four Winds." Among the most precious relics in writing of the Apostolic Age is a little booklet called *The Teaching of the Twelve Apostles,* which dates from the period 80–100. Several of its passages mirror the essence of primitive Catholic piety, and all of these show that the object of their passionate love was the *Church gathered from the four winds and fed upon the Eucharist*. On Sunday worship in general *The Teaching* prescribes:

> On the Lord's Day come together, breaking Bread, and celebrate the Eucharist, after confessing your transgressions, that your Sacrifice may be pure. But let none who has a quarrel with his fellow join in your meeting until they be reconciled, that your Sacrifice be not defiled. For this is that which was spoken by the Lord: "In every place and time offer Me a pure Sacrifice, for I am a great King," saith the Lord, "and My Name is wonderful among the heathen."[1]

Among the prayers suggested for the Eucharistic Mysteries (which, it is decreed, are to be given to none but the baptized), we read:

> Now as regards the Eucharist, give thanks after this manner:
> First, for the Cup: We give Thee thanks, our Father,

---

[1] This is a citation from memory of Malachy's prophecy, i, 11.

for the holy Vine of David, Thy servant,
    which Thou hast made known to us
       through Jesus, Thy Servant.
    To Thee be the glory forever.

And for the Bread that is broken:
    We give thanks to Thee, our Father,
for the LIFE and knowledge Thou hast made known to us
       through Jesus, Thy Servant.
    To Thee be the glory forever.

And as this Bread was [*once*] *scattered over the mountains,*
   and having been gathered together, became one,
     so let Thy Church be gathered together
      from the ends of the earth,
       into Thy Kingdom:
for Thine is the glory and the power through Jesus Christ forever. **ix**

Now after being filled, give thanks after this manner:
    We thank Thee, holy Father, for Thy holy Name,
  which Thou hast caused to dwell in our hearts,
and for the knowledge and faith and immortality
  which Thou hast made known to us
     through Jesus Thy Servant.
    To Thee be the glory forever.

Thou, O almighty Sovereign,
    didst make all things for Thy sake,
Thou gavest food and drink to man, for enjoyment,
    that they might give thanks to Thee.
But to us Thou didst freely give
    spiritual Food and Drink and eternal LIFE,
     through Thy Servant.
Before all things we give thanks to Thee that Thou art mighty.
    To Thee be the glory forever.

Remember, O Lord, Thy Church;
    to deliver her from all evil
    and to perfect her in Thy love.
And gather her together from the four winds,
sanctified for Thy Kingdom which Thou didst prepare for her.
    For Thine is the power and the glory forever.   **xi,1-5**

I Clem. xlvi,5–7   **"Why Tear the Members of Christ?"** To the people of Corinth St. Paul found it good to write in the year 55 his most detailed treatment of the body of Christ. Forty years later that flourishing church was thrown into violent disturbance by the opposition of a small faction to the hierarchy. The pope then reigning was the glorious Clement I, a martyr-to-be, who undertook by letter to compose this schism. After a wistful sketch of the ideal fellowship Corinth had been, famous alike for orthodoxy and a whole litany of virtues, Clement deplores the effect of schism in language that rings familiar:

> Let us take our body: the head is nothing without the feet, likewise the feet are nothing without the head; the smallest members of our body are necessary and valuable to the whole body, but all work to-
>
> *Ibid.* xxviii,5   gether and are united in common subjection to preserve the whole body.
>
> Why are there strifes and passions and divisions and schisms and war among you? Or have we not one God, and one Christ, and one Spirit of grace poured out upon us? Is there not one calling in Christ?
>
> Eph. iv,4–6   Why do you divide and tear asunder the members of Christ, and raise up strife against our own body, and reach such a pitch of madness as to forget we are members of one another?
>
> Rom. xii,5   Take up the *Epistle* of the blessed Paul the Apostle . . .

I Cor. xiii   So Clement goes on to paraphrase the Apostle's golden lyric of love, as we have seen at the end of Chapter I, and bespeaks return of love to *I Clem.* xlix,6   Him "who gave His Flesh for our flesh, His life for our lives." Thus "adult Catholics" of long ago knew that, antecedent to any personal preferences, they actually formed a body, and *therefore* their determination to foster union, and *therefore* their fellowship in the Eucharist, the I Cor. xi,17   eating of which made them all a unity. We learn no more of that trouble at Corinth, so it is likely that this papal quoting of *First Corinthians* restored harmony to the City of the Twin Seas.

    "Branches of the Cross, Members of the Son." A few years subsequent to the events just spoken of, the Catholic world was filled with the brilliant glory of the martyrdom of St. Ignatius of Antioch, who was St. Peter's second successor as bishop of that great city. He was taken from Antioch to Rome to be exposed to the beasts in the capital. En route he wrote seven letters to churches and churchmen in the neighborhood. The faith in Asia Minor was just then threatened by heretical teachers, so that the burden of these celebrated and impassioned letters is always the same, the unity of the Church, which is identical with the *unity of Christ*. To Ignatius Christians are "branches of the Cross, by which *Trall. xi* through His Passion He calls you who are His members." This unity of the members is the fruit of praying together, praying around one altar, *Eph. v,2* and breaking one Bread, professing the same faith, abiding in concord, *Eph. xx,2* and obeying the hierarchy that "the Father may recognize . . . that you are members of His Son." To the Christians of Smyrna Ignatius *Eph. iv,2* pens this passage, in which (incidentally) the expression *"Catholic Church"* occurs for the first time:

> Let no one do anything pertaining to the Church without the bishop. Let that be considered a valid Eucharist which is *celebrated by the bishop,* or by one whom he appoints. Wherever the bishop appears, let the congregation attend; just as wherever Jesus Christ is, there is the Catholic Church. It is not lawful either to baptize or *to hold the Agape* *Smyr. viii,1,2* *without the bishop.*

In addressing the churches of Philadelphia, in Asia Minor, and Ephesus, the future martyr writes respectively:

> Be careful to have [only] *one Eucharist* for there is *one Flesh* of our Lord Jesus Christ, and *one cup* for union in His Blood, *one altar,* as there is one bishop with the presbyters and the deacons, my fellow servants, in order that whatever you do, you may do it according to *Phil. iv* God.
>
> If Jesus Christ permits me . . . in a second despatch [letter] . . . I will instruct you concerning the dispensation of the new man Jesus Christ . . . dealing with His faith and His love, His suffering and His resurrection . . . so that you obey the bishop and the priests with an undisturbed mind, *breaking one Bread,* which is the medicine of immortality, the antidote that we should not die, but live forever in *Eph. xx,1.2* Jesus Christ.

"Wheat of God." To St. Ignatius the Holy Eucharist was not alone the bond of union among Christians, but the instrument of personal sanctification. Fearing that the Christians at Rome would seek to prevent his martyrdom, he begs them to give up such thoughts:

> I am the wheat of God, and I must be ground by the teeth of lions that I may become the pure bread of Christ. . . . I have no pleasure *Rom. iv,1* in the food of corruption or in the delights of this life. I desire the

Rom. vii,3

Bread of God, which is the Flesh of Jesus Christ, who was of the seed of David, and for drink I desire His Blood, which is incorruptible love.

A Bishop's Prayer, a Bishop's Epitaph. If there is an aura of holiness upon the persons of martyrs-to-be, an indefinable fascination attaches to glimpses into their minds and souls. Here is the *catholic* prayer of a bishop arrested at the age of eighty-six. Polycarp, Bishop of Smyrna, ordered food and drink set before the soldiery sent to arrest him (it was just at nightfall), and in turn asked the favor of praying a little. "To this they assented," runs the story of his martyrdom, "and he stood and prayed . . . so that for two hours he could not be silent . . . *remembering all who had ever even come his way, both small and great, high and low, and the whole Catholic Church throughout the world.*" St. Polycarp died by fire in the arena of Smyrna in 155.

Mart. Poly. vii, viii

This chapter could scarcely close more appropriately than by reproducing one more voice from this distant past, a metrical message written for his tombstone by Bishop Abercius of Hierapolis, in Phrygia, about the year 180. Before reading what a Christian bishop thought proper to inscribe upon his tomb even in those days of persecution, let us recall what a wealth of Christian thought is contained in the Greek word for *fish*. As a five-letter acrostic, 'ι-χ-θ-ύ-ς, it yields the initial letters of the Greek words meaning "Jesus Christ, Son of God, Saviour." A symbol so simple and noncommittal in itself, and yet pregnant with such depth of meaning to the initiated, was bound to serve as a watchword in a thousand different contexts. Abercius' uses of the word are easily understood.

> Citizen of a distinguished town,
> This sepulcher I have living made
> That I may sometime lay my body here.
> Abercius is my name, disciple of a Shepherd,
> Who feeds His flocks o'er mountains and o'er plains;
> Whose eyes see all, who taught me words of life.
> He sent me Romewards sovereign majesty to see.
> To see a queen in golden robe and golden sandals shod.
> People everywhere I saw stamped with a gleaming seal.
> In Syria's plains and all her cities, Nisibis beyond Euphrates.
> Brethren everywhere I found, for I was following Paul.
> Faith before me, the FISH she always served me,
> A huge FISH from the fountain, which the chaste Virgin caught.

And this she gives her friends to eat forever and for aye.
Delicious wine she has too, which she serves with bread. . . .

Summary. Besides being our Sacrifice, the holy Eucharist symbolizes
and effects our truest fellowship. Apostolic teaching, the testimony of
pagan adversaries, the writings of the apologists, letters, social customs,
prayers, both public and private, and an epitaph are here adduced to
show that the early Christians were vividly conscious of their social
fellowship as based on their common sharing in the Eucharist.

Seventh-Century Source Material

*(If St. Ildephonse of Toledo in this instruction to newly baptized, of about 657,
passes lightly over transubstantiation, he is crystal clear on the Eucharist
as the bond of Christians.)*

What you see is to the senses bread and a chalice, but what your faith
dictates is this: the bread is the Body of Christ, the chalice [contains]
His Blood. That is quickly said, and may perchance suffice for faith,
but faith desires instruction. . . . You may say to me: "You have
commanded us to believe, but explain it that we may believe." Or such a
thought as this can arise in someone's mind: "We know whence our Lord
Jesus Christ received His Flesh, from the Virgin Mary. Suckled as an
Infant, He was nourished, grew, came to youth, suffered persecution at
the hands of the Jews, was hung on the wood, killed, buried. On the
third day He rose again, and when He chose, ascended into heaven, took
His Body thither, from whence He shall come to judge the living and
the dead, and there He now sits at the Father's right. How is the bread
His Body, or how is that His Blood which the chalice holds? These
things, brethren, are for this reason called Sacraments, because in them
one thing is seen and another thing is understood. That which is seen has
bodily [material] appearance; what is understood has spiritual profit.
If you wish, therefore, to understand the Body of Christ, listen to the
Apostle saying to the faithful:

You are the body of Christ and severally His members.   I Cor. xii,27

If you are the body of Christ and severally His members, this mystery is
placed on the altar of the Lord; you have received this mystery of yourselves, and have responded *Amen* to that which you are. Be a member of
Christ that your *Amen* be true. Therefore in the bread let us offer nothing as of our own; let us hear the same Apostle saying:

           We many are one bread, one body.

Understand and rejoice. We many are unity, love, the truth of the flesh, one bread, one body." — *Lib. de Cogn. Bap.*, c. xxxvii.

Topics for Further Discussion:

The spread of Catholicism was the greatest *revolution* this world has ever known — yet it was accomplished by love.

Anyone may sign himself with the sign of the cross, may say "Amen" and sing "Alleluia," may present himself for baptism, visit churches and help to build them. The only thing which distinguishes the children of God from the children of the devil is love. — *St. Augustine.*

"The Eucharist is what makes men men." — *G. K. Chesterton.*

"The early Christians met constantly to support one another"; the probability of their being able to draw the same support from our assemblies, should persecution break over us.

"The Faithful gather at sacred shrines that they may draw piety thence . . . *by actually participating* in the venerated mysteries and in her public and solemn prayers." — *Pius XI.*

Some reasons for supposing that Catholics of today as a body lack the social-mindedness of the early Church.

That Christian worship, and Eucharistic worship in particular, still offers abundant remedies for the present situation.

Ways in which zealous lay-leadership can make parish organizations, and the parishes themselves real *Agapae,* centers of love.

Readings:

F. Cabrol, *The Prayer of the Early Christians* (New York: Benziger, 1930); "The Eucharist — The Mass," pp. 14–27.

———— *Liturgical Prayer, Its History and Spirit* (New York: Kenedy, 1922); "Primitive Christian Assemblies," pp. 54–61; "Mass at Rome at Beginning of the Third Century," pp. 62–79.

———— *The Mass, Its Doctrine and Its History* (New York: Kenedy, no date), pp. 9–18.

A. Fortescue, *The Mass, A Study of the Roman Liturgy* (New York: Longmans, Green, 1937); "The Eucharist in the First Three Centuries," pp. 1–75.

J. C. Hedley, *The Holy Eucharist* (New York: Longmans, Green, 1907); "The Mass as a Liturgy," pp. 173–195.

J. Husslein, *The Mass of the Apostles* (New York: Kenedy, 1929).

P. Parsch–F. C. Eckhoff, *The Liturgy of the Mass* (St. Louis: Herder, 1936), "Historical Development," pp. 16–38.

J. de Puniet, *The Mass, Its Origin and History* (London: Burns, Oates and Washbourne, 1931); "The Synaxis of the Apostolic Fathers," pp. 40–53; "The Earliest Witness to the Roman Use," pp. 54–66.

Chapter VIII

THE SACRIFICIAL CALENDAR

Some of them
God made high and great days,
and some of them
He put in the number of ordinary days
(Ecclus. xxxiii, 10).

IN CIVIL life we are so accustomed to the prevalence of *our* calendar, as we say, almost everywhere, that any observance of a New Year, other than January 1, strikes us as strangely unreal. Our calendar, called the Gregorian, after Pope Gregory XIII who reformed it in the late sixteenth century, though now so universally adopted, is merely one of many systems in use at different times with which to mark and calculate the progress of time as measured by the solar system. Nor is our civil year merely a norm for *measuring* time: such is man's desire to preserve the memory of past events by attaching them to definite dates that the year becomes a table of annual commemorations of major happenings of former years. Every year thus furnishes a condensed *record* of the great historic past.

Church Year. However universal the Gregorian calendar may be in the civil life of Christian civilization, still we are accustomed to another calendar in our worship: Sunday for Sunday the "date" of the day in the ecclesiastical year is announced in our churches according to our Catholic calendar of worship, which we call the Church Year. The Church Year and the civil correspond in length, but the whole period of twelve months is laid out by the Church in a seasonal arrangement adapted to the measuring of time in its relationship to worship. Such a year in any religious system, pagan, Jewish, Protestant, or Catholic, besides being a unit of cyclic advance, will present a commemorative summary of God's relationships with the religious group in question. In European museums one can still see large marble tablets engraved with the "worship year," so to speak, of this or that pagan deity. In Holy Writ the book called Ecclesiasticus records how, for the Jews primarily, but for all men by implication, this "worship year" is of divine institution:

> Why doth one day excel another,
>   and one light another,
>   and one year another,
> when all come of the sun?

> By the knowledge of the Lord they were distinguished . . .

> And He ordered the seasons,
>   and holidays of them,
>   and in them they celebrated festivals . . .

>   Some of them
> God made high and great days,
>   and some of them
> He put in the number of ordinary days.

Ecclus. xxxiii,
7–10

So we are not at all surprised that the Church of Christ, the fulfillment of *all* imperfect religions, has *its* year of worship, high and great days alternating with ordinary ones. Taken together the days of the Church Year will give a summary of God's relationships with men through their Mediator Christ. And such is the solidarity of human living, that the full sweep of God's relationships with mankind through Christ, even in the case of any single individual, must reach back even to Adam and must look forward even to the resurrection of the body at Christ's second coming. Thus the Church year sums up the record of the Old Dispensation, when men looked forward to Christ, portrays the period of Christ's mortal life, runs through the twenty centuries of our New Dispensation with all men either actually or potentially living as members of Christ, and lastly points ahead to the final consummation and end of mortal living.

Supernatural Pedagogy. Some of the Greek Fathers delighted in calling Christ our "Pedagogue," and one might well begin a study of the Church Year as an institution of supernatural pedagogy. One of the marked characteristics of our worship, especially in the Roman Rite, is this, that while the Mass remains ever the same, it is, week for week, and day for day, given a different tone and setting by being brought into rhythmic relationship with definite historical events, or doctrines, or persons. Sundays, the Lord's days, have all a common aspect, but because of the Scripture readings and prayers proper to each, no two strike exactly the same note, or, one might say, have exactly the same function to perform. Weekdays are generally anniversary commemorations of the saints, men and women who in their manifold ways have signalized themselves in living the Christian life. From time to time occur the great festal commemorations of the epochal events attending our redemption, the celebration of which *inculcates the doctrine* itself, according to an age-old axiom the Church never wearies of citing: "Let the law of praying confirm that of believing." This basic function of feasts in teaching the truths of faith was luminously described by Pope Pius XI at the institution of the Feast of Jesus Christ King: *Cf. Quas primas, 1925*

> For imbuing the people with the faith and leading them by faith to the interior joys of life, the annual celebrations of the sacred mysteries are far more efficacious than even the most weighty documents of ecclesiastical teaching. As a rule these latter reach only the few and the more learned, whereas the former impress and teach all the faithful. The one means, We may say, speaks but once; the other speaks every year and forever. The one touches the mind only; the other effectively appeals to mind and heart, that is, to the whole man. Since man consists of body and soul he should be so moved and interested as to drink in divine doctrines more abundantly through the variety and beauty of the sacred rites, and, converting these into vigor and blood, make them serve him for progress in the spiritual life. *Quas primas*

St. Thomas speaks of the layman's obligation of *explicitly* professing faith in the mysteries of which the Church celebrates feasts, whereas an implicit belief is sufficient for doctrines not so celebrated. Since such feasts have multiplied through the centuries, according to that standard the faith of the twentieth-century layman is much more explicit than it was in St. Thomas' age, just as it was more explicit then than in patristic or apostolic times. Thus, through successive ages are the dogmas of our faith more and more explicitly proposed for our belief. *De Veritate, Q. xiv, a.xi,6*

Prismatic Worship. The round of the Church's feasts is didactic, but for a far higher purpose than the mere imparting of religious information. Worship is primarily for the sake of God, not primarily for the sake of man; but the quality or excellence of our worship, that is to say,

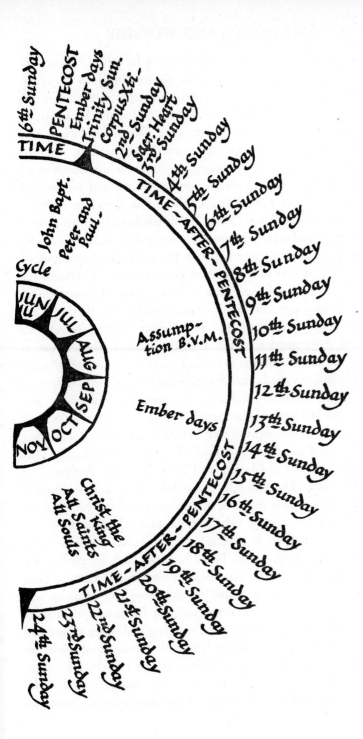

its capacity for glorifying God, since He wishes to be served by our free and intelligent acts, largely depends upon the measure in which we *understand Christianity*. As we see and interpret and apply to ourselves the doctrines of Christ in the work of building up Christian characters, in that degree are we individually enabled to serve Christianity. Now, this mission of Christianity, to promote the glorification of God and the sanctification of souls, is achieved principally through the Sacrifice of Christ, offered once in a bloody manner on the Cross, and renewed in every Mass. The work of sanctifying Christians is therefore summed up in the two words, "Cross" and "Mass." This whole redemptive process is, moreover, the all-embracing lesson each individual must learn and make his own. To enable us more easily to grasp this vast synthesis of truth, the Church Year acts as a refracting prism interposed between the Mass and ourselves. Section by section of Christ's work, the outstanding events of His life long ago, and as continued now in His brethren, are spread out for our separate study and assimilation. During Advent we summarily recall the centuries of the old Dispensation when salvation was by believing in Christ-that-was-to-come. From Christmas until Ascension we study Christ-in-the-flesh. Successively and quickly the first appearance of Christ, His infancy, childhood, the periods of obscurity and public teaching, the incidents of the sacred Passion and Resurrection and final triumphant Ascent into heaven pass before us with their sanctifying graces and blessings. From Pentecost until the end of the Church Year we are studying Christ-in-His-Church, and our own places therein.

Cycles and Units. The Church Year, like the civil year, consists of weeks and seasons; unlike the civil, it is made up of *two concomitant cycles* of feasts and observances. Of these the first relates to God and the mysteries of Redemption; it is called the *dominical* (Lord's) *cycle*. Of the feasts of this cycle, some, like Christmas and Epiphany, are "fixed," that is, they always fall on the same date, while many others, like Easter and Pentecost are "movable" because they can occur on any date within a certain interval. The second series of feasts comprises those of the Blessed Virgin Mary, the Apostles, martyrs, and other saints, and is known as the *sanctoral cycle*. Most feasts of the sanctoral cycle are fixed; hence, there is no special complexity attaching to it. Moreover, these feasts have essentially the same function; they magnify God, "who is wondrous in [us] His holy temples." They demonstrate, "since we

Ps. lxvii,36

have such a cloud of witnesses about us," that the Christian life is cap- Heb. xii,1
able of heroic success at every age and in all walks of life. With this brief
mention we may dismiss the sanctoral cycle and turn to the more complex
dominical one.

The *week*, as such, is a Jewish contribution to civilization, one based
directly on the divine command of a Sabbath rest. By the time of Christ
the week had become common in the Greco-Roman world; in fact, our
names of the weekdays are the old Teuton equivalents of their Latin
names. The Jewish Christians at first continued to frequent the synagogues on the Sabbath, but in memory of Christ's Resurrection observed
the first day of the week as the *Lord's day,* the day of sacrificial worship.
When the final break with the synagogue came, the Sabbath observance
disappeared among Christians.

At the opening of *each of* the four seasons, certain days of fasting are
observed, called *Ember Days* (Old English, *ymbren,* period). With the
Ember Days were sometimes connected observances *pertaining* to harvest-
ing the summer grain, the autumn vintage, the winter yield of olives.
Ember Days were long of great importance, because they were reserved
for a higher kind of harvest, the ordination of the Church's ministers;
to the rank and file of Catholics nowadays they should always serve as
penitential consecrations of each new season.

Nativity Cycle. Both the Church Year as a whole, and its first feast-
cycle, that of *Christmas,* open on the fourth Sunday before the Feast of
the Nativity. This pre-Christian season, called Advent (the coming),
serves as a preparation for the commemoration of Christ's birth by recalling the dire plight of the world before that happy event. The actual birth
of Christ is celebrated continuously, as it were, from December 25 to
January 6, the Feast of the Epiphany, the Manifestation of Christ
principally in His divine nature. The Christmas celebrations are pro-
longed, as it were, on a minor key until February 2 (forty days after
Christmas), on which the presentation of the Child in the Temple of
Jerusalem took place according to the Jewish law. Before taking leave
of the Christmas setting, let us hear an echo from a Christmas sermon
of Pope St. Leo the Great:

> You will celebrate this feast worthily and intelligently [he addresses
> the Romans], if you remember into what body you are incorporated, of
> what Head you are members, lest any discordant jointure mar the
> building up of the sacred edifice. Consider, beloved, and ponder with

prudence, according to the light of the Holy Spirit, who He is who has taken us unto Himself, who He is whom we have received amongst us. For, as the Lord Jesus has taken our flesh by being born, so we have become His body by being reborn [in Baptism]. And therefore also we are members of Christ and the temple of the Holy Ghost, so that the Blessed Apostle says: *"Glorify and bear God in your body."* In sweetly communicating His nature of meekness and humility to us, He imbues us with that virtue by which He redeemed us, as the Master Himself promiseth: "Come to Me, all ye that labor and are burdened, and I will give you rest. Take My yoke upon you and learn of Me, for I am meek and humble of heart, and ye shall find rest for your souls." Let us receive, then, the yoke of guiding Truth, for it is neither heavy nor galling, and let us resemble His humility to whose glory we wish to be configured.

I Cor. vi,20, Douay

Matt. xi,28,29

Serm. iii in Nat.

Paschal Cycle. Surpassing all other events in the Church Year is *Easter,* the *Christian Passover,* the festival of festivals, the day on which Christ rose from the dead. It is the zenith of the Easter cycle, which includes no less than seventeen weeks. It takes us a long way back in history to explain why Easter is a movable feast. The ancient Jewish calendar was based on lunar periods, not solar periods as our own calendar. This lunar year had its quota of months and several extra days, so that, every few years, there was a leap month. This extra month, when inserted, became the first month of the year, and since Easter was held at the full moon of the *first* month, there was thus a full month's interval in which the date of Easter might vary. All the other movable feasts are determined by Easter, and are, so to speak, the satellites of this wandering star. Preparatory to Easter is a forty-day fasting period, called Lent (from an old English root meaning Spring). Before Lent there is again a preliminary quasi-penitential season of two weeks and a half. Lent was called in Latin *Quadragesima,* literally the fortieth. By loose analogy the three Sundays of the pre-Lenten season were named *Quinquagesima* (fiftieth), *Sexagesima* (sixtieth), and *Septuagesima* (seventieth), although Christians for a thousand years and more have puzzled over these inaccurate mathematical implications. Lent is now altogether given up to the commemoration of Christ's Passion and Death: formerly it was also devoted to the final preparation for the public Baptism of Easter Eve. The Paschal Cycle continues on until Pentecost, with its octave (which means a sort of prolongation of the feast for a week).

30494

St. Thomas on Easter. St. Thomas Aquinas ranks as the Church's premier theologian; a passage from one of his paschal sermons should have unique interest.

Peace be with you. Note the threefold peace, internal peace, fraternal peace, supernal peace. Internal peace is that which subdues the inner man, renders him tranquil and peaceable, so that there be no inordinate love in his heart, nor the perplexity of error in his mind: *And the peace of God which surpasseth all understanding will guard your hearts and your minds.* John xx,19

Phil. iv,7

Then there is fraternal peace, to which the Apostle invites us: *Careful to keep the unity of the Spirit in the bond of peace: one body and one Spirit, as also ye were called in one hope, that of your calling.* As if he should say: From the fact that you are one body, among you, as among the members of the body, there should be no quarrel. And since you ought to be one body and one soul, neither should you divide your hearts. For the division of the heart means death. And since ye, as pilgrims and companions, all tend to the same hospice, while ye are on the way there ought not be discord among you. It would be ridiculous if the hand should quarrel with the foot, or the foot with the head. The head are the prelates, the feet are subjects, the hands are others of middle station, who ought all to live together peaceably as in the one body: *Let the peace of Christ stand supreme in your hearts whereunto also ye are called as [members of] one body.* . . . Eph. iv,4

Col. iii,15
Serm. in oct.
Pasch.

Kingship Cycle. The only other feast cycle that need be noted here comes at the end of the Church Year. It presents in one panorama the Feast of *Christ the King,* attended by *All Saints* and *All Souls,* in order that His dominion may be manifested in His own, for, as the Sovereign Pontiff said in instituting the feast, "we are no longer our own since Christ has bought us with a 'great price': our very bodies are the members of Christ." The reasons for the precise position of this feast in the calendar are thus described in the Kingship Encyclical: I Cor. vi,20

I Cor. vi,15

Our reason for designating *Sunday* is that not only the clergy may pay their observances by celebrating Mass and reading the Office, but that the people also, free from their usual occupations, may in the spirit of holy joy, obedience and service give their humble testimony to Christ. The *last Sunday in October,* when the liturgical year is near its close, has seemed to Us more suitable than other days for this celebration. For thus, it will happen that the mysteries of the life of Jesus

Quas primas

Christ commemorated during the year will be completed and fulfilled by the sacred solemnity of Christ as King, and, *before celebrating the glory of all the saints,* the glory of Him who *triumphs in all the saints and elect* will be preached and emphasized.

John i,5

John i,5

II Pet. ii,10

For Christ and Christians alike that is the consummation of the Christian life. If, then, at Christmas we see the light shine into the darkness, and at Easter, how the darkness failed to overcome it, in the Kingship Cycle we see how we are eventually called from this darkness into God's wondrous light.

Dominical Cycle, Origin. Easter and Pentecost were both Jewish feasts to which Christ's death had given a new depth of meaning. The Pasch, "the most joyous night of the year," celebrated the deliverance of the chosen people from the Egyptian bondage. Pentecost, literally *Fiftieth Day,* was the solemn festival in which the Jews commemorated the receiving of the Ten Commandments on Mount Sinai by the sacrifice of the first fruits of the Summer harvest. Now, Jewish Christians, as all the Apostles were, would see the Pasch in retrospect as a bare foretokening of the deliverance of all men from the bondage of Satan and would rejoice in their hearts that Christ chose to inaugurate the New Law of Love by sending the Holy Spirit on the nascent Church on Pentecost. Easter and Pentecost were thus what we might call the positive and negative poles in the ambit of which the Dominical cycle of the Church Year would be formed. Between them there was another great event on a fixed day, Christ's Ascent into heaven. What more natural than that, in the course of time, it should be signaled out for special observance. Ascension is apparently the oldest feast of ecclesiastical origin. It was not long before Christ's Nativity was being observed, and the great cycle has been lengthening its span ever since.

Martyrs' "Birthdays." Were there at that remote date saints' days such as we know them now? There is one clear sign that the motives which later led to the anniversary commemorations of the martyrs were already making themselves felt. The venerable old man, Polycarp, Bishop of Smyrna, who had been a disciple of St. John the Beloved, was burned for the faith at Smyrna, February 23, 155. Within a few months of that event, the Church at Smyrna sent out a circular letter describing the martyrdom, in which we read: "The Lord will permit us to come together . . . and celebrate the birthday of his martyrdom, both in memory of those who have already contested [this was a technical name for martyrdom] and for the practice and training of those whose fate it shall be." This notice is earlier by a half century or more than any similar one, and it will be noted how even at Smyrna Polycarp's birthday was chosen for that of all the martyrs.

Funerary Banquets and Mass. Very early, too, the celebration of the martyrs' anniversaries began to take on a *public* and liturgical character. The circumstances under which this happened merit our best attention. We must begin by saying a word about some of the common mortuary customs of the Greco-Roman world. The will of any man of means in the Empire at that time would, besides designating the property on which his tomb was located, specify certain lands as its perpetual endowment; the testament would then go on to enjoin upon his heirs that on or about March 22 they should meet at his tomb and sprinkle violets over it; on or about May 21 roses in like manner were to be sprinkled over him in their common meeting, and on the *anniversary* of his death the testatees were to gather every year for a *joyous banquet* in his honor. To insure this merriment liberal endowments were provided for wines and all manner of delicacies and appointments. In connection with the tombs themselves there was usually a large hall (*refrigerium*) for this banquet. Now, what the rich could provide for themselves and their families, the poor secured in substance by forming burial associations. So deep rooted was this institution that burial associations were protected by law when a growing despotism had long banned all other forms of association. Thus throughout all the ages of persecution, with one short period excepted, the proscribed Christians were never molested in their common burial places. There they could meet openly and unharmed. Members of a family and close friends could repair thither on the anniversaries of their departed ones and have their modest memorial repasts. What more natural than to connect this with the Agape-repast held in connection with the Holy Eucharist? Thus it was the most natural thing that these family anniversaries early began to include the Holy Sacrifice. Moreover, when the departed was a great personage, or a celebrated martyr, the anniversary began to take on the full character of a local saint's festival, as we know it now. At first of spontaneous and haphazard institution, these anniversaries became fixed and numerous in the third century when severe persecutions greatly increased the number of martyrs. Local churches began to exchange their lists of martyrs, to celebrate one another's martyrs, since, as St. Augustine said: "The solemnities of the martyrs *Serm. xlvii* were exhortations to martyrdom."

Pagan Usages Purified and Adapted. There was another feature of the third century that ought not to be passed over in this survey. It was a local and sporadic movement, but one of far-reaching consequences. In the services of the old, pagan religions, then being abandoned whole-sale despite the fury of the persecutions, were many natural *place* rites and *seasonal observances,* processions, as well as the use of incense, votive lamps, votive offerings at shrines, and the like. To these rites the people through long custom were deeply attached. Realizing that it is only the intention behind these actions that gives them a moral value, churchmen began to propose Christian ideas as substitutes for the former pagan ones. They began, in a word, to Christianize former, natural expressions of religion. This sound principle, so thoroughly in keeping with the whole symbolic nature of Christian worship, has had the effect of enlisting and perpetuating scores of good usages that might otherwise have passed forever from the ceremonial of divine worship. It is fascinating to specu-late along analogous lines, and presume that when the vast nations of the Far East have become Christianized, they, too, will enrich the Chris-tian heritage with all that is good and sound in their present religious mentality.

Influence of Jerusalem. The fourth century brought rapid changes in the Church's fortunes. Hard upon Constantine's Edict of Toleration (313) followed frequent acts of imperial munificence. In the history of Christian worship none of these was of greater moment than the erection of a great basilica on the site of the Holy Sepulcher at Jerusalem. The dedication of this temple in 335 was in a way something like a second inauguration of Christendom. The day of ritual splendor had dawned: henceforth "the beauty of the glory of the Mysteries" was to undergo rapid development. The new movement received wide notice and was all the more effective because of the immortal expositions of the Mass and worship in general by the great St. Cyril, Bishop of Jerusalem, 350–386.

Then, too, the pilgrimages set in and continued in an ever-rising tide. The unique and compelling attraction of the Holy Places made Jerusalem at that date the center of the Church's piety, such as Rome became only when Jerusalem had passed to the domination of Islam. By verbal and written accounts which these pilgrims brought, the ritual glories of Jerusalem were carried to the whole Christian world. To be specific: the great Palm Sunday procession and the adoration of the cross on Good Friday, among other things, are due to the pilgrimage-book of a Spanish nun, Etheria, at the end of this century.

Relic Cult Multiplies Feasts. Devotion to the martyrs continued to grow rapidly throughout the fourth century. Early in the fifth, the discovery of the relics of St. Stephen, the protomartyr, sent a veritable thrill through the whole of Christendom. This led to a diligent search for other relics, and a zealous cultivation of local shrines wherever martyrs were known to lie buried. One important manifestation of this new cult was the desire to have an altar erected over the tomb of the martyr, in order to celebrate the anniversary there with great honor. But there were thousands and thousands of churches not fortunate enough to stand over the tombs of martyrs. An ingenious piety would therefore bring martyrs to these churches, and hollow "tombs" for them beneath the altars. Thus, to make a long story short, it has come about that in the altars of Christendom today are altar stones, wherein are placed in "tombs," the relics of at least two duly authenticated martyrs. St. John's vision in the *Apocalypse* thus finds a strange verification in reality:

> I beheld under the altar
> the souls of those
> who had been slain for the word of God. Apoc. vi,9

It goes without saying that this fresh impetus in the cult of the martyrs brought with it a further multiplication of their feasts. By and by it was deemed proper that other holy men and women be given a place in what was now regarded as "the Church's calendar." By the end of the fifth century the entire Church Year was, so to speak, sketched out. The filling in of details has gone on and still goes on steadily. The first "North American" saints (in the sense that they were martyred in Canada and New York State) are SS. Isaac Jogues, John de Brébeuf, and six others, slain by Indians long ago and canonized in 1930. A detailed and systematic study of the Church Year would reveal how it epitomizes the history of Christianity, since there is scarcely a major event in the long story of the Christian peoples which has not left its monument in the sacrificial calendar.

Summary. The Church Year is designed to further divine worship by focusing attention on the manifold truths of Christianity, and to assist in Christian character building by proposing doctrines linked with examples of how others have already lived them. Of its two cycles, the sanctoral presents saints' anniversaries, the dominical includes the Sundays and the feasts relating to God and Redemption. The whole dominical cycle evolved from the celebration of Easter; that of the saints from a desire to perpetuate their memory after the manner of the mortuary banquets of the ancients.

Eighth-Century Source Material

(How Villagers of France Began the Seasons of the Year: From *Abbot Angilbert's* RITUAL OF THE ABBEY OF ST-RIQUIER.)

For the Greater Litanies [three days before Ascension] let the cross-bearers and processions of the [seven] nearby parishes convene at St-Riquier, namely, . . . and gather before the church of the Nativity, where, the prayer being said, let the crosses be arranged in orderly fashion on either side. The populace shall be drawn up in good order at the gate of Blessed Michael the Archangel, the men on the north, the women on the south.

Then the monks with the choir of the church of St-Riquier shall issue from the church and proceed in this order: First, three with holy-water vessels shall pass out through the above-mentioned gate of St. Michael, then three with smoking thuribles and incense. Then come the seven crosses, the one in the center being that of the Holy Redeemer. These are followed by the great reliquary of the same [church]; on the right of which let there be three priests with lesser reliquaries, and the same on the left. Behind shall follow seven deacons and seven subdeacons, and acolytes, exorcists, lectors and door-keepers, seven of each. Then the monks, seven by seven. We prescribe this marching in seven so that we shall show forth in our work the sevenfold grace of the Holy Spirit: and, besides, so many monks, walking in twos or threes, would be [a line] almost a mile long. Then let the lay boys' choir [of the abbey school] come next with its seven long floating banners in the breeze. Behind these are the noblemen, chosen by the provost or dean, seven by seven; then let the noblewomen observe the same order. Then come the seven crosses [of the neighboring parishes] above-mentioned. Let these be followed by the boys and girls who can sing the *Lord's Prayer* and the *Creed* and such other things as by the help of Our Lord we have caused them to be taught. These are to be followed by the leading citizens of the place, men and women; next the mixed populace, such old and feeble as are able to walk, and these, like the rest, in sevens. Lastly let such of the old and feeble as cannot walk close up the procession on horseback. Arranged in this order, on the first day, let them go through the monastery court by the public road, and circle the wall, going out by the south gate and returning by the north.

The musical program shall be so disposed that when they first go out they shall sing the antiphon: *Exsurge, Domine, adiuva nos.* After the customary prayer is said they file out and all begin the *Exclamemus omnes ad Dominum,* which is followed by three other [antiphons], namely: *Iniquitates nostrae, Domine, multiplicatae sunt; Exaudi nos, Domine;* and *Domine, non est alius Deus praeter te,* until they are beyond the gates. Then let the brethren [monks] sing their psalms in alternate verses, but the boys' choir, and such others as can, sing the *Apostles' Creed,* then after a pause, the *Creed of Constantinople,* then the *Athanasian Creed,* then the *Lord's Prayer.* After this the *General Litany,* which stands at the head of our book, then let the boys' school sing the *Acclamations* for the good estate of all Christendom. When this is finished, let the monks leave off their psalms, and sing along with the boys the several *Litanies,* the Gallic, then the Italian, lastly the Roman. The village boys and girls who have no learning are to have help in joining in from the scholars and the young gentlemen, so that after all they may be able to join in the singing. Thus those behind and ahead, hearing these things, will give thanks to Almighty God.

Care must be taken that everything will be so timed that the items here prescribed be finished when they re-enter the monastery, so that then all may join in the *Te Deum laudamus, te Dominum confitemur,* which they shall complete in alternate verses. If it should happen that they finish too soon, let them sing *Kyrie eleison* and *Christe eleison* until they get to the church of the Nativity. Thus throughout and in all things and by all God shall be praised and honor accorded the Name of our Lord Jesus Christ, who is blessed forever. Amen.

[The ritual goes on to prescribe for the orderly arrangement at Mass after this first day's procession, and ends this section by laying out different routes through the seven villages for the second and third days' marches.]

Topics for Further Discussion:

In the Ages of Faith civil life and civilization itself rested largely upon the sacrificial calendar, "living from festival to festival."

Subsidiary but eloquent ways in which the Church emphasizes the spirit of feasts or seasons; color of sacrificial vestments, use or absence of flowers, incense, number of lights, organ music, use of veils, etc.

The Divine Office in the offices of the saints begins by setting up Christ as the King of the state of life of the saint of the day, King of martyrs, King of confessors, King of virgins, etc.

The practical meaning, as applied to the Church Year, of the expression "Living with the Church."

Ways in which a school year might be organized into liturgical focal points.

Ways consonant with our modern mode of life of giving greater individual and corporate expression to the "spirit of the several ecclesiastical seasons."

Readings:

F. Cabrol, *Liturgical Prayer, Its History and Spirit* (New York: Kenedy, 1922); "The Christian Day," pp. 137–151; "The Christian Week," pp. 152–154; "The Christian Year," pp. 155–169.

———— *The Prayer of the Early Christians* (London: Burns, Oates and Washbourne, 1930); "The Cult of the Martyrs, of the Blessed Virgin, the Angels and the Saints," pp. 125–131.

———— *The Year's Liturgy* (London: Burns, Oates and Washbourne, I, 1938), *passim.*

O. Haering, *Living with the Church, A Handbook of Instruction in the Liturgy of the Church Year* (New York: Benziger, 1930). (For high-school use.)

A. Loehr, *The Year of Our Lord* (New York: Kenedy, 1937); *passim.*

M. S. MacMahon, *Liturgical Catechism* (Dublin: Gill and Son, 1926); "The Liturgical Year," pp. 193 sqq.

C. Marmion, *Our Way and Our Life.* An abridged edition of *Christ in His Mysteries* (St. Louis: Herder, 1927).

C. C. Martindale, *The Mind of the Missal* (New York: Sheed and Ward, 1929); "The Year of Mass," pp. 21–206.

J. Rickaby, *The Ecclesiastical Year*, "My Bookcase" series (New York: Wagner, 1927).

A. Tanquerey, *The Spiritual Life* (Tournai: Desclée, 1930); "The Three Ways and the Liturgical Cycle," pp. 741–750.

H. Thurston, "Calendar, Christian," *CE.*

Chapter IX

THE SETTING OF THE SACRIFICE

We have an altar
from which they are not entitled to eat
who serve the Tabernacle (Heb. xiii,10).

A PAGEANT of progress twenty centuries old is unfolded for us yearly in the Church's sacrificial calendar, and it is a drama in which we see a beneficent Providence constantly enriching man's original capital. If it is true that one of man's fundamental reverences is for the memory of his forbears, what a triumph of Christian solidarity to see ourselves full in this stream of historical worship that links us directly with every Christian that ever lived, or ever shall! In our prayers and rites we reach back through the long Middle Ages, past the Church of the martyrs, even to the Temple and the Synagogue. Christian worship has its historical side, as well as its hyper-historical side, if one may so express it. We have studied Christian worship from the hyper-historical side, the single, changeless service of God in the Person of our Head and Mediator, Himself a man, Christ Jesus. Historically, and in the members I Tim. ii,5 of the Mystical Body, there is the one, holy, Catholic, and Apostolic worship, a vast collection of rites and forms, prayers and thoughts, to which *every civilization and culture,* every race and people, Semite and Syrian, Greek and Roman, Goth and Frank, Celt and Saxon, *have made their own contributions.* In sharing in the present-day Christian Sacrifice anywhere in the world we are thereby caught up not alone with Christ's worship before the Ancient of Days in heaven, but we are carrying forward thoughts and sentiments and rites of all the Christian peoples of our past. Even a superficial knowledge of this fact adds immensely to our appreciation of what may be called the depth of Christian worship.

Thus, some knowledge of the different types of piety manifested by the several Christian peoples and by successive ages in the Church is a necessary condition to understand the ceremonies and rites we now possess.

109

Fifth-century
table ~ altar

from Southern France

For ritual is merely the external expression of the religious sentiment within; and the manifestations of this religious sentiment according to circumstances of time and place may vary widely, though doctrines remain ever the same. This fact is nowhere more clearly in evidence than in the history of the sacrificial altar, to which our attention is now naturally drawn.

God's Representative. Let us begin with a dogmatic consideration, the purpose or function of an altar. The altar receives the sacrificial gift offered to God. It acts as God's agent. It is viewed, therefore, as a sort of representation of the Godhead. It is considered as clothed with God's Majesty, God's Sanctity, even as an ambassador carries the majesty of his sovereign or government. As such the altar is incomparably greater than any merely human gift laid upon it. This truth was driven home vigorously by Christ in speaking to the Jews:

> Ye blind,
> which then is greater,
> the gift, or the altar that halloweth the gift?

Matt. xxiii,19

The House of Sacrifice. The home of the Christian altar is the Christian church. In earliest times the small number of Christians made it possible to celebrate their Sacrifice in private dwellings, a use to which the homes of the better classes were well adapted. But long before the persecutions were over we find the Christians in both East and West in possession of their own church buildings. Not long before the Edict of Toleration a pagan historian, Porphyrius, complains how "the Christians, rivaling the construction of our temples, build vast edifices where they assemble for prayer." Only two years after the same edict, as we learn from St. Optatus, Rome possessed more than forty basilicas. In structure these were simply adaptations of the larger private dwellings of the day. Large, rectangular structures, they had a semicircular, domed apse at the front end raised by steps a little above the level of the nave. In the crown of this apse was an elevated and ornamented throne, the *cathedra*, or bishop's chair, which was flanked on both sides by a row of seats running all around the wall of the apse. From this seat, as St. Augustine said of the bishops, "we can see [you] enter and depart."

Ap. Macar. Magn. iv,22

Ennar. in Ps. cxxvi,3

Table-Altars. At the edge of the apse in the center was a small table, hung (during the Sacrifice) with some precious stuff, and overspread with a linen cloth. This was the primitive Christian altar, the only type of altar known among "the brethren" until about the middle of the ninth century. This altar might be wood, or, from about 350 on, of stone, or even plated with gold and gem incrusted. St. Jerome (died 420) speaks of seeing such altars in the East. Constantine gave St. Peter's basilica, which he erected, a silver altar figured with gold and four hundred gems. Nothing was allowed to be placed upon the altar but the bread and wine, the sacrificial gifts, and for a while at the beginning of Mass the book of the Gospels, this last because it was regarded as representing Christ, and enthroned, therefore, on the altar.

Ciborium or Baldaquin. A modification of this primitive setting, which in the long run had great consequences, dates from Constantine himself. It was the erection over the altar of a permanent, domical baldaquin, or *ciborium* it was then called, resting on four columns. This had at first a practical purpose, which in the West proved passing, but in the East lasts to this day. The religious sentiment of the fourth century felt that the action of sacrifice and even the altar were too holy not to be screened from the public gaze, and so were veiled from the public. The first baldaquin was a vast affair of silver topped with gold, given by Constantine to the Lateran basilica. By and by the impulse to veil the altar disappeared in the West, and then the merely decorative possibilities of the baldaquin were gradually realized. On great days flowers and garlands wreathed the columns, a circle of many lights was suspended by chains over the table, and in similar fashion gold crowns and crosses lent I Cor. x,21 adornment to the "table of the Lord," yet without violating its sacred character by contact. All in all the baldaquin proved a highly satisfactory fixture and was in use for a full five hundred years. But it will be noted that every advance in enlarging or decorating the baldaquin detracted further from the bishop's throne, and put barriers, even if of silver and gold, between the body of the people and the sacred ministers.

Priest's Position at Altar. It is often made a matter of objection to Catholic worship that the officiating minister, priest or bishop, sacrifices and conducts services generally with his back to the people. Non-Catholic objectors, who know something of the great Roman basilicas, can even find in this fact an argument of "corruption," since the papal altars, they point out, are erected so that the celebrant faces the people. Well, to begin with, it is more logical that the officiant, as spokesman of the other worshipers, should stand at their head, and they behind him, as he addresses their common homage to God. Too, there is a reason based on a once common historical consideration that taken by itself would weigh lightly with us nowadays. The early Christians, who were so keenly expectant of Christ's second coming to judge mankind, always prayed with eyes to the East, facing the orient from whence

> He shall rise and visit us from on high. *Luke i,78*

If the church building had its entrance façade at the East end, the officiant faced toward the congregation (*they,* then, at times during the service, faced away from him!) at worship. Outside of Italy the more common arrangement was that the Church had its altar at the eastern end, and in that arrangement the relative positions of priest and people were the ones common to us now. It is only custom, not prescription, that dictates that the altar be located as we know it, with the priest facing away from the congregation. The rubrics of the missal still contain this direction, as an aid to the celebrant in accommodating himself to whatever arrangement he finds:

> When the altar is erected eastwards and towards the people, since he is already facing them, the priest does not turn his back to the altar when he is about to say; *Dominus vobiscum, Orate Fratres, Ite missa est,* or when he gives the blessing. But he kisses the altar in the center, extends and rejoins his hands, as directed above, and gives the salutation and the blessing. *Rit. Cel. v,3*

Altar and Relic Shrine. The *Acts* of the martyrdom of St. Lucian, who was martyred on January 7, 312, at Nicomedia, preserve a beautiful instance of Mass offered on the altar of the living breast of a martyr-to-be. It had been arranged that Lucian once more offer the mystic Sacrifice before complementing It with his own bloody one, but when the time came he lay perforce on his back, his feet being fastened in the stocks. So the sacred elements were laid upon a pall upon his breast, and with assistants supporting his head and hands, he sacrificed in that fashion and broke the Bread of everlasting life. But in those ages of persecution *Ruinart, III, 182* prior to Constantine we know of no relics in direct connection with the altars, but the structure of the catacombs itself allowed a Mass on a martyr's anniversary to be celebrated near, or even upon, the tomb itself. In the fourth century, the first of official freedom, *permanent altars* began to be erected at famous tombs, those of SS. Peter and Paul being among the first such known. Within a century this custom of an altar at the martyr's tomb was common everywhere. Devotion to the martyrs found expression in lavishly adorning these shrines; *ex voto* offerings, in token of favors received, further enriched them. In the turbulent times of the barbarian invasions these numerous shrines were choicest prizes for plunder, all the more so, since the tombs were outside the cities and utterly defenseless. In the case of Rome, for instance, it was seldom that the barbarians actually penetrated into the city, but again and again, they swept up to its gates and they did plunder the Roman catacombs at will. As most of the barbarians were themselves Arian Christians, they felt a special joy in possessing themselves of the relics of famous martyrs. In 537 the Goths thus violated many of the holiest graves: the trampling Lombards in 756 worked such awful havoc in the catacombs that Pope Paul I in 761 resolved upon the wholesale transfer of the bodies of all known martyrs to the crypts of the Roman churches. Besides tombs in the crypts, graves were dug in the pavement of the churches, and even in the stone footing of the altar-tables.

A Barrier of Relics. This work of transferring the martyr's relics, interrupted more than once, was spread over a full century, 761–855. Solemn "translation" processions "with hymns and spiritual songs" were almost a daily feature of Roman life at that time. Now this period 761–855 just coincides with the real greatness of the Carolingian dynasty, the princes of which, accompanied by numerous ecclesiastics, were so frequently visitors at Rome. Seeing the Romans every day enriching their churches with the relics of the martyrs, these Frankish bishops and abbots began to think of their own faraway churches and sought *to secure relics for them.* At that time it was felt unseemly to divide the body of a martyr, so that a reliquary was the shape and size of a coffin, and usually larger because ornamented with metal plating finely wrought. Such relic cases were now taken over the Alps in great triumphant processions and were, with great fanfare and solemnity, installed — where? In hidden, out-of-the-way crypts? Not at all. They were put where they would be most conspicuous, *at the altar.* Now the other local churches, which possessed founders' or martyrs' relics, hastily disinterred them, made costly shrines, and set them on display. As it happened, a great many churches were rebuilding then, as a consequence of the Norse raids, and so it was not long before enterprising churches far and near had new and strange-looking altars.

Relic Shrines Upon the Altar. These churches of the North, unlike those of Rome and Italy, were for the most part orientated in the traditional manner, so that the priest, facing the East, had his back to the people. Here there was no need of passing behind the altar, nothing therefore to prevent the relic shrine or chest being set upon a platform behind the altar, at right angles to it, so that the end of the shrine would rest *upon the altar itself.* "Let nothing be placed upon the altar," runs a famous Frankish decree of this date, *"except* reliquaries of the saints, or perchance the four holy Gospels of God, or a pyxis with the Body of our Lord." Here the age-old sanctity of the altar was silently invaded, a fact which itself testifies to a change in religious sentiment.

Subsequent Development. The first consequence of the new arrangement was that the altars now had a fixed front, quite independently of the old idea of facing eastward. It was no longer possible to stand at the altar except in front of the relic shrine. The throne, too, was now invisible. This resulted before long in setting the throne at the side, and the shrine and altar back against the wall, where the throne had been. Again, the new setting, throwing the emphasis on the relic shrine and not on the table as formerly, made the baldaquin hard to handle. It was first moved back over the relics and then discarded generally. With the passing of the baldaquin the way was opened to putting *upon* the altar the cross, candles, flowers, and other objects of adornment, all of which were formerly suspended from the baldaquin or its columns. This necessitated additional space, and so steps, shelves one might almost say, were constructed for these accessories at the sides. In the vast churches of the Middle Ages this departure alone provided unlimited possibilities for decorative superstructures. Lastly, a small, square altar looked incongruous in conjunction with such large relic shrines. Thus, as the altars little by little grew taller, they also became longer in proportion.

The Tabernacle Introduced. Nothing has been said in the foregoing paragraphs about what is now regarded as the central feature of the altar, the tabernacle. *The altars then had no tabernacles.* The whole realm of non-sacrificial worship of the Eucharist was beginning to manifest itself only in the eleventh and twelfth centuries. Moreover, even after this type of devotion developed and was spread rapidly (as a consequence of the establishment of the feast and public procession of Corpus Christi in the thirteenth century), there was still no need of a tabernacle *at the altar,* because the new devotion was non-sacrificial. There was need, indeed, to remove the Blessed Sacrament, which had hitherto been kept in some inconspicuous place, to some sort of tabernacle, where it could be publicly "visited," worshiped, prayed to. But since people did not communicate more than a few times a year, at the great feasts, there was not yet need of a tabernacle at the altar itself, and the first tabernacle took various forms, such as a silver dove suspended in plain sight somewhere, or a specially constructed Sacrament house against the wall, or a grill opening in a pillar. The practice of frequent Communion began to spread again in a noticeable way in the late sixteenth century. Throughout the following century this was one of the most noted characteristics of the Catholic revival. The twentieth century brings us in this matter "the fullness of time," since we are now once more in the spirit of the early Church. "Let the faithful be exhorted frequently, even daily, to partake of the Eucharistic Bread, and when present at Mass . . . to communicate sacramentally," runs the text of the current legislation. The restoration of frequent Communion has given us our modern tabernacle.

Canon 863

Table-Altars Once More. How this advance in religious sentiment is at present affecting the construction of our altars becomes more evident every year. The more conscious emphasis now directed to the sacrificial Gift is reflected in fashioning the altar which receives that Gift. Modern adaptations of the old table-altar are becoming common. In some localities the closer fellowship now felt in worship is bringing in a free-standing altar with the celebrant facing the people.

Sacred Vestments. The ministers at the Sacrifice wear garments such as we now see nowhere else. These are modifications of the ordinary civil dress of the late Empire, say of the fourth century. Some of the priestly vestments are garments properly so called, others are insignia of office. A few paragraphs on this sacrificial vesture may well conclude the present topic.

Amice. In the order in which the vestments are put on, the first is a white, rectangular linen cloth put upon the shoulders and wrapped about the neck. This vestment is called an *amice* (*amicta*). It is a survival of the customary neckerchief or *scarf* of the ancients; by the older authors it is often called "the protection of the voice." Originally meant to serve purely practical purposes, to cover the neck, and to protect the other vestments from the hair, the amice became a very conspicuous item in the Middle Ages, when it was decorated with a wide, rich band of embroidery and allowed to show outside the other garments. Up to a certain point in the Mass, it was even worn over the head, a usage that survives still in some monastic Orders. With the disappearance of this rich ornamentation, the amice went back to its original, humbler form.

Alb. In the whole of the ancient Roman Empire of the fourth century the customary body-garment of both sexes and all classes was a sleeved *tunic* reaching well below the knees and caught at the waist with a girdle. It was of white linen. Later a short tunic became commoner in civil life, but churchmen kept to the longer form in their official functions. This old tunic lives on in our *Alb* (Latin for *white*). Like the amice, the alb was often adorned with rich embroidery attached to the wrists, to the lower parts, or to the hem. The use of lace on the alb is a modern departure from tradition, and destined, it would seem, to disappear before long.

Tunic and Dalmatic. The decorated outer vestment worn by the subdeacon, called a *tunic,* as well as the (now) identical vesture of the deacon, called a *dalmatic,* are in origin outer tunics, with shorter, wider sleeves, and shorter body. The dalmatic is so called because this style of highly ornamented tunic came from Dalmatia.

Maniple. The *maniple,* a band of colored, decorated fabric laid across the left forearm, is a relic of a *handkerchief* carried as an emblem of office by Roman officials. The consul carried such a ceremonial handkerchief and with it gave the signals for the opening of games and other functions. In the first detailed description of a Roman Mass we have, the Pope's handkerchief is used to give the signal to begin Mass. The maniple was formerly made of linen, and by reason of its humble origin was called a *sudarium,* a sweatcloth, or because carried in the hand, a *manual.* Until about the year 1000 this clerical emblem of office was carried in the hand (usually the left); then began the custom of wearing it upon the wrist or forearm. When that happened, its original purpose was lost sight of, and instead of white linen, it was made of a colored and ornamented fabric.

Stole. Quite a different mark of the clerical order is what is now called a *stole* (a Greek word for garment in general). This was in ancient times called the *orarium* (literally, the mouth-cloth). How it was that a long, flowing band, slung over one or both shoulders and hanging loosely about the body, and originally destined for such humble purposes, should have become a highly prized symbol of the clerical order, remains in the present stage of our knowledge an unanswerable question. Old mosaics and pictures show the stole worn in many different ways, even as now it is worn in distinctive ways by bishop and priest and deacon respectively.

Chasuble. The most conspicuous of the sacrificial garments is the *chasuble,* as we say, from the Latin *casula,* a little house; so called, said St. Isidore of Seville, because it covered the whole man. It is a modified form of the ancient *paenula,* a cone-shaped outer garment, reaching down, more or less, the full length of the body all around, and provided with an opening and hood for the head. Designed for protection against all weathers in traveling, it finally became the ordinary outdoor garment for all wear, even replacing the toga of the high officials. At Rome it continued to be the ordinary outer garment for both sexes and all classes until the end of the sixth century or later. Thus everyone in a Roman church then wore a chasuble. St. Augustine speaks of it as the clothing of even the poor, but of course, it could be something very fine, and only a generation or so later St. Fulgentius will not have a colored chasuble because he thought that something for wealthy people. But Fulgentius was a monk and wore his monk's robe at the altar. In the new European nations the chasuble was at first the ordinary garment of clerical attire for church, street, and domestic uses. In the course of time it became reserved for priests and later still, for priests at the time of Mass only.

Not Now a "Little House." The ordinary chasuble of today represents a very *truncated* form of the ample "little house" of former ages. The garment, to allow freedom to the hands, had to be caught up over the forearms. Even in classical antiquity the chasuble was often cut somewhat shorter at the sides to facilitate freer movement. As long as pliable silk, the prescribed material for this vestment, continued to be used in making it, there was no great need of radical altering, but it was another thing entirely when stiff brocaded velvets, themselves heavily embroidered, began to be substituted for the silk. Then it was necessary to *cut* and *trim* away all that should have folded. The nadir of the trimming process was reached in the eighteenth century, when the attenuated vestment of today made its appearance. Since that day a gradual reversion to the traditional garment has been making itself felt. This movement will probably be slow in progressing, because it depends in last instance upon the slow-growing, inner religious sentiment, to which all change in external features of worship corresponds.

Summary. The Christian Sacrifice has its setting in a building adapted from the private homes of classical antiquity. In the twenty centuries of Christianity its altar has undergone many accidental modifications of size and structure, all of which are instructive reflexes of changing modes of religious thought. In the priestly vestments of today the civil dress of the late Empire lives on, hallowed by the religious associations of all the Christian past.

Ninth-Century Source Material
(From Walafrid Strabo's precious work, ON THE ORIGINS AND DEVELOPMENTS OF USES PERTAINING TO WORSHIP.)

Altars were erected to the Lord, as we read, by Noah, Abraham, Isaac, and Jacob, while Moses was the first to erect a Tabernacle for the sons of Israel freed from the Egyptian servitude. This he did in the desert of Sinai, and according to plans made known by heaven. Afterwards, when the same Jews had long dwelt in the Land of Promise . . . Solomon at great outlay erected and adorned that marvelous Temple of Jerusalem. In both Tabernacle and Temple were placed the Ark of the Covenant, and altars with their vessels, and the manifold other appurtenances corresponding to the religion of that time . . . (Ch. I).

Afterwards came the day when worshipers in spirit and in truth (John iv) began to adore the Father spiritually, and not locally only in Jerusalem or on the mountain of Samaria, when the doctrine of salvation was sent out unto all peoples. The faithful then began to search out "clean" places, and such as were removed from the noise and business of carnal affairs, in which they might offer "clean" prayers, and the holy Mysteries, and celebrate the comforts of mutual edification. . . . Not only were new houses erected for prayer, but even pagan temples, their unclean cults and idols being swept clean away, were changed into churches of God (Ch. III).

And because the diversity of idolatrous worship had built temples in different manners, the faithful of that age were at no great pains as to

Classical Antecedents

Greek charioteer
in girded tunic
(alb)

Greek boy
in wide-sleeved ungirt tunic
(dalmatic)

Roman sailor with
amice (neck cloth)
and chasuble

Chasuble serves goatherd as a little house

—Reproduced from photographs by courtesy of Dom Raymond James, O.S.B.,
and *Orate Fratres*.

Roman father and son in chasubles over
banded tunics

Roman consul wearing
tunics and stole and
holding maniple

Mercury in chasuble

what direction the houses of prayer faced, provided only that the omnipresent God, Creator of all things, be worshiped and adored where the filth of demons had been removed. Of course the learned will say that we ought to face the East in worshiping (and in fact this is a fitting and salutary institution) . . . (Ch. IV).

[To those prompted to give "unclean" money for the construction or ornamentation of churches, Walafrid addresses strong words:]

It is to these the Saviour saith:

> Woe to you,
> scribes and Pharisees, hypocrites;
> because ye tithe mint and dill and cummin,
> and ye have neglected the weightier things of the Law,
> justice and mercy and faith.

Matt. xxiii,23

We do not say this to blame the devotion of those who build and adorn churches, but to show that almsgiving to the needy is to be preferred. As Blessed Jerome says: "It is a mere external observance to have the wall bright with gold, while Christ at the entrance suffers from hunger and nakedness." And when He comes in judgment, He will not ask if we have built churches, but whether we have done good to His least brethren . . . (Ch. XIV).

Matt. xxv

Nothing could be found more appropriate than these Species for showing forth the union between Head and members. Because, as the bread is one body made of multiple grains of wheat moistened with water, and the wine is pressed from many grapes, so the body of Christ is filled up by the unified multiplicity of the faithful [saints] . . . (Ch. XVI).

The hour of celebrating Mass varies according to the rank of the solemnity. Sometimes Mass is offered in the forenoon, sometimes about three in the afternoon, or again at sundown, at times, even at night . . . (Ch. XXIII).

The vessels in which our Sacraments are prepared and consecrated are chalices and patens. . . . Boniface, martyr and bishop, when asked if it were lawful to consecrate in wooden chalices, replied: "Formerly priests of gold consecrated in wooden chalices, now priests 'of wood' use golden chalices."

Pope Sylvester established that the Sacrifice should be offered, neither on silk, nor a shabby cloth, but only on clean linen "born" of the earth. . . . The sacred vestments have developed by gradual stages to the ornamentation of the present day. At first priests offered Mass in every-day garments. . . . Stephen, the twenty-fourth pope, prescribed that priests and deacons should not use sacred vestments when engaged in profane occupations, but only in church. And Pope Sylvester ordained that deacons should wear dalmatics in church. . . . And others made still other additions to the sacred vestments, either by way of imitating what ancient priests had worn, or to express some mystical significance (Ch. XXIV).

Topics for Further Discussion:

The entire altar-table is ideally one piece of natural stone, containing a "sepulcher" of relics of martyrs, and resting on stone supports: only such an altar is a "fixed" or "permanent" altar.

If made of any other material, provision must be made for the location of an altar-stone (containing relics). Technically, only this altar-stone is the pre-scribed altar: it is known as a portable altar.

Altars are by prescription consecrated by a bishop, or, in some cases, a prelate of lower rank designated for the purpose by the bishop.

Altars lose their consecration by being cracked seriously, by any damage to the "sepulcher," etc., and in such cases must be reconsecrated after being repaired.

The latest American altars are reverting to the simple table type: cf. photo-graphs in *Liturgical Arts* (quarterly).

Advantages from the social point of view of the free-standing altar, at which the sacrificing priest faces the people.

Readings:

D. Attwater, "Vestments of the Western Church," *Thought*, II (1927–28), pp. 98–113.

E. Bishop, *Liturgica Historica, Papers on the Liturgy and Religious Life of the Western Church* (Oxford: Clarendon, 1918); "The Christian Altar," pp. 20–38.

J. Braun, "Vestments in Western Europe," *CE.*

H. E. Collins, *The Church Edifice and Its Appointments* (Philadelphia: Dolphin, 1936); "Altar," pp. 43–69; "Sacred Vestments," pp. 167–174.

M. M. Hassett, "Altar, History of the Christian," *CE.*

H. Lucas, *Holy Mass, the Eucharistic Sacrifice and the Roman Liturgy* (St. Louis: Herder, 1914); I, "The Christian Altar," pp. 14–23.

A. Roulin, *Vestments and Vesture* (St. Louis: Herder, 1931); "The Chasuble (1): From the Beginning to the XIX Century," pp. 56–71; *passim.*

A. J. Schulte, "Altar (in the Liturgy)," *CE.*

C. L. Souvay, "Altar (in the Greek Church)," *CE.*

G. Webb, *The Liturgical Altar* (New York: Benziger, 1939); *passim.*

Chapter X

HIGH MASS WITH ST. GREGORY THE GREAT

The cup of blessing, which we bless,
is it not fellowship in the Blood of Christ?
(I Cor. xi,26.)

WHEN Alaric and his Visigothic hosts sacked and pillaged Rome in the summer of 410, the national pride of the Romans was cut to the quick. In the provinces no less than in the city, Christians as well as pagans were amazed and dumbfounded to see the Eternal City, "the mistress of the world," violated and plundered by the hands of barbarians. It was not long before the still remaining adherents of paganism raised the cry, "This happened because Rome turned from her ancient gods to adopt Christianity!" This charge drew from St. Augustine, then bishop of an African town, the greatest of all his works, *The City of God.*

After refuting the old calumny that pagan worship was necessary for temporal happiness or prosperity, Augustine passes to a positive defense of Christianity, which he calls in Scriptural language "The City of God." In his tenth book he deals at length with the true nature of worship, of sacrifice, and in particular of the sanctifying value of the Sacrifice of the Mystical Body. We find him here forcibly restating the language of the New Testament, and its earliest exponents, as already summarily reviewed in these pages. Here we shall allow ourselves only a short quotation from his thought. He says:

> We owe [God] that worship which the Greeks call *latria*, both in external symbols and in our own selves, for we are all His temple . . . our hearts elevated to Him are His altars; His only Son is the Priest by whom we are made pleasing to Him.
>
> The whole ransomed city, that is, *the Church and the communion of saints, forms the universal sacrifice* offered to God by the High Priest,

who in His passion gave up His life that we might become the Body of so great a Head. . . . This is the Christian's Sacrifice: we being many are one Body with Christ, as the Church in the Sacrament of the Altar, so well known to the faithful, wherein is shown that in that oblation *the Church is offered.*

Chap. vi

This entire part of *The City of God* is the classic presentation of what full Christian worship implies.

Gregory the Great and Our Worship. It may, therefore, come as a surprise to learn that all through the Middle Ages people called *St. Gregory the Great* (pope, 590–604), "the Father of Christian Worship." This was because that great pontiff, who so uniquely embodied the Roman genius for organization, revised the Roman worship of his day with a result so satisfactory that Rome has kept to it ever since. What Augustine sketched in theory in the early fifth century, Gregory at the end of the sixth reduced to perfect practice. It happens that we possess a detailed account of a papal feast-day Mass of an age not long after Gregory's, and scholars agree that, barring a detail here and there, it shows us Gregory's own Mass. On reading this ancient sketch of Gregory's Mass, one does not wonder that the Church for more than thirteen hundred years has regarded it as the most perfect expression of her Eucharistic worship ever realized. The full *sacrificial consciousness* on the part of the worshipers there had its counterpart in the chief fruit of their worship, an ennobling *sense of the Christian solidarity.*

Approaching the Station. On great days the Roman Mass was a "stational" affair, that is, a papal Mass in some particular church of the city designated beforehand, to which clergy and people of the whole city came. At meeting places in each of the seven ecclesiastical "wards" the populace assembled, where with a prayer they fell in behind the Christian standard, the cross, and set off in processions for the station. There they found, ranged along the bench of the apse, to right and left respectively of the papal throne, the seven suburban bishops and the city's twenty-five pastors. Numerous monks would be already there, probably reciting, or singing, their psalms, and there would be found soldiers from the Roman garrisons. Meanwhile from the Lateran palace a striking procession would be approaching. Carrying sacred vessels and vestments, came various minor clerics on foot; on horseback rode deacons and subdeacons (one from each of the seven regions), the papal chancellor, and notaries. In a second troop rode the Pontiff attended by his major-domo, his sacristan, and his almoner. Dismounting at the entrance, all vested in the sacristies, located in front of the main entrance to the basilica. Their ceremonial garment was the chasuble, in cut and shape the same as in civil life, but of finer texture and adornment, and now beginning to take on a sacred character because these particularly fine specimens were reserved for the sacred functions. Two choirs of singers would already be in place on either side at the front, with the men standing behind the boys. A sub-deacon, attended by an acolyte, would enter and "place the Gospel-book honorably upon the altar." When all was ready, a subdeacon, carrying as a badge of authority the Pope's ceremonial handkerchief, the maniple, would give notice to the choir to begin the chant. The Introit, a Psalm with a short refrain intercalated between the verses, thereupon began, and the great procession moved into the basilica.

ROMAN CONSUL WITH OFFICIAL HANDKERCHIEF
The priest's *maniple* is a development of the official handkerchief, an insignia of office, with which high Roman officials opened and closed games, sessions, etc.

Torches of Honor. When high magistrates of Rome entered their courts, they were preceded by attendants carrying *torches*, and a *brasier* of coals, for relighting the torches should these be extinguished. St. John the Evangelist no doubt often saw such processions, and memories of them may have subconsciously shaped his vision in the *Apocalypse* of "the One who walked in the midst of the seven golden lamps." Be that as it may, the Pontiff is now preceded by seven acolytes each bearing a gold or silver candlestick, by the seven deacons, and the seven subdeacons, one of whom holds a fuming censer.

Apoc. ii,1

Beginning the Mass. As the imposing procession approached the presbytery, the acolytes separated, three on one side and four on the other, to allow those behind to pass up through their midst. Then the subdeacons would do the same, and at the foot of the altar the deacons likewise. As the Pope proceeded to the altar, two acolytes approached, carrying a casket in which a fragment of the consecrated Species from a

GROUP OF CLERICS VESTED
The clerics, vested in alb, stole, tunic, and chasuble carry maniples in right or left hand indifferently. (From a ninth-century Bible Codex.)

former Mass was preserved. The Pontiff would inspect, and, presumably with a bow, salute, the Sacred Species. Also with a bow he saluted the altar, and prayed silently for a moment. Thereupon he made the sign of the cross on his forehead, gave the kiss of peace to one of the suburban bishops, to the archpriest, and to the seven deacons. Then he motioned the precentor to end the Introit Psalm. While awaiting its conclusion, he would kneel for a few moments in prayer. During the interval the deacons had approached the altar two by two and kissed its extremities. The Pontiff now ascended, kissed the Gospels and then the altar. Thereupon he went to his throne, where he stood facing eastward, away from the people. The choirs continued singing the *Kyrie* alternately until a signal was given them to stop. Turning to the assembly, the Pontiff would now intone *Gloria in excelsis Deo* (Glory be to God on high), and at once face eastward again while this was being sung throughout by the chanters. Again turning, the Pontiff saluted the throng with *"Peace be with you,"* and intoned the short Collect prayer. This over, he would seat himself and motion to the bishops and priests to do the same.

The Scripture Lessons. A subdeacon appointed beforehand now went without accompaniment or ceremony into a pulpit and read the Epistle. When he descended, a singer went up and chanted a Psalm, to the several verses of which the entire congregation answered with a short, simple refrain, as, for instance, *Alleluia.* The chanting of the Gospel was, so far as external ceremonials is concerned, the high point of the entire function. In much the same manner as now, with lights and incense, a procession moved to a second pulpit on the opposite side, where the deacon chanted the sacred message. At its close, the Gospel-book was kissed by everyone in the presbytery.

Bringing the Gifts. Two deacons now approached the altar, one of them holding a cloth. This "he lays on the right side of the altar, throwing the other end of it to the second deacon in order to spread it." The choir again began a Psalm, the verses of which were again marked off by some simple refrain. The Pope now went down with his attendants to receive the offerings of the people. The men come on the north side, the women on the south, carrying their gifts, little loaves of bread, and little flagons of wine. The bread they put directly into the hands of the Pontiff, and it was then put upon a cloth held by attendants. The wine was poured into a great, two-handled chalice, from which, when filled, it was poured into large bowls carried by acolytes. Everyone in the congregation would make an offering to express his or her participation in the common Sacrifice, and to symbolize in these gifts the dedication of their lives to Almighty God and to Christian ideals. It was the privilege of the choir boys, who were for the most part orphans, to offer the water that was required for the sacrifice.

A Papal Basilica.

suburban bishops
visiting bishops
minor clergy
papal throne
altar
city pastors
minor clergy
ambo   ambo
boys   boys
choir choir
men   men
women   men
door
sacristy
lavabo
sacristy
door

After receiving the offerings, the celebrant returned to his throne and washed his hands. The archdeacon meanwhile arranged some of the loaves upon the altar. Next, the offerings of the clerics were received, rank by rank. The chalice was placed upon the altar and water added to it. The Pontiff approached the altar and received his own oblation, two small loaves brought for this purpose from the Lateran. The signal was then given to end the Psalmody.

Dedicating Self Through Gifts. With the heaped-up altar between himself and his flock, and with the attendant bishops, priests, the minor clerics ranged in order about him, while all bowed deeply in reverence, the Pontiff recited in an audible voice the prayer now called the Silent Prayer. This brief prayer varied from day to day, but it always echoed the thought that the gifts now laid upon the altar represented the persons who had made them. In direct, concise form, the wish was expressed that in return for these gifts, God would deign to grant some blessing in return. For instance, the prayer that follows was said each year by Gregory on the Tuesday of Passion Week:

> O God, our Lord, who in these objects especially, which Thou hast created for the support of our weakness, hast commanded gifts to be offered; grant, we beseech Thee, that they may become the support of the present life, and a symbol of life everlasting. Through Jesus Christ, Thy Son our Lord.

Another train of thought, which often recurs in these Offertory-prayers, and also dates from St. Gregory at the latest, is this; we repeat it on the seventh Sunday after Pentecost:

> O God, who hast enacted one perfect Sacrifice in place of all the victims that were under the Old Law, receive this Sacrifice offered by Thy devout servants, and sanctify it as Thou didst sanctify the offerings of Abel, that *what they have severally offered to the honor of Thy Majesty, may avail them all unto salvation.* Through, etc.

A Sacrifice of Thanksgiving. The Pontiff raised his voice to chant the final words: "Through endless ages of ages." The subdeacons stood erect to respond, "Amen." Then as now *Sursum corda* (Lift up your hearts), and *Gratias agamus* (Let us give thanks to the Lord our God), led up to the Preface, which, then as now, was followed by the *Sanctus*, at the singing of which all again bowed the head profoundly. The most noticeable difference between a High Mass of the sixth century and our own of today was the manner of praying during the Canon. The *Sanctus* over, the celebrant alone stood erect and began the Canon. While up to this point there had been constant movement and chant, now the Act progressed in comparative quiet, while all bowed profoundly. There was thus the same profound sense of deepest reverence before God during the entire period of the Canon as marks, in our Mass, the fleeting moment of consecration. No bell, or incensation, or elevation gave external sign of that moment when the transubstantiation changed the poor gifts of bread and wine into the supreme Gift of the Body and Blood of Christ. The people merely knew when the Pontiff raised his voice once more, that this change had been effected, and the perfect Gift ritually offered before God's Majesty. The Pontiff would call upon the people to signify their common assent to this sacrificial Action by joining in the "Amen." The sacrificial ritual was here complete.

A Portion for the Absent. The Pontiff now returned to his throne to say, as a special preparation for Communion, the *Our Father*, and a subsequent short prayer. The remnant of the consecrated Species from a former Mass, held all the while on a paten by an acolyte, was now dropped into the chalice. This was done to symbolize the oneness of the Christian Sacrifice, and this same idea lies behind another action that followed. If any of the priests of the city happened to be absent from the stational Mass, *a portion of the Eucharist* was broken off, one of the Pope's own oblations being used for this purpose, to be sent to the absentee as a token of union. The Eucharist means *fellowship* in Christ above all else. After the actions just described, the time and place of the next "station" would be announced by the archdeacon as: "Tomorrow the station will be at the Basilica of St. Peter, the chief of the Apostles." To this the people responded, "Thanks be to God."

Breaking the Bread. The general *breaking of the Bread* was an impressive ceremonial preparation for Communion. Acolytes, carrying the Bread in little linen bags around their necks, passed up and down the presbytery, allowing bishops and priests to take the Bread. At a signal from the Pontiff, all would join with him in breaking the Bread in unison. It was then returned to the altar, for distribution at the sacrificial Banquet which followed forthwith. The Pope communicated himself at his throne, the archdeacon supporting the Chalice, of which the Pontiff partook.

Then the bishops and higher clergy came before the Pope to receive in their hands the species of Bread, while at the altar a bishop proffered them the Chalice. The singers once more intoned a Psalm with a fixed refrain after every verse. The people came forward as before, called now to the Table of God as guests, to receive as from His hand the visible token and pledge of the acceptance of their gifts.

The biography of St. Gregory enshrines a tiny anecdote, which illustrates how closely gift and Return-Gift might chance to be linked together. A certain noble lady had smiled just as Gregory was about to communicate her. On being taken to task for this afterwards, she said: "I recognized the Fragment to be of the very oblation-loaf which I made myself with my own hands and offered you."

Bk. iv,10

On the palm of the right hand of the communicant the Pontiff laid the Bread, and the archdeacon offered each in turn the Cup of fellowship in the Blood of Christ. The Communion of the lower clerics followed upon that of the people.

The Fruit of Union. After the Communion the celebrant went to the altar to say the prayer now called "Postcommunion." This links up in a brief compass the thought of the Sacrament just received and the fruits of that Sacrament to be perceived in a better living of the Christian life. The following short form still keeps its place in St. Gregory's Mass Book, on the Saturday before Laetare Sunday:

We beseech Thee, Almighty God, that we may ever be numbered among *His members,* in whose Body and Blood we have communicated. Through the same Jesus Christ Thy Son our Lord.

The Gregorian Postcommunion we say now on the sixth Sunday after Epiphany runs:

Fed as we have been, O Lord, on heavenly delights, we pray Thee that we may ever have a longing for the same *by which we truly live.* Through Jesus Christ Thy Son.

These last words re-echo a celebrated passage of St. Augustine in which he says. "O sign of unity! O bond of charity! Whosoever would live, hath here where to live, hath here whereof to live. Let him come, let him believe; let him be incorporated, that he may be enlivened. Let him not shrink from the *whole* into which *the members* are compacted together. . . . Let him cleave to the body, let him live to God by God."

Hom. xxvi in loan.

Recessional. After the Postcommunion the deacon sang: *Ite missa est* (Go, it is the time of dismissal), to which the entire congregation responded: "Thanks be to God." Whereat the long procession, swelled this time by the monks and the soldiers, formed and marched down the basilica, the Pontiff bestowing blessings as he went.

A Reflection. In this sketch of High Mass in St. Gregory's day we realize that the substantial rites have changed but little. But everyone will also realize that the intervening centuries have brought a profound difference in the general attitude of the congregation toward those rites at the altar. Then everyone, high or low, publicly *expressed* his or her *individual homage in a social, public gift-offering,* and similarly everyone high or low felt prompted by an enlightened self-interest, so to speak, to partake of God's *Return-Gift,* Communion.

How forcibly did not this rite portray the fellowship of the Church, and its corporate spirit! By reason of the general obscuring of the sacrificial consciousness, Christians of the present day are much poorer than those of Gregory's time. True, the Sacrifice is essentially the same, and is *in a measure* profitable to us by its own intrinsic value, however we may lack what a modern phrase would call "sacrificial-mindedness." But inasmuch as our service of God must be reasoning and intelligent, we shall share in the unspeakable riches of the Eucharist in proportion as we penetrate its social and sacrificial character. That is the task of twentieth-century Christianity.

Summary. In two important respects social participation in Eucharistic worship has diminished since the end of the sixth century; first, the individual worshipers no longer make a personal gift-offering of the sacrificial elements, and second, the reception of Communion is not now regarded as a necessary adjunct of assistance at the Sacrifice.

Tenth-Century Source Material

(Our better-informed age may improve a little on the faulty history but not on the faith or piety of Remigius of Auxerre in his work: ON THE CELEBRATION AND MEANING OF THE MASS.*)*

Mass is celebrated in memory of the Passion of Christ. He Himself, in giving them His Body and Blood, bade the Apostles, "Do this in memory of Me" (Luke xxxi,19), that is, in memory of My Passion. As if He should say, what I have suffered for your salvation, do you recall, and take pains to do the same thing for the weal of yourselves and yours. Peter is said to have been the first to celebrate this Sacrifice, at Antioch, using (in that beginning of the faith) only three prayers, beginning at that place [in the Canon] where it is said: *Hanc igitur oblationem.* . . .

First of all the antiphon at the introit is said. Now "antiphon" is a Greek word, of which the Latin equivalent is "reciprocal," two singing alternately, the one after the other in order. The Greeks are reputed to have invented this mode of singing. This antiphon is called "at the introit [entrance]," because through it we enter the divine mystery, as one enters through the doorway into the interior part of the house. . . .

The chanter beginning *Kyrie, eleison,* the candles are arranged by an acolyte in a row from south to north, thus showing forth in what order the Lord Almighty had mercy on the world. [*R. was writing near the then "North Pole" of European civilization.*] . . . The Latins sing in Greek, "Kyrie, eleison," and the Greeks in Latin . . . that we may show ourselves as one people, and that both races believe in one God. Kyrie, Lord, eleison, have mercy, *Christe,* eleison, that is, Thou who art anointed, not with visible oil, but with the plenitude of the Godhead, have mercy, for *chrism* is anointing.

Then the priest begins *Gloria in excelsis Deo,* the hymn sung by the angels at the birth of the Saviour, and later completed, as it were, by Blessed Hilary of Poitiers, and after the manner of the angels, to show that we worship the same Lord on earth whom the angels venerate in Heaven. . . .

Thereupon the priest says *Dominus vobiscum,* greeting the people and praying that the Lord be with them, as He deigned to say by the Prophet, II Cor. vi,16 "I will dwell amongst them" and the rest, and as the Saviour said to His Matt. xxviii,20 disciples, "Behold I am with you." This salutation is not of human composition, but is taken as used by the authority of Sacred Scripture, where one often reads it both in the singular and plural forms. . . .

Then he says *Oremus,* inviting the people to pray with him. . . . There follows the *Collect,* so called from the act of collecting . . . because from many words one prayer is gathered up. . . .

After the recitation of the Gospel, the priest again greets the people, praying that the words they have heard of the Lord may be strengthened in their hearts, and inviting them to pray, saying *Oremus.* And although in our rite this Collect between the Gospel and the Offertory is no longer said, it is retained by the Greeks. Our custom may be understood in this manner: that the people is enjoined to make its offering, and the offerers should make their intention, that their oblations be pleasing to the Lord. . . .

Then follows the Offertory itself, which derives its name from the circumstance that the people present their gifts. . . . Meanwhile the priest receives the gifts of the people, that he who stands as mediator between God and the people, may present their prayers and wishes to the Lord. In this offering water is mixed with the wine. Christ is signified in the wine, the people in the water. If wine were to be offered without water it would signify that the Passion of Christ had not benefited the human race; but if water without wine, it would mean the man could have been redeemed without Christ's Passion. . . .

The *thanks* which it is fitting for us to offer are to be rendered through our Lord Jesus Christ, who is Mediator between God and us, and High-priest of highpriests. . . .

Cum quibus et nostras voces, and so forth. The voices of the angels hymn their Maker in the very ecstasy of intuitive contemplation. What should be the character of *our* voices, that we beg to be admitted, that is introduced, into the angelic choirs before the Face of God? . . . Our *words* do not carry our voices unto the inmost ears of God, but *our desires do,* and because the heavenly city is peopled by angels and men, the holy Church, which is to be joined with them in Heaven, and carry on with them the praises of God, the Church is right, I say, in even now praising God with those very same voices on earth with which the holy angels sing in paradise. . . .

Topics for Further Discussion:

Advantages to society now lost to us, derived by the Christians of St. Gregory's day from their type of Mass celebration.

Limited ways and means by which popular participation in the public functions of the Church can be reproduced in collegiate and parish services.

"In order that the faithful may participate more actively in divine worship Gregorian chant in that which pertains to the people must be given back to them." — *Pius XI.*

"Do not pray at Mass, pray the Mass." — *Pius X.*

The so-called Dialogue Mass, or *Missa Recitata,* and its advantages.

The justice of the saying, "Ceremonial is to public worship as the body to the soul."

The suitability of the materials in this chapter for a Mass pageant of medieval civilization.

The possibility of dramatic representation of modern American youth presenting in symbolic tokens their lives of work and play.

Readings:

C. F. Atchley, *Ordo Romanus Primus,* Text, Translation, Notes (London, 1905).

E. Bishop, *Liturgica Historica, Papers on the Liturgy and Religious Life of the Western Church* (Oxford: Clarendon, 1918); "The Genius of the Roman Rite," pp. 1–19.

L. Duchesne, *Christian Worship, Its Origin and Evolution* (New York: Macmillan, 1923); "The Roman Mass," pp. 161–188.

A. Fortescue, *The Mass, A Study of the Roman Liturgy* (New York: Longmans, Green, 1937); "The Mass since Gregory I," pp. 172–177.

J. Kramp, *Eucharistia, Essays on Eucharistic Liturgy and Devotion* (St. Paul: Lohmann, 1926); "The Visible Ceremony of the Christian Sacrifice," pp. 22–40.

J. de Puniet, *The Mass, Its Origin and History* (London: Burns, Oates and Washbourne, 1931); "The Setting of the Roman Mass in the Time of St. Gregory the Great," etc., pp. 81–95, sqq.

Chapter XI

SACRIFICIAL-MINDEDNESS LARGELY LOST — AND FOUND

Take ye and eat (Matt. xxvi,26).

REFERENCE has been made several times in these pages to the gradual but profound changes affecting the religious outlook of succeeding ages. In particular a good deal of the sacrificial and Eucharistic atmosphere of the early Church seems remote from us, not only in time, but in concept and feeling. A little puzzled, we ask ourselves how it could be that, while the faith in the Eucharist remained quite unchanged, the Christian mentality toward it could undergo far-reaching changes. How did it come about that *we* are inclined to regard attendance at Mass as an irksome duty, while it was originally considered as the exercise of the *supreme right* of the Christian man and woman? Or how was it that the Church was forced to make a matter of law binding under mortal sin the annual reception of Communion, when once men and women, and usually even infant children, communicated at every Mass, and privately in their homes when there was no Mass?

Why Piety Changed. These questions are partly answered by saying, "The piety of the people grew cold and formal, and so these changes resulted." Besides being incomplete, such an explanation is partly incorrect, since there has never been a lack of seraphic saints in the Church. The full truth of the matter must take account of the fact that in the course of time the piety of the people gradually grew *different*. There is no more important or instructive chapter in the Church's inner history than the beginning of this very process, whereby what is pre-eminently the sacrament of love and union, became invested with attributes of dread and fear. What is really at stake here is the concept of Christ as the *Bridge-Builder*, the very notion of mediatorial worship of God *through* the New Man, His Son.

137

Daily Communion, the Common Thing. In the first centuries, Christ's unique position as Mediator of the New Law was the focal point of the Glad Tidings of Salvation. Therein men found an unfailing source of individual strength and peace and "confident access unto God." *Eph. iii,12* The Eucharistic Food united them with God through Christ, and so it was eagerly and ardently eaten on rising every morning. Even though Mass was, as a rule, celebrated but once or twice a week in the earliest ages, Christians kept the Eucharist in their homes and communicated themselves at their morning prayer. Tertullian, in urging upon women not to marry pagans, speaks of the misunderstandings inevitably to arise out of the fact that the pagan husbands will know, but not understand, *Ad Ux. ii,5* what it is they eat on rising. The words of St. Hippolytus of Rome, about 225, speak volumes by implication: "Let each of the faithful hasten, before eating any other food, to partake of the Eucharist . . . and let each be solicitous lest any unbeliever share of it, or that a mouse *Apos. Trad.* or any other animal touch it, or that any of it fall [to the ground] and *lxxvii–viii* perish."

A SECOND-CENTURY EUCHARISTIC FRESCO
A symbolic representation of the Holy Eucharist, the fish supporting a basket of bread and glass of wine. (Crypt of Lucina, Catacomb of Callistus.)

Carried in Wicker Baskets. In inveighing against the pagan theaters, at least one preacher spoke of the shamelessness of Christians appearing at them "as they return from the Sacrifice, carrying the Eucharist, as is *De Spectac.,* ▼ customary." In the mural decorations of the catacombs a frequent theme is that of a fish bearing on its back a basket of small loaves, among which one can discern a glass vessel of wine. The fish, of course, stood for Christ, as was explained previously, and the loaves and wine were unquestionably the Eucharistic Species. The Christians were constantly taught to interpret the words, "Give us this day our daily bread," as referring primarily to the Food that had become Christ's Body in their public Sacrifice of thanksgiving. If there is one thing that stands out clearly in the meager records of early Christianity, it is this popular hunger and thirst for the Eucharist as affording "confident access unto God."

The Bridge Broken — or Unused. This primitive attitude lasted unchanged until, at the turn of the fourth century, Arianism appeared in the Orient, fiercely denying the divinity of the Word, and hence of Christ. In the ensuing struggle, one of the wildest and bitterest of the Church's long history, every move made by Arians to insist on the humanity of Christ was parried by a counterstroke of the Catholics emphasizing His divinity. In this process many an old prayer expressive of Christ's *mediation,* now deemed *capable* of an Arian interpretation, was changed so as to bring out with unequivocal clarity Christ's divine nature equal with the Father's. Thus, an old form of the common doxology, "Glory to the Father, *through* the Son . . ." was altered to "Glory to the Father, *and* to the Son. . . ." When the violence of this storm had passed, the Oriental Churches had developed a quite different *attitude toward Christ.* Arians no longer worshiped God *mediatorially* through Christ, for to them Christ was a mere man; Christians, by focusing all attention on the divine nature of Christ, were also losing the *practical consciousness* of His office of Bridge-Builder. "Now Christ no longer stands by man's side, as the representative of mankind, and no longer as *the* man, Christ Jesus, and the First-born of His brethren, offers the Sacrifice of mankind to the Triune God. He has, so to speak, crossed over, and is now by God's side, and Himself is the awful and unapproachable God."[1]

Origin of "Cultual" Dread. Within a generation this new attitude brought about epoch-making consequences in the primitive outlook toward the Eucharist. It surrounded both Sacrifice and Communion with a *sense of awe and dread.* Thus, within twenty years of the condemnation of Arianism, we find a Council at Antioch (341), and one at Sardica, in Thrace (343), threatening to cut off Christians from the Church because they had begun *to abstain from the reception of Communion at public worship.* The famous *Catechetical Instructions* of St.

---

[1] K. Adam, *Christ Our Brother* (New York: Macmillan, 1931), p. 49.

Cyril of Jerusalem date from the year 348: In them the period of the
xxxiii,iv Canon of the Mass is called "that most awful hour." This "awfulness"
is a note that will echo louder and louder in the preaching of subsequent
ages: The Holy Eucharist was in the East fast becoming "the dread
Mysteries," at the celebration of which the Christians were bid to stand
"in fear and dread." For the reception of the "awful Body" preachers
were beginning to find that no preparation really sufficed, and they
began attaching hard and oftentimes insupportable *conditions* to the reception of Communion. So swift were matters moving in the East that at the
end of the century, St. John Chrysostom complains at Constantinople:

> In vain is the daily Sacrifice, in vain do we stand before the altar,
> and there is no one to partake: Everyone that partaketh not of the
> Mysteries is standing here in shameless effrontery. . . .

But almost the next words on the lips of this strict preacher were hardly
adapted to bring the people in numbers to the Communion Table.

> These things I say to you, not to induce you to come in any which
> way, but that you should render yourselves worthy to partake. . . .
> It is sincerity and purity of soul. With these approach at all times,
Hom. iii in Ephes. > *without them, never!*

Jerome's Influence. The great St. Jerome was a Roman by training,
but at this time he had long been a resident in the East, and he was
imbued with these Eastern ideas. He was more than once asked by cor-
respondents if they should communicate daily "as the Roman and Spanish
churches do." In his replies Jerome "*neither praises nor blames the Roman
custom,*" but for the rest, "let his questioners follow the usages of their
localities," that is, let them abstain from Communion, if that be the local
usage. Moreover, St. Jerome found, as he thought, Scriptural reasons
for supporting the hard conditions that were then being attached to the
reception of Communion. When we recall that Jerome's authority in
matters of Scripture was supreme, it is clear that his influence tended to
accelerate the common abstention from Communion.

West Feels Cultual Dread. Before very long this new spirit had
penetrated into the West, partly through the spread of Arianism, but
probably more by reason of the pilgrimages to the Holy Places. A
council at Saragossa, Spain, in 381, found it necessary to excommunicate
those who received the consecrated Bread into their hands as usual *but*

refrained from eating it. How the new ideas filtering in from the East   *Mansi* iii,634
were being combated in the West is clearly shown in many contemporary
documents. Probably no passage so briefly and so cogently states the
whole case as the lines quoted below. They are from a little treatise *On
the Sacraments* written somewhere in the north of Italy during the episcopacy of the great St. Ambrose at Milan. Some scholars consider them
as a stenographic report of Ambrose's sermons.

> *Give us this day our daily bread.* As often as Christ's Blood is shed
> (it is shed for the remission of sin), I ought daily to receive Him; for
> since I continually sin, as continually should I drink of His
> medicine.
>
> For if it is *daily* Bread, *why do you receive it but annually, as the
> Greeks are wont to do?* Receive daily what will daily help you. So live
> that you may be fit to receive daily. *He who is unfit for daily Com-
> munion is equally unfit to receive but once a year.*

St. Augustine in Africa, St. Hilary of Poitiers, France, St. Zeno of
Verona, Italy, and other great pastors of this time were protecting their
local churches from the new spirit. How one's own attitude may be
misinterpreted is well illustrated by an incident in the life of St. Augustine. On being asked by a certain correspondent just what the spirit of
the Church in this matter of frequent Communion was, Augustine composed a very gracious answer in which he set down the customs of various
churches.

> Some receive the Body and Blood of the Lord every day; others on
> certain days only; in some places no day passes on which the Sacrifice
> is not offered; in others on Saturday and Sunday only, in others on
> Sunday only.

Augustine goes on to offer a kindly interpretation for those who received
seldom as well as to commend those who received daily. The one party
resembles Zachaeus of the Gospel, who received our Lord rejoicing into   Luke xix,6
his house; the other is likened to the centurion, who thought himself   Matt. viii,6
unworthy of that honor. Unfortunately, at a later date, this letter was
quoted and requoted as showing Augustine's approval of a rare reception
of Communion.

The Barbarian Invasions. When matters stood thus, the fifth century ushered in the barbarian invasions. In a generation the whole of
the Western Empire, barring the city of Rome, and a few such "islands,"

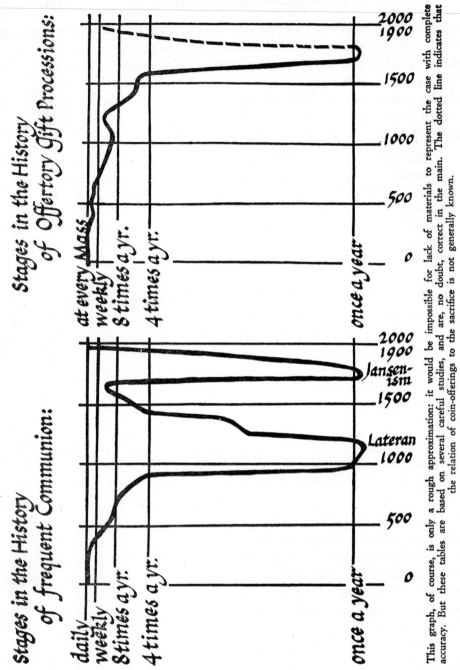

Stages in the History
of Frequent Communion:

Stages in the History
of Offertory Gift Processions:

at every Mass
weekly
8 times a yr.
4 times a yr.
once a year

daily
weekly
8 times a yr.
4 times a yr.
once a year

Jansen-
ism
Lateran

This graph, of course, is only a rough approximation: it would be impossible for lack of materials to represent the case with complete accuracy. But these tables are based on several careful studies, and are, no doubt, correct in the main. The dotted line indicates that the relation of coin-offerings to the sacrifice is not generally known.

was overrun by semicivilized people, who were fanatical, if ignorant, Arians. The work of winning them to Catholicity lasted over a century. It should not, therefore, be very surprising that when the new nations arose, they were pretty generally imbued with the "fear-and-dread" attitude toward the Holy Eucharist.

The Losses Heavy. The result was, that with the exception of Rome and a few such centers of the old traditions, Communion was ceasing to be in the minds of the people the *Return-Gift* of the Sacrifice. This led to the obscuring of the popular notion of sacrifice and sacrificial worship. Fast fading, too, was the concept of the Eucharist as the Christians' bond of union. Suppose we here sketch the main stages in this obscuring of the sacrificial concept by noting the gradual disappearance of the Offertory procession, that solemn external act by which the people's sacrificial purpose was expressed.

One of the first manifestations of the spirit of dread and fear in Eucharistic worship, as we saw, was that whereby people received the Species in their hands as before *but did not communicate.* In other words, they still offered their own sacrificial gifts, but they *hesitated to accept the Return-Gift of God.* Since the individual's offering of a gift is, after all, the very basis of the whole sacrificial system of worship, this idea would naturally persist even a long time after a feeling of unworthiness had constrained the worshiper not to accept God's Gift in return. But by the time Communion had come to be received only three or four times a year, several ominous phenomena make a simultaneous appearance.

Sunday Mass, an Obligation. In place of the early Christians' eagerness to be present at the Sacrifice, lest their absence should *"cause the Body of Christ to be short a member,"* Christians now had to be Didascalia xiii compelled by a *precept under sin* to assist at Mass. Again, preachers now felt it necessary to tell the people that they must not leave the church *after the sermon,* but that Catholic worship was really the Sacrifice. Lastly, from this time on the people are being urged and urged with endless repetition to make the bread-and-wine offerings at the altar. The first traces of positive legislation on all these points are found in the south of France, where, just then, the spirit of the Orient had entered by way of the monasticism imported from the East. The precept of assistance at Sunday Mass, and particularly that of making sacrificial offerings, was destined to echo wearily through the acts of Church councils for centuries.

Gift-Processions Repeatedly Enjoined. These first conciliar enactments had some temporary effect in checking the disastrous decline of the sacrificial concept. But at the end of the sixth century, which was at Rome just the golden age of St. Gregory the Great, we find these decrees being reaffirmed in new French councils. Throughout the seventh, eighth, and ninth centuries these canons are enjoined again and again, a clear sign that, despite all efforts, pastors could not bring their people to maintain the Offertory procession. When things had reached the pass when *men* no longer brought gifts, it was urged upon their *womenfolk* to make the offerings for themselves and their male relatives.

In this whole matter one must *not* think of these offerings as made *for the support of the churches* or clergy. *That* type of offering was being made, and generously. What is here in question wholly concerns sacrificial gifts, the visible tokens of self-dedication publicly offered to God and in the transubstantiation linked up with the self-oblation of Christ upon the cross.

Communion Ever Rarer. But along with these repeated urgings to continue the sacrificial gifts, there were parallel enactments surrounding the reception of the Eucharist with conditions which made it extremely difficult for people living in the world. The two tendencies develop side by side. Communion comes to be regarded as a spiritual reward to be won at great cost on the three or four principal feasts, and the gift procession dwindles until it is no more a public, social affair, but an occasional sight, a relic come down from times long past.

Unleavened Bread Adds New Difficulty. In the period 800–1000 the use of *unleavened bread* at the altar was spreading throughout the West. This was a further hindrance to the bringing of gifts, for now ordinary table bread would no longer serve for the offering. About the year 1200 money first began to be brought to the altar as a substitute for the old gifts of bread and wine. For a time this made the gift-procession easier, and in places helped to restore it for a while.

Yearly Communion Obligatory. By this date the reverential awe surrounding the reception of Communion had brought it about that even the greatest saints, and whole religious orders in the first fervor of their foundation, communicated only three or four times a year. Many people living in the world put off Communion for years at a time. In the face of these conditions, the Lateran Council in 1215 enjoined the annual

Easter Communion under pain of excommunication (the penalty of excommunication has since been removed). The same Council spoke of priests "who celebrate Mass only three or four times a year."

Opinions of Theologians. This was the age of the great theologians, and it is interesting to see how they face the question of frequent Communion. St. Thomas sees too clearly to doubt the *lawfulness* of frequent or even daily Communion, but finds that "in the case of the majority of men there are so many obstacles to the [requisite] devotion . . . [that] it is not praiseworthy to receive this Sacrament daily." His celebrated contemporary, St. Bonaventure, leaves the burden of final decision to another, but clearly indicates on what strict principles the judgment would rest. *S.T.* III. Q. lxxx, *a.*10

> Should one receive Communion frequently? If one finds oneself in the state of the primitive Church, one should: but if you find yourself in the state of the Church in its last stage, namely cold and sluggish, you should go rarely; if in a middle state, one should go from time to time, and sometimes stay away to learn reverence, and sometimes go to be inflamed with love. *In IV Sent. Dist.* xii, *punct.* ii, *a.*2, *q.*2

This age reached the lowest point in the history of the Eucharist as Communion. But let us not forget that the same age witnessed a deep and widespread enthusiasm for the Blessed Sacrament in non-sacrificial forms of devotion. It was St. Thomas who composed the marvelous hymns and Office for the Feast of Corpus Christi then recently instituted. Stamped with the spirit of the age, the newer forms of devotion were non-mediatorial in character: practically speaking, they leave the Blessed Trinity as such quite out of consideration.

End of Gift-Processions. As one approaches the sixteenth century, the Offertory procession becomes rarer and rarer. Whereas, at the beginning of the fifteenth century, synods could still prescribe eight such processional gift-offerings of money annually, by the end of that century they could enjoin no more than four. Then came the religious upheavals of the sixteenth century. These *swept away all but the last vestiges* of the old gift-processions. In our day a few faint traces of the old usage remain as ceremonies on certain high occasions. When a bishop is consecrated, for example, he makes an offering of two candles, two miniature barrels of wine, and two loaves of bread. At a papal Mass for a canonization, and at a priest's ordination Mass, there is likewise a gift-offering made at the altar. In some rural districts of Germany a gift-procession of money-offerings is made at funerals, but these offerings are for *other* Masses, not for the one being celebrated. In the Cathedral of Milan on a few feast days ten old men and ten old women, clad in garments of an age long past, present gifts of bread and wine at the altar. But to all intents and purposes the once universal offering of bread and wine as sacrificial gifts has disappeared from Christian worship. Our "Offertory collections" are made directly for the support of the Church: the *internal connection* of gifts with the Sacrifice *is seldom made clear.*

Turn of the Tide. As the gift-procession tapered off toward disappearance, the restoration of Communion as something *to be received* slowly progressed. In this matter as in others the pontificate of Innocent III (1198–1216) was a turning point in history. After the Lateran Council under his presidency had prescribed the reception of Communion once annually as a minimum, the ideal of more and more frequent, even daily, Communion, again came to the fore. St. Catherine of Siena, one of the most influential women the church has known, was with papal approval a daily communicant. Particularly in Italy and in the sphere of the Spanish Dominicans the frequentation of the Holy Table was slowly spreading. Thus a Eucharistic springtime, as far as the reception of Communion was concerned, was under way before the outbreak of the sixteenth-century Protestant revolts. In the face of that great apostasy this preaching was continued with renewed zeal. The members of the newer religious institutes, the Theatines, the Capuchins, the Oratorians, and the Jesuits brought this movement to the masses, so that, as was said of St. Philip Neri's church at Rome, "every morning looked like Easterday." St. Ignatius Loyola's *Book of the Spiritual Exercises,* than which in God's Providence there was scarcely a more timely instrument in effecting the Catholic Counter-Reform, embodied certain rules for enabling one "to follow as we ought the true mind of the Militant Church." Conspicuous among these was the injunction: "To praise . . . the reception of the Most Holy Sacrament once a year, and much more every month, and *much better every week.*" The full mind of the Saint in this matter was manifested in a letter to a Spanish nun in 1543:

> . . . As to communicating every day, let us recall that in the primitive Church all communicated daily, and from that time to this there is no order or writing of our holy mother, the Church, or of her holy doctors,

scholastic or positive, forbidding those whose devotion so prompts them, to receive Communion every day. Then, too, the blessed St. Augustine says that he neither praises nor blames those who communicate daily, adding elsewhere that he exhorts all to communicate every Sunday. In another passage, speaking of the most blessed Body of Christ Our Lord, he says: "This is daily Bread: live therefore in such wise as to be able to receive it daily."

All this being so, even if there were not at hand so many indications of good, and so many wholesome motions of grace, there is the criterium of the testimony of a good conscience: To wit, if you are persuaded, first of all, that it is licit in Our Lord, *since you are free from known mortal sins or what you may regard as such;* then, if you judge that your soul is advanced and inflamed by love of your Creator and Lord; then, if communicating with such an intention, and finding out by experience that this sacred and celestial Food gives you nourishment, peace of soul, and lastly, if persevering in this practice, you advance in God's greater service, worship and glory, then, *without any doubt it is allowed and it is the better thing for you to receive Communion every day.*

Mon. Ign. Ep. 73

Council of Trent. With half or more of its entire membership lost through defections, the Militant Church mustered its spiritual forces in the great Council of Trent (1545–63), wherein the whole economy of salvation was reaffirmed, original and personal sin, justification, the Sacraments, etc. Of the Tridentine definitions three points only need concern us just now. First of all, *justification,* described as "the translation from that state wherein man is born a child of the first Adam to the state of grace and of the adoption of the sons of God through the second Adam, Jesus Christ," gives the "new man" *vital contact* with the life-force of Christ,

Col. i,12

. . . since Jesus Christ Himself, as the Head [acting] on the members, and as the Vine [vivifying] the branches, ceaselessly communicates a life-force to the justified, and this life-force always precedes, accompanies and follows their every good action.

Eph. iv,15
John xv,5
Sess. vi, 1547

Again, in speaking of the reasons that prompted Christ to institute the Sacrament of the Altar, the conciliar Fathers touch this same note of social solidarity:

He [Christ] wished [this Sacrament] . . . to be a symbol of that

I Cor. xi,3
Sess. xiii, 1551
one body whereof He is the head, and to which He would fain have us as members united by the closest bond of faith, hope and charity.

Most pertinent to our present consideration is Trent's handling of the Mass, and the relation of Communion to integral sacrificial worship. The *true doctrine*, the *ultimate goal*, and the *temporary, regretful acquiescence* in current customs are all clearly expressed in this paragraph:

> The sacred and most holy Synod would fain indeed that, *at each Mass, the faithful* who are present *should communicate*, not only in spiritual desire, but also by the sacramental participation of the Eucharist, that thereby a more abundant fruit may be derived to them from this most holy Sacrifice: but not, therefore, if this be not always done, does it condemn, as private and unlawful, but approves of, and therefore commends those Masses in which the priest alone communicates sacramentally; since those Masses ought also to be considered as truly common; partly because the people communicate spiritually thereat; partly also because they are celebrated by a public minister of the Church, not for himself only, but for all the faithful who belong to the body of Christ.

Sess. xxii, 1562

To interpret its own decrees, the Council of Trent ordered that an official commentary, the so-called *Catechism of the Council of Trent* (published 1566), be put into the hands of all priests. This most authoritative document mirrors the program of the Catholic Counter-Reform for the restoration of the reception of Communion. Thus, we read:

THE CHURCH DESIRES THE FAITHFUL TO COMMUNICATE DAILY

> Let not the faithful imagine that it is enough to receive the Body of the Lord once a year only, in obedience to the decree of the Church. They should approach oftener; but whether monthly, weekly, or daily, cannot be decided by any fixed universal rule. St. Augustine, however, lays down a most certain norm: *Live in such manner as to be able to receive every day.*

II, Euch. a.14

Thus, the Church was engaged with the restoration of Communion: it was hoped, and we see this hope realized in our own day, that time would effect the popular recovery of full sacrificial-mindedness, the mediatorial position of Christ, and the internal relation of Communion *as a part of Mass.*

Blight of Jansenism. Hardly had the primitive attitude toward the Eucharist begun to take possession of the collective consciousness of Europe, when a backwash of the spirit of exaggerated awe again swept over Christendom. This was the application to the Eucharist of Jansenist ultra-rigorist views, and was brought to a head by the publication of a treatise *On Frequent Communion* by Anthony Arnault in 1643. By an unhappy alliance Jansenism became linked with State polity in France and subsequently in other Bourbon courts, such as Spain and Portugal. Almost two centuries elapsed before this corrosive element could be entirely eliminated. In that long and sometimes very bitter conflict progress toward daily Communion as the goal for all Catholics marked slow advancement.

Pope Leo XIII. In our modern age events move more rapidly, even in the realm of the spiritual realities here in question. In 1902 the great Pope Leo XIII published an encyclical letter on the Most Holy Eucharist. This gave the *coup de grace* to the Jansenist position:

> Away then with the widespread but most mischievous error . . . that the reception of the Eucharist is in a manner reserved for those narrow-minded persons (as they are deemed) who rid themselves of the cares of the world in order to find rest in some kind of professedly religious life. For this gift, than which nothing can be more excellent, or more conducive to salvation, is offered to all those, whatever their office or dignity may be, who wish — as every one ought to wish — to foster in themselves that life of divine grace whose goal is the attainment of the life of blessedness with God.

Mirae caritatis

No message from Pope Leo went far in its unfolding without deploring "frequent disturbances and strife between class and class: arrogance, oppression, fraud on the part of the more powerful: misery, envy and *Ibid.* turbulence among the poor." The Vicar of Christ was persuaded that against such evils it is vain to seek remedies in legislation, or any device of merely human prudence. But the remedy was to be the social appreciation of the Eucharist:

> All of which is confirmed by the declaration of the Council of Trent that Christ left the Eucharist in His Church "as a symbol of that unity and charity whereby He would have all Christians mutually joined and united . . . a symbol of that one body of which He is Himself the Head, and to which He would have us, as members, attached by the

Sess. xiii   closest bonds of faith, hope, and charity." The same idea had been expressed by St. Paul when he wrote:

I Cor. x,17

We many are one bread, one body,
for we all partake of the one Bread.

Very beautiful and joyful too is the spectacle of Christian brotherhood and social equality which is afforded when men of all conditions, gentle and simple, rich and poor, learned and unlearned, gather round the holy altar, all sharing alike in this heavenly banquet. And if in the records of the Church it is deservedly reckoned to the special credit of its first ages that the multitude of believers were of one heart and soul, there can be no shadow of doubt that this immense blessing was due to their frequent meetings at the divine table; for we find it recorded of them:

Acts iv,32

They persevered in the teaching of the Apostles
and the fellowship,
the breaking of Bread and the prayers.

Acts ii,42

Leo's determination "to bend all our efforts to that point, that the frequent use of the Eucharist be widely revived among Catholic peoples," soon issued in the decrees of Pius X, 1905, that all Catholics, the world over, of every condition and walk of life, provided only they have a right intention and be *free from known mortal sin,* must be allowed to communicate when present at Mass. Indeed under Pius X, as a subsequent chapter will disclose more in detail, the papal program was broadened out to include the *most active possible participation in the Mass,* of which communicating is but the main feature. Under Pope Pius XI the movement has reached full circle, when the advocacy of integral Eucharistic worship begins by dedication of self to God in the symbol of the sacrificial-gift. Centuries had elapsed since the Father of Christendom addressed to all his children such a message as this from the Encyclical On Reparation to the Sacred Heart:

Mirae caritatis

The more our oblation and sacrifice of self resemble the sacrifice of Christ, in other words the more perfect the immolation of our self, and of our passions . . . the more abundant are the fruits of propitiation and expiation which we receive for ourselves and others. . . . To this most august Eucharistic Sacrifice *ministers and faithful must join the offering of themselves* as victims "living, holy, well-pleasing to

God." Therefore St. Cyprian did not hesitate to say: "The Sacrifice of Our Savior *is not celebrated with the requisite sanctity if our own offering* and our sacrifice of self *do not correspond* with His Passion." Rom. xii,1

Ep. lxiii

Mis. Redemptor, 1928

Summary. As a consequence of the widespread Arian heresy, Christians in their worship so emphasized the divinity of Christ, that His position as Bridge-Builder, between God and men, so far as piety is concerned, was popularly obscured. The resultant relationship induced feelings of awe and dread, which began by keeping people away from Communion, and ended by obscuring the very concept of sacrificial worship. In the Catholic revival of modern times the old ideas are being rapidly recovered.

Eleventh-Century Source Material

(Although repeating the familiar teaching of the Eucharist as the bond of the mystical Body, Peter Damian does not urge the reception of Communion in this passage from his book, THE LORD BE WITH YOU.)

The Sacrifice Offered on Our Altars is That of Women Alike and Men. That is the reason why, in the very celebration of the Mass, is said: *"Be mindful, O Lord, of Thy servants and handmaids,"* and, as is added shortly "for whom we offer, OR who offer up to Thee, this sacrifice of praise." These words clearly show that the Sacrifice of praise is offered by *all* the faithful, not men only, but women also, although it is seen to be offered by one priest in a special manner. What he holds in his hands presenting unto God, that the whole multitude of the faithful by their devout intentions commends and offers. This is further shown again when it is said, "We therefore beseech Thee, O Lord, graciously to accept this oblation of our servitude *and that* of Thy whole family." It is as clear as light in these words that the Sacrifice put on our holy altars by the priest is the joint gift of the entire family of God.

The Apostle openly declares this unity of the Church, when he says, "We many are one body, one Bread." So great is the unity of the Church in Christ, that the bread of the Body of Christ is one throughout the whole world, and one is the chalice of His Blood. For just as the Divinity of the Word is one, which fills the universe, so, even though the Body is consecrated in different places and on many days, there is but one Body of Christ. And as the bread and wine are really changed into the Body of Christ, so all who worthily receive It in the Church, become beyond all doubt the one body of Christ, as He Himself saith: I Cor. x,17

He that eateth My Flesh
and drinketh My Blood,
the same abides in Me,
and I in him.

John vi,57

If therefore we are all one body of Christ, and, although we seem to be separated by corporeal appearances, we cannot be separated from one another, as long as we remain in Him. There is no disadvantage that I see in abiding always in this symbol of individual unity, and one and all holding the common custom of the Church. For when I alone speak the common words of the Church, I show myself to be one with her, and testify that the Spirit really abides in me. And if I am truly her member, it is but proper that I promote the well-being of my "whole."

Topics for Further Discussion:

The propriety of receiving Communion fasting.

As the temptations surrounding youth today are more evident and alluring than since the ages of paganism, so, too, are the sacramental helps of the Church.

Since all Christians are to be urged to communicate daily, the moral responsibility of collegiate-trained lay people in this matter.

The dogmatic and social values of reviving the thought connection between the offering made at Mass and intrinsic participation in the Sacrifice.

The effects of Pius X's recommendations in America, where older people in certain localities object to (a) children receiving Communion before the age of twelve; (b) frequent, especially daily, Communion for lay people. What arguments could be adduced, besides the Pontiff's pronouncements, to make them change their attitude?

Readings:

K. Adam, *Christ Our Brother* (New York: Macmillan, 1931); "Through Christ Our Lord."

G. Dix, *A Detection of Aumbries* (Westminster: Dacre, 1942), "Reverence for the Reserved Sacrament," pp. 42–68: The author is an Anglican.

J. B. Ferreres, *The Decree on Daily Communion* (St. Louis: Herder, 1910), "Historical Sketch," pp. 34–102.

J. C. Hedley, *The Holy Eucharist* (New York: Longmans, Green, 1907); "On Frequent Communion," pp. 129–146.

J. C. Husslein, "Communion in the Early Church," *The Ecclesiastical Review* (81), 1929, pp. 491–509.

E. King, "Holy Communion in the Early Church," *The Month* (108), 1906, pp. 1–13.

J. Kramp, *Eucharistia, Essays on Eucharistic Liturgy and Devotion* (St. Paul: Lohmann, 1926); "The History of Eucharistic Adoration," pp. 111–157.

———— *The Liturgical Sacrifice of the New Law* (St. Louis: Herder, 1926); "The Notion of Sacrifice and Christian Holiness," pp. 201–214.

Chapter XII

HEIRS OF THE SYNAGOGUE

Jesus went about the whole of Galilee,
teaching in the synagogues (Matt. iv,23).

AT THE head of the Roman Mass Book there has been printed since 1634 a Bull of Pope Urban VIII which begins, "If there is one thing in human life absolutely divine, one thing that the citizens of Heaven might envy, if envy were consistent with their state, it is the holy Sacrifice of the Mass. . . . Accordingly, the more must men endeavor to hold a privilege so great in becoming honor and reverence." Of the singular privilege of sharing in this sacrificial worship through the mediation of the Man, Christ Jesus, much has been said in this course, and from more than one point of view. This must now be completed by a brief study of the august rite as we possess it today, after nineteen centuries of such universal and frequent use.

The Name "Mass." The first circumstance that attracts attention concerns the name now so common in modern languages, the *Mass.* This term illustrates how factors, trivial and inconsequential in themselves, may come to have far-reaching effects. The Christian Sacrifice, like all public functions, has a formal opening and a formal ending. The formal ending, in imitation of the Jewish synagogue rites, took the form of a ceremonial dismissal, or leave to depart, proclaimed by the officiating ministers. At a certain point the announcement was made from the altar, as indeed it is still so made, *Ite, missa est* (Go, this is the dismissal). *Missa* here is low Latin for *missio,* sending away or dismissal. Again, when adherents of the Jewish religion, or pagans or those preparing for baptism, were present at a service of prayer and instruction, which was to be followed by the Sacrifice, all these had to be dismissed before the sacrificial Action began. Thus, a conspicuous element of the rite was *this* dismissal also. People began before long to refer to the

Plan of a Synagogue.

Circle of lamps → **Ark** ← for Scripture

Elevated Platform

Lectern

women   men

Scripture ↘
kissed
on entrance

— **door** —

water

whole rite in both cases as the *Missa,* the Dismissal of the Catechumens and the Dismissal of the Faithful. In popular speech, this term was soon synonymous with the more formal designations of the Sacrifice. From *missa* are derived our English word "Mass," and cognate terms in the other modern languages.

Types of Worship in the Mass. The next feature to be noted is that our Mass of today represents the union or combination of two types of worship, the non-sacrificial and the sacrificial. Just as the Jews had sacrificial worship only in the Temple of Jerusalem, but non-sacrificial worship in countless synagogues everywhere, so in the primitive Church there was a clear-cut distinction between sacrificial and non-sacrificial worship. True, the Christian Sacrifice was not limited to Jerusalem, or any other place, but it was, from the outset, limited to certain days, and very strictly limited to Christians only. On the contrary, non-Christians were admitted to, and by all honest arts of persuasion urged to attend, the more frequent Christian gatherings for instruction and prayer in common. In course of time the custom grew of having the Sacrifice immediately after the non-sacrificial rites. The old forms of non-sacrificial worship are preserved, abbreviated, it is true, but in no way substantially changed, in the first part of our Mass. We call it, for that reason, the Mass of the Catechumens, that is, the rites which persons preparing for Baptism were allowed to attend. The original Christian rites of sacrifice, as modified by later ceremonial developments, remain our Sacrifice proper. In our Mass of the Catechumens, or as it might be designated, the Ante-Mass, we have the continuation of that synagogue service at which Christ did so much of His teaching in the period of His public life.

The Synagogues of Israel. Since the Jews not resident at Jerusalem could participate in the Temple rites very seldom, the local synagogue was in great measure the *focal point of their religious,* civil, and national *life.* With the civil or juridical position of the synagogue we are not now concerned: our interest is its worship. It had become a tradition that the synagogue should be built on the highest spot in the community, and that it should outrank all other structures in dignity. Circumstances permitting, it was built facing eastward. On completion the new synagogue was ceremoniously consecrated to the purposes of worship. Within, at the end opposite the entrance, was the Ark, wherein the Sacred Scrip-

CHART SHOWING HOW OUR ANTE-MASS IS THE SYNAGOGUE SERVICE SLIGHTLY AMPLIFIED

Jewish Synagogue	New Testament	Apostolic Times	Roman Missal
1.	1.	1. "Come together after confessing your transgressions." — *Teaching* (80).	1. Preparatory prayers: A. Psalm. *Judica* — Judge me. B. *Confiteor* — I confess.
2.	2.	2.	2. Ascending the altar *Aufer* — Take away.
3.	3.	3.	3. Priest kissing altar *Oramus te* — We beseech.
4.	4.	4.	4. *Introit* — Antiphon and verse.
5.	5.	5.	5. *Kyrie* — Lord, have mercy.
6.	6.	6.	6. *Gloria* — Glory be to God.
7. Opening prayers, standing facing place of sacrifice.	7.	7.	7. *Collect* — prayer standing facing East.
8. First Lesson — Moses.	8. "Moses . . . in the synagogues being read every sabbath" (*Acts* xv,21).	8. [Or] "the writings of the prophets are read as long as time permits." — *St. Justin* (150).	8. First Scripture Lesson Epistle (usually).
9. First Psalm chant.	9. "Teach and admonish one another, and in Psalms, hymns and spiritual canticles sing in your heart" (*Col.* iii,16).	9. "Saying they had been accustomed to assemble on a fixed day before daylight and sing by turns a hymn to Christ as a god." — *Letter of Pliny to Trajan* (112).	9. Chanting of Gradual Psalm.
10. Second Lesson — Prophet.	10. "Prophets, which are read every Sabbath" (*Acts* xiii,27).	10.	10. [Lesson formerly here now dropped.]
11. Second Psalm — chant.	11.	11.	11. Alleluia verse.
12.	12.	12.	12. Preparation for Gospel. A. *Munda cor* — Cleanse. B. *Dominus sit* — May the Lord.

13.	13.	13. "The Memoirs of the Apostles are read." — *St. Justin.*	13. Scripture Lesson — The holy Gospel.
14. Sermon by someone invited to preach.	14. "The presidents of the synagogues sent word to them saying: 'Brethren, if ye have any words of exhortation unto the people, speak'" (*Acts xiii,15*).	14. "When the reader has ceased, the president orally admonishes and exhorts us to imitate these excellent things." — *St. Justin.*	14. Sermon.
15.	15.	15.	15. *Credo* — I Believe.
16. Great intercession for needs of each group in community.	16. "I urge that petitions, prayers, intercessions, thanksgivings be made on behalf of all men" (*II Tim. ii,1*).	16. "We rise . . . and offer prayers . . . making earnest prayers in common for ourselves . . . and for all others everywhere" — *St. Justin.*	16. *Oremus* — Let us pray. [These prayers are now omitted. They were like the series we say on Good Friday.]
17. Solemn Blessing.	17.	17.	17. Blessing now given at end of Mass.
18. Prayer for peace and union (kiss).	18. "Greet ye one another with the kiss of charity" (*I Pet. ii,14*).	18. "We salute one another with a kiss when we conclude our prayers." — *St. Justin.*	18. Kiss of peace now given before Communion.
19. Almsgiving, gifts of money and in kind.	19. "Concerning the collection for the saints [at Jerusalem]. . . Upon the first day of [every] week let each one of you put by whatever he may well spare" (*I Cor. xvi,1*).	19. "They who are well-to-do and willing give what each thinks fit." — *St. Justin.*	19. Almsgiving now united with Offertory oblation.
20. Dismissal.	20.	20.	20. Dismissal of catechumens formerly took place.

tures were kept. This Ark might take many forms, from a simple niche in the wall, to an elaborate chest set upon a dais. Before the Ark one or more lamps burned constantly. Upon a raised platform near the Ark, or on the same platform, was a lectern, at which the Scriptures were read, and a chair for the preacher. Seats were ranged all about, those in front for the "presidents of the synagogue" and their associates, the elders. The seats for the populace were so disposed that the men and women occupied separate sections.

Acts xiii,15

Service of Prayer and Sacred Reading. In such synagogues, on the Sabbath all the Jews came together. Before entering they purified their hands; after entering they kissed a copy of some portion of the Scriptures set upon a stand near the entrance for that purpose. The services opened with common prayers, led by a "ruler"; these prayers were said standing, and facing toward Jerusalem, the place of sacrifice, after which all sat down to listen to the Scriptures. Seven designated readers were attached to the staff of the synagogue, and since several passages were to be read, they took turn and turn about at the lectern. Or, the president or officiant might invite a stranger, or one he wished to honor, to take this charge. Passages from the Books of Moses, or the Law, as they were called collectively, alternated with corresponding readings from the Prophets. As the sacred scrolls were replaced in the Ark, some of David's prayer-poems, the Psalms, were sung. A precentor sang a verse in solo, and the congregation answered the alternate ones. This mode of antiphonal singing still in use among us, was used by the Babylonians and many Eastern peoples. Besides the Psalms and Scriptural canticles, hymns were also used on occasion.

The Scriptures Expounded. The Scripture passages read had now to be expounded to the people. Here, too, the synagogue service lent itself to a certain variety and promoted social unification, since anyone might be invited to preach or address words of exhortation to the assembly. The sermon was followed by a series of short prayers, cast in the form of blessings on behalf of all the classes of the people, and their several needs. Thus, the priests, the doctors, and scribes, and the young students of the Law, the rulers of the synagogue, the elders, and the congregation in general, were in turn prayed for. Those who gave oil for the lamps before the Ark, those who gave hospitality to strangers, also to the poor, the aged, the sick, in fact all ranks and classes of the community were commended to God, the voice of the rabbi being supported by the "Amens" of the people. After a final blessing for the peace and union of the congregation, the worshipers were dismissed. At some undetermined point in the rite, alms were collected for the needy.

The Christian "Synagogue" Service. A careful scrutiny of the chart of pages 156, 157 shows how the old *Jewish synagogue service is reproduced* in our Ante-Mass. The opening prayers, the Scripture lessons alternating with psalmody, the sermon, all, despite the long ages since Church and Synagogue have parted company, are preserved in a manner a Jew would instantly recognize. In addition, we now find in our Ante-Mass some few distinctly Christian features at the beginning. Again, toward the end, and as a result of combining this non-sacrificial rite with the more important sacrificial one, certain elements of the Jewish rites have been transposed to positions within the Christian Sacrifice proper.

Only one important item of the synagogue ritual has now quite disappeared; that is the long, litany-like intercession for all the classes of society. As late, however, as the time of St. Augustine (fifth century), these prayers were still to be found in the Ante-Mass. His letters have several accounts of them. Infidels were prayed for, the Jews, the catechumens, the several ranks of the clergy, and the whole Church of God. The series of such prayers we now say publicly only on Good Friday is, in all likelihood, the last relic of this Jewish rite, so eloquent in its appeal, but eventually abandoned for the sake of greater brevity.

Growth without Change. The surplus items in the column to the extreme right of the chart show at a glance the accretions to the Ante-Mass since it was taken over from the Synagogue. An examination of the individual items, as to their content and spirit, to which we now pass, will also disclose a remarkable fidelity to the structure and function of the original parts, however much in the course of centuries the actual message of some of the parts, particularly the chanted ones, may have become obscured. The Ante-Mass remains what the Synagogue Service was, the worship of public prayer, followed by an instruction drawn from Holy Writ.

COMMUNION *we receive*		*Sacrificial meal*
CONSECRATION (CANON) *we offer through Christ*		*Sacrifice*
OFFERTORY & COLLECTION *gift symbolizing self*		*Preparation of Sacrifice*
CREDO	4	
SERMON	3	*Service of Instruction*
GOSPEL	2	
EPISTLE OR LESSON	1	*(we learn)*
COLLECT *petition*	4	
GLORIA *praise*	3	*Service of Prayer*
KYRIE *plea for mercy*	2	*(we pray)*
PRAYERS AT FOOT OF ALTAR *contrition*	1	

—Adapted from Parsch-Eckhoff's *The Liturgy of the Mass*, by courtesy of B. Herder Book Company.

THE ORDINARY OF THE MASS: FIRST PART[1]
Prayers at Foot of Altar

"Cleanse Me from Sin" (Ps.
l,4). The preparatory prayers are
an outgrowth of that sense of unworthiness felt by a priest approaching the altar of Sacrifice,

> Since he is himself encompassed
>   with weakness,
> and because of it must make
>   offerings for sin,
> not merely on behalf of the
>   people,
> but *also for himself* (Heb. ii,3).

These prayers were originally the
priest's private prayers of preparation, and were said in silence, or in
whispered dialogue with his attendants, as he proceeded to the altar.
Later they came to be regarded as
part of the public rite. Psalm 42
recited here, expressed the longing
of a priest, whom enemies (sins)
have driven far from the Temple,
as he recalls the enthusiastic joy of
his youthful ministrations at God's
altar.

> That I may go to the altar of
>   God!
>   To God, who was the joy of
>   my youth,
> That I may praise Thee with the
>   harp,
> O God, my God!

IN THE name of the Father, and
of the Son, and of the Holy
Ghost. Amen.
Ant. I will go unto the altar of
God.
R. To God, who giveth joy to my
youth.
P. Judge me, O God, and dis-
tinguish my cause from the nation
that is not holy: from the unjust
and deceitful man deliver me.
R. Since Thou, O God, art my
strength, why hast Thou cast me
off? And why do I go sorrowful,
while the enemy afflicteth me?
P. Send forth Thy light and Thy
truth: they have conducted me and
brought me to Thy Holy Mount,
and into Thy Tabernacles.
R. And I will go unto the altar of
God, to God who giveth joy to my
youth.
P. I will praise Thee on the harp,
O God, my God: why art thou sad,
O my soul, and why dost thou
disquiet me?
R. Hope in God for I will praise
Him, the salvation of my countenance, and my God (Ps. xlii,1–6).
P. Glory be to the Father, and to
the Son, and to the Holy Ghost.
R. As it was in the beginning, is
now, and ever shall be, world with-
out end. Amen.

---

[1]The variable, or "proper," parts of the Mass are from the new votive Mass of Jesus
Christ, Supreme and Eternal Priest.
Short citations from Scripture incorporated into the prayers are indicated by italics.

Psalm 42, as St. Ambrose describes for us, was used as a hymn sung by newly baptized Christians as they marched into Church for their First Communion Mass on Easter. It is not clear just how it came to be chosen by way of putting the priest into the proper frame of mind in which to approach the altar, but baptismal memories are the very best preparation in which to come to the Holy Eucharist, the fulfillment of that of which Baptism is but the pledge.

The *Confiteor* is an act of contrition, a mutual public confession of sin couched in general terms. This was a preliminary to sacrificial worship from the dawn of Christianity, as we saw in the *Teaching of the Twelve Apostles:* "On the Lord's Day come together, breaking Bread and celebrate the Eucharist, *after confessing your transgressions,* that your Sacrifice may be pure" (Chap. xiv). The *Confiteor,* as we have it, is one of the many variant forms current in past ages: even yet some of the old monastic Orders, like the Carthusians and the Dominicans, recite an older version of this prayer.

P. I will go unto the altar of God.
R. To God, who giveth joy to my youth.

(Frankish)

P. Our help is in the name of the Lord.
R. Who hath made heaven and earth.
P. I confess, etc.
R. May Almighty God be merciful to Thee, and, forgiving thy sins, bring thee to everlasting life.
P. Amen.

R. I confess to almighty God, to blessed Mary ever Virgin, to blessed Michael the archangel, to blessed John Baptist, to the holy Apostles Peter and Paul, and all the saints, and to you, Father, that I have sinned exceedingly in thought, word and deed, *through my fault, through my fault, through my most grievous fault.* Therefore, I beseech the blessed Mary ever Virgin, blessed Michael the archangel, blessed John Baptist, the holy Apostles Peter and Paul, and all the saints, and you Father, to pray to our Lord God for me.
P. May Almighty God be merciful to you, and, forgiving your sins, bring you to everlasting life.
R. Amen.
P. May the almighty and merciful Lord grant us pardon, absolution, and remission of our sins.
R. Amen.

(Irish? Frankish?)

These ejaculatory prayers serve to illustrate how Christians of an older age constructed their prayers. They knew that Christ had known and loved the divinely inspired words of the Psalter, and so they combed the Psalter for expressions suited to their prayer-needs and linked them together in doublets, a verse, as we call it, answered by a response.

P. *Thou, O God, being turned, wilt enliven us.*
R. *And Thy people will rejoice in Thee* (Ps. lxxxiv,7,8).
P. *Show us, O Lord, Thy mercy.*
R. *And grant us Thy salvation.*
P. *O Lord, hear my prayer.*
R. *And let my cry come unto Thee* (Ps. ci,2).
P. *The Lord be with you* (Ruth ii,4).
R. *And with Thy spirit.*

(Frankish)

There is utilized here an old Roman Collect, which, written for Lent, continues the same train of thought as in the foregoing, namely, self-purification at approaching the altar.

An important *difference in outlook* marks this prayer, in that the priest prays *in the singular number.* This is a relic of an era when Mass was often regarded as a private affair of the priest's.

It is doubtless in imitation of the prescription of the Old Law, that the High Priest must not approach the Holy of Holies without incense, that this use was introduced (Lev. xvi, 12).

Take away from us our iniquities, we beseech Thee, O Lord, that we may be worthy to enter with pure minds into the *Holy of Holies* (Exod. xxx,10). Through Jesus Christ our Lord. Amen.
(Frankish adaptation of Roman prayer)
We beseech Thee, O Lord, by the merits of Thy saints, whose relics are here, and of all Thy saints, that Thou wouldst vouchsafe to forgive me all my sins. Amen.

(Frankish)

(At High Mass): Blessing of Incense.
Be thou blessed by Him in whose honor thou shalt burn. Amen.

(Frankish)

Entrance, Introit

It will suffice to refer back to the description (at page 127) of St. Gregory's High Mass by way of recalling the very important dramatic function of the Entrance Chant, or Introit, now preserved in its barest outline. This element of Psalmody was introduced at Rome to add solemnity to the entrance of the ministers, and their "marching music" was given an accompaniment of song, choir alternating with choir, in such wise that a refrain was sung after *each verse* of the psalm, or psalms, required to fill up the interval of the entrance.

(Antiphon) Ps. cix,4
The Lord hath sworn and He will not repent:
"Thou art a priest forever after the manner of Melchise·dech."
(Ps. cix,1): The Lord said to my Lord:
"Sit Thou at My right hand."
V. Glory be to the Father, and to the Son, and to the Holy Ghost.
R. As it was in the beginning, is now, and ever shall be, world without end. Amen.
(Antiphon repeated):
The Lord hath sworn and He will not repent:
"Thou art a priest forever after the manner of Melchisedech."

(Roman)

Kyrie

The Greek words betray the Hellenic source of this popular acclamation for mercy. Recent research has shown good reason for ascribing its relation to the Roman Mass to the time of Pope Gelasius (492–96). When Gregory I was pope (590–604), he introduced the *Christe, eleison.* Our precise three-three-three arrangement is a later modification.

P. Lord, have mercy on us.
R. Lord, have mercy on us.
P. Lord, have mercy on us.
R. Christ, have mercy on us.
P. Christ, have mercy on us.
R. Christ, have mercy on us.
P. Lord, have mercy on us.
R. Lord, have mercy on us.
P. Lord, have mercy on us.

(Greek)

Gloria

Those who have studied the *Gloria* find it is an enlargement of the message at Christ's nativity

GLORY be to God on high, and on earth peace to men of good will (Luke ii, 4).

(Luke ii,4) by a marvelous array of old ejaculations and expressions drawn from New and Old Testament sources, and other documents of the most venerable Catholic antiquity. Such a text was, naturally, the product of evolution and addition, but by the fourth century it had reached, practically speaking, the finished form we now have. It was a morning hymn of Greek-speaking Christians, and, as such, was recommended by St. Athanasius to the consecrated virgins for their morning devotions (*De Virg.*).

Under what circumstances the *Gloria* came into our Latin Mass is not known. At first its use seems to have been limited to the Supreme Pontiff and for the Christmas Midnight Mass. Pope Symmachus (498–514) allowed it to be chanted on Sundays and martyrs' feasts. Later restrictions, as to bishops' Masses, or to priests on Easter only, gradually fell away, until, about the twelfth century, the present custom of using it in all Masses of a joyous character was adopted.

We praise Thee,
we bless Thee,
we adore Thee,
we glorify Thee.
We give Thee thanks for Thy great glory.
O Lord God, Heavenly King,
God the Father Almighty.

O Lord Jesus Christ,
the only-begotten Son,
O Lord God, Lamb of God,
Son of the Father (II John 3),
who takest away the sins of the world (John i,29),
have mercy on us.
Who takest away the sins of the world,
receive our prayers.
Who sittest at the right hand of the Father (Col. iii,1),
have mercy on us.
For Thou alone art holy,
Thou alone art the Lord.

Thou only, O Jesus Christ,
together with the Holy Ghost,
art most high (Ps. lxxxii,19)
in the glory of God the Father.
Amen.

(Greek)

Prayer, or Collect

This prayer, which fulfills the all-important function of sounding the worship-motif of the feast or occasion, preserves in its name a link with a vanished usage, the stational Mass. For this the Romans met in one church, called

O GOD, who unto the glory of Thy Majesty and the saving of our race, *hast set up Thy Sole-Begotten Son* sovereign and *ever-lasting Priest* (Heb. v), "church of the assembly or *Collecta*," and then marched to the church of the Mass. Before setting out, a prayer was said, *Oratio ad collectam*. Later on, the prayer itself came to be known by the name of *Collecta*. Almost invariably these prayers are addressed to God the Father, who is approached *through* our Mediator, His Son.

grant that
 those chosen by Him as *helpers*
 and almoners of His Mysteries
 (I Cor. iv,1).
may in the allotted tasks be found
faithful (I Cor. iv,2).
through the same our Lord Jesus
Christ
Thy Son,
who liveth and reigneth with Thee,
in the unity of the Holy Ghost,
God, world without end.
R. Amen.

Lesson

Scripture reading was of the very essence of the Synagogue service, and St. Luke gives us a graphic description of how Christ one Sabbath read and expounded Holy Writ for His townsmen of Nazareth.
He writes:
 He came to Nazareth,
 where He had been brought up;
 and according to His custom
 He entered the synagogue
 upon the Sabbath day and rose
 to read.
And the volume of the Prophet Isaiah was handed to Him.
And He opened the volume and *found the place*
 where was written:
 The Spirit of the Lord is upon
 Me, for He hath anointed Me;
To evangelize the poor He hath sent Me . . .
And He rolled up the volume
 and returned it to the attendant
 and sat down.

LESSON from the Epistle of the blessed Paul the Apostle to the Hebrews (v,1–11).
Brethren: Every High Priest taken from among men
is appointed as a representative of men in the things that refer to God,
that he may offer gifts and sacrifices for sins;
as one who can be mild
with the ignorant and erring,
since he himself is encompassed with weakness,
and because of it must make offerings for sin,
 not merely on behalf of the people, but also for himself.
And none taketh to himself the honor, but one who hath been called by God,
as was Aaron.
So, too, Christ did not appoint Himself to the honor of becoming High Priest, but He who said to Him:

ORDINARY OF MASS: FIRST PART   167

And the eyes of all in the synagogue were gazing upon Him.
And He began to say unto them,
"Today in your hearing
is this Scripture fulfilled" (Luke
iv,16–21).

In that passage we see how Christ
deliberately chose a definite portion of the Sacred Writing with a
view to its suitability to the occasion. And, whereas in the Divine
Office the Scripture passages are
for the most part read continuously from day to day, in the Mass the
Church carefully selects definite
passages for every occasion.

Formerly the Roman Mass
always had *two* Lessons before the
Gospel, but now on Sundays there
is never more than one, and since
this is invariably from the canonical
Epistles, the lesson is itself called
the Epistle.

"Thou art My Son: this day I
have begotten Thee."
As He elsewhere saith:
"Thou art a Priest forever
after the manner of Melchisedech."
In the days of His flesh
He offered up prayer and supplications to Him who could save
Him from death,
with a loud cry and tears,
and was heard because of His devout submission:
and though He was Son,
He learned obedience from that
which He suffered:
Himself being made perfect,
He became for all who obey him
the Author of eternal salvation,
designated by God as High
Priest "after the manner of Melchisedech."
On that point we have much to say,
and it is difficult to expound
it.

Gradual

Called *Gradual* because once led
by a chanter standing on a *step
(gradus)* of the pulpit, this alternate singing of a psalm-verse by
the soloist and the recurring refrain
by the people served to emphasize
what had been read.

(Luke iv,18, *Vulgate*):
The Spirit of the Lord is upon
Me, for He hath anointed Me;
V. To evangelize the poor He hath
sent Me,
and to heal the broken of heart.

Alleluia Anthem

The Alleluia-verse, which originally replaced the psalm-chanting
after the *second* Scriptural lesson,
is musically the most brilliant part

Alleluia.
Alleluia.
V. (Heb. vii,24):
Jesus, because He remaineth for-

of the entire Mass, and has for its function to attune the minds for the hearing of Christ's own words in the Gospel.

ever, hath an unchangeable priesthood. Alleluia.

Preparation for Gospel

The impending proclamation of Christ's message evokes anew a sense of guilt and unworthiness in the human herald, and so he makes bold to pray that his lips might be cleansed as by fire! The prayer dates as of about the year 1100.

Cleanse my heart and my lips, O Almighty God, who didst *cleanse the lips of the prophet Isaias with a burning coal* (Isa. vi,6); and vouchsafe, through Thy gracious mercy, so to purify me, that I may worthily proclaim Thy Holy Gospel. Through Christ our Lord. Amen.

(Frankish)

In the foregoing formulary, and this adaptation to himself of the blessing given to the deacon at Solemn Mass, the first-person singular marks medieval origin.

Lord, give Thy blessing. May the Lord be in my heart, and on my lips, that I may worthily, and in a becoming manner, proclaim His holy Gospel. Amen.

(Frankish)

Gospel

"And Esdras opened the book before all the people: for he was above all the people: and when he had opened it, all the people stood" (II Esd. viii,5). The little picture from Old Testament times could serve as a partial description of the impressive and rich ceremonial surrounding the reading of the Gospel, the Good Tidings of God spoken by His Son. If to the act of standing as a mark of deepest reverence, were added the carrying of candles and incense, the use of a pulpit (or altar-corner at low Mass), the kissing of the sacred page, the signing it with

P. The Lord be with you.
R. And with thy spirit.
P. The continuation of the Holy Gospel according to St. Luke (xxii,14–20).
At that time: Jesus laid Him down at table,
    and the Apostles with Him.
And He said unto them,
    "With desire have I desired
to eat this passover with you before I suffer;
    for I say to you,
    that I shall eat of it no more
until it is fulfilled in the kingdom of God."
    And He took a cup,

the Cross, and so forth, the enumeration of rites in honor of the Gospel would be more what we see at Mass. All this serves to show the intimate connection between even the most didactic parts of our service and the latreutic purpose of worship.

In the Gospel-lesson the Ante-Mass reaches its structural climax: God has spoken by New and Old Testament heralds, here He speaks Incarnate. The sermon is as a commentary on the *Gospel* (O.E., *god spel*, Good Tidings).

and after giving thanks, He said,
"Take ye this, and share it
   among you;
   for I say to you,
I shall not drink henceforth of the fruit of the vine.
   until the kingdom of God
   come."
And He took bread and gave thanks
   and brake and gave to them, saying,
   "This is My Body,
   which is being given on your behalf;
this do ye, in remembrance of Me."
He took also the cup in like manner
   after the supper, saying,
"This Cup is the New Covenant in My Blood,
   which is being shed on your behalf."
R. Praise be to Thee, O Christ.
           (*Jewish*)

Creed

The Creed. In an age when heresies were as common as books were rare, it was essential to have clearly articulated creeds available for everyone. This feeling led a certain archbishop of Antioch, called John the Fuller, to introduce the recitation of an official *Credo* in his Mass early in the fifth century. This custom spread over the East, and penetrated into Europe where so much from the East has found entrance, through the Spanish

I believe in one God, the Father almighty, maker of heaven and earth, and of all things visible and invisible. And in one Lord Jesus Christ, the only-begotten Son of God, and born of the Father before all ages; God of God, light of light, true God of true God; begotten, not made; consubstantial to the Father, by whom all things were made. Who for us men, and for our salvation, came down from Heaven, and became incarnate by peninsula. From this new point of radiation, the practice spread until by the ninth century it had covered all of Europe. But, oddly enough, it was as a protection against a new Moslo-Christian error, that Christ was an adopted Son of God, then ravaging the Spanish Church, that the Creed was added to our Mass. It has recently come to light that this was done about 798 by one of Charlemagne's great advisers, St. Paulinus of Aquileia. Paulinus is the author of the Latin formula of our missals. This Creed is often called the Nicene Creed, and a long passage of it, referring to the consubstantiality of the Son, was solemnly promulgated at the Council of Nicaea, 325. Again, it is referred to as the Niceo-Constantinopolitan Creed, because the final section on the Holy Spirit are repeated as solemnly defined in the Council of Constantinople of the year 381.

After repeating the salutation, and intoning *Oremus — Let us Pray,* the Ante-Mass abruptly ends. Formerly the Prayers For All Classes were said here, a medieval substitute for which we give below.

the Holy Ghost, of the Virgin Mary, AND WAS MADE MAN. He was crucified also for us, and suffered under Pontius Pilate, and was buried. And the third day He arose again according to the Scriptures; and ascended into heaven, sitteth at the right hand of the Father; and He is to come again with glory, to judge both the living and the dead, of whose kingdom there shall be no end. And in the Holy Ghost, the Lord and giver of Life; who proceedeth from the Father and the Son; who, together with the Father and the Son, is adored and glorified; who spoke by the prophets. And one holy, Catholic and Apostolic Church. I confess one Baptism for the remission of sins. And I expect the resurrection of the dead, and the life of the world to come. Amen.

(Greek)

P. The Lord be with you.
R. And with thy Spirit.
P. Let us pray.

(Jewish)

End of the Ante-Mass.

Summary. Viewed as a whole, the Ante-Mass is seen to be a slightly modified form of the non-sacrificial worship of Israel, a continuance of the old synagogue rites. By attending these "according to His custom on the Sabbath," Christ Himself was carrying forward usages of a venerable antiquity.

Luke iv,16

When the Ante-Mass and the Mass had come to be looked upon as one service, a few features of the former rite were transferred to the latter. Lastly, with the passing of the organized catechumenate, there disappeared, too, the dismissal of the catechumens, of which a very tactful and polite form closes one of St. Augustine's sermons.

Twelfth- or Eleventh-Century Source Material

(At parochial Masses on Sundays, after the Offertory, the priest turned to the people and led the so-called Bidding Prayer, of which a specimen is appended from Bridgett's HISTORY OF THE HOLY EUCHARIST IN GREAT BRITAIN.)

Let us pray God Almighty, Heaven's high King, and St. Mary and all God's saints, that we may God Almighty's will work, the while that we in this transitory life continue; that they us uphold and shield against all enemies' temptations, visible and invisible: Our Father.

Let us pray for our Pope in Rome, and for our King, and for the Archbishop and for the Alderman; and for all those that to us hold peace and friendship on the four sides toward this holy place; and for all those that us for pray within the English nation, or without the English nation: Our Father.

Let us pray for our godmothers, and for our godfathers, and for our guild-fellows and guild-sisters, and all those people's prayer who this holy place with alms seek, with light and with tithe; and for all those whom we ever their alms receiving were during their life and after life: Our Father.

[*In later specimens this petition was often found:* For all women that be in our Lady's bonds, that God almighty may send them grace, and the child to receive the Sacrament of Baptism, and the mother churching.]

Pray we for [*here the bede-roll was recited*]. For Thorferth's soul pray we a Pater Noster, and for many more souls, and for all the souls that Baptism have undertaken, and in Christ believed from Adam's day to this day: Our Father. — Quoted by permission of Burns, Oates & Washbourne. This form antedates the Conquest but its use must have continued into the twelfth century.

Topics for Further Discussion:

With the aid of the missal, list the places where the ideas of the "Great Intercession for All Classes" are now scattered throughout the Mass.

The drama of today descends from the medieval mystery plays, which originated as musical tropes in connection with the Alleluia-verse.

"The Mass is the greatest synthesis of beauty that man has ever achieved." — *Cram*. The history of modern painting, or sculpture, or architecture are chapters in the history of the Mass.

"Before one can preach the Catholic solutions of modern economic problems, he has to indoctrinate his audience with the notion of the mystical body."

Entirely apart from all question of church support, what is the idea underlying almsgiving as a form of worship?

Readings:

F. Boeser, *The Mass-Liturgy* (Milwaukee: Bruce, 1932); "The Mass of the Catechumens," pp. 19–37.

F. Cabrol, *The Mass, Its Doctrine, Its History, The Story of the Mass in Pen and Picture* (New York: Kenedy, no date); "The Mass of the Catechumens," pp. 24–26.

W. Drum, "Synagogue," *CE.*

A. Fortescue, *The Mass, A Study of the Roman Liturgy* (New York: Longmans, Green, 1937); "The Influence of Jewish Ritual," pp. 70–75.

J. Husslein, *The Mass of the Apostles* (New York: Kenedy, 1929); *passim.*

H. Lucas, *Holy Mass, The Eucharistic Sacrifice and the Roman Liturgy* (St. Louis: Herder, 1914); I, "The Liturgy," etc., pp. 46–111.

N. Maas, *The Treasure of the Liturgy* (Milwaukee: Bruce, 1932); "The Beginning of the Mass," pp. 37–68.

M. S. MacMahon, *Liturgical Catechism, The Church, The Mass, The Year* (Dublin: Gill and Son, 1926); "The Mass of the Catechumens," pp. 87–98.

P. Maranget, *The Roman Mass* (St. Louis: Herder, 1928); "The Mass of the Catechumens," pp. 16–37.

C. Marmion, *Christ the Life of the Soul* (St. Louis: Herder, 1923); "The Eucharistic Sacrifice," pp. 257–278.

C. C. Martindale, *The Prayers of the Missal: I, Collects* (New York: Sheed and Ward, 1937); *passim.*

V. Michel, *The Liturgy of the Church* (New York: Macmillan, 1937); "The Liturgical Sacrifice," pp. 149–170.

T. H. Moore, *Beyond the Altar Rail* (New York: Fordham Univ., 1939); "Mass of the Catechumens," pp. 39–50.

P. Parsch–F. C. Eckhoff, *The Liturgy of the Mass* (St. Louis: Herder, 1936); pp. 46–152.

M. Perkins, *Speaking of How to Pray* (New York: Sheed & Ward, 1944); "An Oblation and a Sacrifice to God," pp. 156–166.

J. Putz, *My Mass* (Ranchi: Cath. Press, 1938); "The Offertory," pp. 7–18.

Chapter XIII

THE MYSTERY OF FAITH

You proclaim the death of the Lord
until He come (I Cor. xi,2).

WE RENDER *thanks* to the Lord our God, and this is the great rite in the Sacrifice of the New Covenant, touching which you will learn, when you are baptized, *what* it is, and where, and when, and *how* it is offered." So wrote St. Augustine to a Epis. cxl,48 prospective convert, because in his day the truths of the Eucharist were revealed to neophytes only *after* Baptism. "If we ask a catechumen," said the same Augustine on another occasion. " 'Do you believe in Christ?' he will answer, 'I believe,' and he signs himself the while with the Cross of Christ: he bears the Cross on his forehead and he is not ashamed of the Cross of his Lord. See, he believes in His Name. Let us ask him, 'Do you eat the Flesh of the Son of Man, and do you drink the Blood of the Son of Man?' and he knows not what we are talking about." In the words Tract. in Ioan. xi of the first quotation the great bishop touched upon themes that may well engage us now: the thank-offering, the essence of the Sacrifice of the new and eternal Testament, and something of the rite of its offering.

Christian Passover. In God's relations with His chosen people, He once delivered them from captivity and slavery in Egypt under circumstances familiar to us all. The Jews had been told to sacrifice lambs, and to sprinkle the lintels of their houses with some of the blood. That night, as the Israelites, girded and ready for a journey, hurriedly ate of their sacrifices, angels of God's wrath slew the first-born of all the Egyptians, but *"passed over"* the homes sprinkled with blood. This awful visitation of God compelled the reluctant Pharaoh to grant permission for the departure of the Jews under Moses. By divine ordinance, the Jews kept henceforth the annual remembrance of the Passover as the most sacred token of God's covenant with their race. The Pasch was the pole star

173

around which revolved the whole religious life of Israel. For over two thousand years it was held with its own sacred rites as "the most joyous night of the year," as the ancient *Mishna* phrased it. The paschal lambs were sacrificed to God in thanksgiving for His numberless mercies and provident care. They were eaten in the family circles with an elaborate ritual, wherein the countless benedictions of God were chanted in the sublime poetry of King David. The mercies of God to Israel were told over one by one, and, as each divine favor was recounted, all answered

Cf. Ps. cxxxv in song: "For His goodness endureth forever!"

I Cor. x,11 **Reality Succeeds Figure.** "Now these things befell them in a figure." Not Israel alone, but *all mankind was to be delivered from Satan's bondage,* one worse than Pharaoh's. Therefore Christ, "the Lamb that

John i,29 taketh away the sins of the world," chose the setting of the Jewish thanksgiving supper at which to institute the new Sacrifice of Blood for the sealing of the New Testament. It was thus in an atmosphere of thanksgiving, one still echoing with the hymns of God's endless mercies to mankind, that Christ gave Himself for us. What should not be man's thankfulness in accepting that boon from the hand of the Mediator! "This do ye in remembrance of Me," the command accompanying the great Gift, gave us the Sacrifice of the Mass.

A Thank-Offering. In breaking the Bread the Christians were thrilled by many emotions, but their cardinal impulse was *thankfulness.* This is proved in a telling manner in the name they gave this Sacrament: it is the *Eucharist,* which is Greek for *thank-offering, thanksgiving.* "We render thanks to the Lord our God," to quote St. Augustine's words once more, "and *this is the great rite* in the Sacrifice of the New Law." From the dawn of Christianity, the Sacrifice has been a public and solemn thanksgiving. The great prayer of the Canon of the Mass has always been one wherein gratitude to God for all His mercies, and especially for our Redemption, is a leitmotif. The first written Mass prayers we have, those of St. Hippolytus of Rome, about 225, begin, *Sursum corda —* "*Lift up your hearts, Let us give thanks to the Lord our God.*" Day for day, and year for year, whether in the exaltation of joy or in the bitterness of sorrow, the sacrificial Action is uniformity prefaced with the thought:

It is truly meet and just, right and available to Salvation that we should at all times and in all places give thanks to Thee, O holy Lord, Father almighty, everlasting God.

Saint Hippolytus
Martyr

Thanksgiving *is* the great rite of the Christian Sacrifice; we can never be sufficiently grateful for our sharing in that unique worship.

Calvary and the Mass. Let us take up the consideration of the *essence* of the Mass. Every Catholic knows those points of identity between the Mass and the sacrificial death of Christ upon the Cross; that *the Mass renews the Oblation of the Cross,* because Victim and Priest in both are the same; namely, Christ. Not so prominent in the popular consciousness are two points of dissimilarity between the Cross and the Mass. First, on the Cross, although acting on behalf of all mankind, Christ necessarily acted *alone;* in the Mass, while still acting on behalf of all men, Christ sacrifices *with* His whole Mystical Body. Nay, more: in the Mass Christ sacrifices only *through* His Mystical Body, only as conditioned by the Mystical Body. That is to say, unless the Mystical Body "does this in

memory of Him," the great High Priest Himself must remain inactive. Second, the Mass is a never-failing *reminder* of the Cross. The Mass is thus more than a Sacrifice; it is the ritual *commemoration* of Christ' death on Calvary. Every Mass announces the Good Tidings yet once more, and will do so until Christ comes in power and majesty to gather His kingdom from the four quarters of the world and presents it to the

I Cor. xv,24   Father.

Groping in Mystery. Clear as these points are in themselves, there are other pertinent factors not so readily explained. The full exposition of *how* the Mass reproduces the Sacrifice of Calvary is not revealed to us, and remains in part a mystery. We can help ourselves somewhat by study, but after the last analysis, we must be content to accept this as the great *"mystery of faith,"* words which the Church applies to the Eucharist in the very moment of transubstantiation. On a former occasion we had an opportunity of studying the concept of a sacrifice. There we saw that, while the sacrificial process embodies several ideas, its essence consists in the transfer of a symbolic gift to God. The technical expression for this gift-offering is *oblation.* If the sacrifice be a bloody one

"unto the remission of sins," the victim is killed, or *immolated,* as the ritual formula puts it, sometime during the course of the rite.

Oblation, Immolation. Now these two acts, *oblation* and *immolation,* were in the Old Law combined in three distinct ways in different sacrifices, but, of course, the sacrifice was not completed until *both* acts had been performed. First, the oblation could *precede* the immolation, that is, the victim could be sacrificially dedicated unto God by the sacrificing priest, and killed only later on. Again, oblation and immolation could be *simultaneous,* and effected by one and the same act. Lastly, the immolation could be effected first, and the lifeless victim, or its blood, later offered by the priest. Now, one of the explanations theologians have devised for interpreting the sacrificial character of the Mass is based on the analogy of that Jewish usage. Christ, they say, *offered* Himself (oblation) at the Last Supper, and this dedication unto death was completed by Christ's being killed (immolation) on the Cross. The Last Supper and the Cross thus taken together completed each other, and together made up the sacrificial Act by which we were redeemed. Now, Rom. vi,9 it is revealed that Christ, being risen from the dead, can die no more. Again, at the Last Supper Christ commanded the Apostles to do that which He was then doing. Therefore, it is concluded, the Mass repeats the *oblation* of Christ, which is itself completed once and forever by the Apoc. v,12 permanence of "the Lamb that was slain" on Calvary.

"My Sacrifice and Yours." All that has been said thus far has reference primarily to the Mass as *Christ's* Sacrifice. But the Council of Trent tells us that it is also *our* sacrifice, and that "no other work can be Sess. xxii *performed by the faithful* so holy and divine as this tremendous Mystery." It behooves us, therefore, to examine carefully, as we proceed, the part the ordinary member, man, woman, or child, has in the great priestly Act of the Head of the mystical body.

ORDINARY OF THE MASS: SECOND PART, OBLATION OF GIFTS

Offertory Anthem

Eloquent of the spectacular setting of the gift-bringing of old, and of the *ceremonial* insignificance it holds today, is the Offertory Anthem. This is the surviving refrain, sung with psalmody, as the people presented their bread and wine.

Christ, having offered one sacrifice for sin,
  "hath taken His seat forever
    at the right hand of God"
    (Ps. cx,1):
      for by a single offering
      He hath forever perfected
      those that are made holy
      (Heb. xii,12,14).

Offering of Bread

It has been said that, while the layman's Offertory was formerly *an act,* now it is a prayer. It would be more accurate to say that it was formerly a *prayer-expressed-in-action,* but now, at most, a *prayer.* The interior act of self-surrender, symbolized in the presentation here of the bread, a moment later, of the wine, is given a suitable verbal accompaniment by the Offertory prayers.

Accept, O holy Father, almighty and eternal God, this unspotted Host, which I, Thy unworthy servant, offer unto Thee, my *living and true God* (I Thess. 1,9), for my innumerable *sins* (Heb. vii,27), offenses, and negligences, and for all here present, as also for all faithful Christians, both living and dead; that it may avail both me and them unto life everlasting. Amen.

(Frankish)

Mixing Wine and Water

Of this symbolic act of mixing water and wine the Council of Trent says: "It has been enjoined by the Church on priests to mix water with the wine that is to be offered in the chalice; as well because it is believed that Christ the Lord did this (John xix,34) . . . and, whereas in the Apocalypse of blessed John (Apoc. xvii,15) the

O God, who in creating human nature, hast wonderfully dignified it, and still more wonderfully reformed it; grant that by the mystery of this water and wine, we may be made partakers of His holy nature, who vouchsafed to become partaker of our human nature, namely, Jesus Christ our Lord, Thy Son, who with Thee and the Holy peoples are called waters, the union of that faithful people with Christ their Head is hereby represented" (*Sess.* xxii).

Ghost, liveth and reigneth one God, world without end. Amen.

(Frankish adaptation of Roman prayer)

Offering of the Chalice

The end of all sacrificing, of course, is that God deign to accept the gift-offering. *Christ's* gift God is bound to receive, and so we multiply petitions that He accept ours in one and the same act.

We offer unto Thee, O Lord, the chalice of salvation, beseeching Thy clemency, that it may ascend before Thy divine Majesty, *as a sweet odor* (Eph. v,2) for our salvation, and for that of the whole world. Amen.

(Frankish)

Offering of Ourselves

"The sacrifice which is offered externally," says St. Thomas, "betokens the internal, spiritual sacrifice, by which the soul surrenders itself to God" (*S.T.* II, II. Q. lxxxv,*a*.2). This *self-oblation* is here voiced in the words of the three youths cast into fire for God's law!

We think now of what is symbolized by the bread and wine — our own interior dispositions, which so need God's sustaining aid.

When the priest bows before the altar.
May we be received by Thee, O Lord, *in the spirit of humility and contrition of heart; and grant that the sacrifice we offer this day in Thy sight, may be pleasing to Thee,* O Lord God (Dan. iii,39 40).

(Frankish)

Come, O almighty and eternal God, the Sanctifier, and bless this sacrifice, prepared for the glory of Thy holy Name.

(Frankish)

Blessing of Incense

Incense, a natural symbol of prayer, and itself often one of the symbolical gifts in sacrificial worship, is here to be used in a solemn rite expressive of several ideas. But before being offered, the incense is blessed with a prayer that its sweetness delight God.

By the intercession of blessed Michael the *Archangel, standing at the right hand of the altar of incense* (Apoc. viii,3), and of all His elect, may the Lord vouchsafe to bless this incense, and receive it as *an odor of sweetness* (Eph v,2). Through Christ Our Lord Amen.

(Frankish)

Incensing the Oblations

This censing of the oblations on the altar is best understood as a signal mark of honor shown to them.

May this incense, which Thou hast blessed, O Lord, ascend to Thee, and may Thy mercy descend upon us.

(Frankish)

Incensing the Altar

The first verse of this Scripture passage is the keynote of the elaborate action of incensing, first the crucifix, then the altar, back, table, ends, base. One is thinking mostly of *prayer*, secondarily of incense. It is prayer that pleases God, prayer that is the evening sacrifice, prayer that is the watch set over our unruly inclinations.

Let my prayer, O Lord, be directed
  as incense in Thy sight:
and the lifting up of my hands
  as the evening sacrifice.
Set a watch, O Lord, before my mouth,
  and a door round about my lips,
That my heart may not incline
  towards evil words,
  to make excuses in sins (Ps. cxl,2–4).

(Frankish)

Returning Censer

The incensing of celebrant, ministers, and laity is again an expression of honor paid to the members because of the Head.

May the Lord enkindle in us the fire of His love, and the flame of everlasting charity. Amen.

(Frankish)

Lavabo

When the laity made their gift-offerings in kind and directly into the hands of the celebrant, practical considerations dictated a washing of the hands at this point. Now that the oblations are no longer presented in the ancient manner this washing of the hands has a purely symbolical meaning. The closer the moment of sacrifice approaches the more the priest multiplies his efforts to purify his soul —

Washing his hands he says:
I will wash my hands among the innocent:
and will encompass Thy altar, O Lord,
That I may hear the voice of Thy praise,
and tell all Thy wondrous works.
I have loved, O Lord, the beauty of Thy house,
and the place where Thy glory dwelleth.

and to that end washes yet once again his hands.

Those who are near enough to see this action clearly will note that the priest washes not the entire hands, but only the thumbs and forefingers. These were especially anointed at his ordination, and with these only does he handle the Holy Eucharist.

Take not away my soul, O God, with the wicked,
and my life with bloody men.
In whose hands are iniquities;
and their right hand is filled with gifts.
But I have walked in my innocence: redeem me, and have mercy on me.
My foot hath stood in the direct way:
in the churches I will bless Thee, O Lord. (Ps. xxv,6–12.)
Glory be to the Father, etc.

(Frankish)

The prayer before us, which is of rather late medieval composition, embodies a quotation from the Canon of the Mass, "in memory of the Passion, Resurrection and Ascension." Almost the whole theology of sacrifice is sketched in this one short formula:

we offer
a tangible gift
to God alone
in memory of Christ's death
in honor of Mary and the saints
with a prayer for its acceptance
unto our salvation
through our Mediator Christ
Jesus.

Bowing in the middle of the altar, he says:
Receive, O holy Trinity, this oblation which we make to Thee in memory of the Passion, Resurrection, and Ascension of our Lord Jesus Christ, and in honor of the blessed Mary ever a Virgin, of blessed John Baptist, the holy Apostles Peter and Paul, of these and of all the saints; that it may be available to their honor, and our salvation; and that they may vouchsafe to intercede for us in heaven, whose memory we celebrate on earth. Through the same Jesus Christ our Lord. Amen.

(Frankish)

Orate Fratres

This mutual exhortation to prayer is found in a wide variety of forms in old missals. The encouraging response to it is a still later addition, and is not found, for in-

Brethren, pray that my Sacrifice and yours may be acceptable to God the Father Almighty.
R. May the Lord receive the Sacrifice from thy hands, to the praise

stance in the Rite of the Dominican Fathers.

and glory of His Name, to our benefit, and to that of all His holy Church.

P. Amen.

(Frankish)

Silent Prayer

This Silent Prayer, the oldest Offertory prayer, has for purpose to express our double role of co-priests and co-victims. St. Albert the Great characterizes it as expressing nothing other than the people's oblation of itself in these gifts and through these gifts to God for "incorporation in the unity of the Body of Christ" (*De Off. Miss.* III,2,5).

These gift-offerings, Lord,
may our *Mediator Christ Jesus* (I Tim. ii,5) make to please Thee,
   and our own selves, along with Himself,
may He to Thee as gracious victims show,
   Who liveth and reigneth with Thee,
   in the unity of the Holy Ghost, God.

(Roman)

CANON OF THE MASS: FIRST PART

Dialogue

This dialogue before the Preface is found in identical terms in all the oldest rites. Tradition ascribes it to apostolic times. "You were invited to *lift up your heart* on high," says St. Augustine to neophytes. "That is proper for members of Christ, for our Head is in heaven" (*Serm.* ccxxvii).

P. World without end.
R. Amen.
P. The Lord be with you.
R. And with thy spirit.
P. Lift up your hearts.
R. We have lifted them up to the Lord.
P. Let us give thanks to the Lord our God.
R. It is meet and just.

(Jewish)

Preface

In our minds "Preface" is associated with the introductory statement at the head of a book, and the connotation is here a danger insofar as the Preface of the Mass may come to be regarded merely

It is truly meet and just, right and profitable unto salvation, that we should at all times and in all places, give thanks unto Thee, O holy Lord, Father Almighty, everlasting God.

as something preliminary to and introducing the Canon itself. The word "Preface," as used in the Mass, was formerly, it would seem, applied to the *entire Canon,* and not merely this chanted opening of it. Obviously, then, it is used in an unusual meaning; it is a solemn *address before* (prae-fatio) God. Thus far, in the Roman Mass, there has been very little said or sung that is the exclusive part of the celebrant. But now comes his "grand and solemn prayer" on the improvisation of which the first Christians set such store.

Who didst set the salvation of mankind upon the tree of the Cross, so that whence came death, thence also life might rise again, and that he that overcame by the tree, on the tree also might be overcome through Christ our Lord.

Through whom the angels praise Thy Majesty, the dominations adore it, the powers are in awe. Which the heavens and hosts of heaven together with the blessed seraphim joyfully do magnify. And do Thou command that it be permitted us to join with them in confessing Thee, also, while we say with lowly praise:

(Jewish)

The Hymn of Thanksgiving is here interrupted by the "Holy, holy, holy." This is almost word for word from Sacred Scripture, recalling the visions of Isaias and St. John the Apostle. The last line is the Palm Sunday acclamation slightly modified.

Holy, Holy, Holy, Lord God of Hosts. Heaven and *earth are full of Thy Glory* (Isa. vi,3). *Hosanna in the highest. Blessed is He that cometh* (Apoc. iv,8) in the name of the Lord. *Hosanna in the highest* (Mark xi,9,10).

(Jewish)

CANON OF THE MASS: SECOND PART

Canon means in the Greek a fixed rule, or norm, or standard. The Canon of the Mass is a fixed norm of consecratory prayer, which remains substantially what it was in the time of St. Gregory the Great. It is particularly interesting to note with what terms of deepest reverence the Fathers of Trent speak of the Canon: "Of all holy things this sacrifice is the most

WE THEREFORE humbly pray and beseech Thee, most merciful Father, through Jesus Christ Thy Son, our Lord, that Thou wouldst vouchsafe to accept and bless these gifts, these presents, these holy unspotted sacrifices, which, in the first place, we offer Thee for Thy holy Catholic Church; to which vouchsafe to grant peace, as also to preserve, holy; to the end that it might be worthily and reverently offered and received, the Catholic Church instituted, many years ago, the sacred Canon, so pure from every error, that nothing is contained therein which does not in the highest degree savor of a certain holiness and piety, and raise up unto God the minds of those that offer. For it is composed out of the very words of the Lord, the traditions of the Apostles, and the pious institutions also of holy pontiffs" (*Sess.* xxii).

In the *First Book of Machabees* we read in Jonathan's celebrated letter to the Spartans:

We therefore at all times without ceasing,
   both in our festivals
   and other days wherein it is fitting,
remember you in the sacrifices that we offer,
   and in our observances,
as it is meet and becoming to remember brethren (I Mach. xii, 11).

The same propriety dictates that we, in our grateful gift-bringing, think of the whole Church, her visible head, the pope, her local shepherd, the bishop, and all its members everywhere. This prayer, and the several "remembrance

unify, and govern it throughout the world, together with Thy servant N. our Pope, N. our Bishop, as also all orthodox believers and professors of the Catholic and apostolic faith.

Be mindful, O Lord, of Thy servants, men and women, N. and N., and of all here present, whose faith and devotion are known to Thee; for whom we offer, or who offer up to Thee this Sacrifice of praise for themselves, their families and friends, for the redemption of their souls, for the health and salvation they hope for; and for which they now pay their vows to Thee, the eternal, *living and true God* (I Thess. i,9).

We pray in union with, and we honor the memory especially of the ever glorious Virgin Mary, mother of our Lord and God, Jesus Christ; as also of the blessed Apostles and Martyrs, Peter and Paul, Andrew, James, John, Thomas, James, Philip, Bartholomew, Matthew, Simon and Thaddeus, Linus, Cletus, Clement, Xystus, Cornelius, Cyprian, Lawrence, Chrysogonus, John and Paul, Cosmas and Damian, and of all Thy saints, through whose merits and prayers, grant that we may be always defended by the help of Thy protection. Through the same Christ our Lord. Amen.

prayers" are additions to the original Canon of the Roman Mass.

For the sake of comparison we here give the oldest Mass Canon extant, that of Rome about 225, when the Mass there was still in Greek. A discerning reader will find all the ideas, except the "Mementoes," expressed in our Canon.

Roman Canon of about 225

The deacons bring him [the bishop] the oblation . . . he lays his hands upon it with all the priests and gives thanks saying:

"The Lord be with you."
And all answer:
"And with thy spirit."
"Lift up your hearts."
"We have lifted them up to the Lord."
"Let us give thanks to the Lord."

And he thus continues:
"We give thanks to Thee, O God, through Thy beloved Son Jesus Christ, whom in these last days Thou hast sent to us [to be] the Redeemer and Saviour and Messenger of Thy will; who is Thy inseparable Word, through whom Thou didst create all things, and who was acceptable to Thee; whom Thou didst send from heaven into the Virgin's womb, and who in her womb was made Man and was manifested [as] Thy Son of the Holy Ghost and born of the Virgin; who fulfilling Thy

Spreading his hands over the Oblation, he says:

We therefore beseech Thee, O Lord, graciously to accept this oblation of our servitude, as also of Thy whole family and to dispose our days in Thy peace, preserve us from eternal damnation, and rank us in the number of Thine elect. Through Christ our Lord. Amen. Which oblation do Thou, O God, vouchsafe in all respects to make blessed, approved, ratified, reasonable and acceptable: that it may be made for us the Body and Blood of Thy most beloved Son Jesus Christ, our Lord.

Who the day before He suffered, took bread into His holy and venerable hands; and, with His eyes lifted up towards heaven, giving will, and buying for Thee a holy people, stretched forth His hands, when He suffered, that by His passion He might deliver those who believed in Thee; who when He was delivered over to His passion of His own will, to destroy death, to break the bonds of the devil, to trample upon hell, to enlighten the just, to set a term and to manifest His Resurrection, taking bread, giving thanks to Thee, said:

TAKE YE, THIS IS MY BODY, WHICH SHALL BE BROKEN FOR YOU.

And taking likewise the chalice, saying:

THIS IS MY BLOOD, WHICH IS SHED FOR YOU; WHEN YOU DO THIS, YE MAKE COMMEMORATION OF ME.

"Mindful therefore of His death and resurrection, we offer Thee this Bread and Chalice, giving thanks to Thee, because Thou hast held us worthy to stand before Thee and to minister to Thee. And we beg, that Thou wouldst send Thy Holy Spirit upon the Oblation of the holy Church, and gathering into one all who have received [It] in the fullness of the Holy Ghost unto the confirmation of the faith in truth. That we may praise and glorify Thee through Thy Son Jesus Christ, through whom is to Thee glory and honor, to the Father and the Son with the Holy Spirit, in Thy holy Church both

thanks to Thee, Almighty God, His Father, He blessed it, broke it, and gave it to His disciples, saying: *Take and eat ye all of this; for*
THIS IS MY BODY

Kneeling, the priest adores, and then elevates the Sacred Host.

In like manner, after He had supped, taking also this *excellent chalice* (Ps. xxii,5) in His holy and venerable hands, giving Thee also thanks, He blessed, and gave it to His disciples, saying: *Take and drink ye all of this; for*

THIS IS THE CHALICE OF MY BLOOD OF THE NEW AND ETERNAL TESTAMENT, THE MYSTERY OF FAITH (I Tim. iii,9);
WHICH SHALL BE SHED FOR YOU, AND FOR MANY, TO THE REMISSION OF SINS.

As often as ye do these things, ye shall do them in remembrance of Me.

now and forever. Amen" (Hippolytus).

The narrative of the Last Supper puts on the lips of Christ the words of institution and the injunction so to keep His memory. In that one Act our gift is offered to God, becomes the Body and Blood of Christ, proclaims His death on the Cross, and is accepted by the Father as pledge of the new, eternal testament. The essence of the Mass is in the twofold consecration.

It is a commonplace division of the Mass of the Faithful to speak of three principal parts, Offertory, Consecration, and Communion. The division would be misleading if one were to imagine that the offering part of the Mass was over and finished *before* the Consecration. The commemoration prayers excepted, practically every verb used in the entire Canon, before *and after* the Consecration expresses oblation. Let us look at them: "Vouchsafe to accept," "beseech Thee to accept," "make ratified and acceptable," "offer," "accept," "command to be carried on high," etc. If we are to understand the mind of the Church here, two things must be remembered. The first is that the *offering* continues straight through the Canon. By the consecration the gifts offered achieve incomparably higher worth and value, as being Christ's excellent and precious Body and Blood. But the act of sacrificing continues to be that of offering as

After the priest elevates the Chalice, he says:

Wherefore, O Lord, we Thy servants, as also Thy holy people, calling to mind the blessed Passion of the same Christ Thy Son our Lord, His Resurrection from the dead, and admirable Ascension into heaven, offer unto Thy most excellent Majesty, of Thy gifts bestowed upon us, a pure Host, a holy Host, an unspotted Host, the holy Bread of eternal life, and *Chalice of* everlasting *salvation* (Ps. cxv,13).

Upon which vouchsafe to look with a propitious and serene countenance, and to accept them, as Thou wert graciously pleased to accept the gifts of Thy just servant *Abel* (Gen. iv,4), and the sacrifices of our patriarch *Abraham* (Gen. xxii), and that which Thy high priest *Melchisedech* (Gen. xiv, 18), offered to Thee, a holy sacrifice and unspotted victim.

We most humbly beseech Thee, Almighty God, to command these things to be carried by the *hand of Thy holy angel to Thy altar on high* (Tob. xii,12), in the sight of Thy divine Majesty (Apoc viii,3); that as many as shall partake of the most sacred Body and Blood of Thy Son at this altar may be filled with every heavenly grace and blessing. Through the same Christ our Lord. Amen.

Be mindful, O Lord, of Thy

before; it is the same Act elevated to a much higher plane but continuing in the same direction. Again, it is essential to see in all this how the Church regards the Mass not only as Christ's gift to the Father, but ours as well. The Mass, as Christ's gift, is perfect in all respects, but as ours, the token of our internal disposition, "it may displease God," as St. Robert Bellarmine says. "This therefore is why we ask that God deign graciously to regard this Gift *as it is offered by us*" (*Cont.* II,24).

To that end we beg for part and fellowship with the faithful on earth, below the earth (Purgatory), and in glory, saint and angel, and in one last, supreme gesture we again identify ourselves with the Divine Liturgist fitted to our needs, through Christ, with Christ, and in Christ, as we offer Christ-and-ourselves. It is the climax of *our* part of the Mass. To it the people say "Amen."

This "Amen," as the popular ratification of the Sacrifice, is famous, and has echoed through all the Eucharistic literature. Of it St. Justin says so pointedly: "And when he has ended . . . the thanksgiving, the whole people assent, saying 'Amen.' Now the word 'Amen' in Hebrew language signifies 'So be it'" (c. lxv). St. Ambrose interprets it as follows: "You now say 'Amen,' that is, 'It is true.' Let the ear confess within

vants, N. and N., who are gone before us with the sign of Faith, and rest in the sleep of peace. To these, O Lord, and to all that sleep in Christ, grant, we beseech Thee, a place of refreshment, light, and peace. Through the same Christ our Lord. Amen.

(An Irish? Frankish? interpolation of the Canon)

Also to us sinners, Thy servants, confiding in the multitude of Thy mercies, vouchsafe to grant some part and fellowship with Thy holy Apostles and Martyrs; with John, Stephen, Matthias, Barnabas, Ignatius, Alexander, Marcellinus, Peter, Felicity, Perpetua, Agatha, Lucy, Agnes, Cecily, Anastasia, and with all Thy saints; into whose company we beseech Thee to admit us, not in consideration of our merit, but of Thy own gratuitous pardon. Through Christ our Lord.

By whom, O Lord, Thou dost always create, sanctify, quicken, bless, and give us all these good things. BY HIM, AND WITH HIM, AND IN HIM, IS TO THEE, GOD THE FATHER ALMIGHTY, IN THE UNITY OF THE HOLY GHOST, ALL HONOR AND GLORY.

P. FOR EVER AND EVER.

R. AMEN.

(Entire Canon, Roman, except "Be mindful . . ." above)

what the tongue openly: What your voice proclaims, that let the affections feel" *De Mys.* liv. Listen to St. Jerome's rhetorical question: "Where can the 'Amen' be heard to resound as it resounds in Rome?" *Ad Gal.* II. St. Augustine dwells on it, and other Fathers also.

Summary. "Our prayer is public and social," says St. Cyprian, the glorious martyr-bishop of Carthage (258). "When we pray, we pray not for one, but for the whole people, because we the whole people are one. . . . It is the law of prayer." This law of Christian prayer finds its supreme exemplification in their Sacrifice. This Gift is proffered by the last and the least of the faithful as really as by the New Man and *De Dom. Orat. 9* Mediator of the New Testament.

Thirteenth-Century Source Material

(Of all the successors to St. Peter, Innocent III is judged to have had the most brilliant pontificate. He was also great as an author, and his book on the Mass, here cited, is the medieval classic in this field.)

There are in this Sacrament three separate elements; namely, the visible form, the real Body, and the spiritual strength: There are the species of bread and wine, the true Flesh and Blood, and the bond of unity and charity. The first is seen by the eye, the second is grasped by the mind, the third is felt by the heart. . . . For indeed the species of bread signifies the dual Body [flesh] of Christ, the real and the mystical. It both signifies and contains Christ's real Flesh. It also typifies, but does not contain, Christ's Mystical Body. As a loaf of bread is made from many grains of wheat, and a cup of wine is crushed from a great number of grapes, so Christ's Church is made up of different classes; in the predestined, the elect, the justified, and the glorified. For

He predestined those whom He called,
Rom. viii,30,31   and He called them and justified them.

And, therefore, the Apostle says:

> We many are one bread and one body.   I Cor. x,12

As a type of this, the ark of the Lord was made from setim wood — an incorruptible substance like white thorn. The wine, as fluid and red, Exod. xxv,10 suggests blood. In its warmth and fragrance it symbolizes charity. And in quickening the blood and exciting love it rejoices the heart of him who partakes of it. It follows, therefore, that the substance of Christ's Body and Blood is both the Sacrament and the effect, though the bond of union and charity, which is the effect, comes from the Sacrament, and the Sacrament itself is the symbol of this bond. The substance, then, belongs to the bread and wine as it is both contained and signified by them under the visible Species; and the substance is the Sacrament or sign of the bond, signifying and effecting as it does, the oneness of the Church (Bk. IV, ch. 36).

For He is one and the same, the Son of God who descended from heaven, and the Son of Man who ascended into heaven. To Christ Jesus, John iii,13 as to their Head, are joined all the members of the body — those who through faith in the Eucharist

> keep the unity of the Spirit in the bond of peace.   Eph. iv,3

And as one body, one person, the one Christ with His members ascends into heaven. In triumph He represents the glorious Church, and manifesting the oneness of its members with His Person, He cries out to God the Father:

> This now is bone of my bone and flesh of my flesh: Gen. ii,24
> They will be two in one flesh.

This is, as the Apostle says,

> A great mystery in reference to Christ and to the Church.   Eph. v,32

The Eucharist both effects and symbolizes [prefigures] what the Lord said:

> He who eats My Flesh and drinks My Blood
> abides in Me and I in Him.   John vi,57

By virtue of our human nature which He assumed, we receive from

Him an indissoluble bond of union, so that He who is ineffably united with the Father, is marvelously one with us, and through Him (He mediating between both extremes), we are made one with the Father. He says:

> Holy Father, keep them in Thy Name,
> whom Thou hast given Me,
> that they may be one as We.
> Not for them only do I ask,
> but for them also
> who shall believe
> through their word in Me,
> so that they may be one in Us,
> and the world may believe
> that Thou hast sent Me.

John xvii,20,21,
Douay

Unity asks for union, the Word is one with His Father in nature, man with the Word is one in person, the members are one with the Head (Bk. IV, ch. 44).

Topics for Further Discussion:

"Sacrifice is positive, not negative; something given, not given up."

The Offertory Anthem and psalmody were introduced into the Latin Mass by St. Augustine, which is an additional reason for regretting their decadence.

If sacrifice is basically the service of God by gift-giving, is there a much more profound idea in the coin collection than any question of contributing to the support of the church?

Let the group formulate a list of the *social aims* for which alert, intelligent Catholics offer themselves at Mass.

Two people who have quarreled bitterly, see each other at Mass: think out a suitable Offertory oblation for either one of them.

Readings:

F. Boeser, *The Mass-Liturgy* (Milwaukee: Bruce, 1932); "The Mass of the Faithful," pp. 38-99.

F. Cabrol, *The Mass, Its Doctrine, Its History, The Story of the Mass in Pen and Picture* (New York: Kenedy, no date); "The Mass of the Faithful," pp. 27-36; *passim.*

J. Kramp, *The Liturgical Sacrifice of the New Law* (St. Louis: Herder, 1926); "The Structure of the Liturgical Action of Sacrifice," pp. 95-158.

——— *Eucharistia, Essays on Eucharistic Liturgy and Devotion* (St. Paul: Lohmann, 1926); "The Internal Structure of the Mass-Drama," pp. 42-68.

E. Leen, *The True Vine and Its Branches* (New York: Kenedy, 1938); "The Sacred Sign of Calvary," pp. 48-62; "The Sacred Sign of the Christian Altar," pp. 63-77.

G. Lefebvre, *Catholic Liturgy, Its Fundamental Principles* (St. Louis: Herder, 1937); "The Holy Sacrifice of the Mass," pp. 63–76.

H. Lucas, *Holy Mass, The Eucharistic Sacrifice and the Roman Liturgy* (St. Louis: Herder, 1914); II, "The Preface," etc., pp. 1–68.

N. Maas, *The Treasure of the Liturgy* (Milwaukee: Bruce, 1932); "The Offertory," etc., pp. 69–99.

M. S. MacMahon, *Liturgical Catechism, The Church, The Mass, The Year* (Dublin: Gill and Son, 1926); "The Mass of the Faithful," pp. 99–138.

P. Maranget, *The Roman Mass* (St. Louis: Herder, 1928); "The Eucharistic Prayer," pp. 38–73.

V. Michel, *The Liturgy of the Church* (New York: Macmillan, 1937); "The Sacrifice-Oblation," pp. 171–191.

T. H. Moore, *Beyond the Altar Rail* (New York: Fordham Univ., 1939); "Bread and Wine," pp. 51–62; "The Consecration," pp. 63–76.

P. Parsch–F. C. Eckhoff, *The Liturgy of the Mass* (St. Louis: Herder, 1936); pp. 153–256.

M. Perkins, *Speaking of How to Pray* (New York: Sheed & Ward, 1944); "An Oblation and a Sacrifice to God" cont'd, pp. 167–177.

J. de Puniet, *The Mass, Its Origin and History* (London: Burns, Oates and Washbourne, 1931); "The Mass of the Faithful," etc., pp. 110–170.

J. Putz, *My Mass* (Ranchi: Cath. Press, 1938); "The Consecration," pp. 19–32.

F. J. Sheed, *A Map of Life* (New York: Sheed and Ward, 1933); "The Mass," pp. 111–117.

M. de la Taille, *The Mystery of Faith, An Outline* (London: Sheed and Ward, 1930); *passim*.

M. Zundel, *The Splendour of the Liturgy* (New York: Sheed and Ward, 1939); "The Liturgy of the Supper," pp. 125–204.

Chapter XIV

TABLE-GUESTS OF GOD

> *We many are one bread, one body,*
> *for we all partake of the one Bread . . .*
> *Have not they who eat the Sacrifices*
> *fellowship with the altar?* (I Cor. x,17,18.)

PERFECT sacrificial worship has always been accompanied by a sacrificial banquet. The idea of sacrifice implies this banquet in which the worshipers partake of the sacrificial gifts, in order to achieve fellowship with the altar, that is, with God, who accepts the gifts put upon the altar. The logical and psychological processes of this ritual are as follows: first, the worshipers make an offering of foodstuffs, as a social symbol of self-consecration to God; in case a living victim be offered, it is put to death in token of God's sovereignty. These self-symbolizing foodstuffs become a savory banquet for the Divinity. Then, in return, God admits us to this banquet, and thus portrays in symbol the benefits that flow to man in serving Him. God's foodstuffs in His sacrificial banquet thus betoken these three things:

A. The happiness of future union with God in heaven.

B. The sanctification of self through union with God on earth.

C. The intimate union or unity of the whole divine family, "on earth as it is in heaven."

These things are called the "fruits" or the "effects" of sacrificial worship. Since God, moreover, is glorified through the same processes by which man is sanctified, these things constitute the whole why and wherefore of such worship.

"Gifts of Unity and Peace." It is essential to draw out in some detail the intrinsic relation of God's Gift-in-Return, which is Communion, to our gift-bringing, which is sacrifice. At the Offertory we together presented God with what St. Thomas called our "gifts of unity and peace," in the Silent Prayer which he composed for the Mass-formulary of the Feast of Corpus Christi. The Canon of the Mass speaks of them as the *oblation of our service*. But *for what* are we offering and dedicating ourselves to God in every Mass? Our adoration, thanksgiving, petition, and reparation are rendered to God in token of our *acknowledged dependence* upon Him. We are symbolically and dramatically expressing our complete willingness to accept whatever God's service entails *now*. That inevitably entails putting up with much minor unpleasantness from those about us, involves self-renunciation at home, in the classroom, in office, factory, at the theater, at the dance. This oblation of our service is a big order, in fact, our every relationship is part of it. Of itself it isn't easy, much less, is it pleasant. God therefore wished to make it tolerable (and even easy) by drawing us all together into a *living union* with His Son, who will give us the necessary life-force for the task.

Function of Eucharist. Let us ponder the reasons given by the Fathers of Trent "for the institution of this most Holy Sacrament":

> Wherefore our Saviour, when about to depart out of this world to the Father, instituted this Sacrament, in which He poured forth, as it were, the riches of His Divine love towards man, making a remembrance of His wonderful works;

> and He commended us in the participation thereof to venerate His memory, and to show forth His death until He come to judge the world.   I Cor. xi,24 / I Cor. xi,26

> And He would also that this Sacrament should be received as the spiritual food of souls, whereby may be fed and strengthened those that live with His life who said: Matt. xxvi,26

> > He that eateth Me,
> > the same shall live by Me;   John vi,58

> And as an antidote whereby we may be freed from daily faults and preserved from mortal sins.

> He would, furthermore, have it to be a pledge of our glory to come and everlasting happiness, and thus be *a symbol of that one body whereof He is the Head, and to which He would fain have us as members united* by the closest bond of faith, hope, and charity.   I Cor. ii,3 / Sess. xiii

The last and highest function of the Holy Eucharist is its cementing and unifying one: Communion is to be the real Communion Breakfast, where

I Cor. x,17 we are made one body by partaking of the one Bread. And this, Trent tells us, is in God's purpose the great symbol of the mystical body of Christ.

Integrated with Sacrifice. Present-day Catholics fall into three classes, which might be called respectively, Mass-Catholics, Communion-Catholics, and Mass-and-Communion Catholics. The first, and very large, group regard Mass for the layman as quite complete in itself without Communion, which is something extra one can add on for occasions. The second, fortunately small, group regard Mass, as such, subordinate to Communion, even existing for the sake of Communion. The third, ever increasing group see Communion in the setting in which Christ gave it to the Church, as a complementing, integral part of sacrificial worship. Only these last have a perfectly balanced appreciation of Communion, and are in a position to derive at once the greatest fruit from the use of the Sacrament. Only they can understand the language of Trent about the divinely planned symbolism of the Sacrament of the Eucharist. "The reception of Holy Communion," Bishop C. D. White (Spokane) reminds us, "at whatever time permitted has its own immeasurable advantages, but should not insistence also be laid on the intimate relation that exists between the Sacrament and the Sacrifice? On the fact that the reception of Holy Communion *during* Mass is an integral part of perfect assistance at Mass, that as the faithful are co-offerers with the celebrant so also they should receive with him the Eucharistic Bread? Both liturgy and canon law, not to speak of dogmatic

1930 treatises, aim in various ways to impress this truth."

The Gift-in-Return. Sacrifice, we recall, is essentially a method of approach to God; hence, it is not an end in itself, but a means. So the *sacrificial banquet* is not an end in itself, much less a separate act of worship in itself, but a *means of participating* in the fruits and blessings of the Sacrifice. Even when Holy Communion is carried a long way to the sick, and at any hour of the day or night, this is merely an extraordinary manner of allowing them to share in the completed Sacrifice. The very concept of Communion remains incomplete if it does not include this relation to the Gift that has been offered to God. St. Paul used only four terms to refer to the Holy Eucharist, "eating the Sacrifice," "shar-

I Cor. x,xi ing in the altar," "partaking of the Table of the Lord," and "eating the Lord's Supper." As the natural complement of the Sacrifice, this sacrificial banquet is the divinely instituted channel through which God gives man His Gift-in-Return. Thus, to assist at, and share in the Sacrifice, and then needlessly abstain from communicating (it is *always* possible to communicate spiritually), is like presenting a check for payment at the bank, and then walking away without waiting for the money.

Fuller Sharing in Christ-Life. Every aspect of this exalted subject merits our best attention, but none more than the *ultimate meaning of Communion*. In Communion we are sacramentally united with the Person of Christ; but that sacramental union is transitory, even momentary. It is itself designed as a means toward something ulterior, the abiding spiritual fellowship of ourselves in Christ and of Him in us;

> He that eateth My Flesh
> and drinketh My Blood
> abideth in Me
> and I in him.

John vi,56

Food must be converted into living flesh and blood and sinew; it must become alive and part of ourselves. The Son of Man came that we might have life, and He communicates this life by causing us to eat His Flesh and drink His Blood, whereby He shares with men the life He has from the Father. Here one acquires *Christ-life* at its very wellspring and fountain:

John x,10

> As I live by the Father,
> so he that eateth Me,
> the same shall live by Me.

John vi,57

"Africans do well," said St. Augustine, "to call baptism by no other name than 'Salvation,' and the Sacrament of Christ's Body none other than 'Life.'" And this usage he himself more than once follows, as in this sermon on St. John's Gospel:

De Pecc. Mer.
1,24

> Let him who will eat, let him who will drink; let them hunger and thirst; they eat life, they drink life. This "eating" means to be nourished, but one is so nourished that that is not diminished whence you are nourished. The "drinking," what is it but "living"? Eat life, drink life, and you shall have life, and your life shall be whole and entire. Then shall it be, that the life force of each will be the Body and Blood of Christ.

Closer Bond with Fellow Christians. The first consequence of this

Serm. cxxxi,1

"IS CHRIST DIVIDED?"
asks Saint Paul.

*"We many are one body
for we all eat one Bread"* says Saint Paul.

vital union with Christ, in the order of importance, is this: the selfsame act which thus unites the Christian with Christ, and through Christ with God, equally unites him *with all other Christians,* for all are equally by the same token fellow table-guests of God. Fellowship with the physical Body of Christ means fellowship with the Mystical Body of Christ. The very same bond that links the individual with Christ, the Head, links him with the other members of Christ's Mystical Body. Communion is food for the soul of the individual Christian; no less is it the food for the building up of the Mystical Body:

> Because one is the Bread,
> one body are we the many,
> who partake of the one Bread.

I Cor. x,17;
variant reading

"The effect of this Sacrament," says St. Thomas, "is union with the Mystical Body. . . . The unity of the Mystical Body is the consequence of the real [physical] Body sacramentally received."

S.T. III. Q. lxxiii,
a.3
Ibid. lxxxii, a.9

The thought of the bread made from numberless grains of wheat, and the wine pressed from countless grapes, *as symbolizing the living unity of Christians,* echoes through the whole of the early Christian literature. We shall limit ourselves here to one citation, the kernel of an Easter sermon by St. Augustine, preached to the "infants" baptized the previous night.

> When you were enrolled as catechumens [says St. Augustine], you were stored in the Christian granaries. Later, when you handed in your names as candidates for Baptism, you began to be ground by the millstones of fasting and exorcisms [in the Lenten exercises of the catechumenate]. Then ye came to the font, and were moistened and made one paste; and then the fire of the Holy Spirit coming upon you [in Confirmation], ye were baked and became the Lord's Bread. See what you have received. *See how this unity has been brought about,* and be of one accord, cherishing one another, holding to one faith, one hope, and love. . . . Thus, too, the wine was once in many grapes, but now is one. . . . Ye now dine at the Lord's Table, and ye there share in His Cup. We are there with you; *together* we eat, *together* we drink, for we live *together.*

Serm. ccxxix

The highest function of the Christian life on earth is this harmonious activity of the Mystical Body of Christ: its last goal is the brotherhood of the sons of God in the homeland of heaven.

Communion Rites Long Varied. Before reviewing in detail the text or rites of this part of Holy Mass, which might well be called "The Communion Service," it is well to point out a general peculiarity, in which it differs from the Canon, or even the Ante-Mass. The *present rites* were not definitely fixed, or imposed as obligatory, until *comparatively recent* times. It was only at the appearance in 1570 of the reformed edition of the Roman Mass Book requested by the Council of Trent, that this part of the Mass lost the freedom of local variation. Up to that time ceremonial usages, while following the same general lines throughout Latin Christendom, still differed widely in matters of detail. The prayers we now have, therefore, result from a final, selective adoption of elements old and new.

THE ORDINARY OF THE MASS: THIRD PART, SACRIFICIAL BANQUET

This little introductory formula to the Lord's Prayer is found in the writings of St. Jerome (4th cent.) (*Cont. Pelag.* III, 15).

LET us pray. Instructed by Thy saving precepts, and following Thy divine directions, we presume to say:

(Roman)

Lord's Prayer

We owe it to St. Gregory the Great that the preparation for Communion begins with the *Our Father* (PL. lxxvii,956). In that prayer of divine composition the first petition is for "our daily bread," a request which Origen, Tertullian, Cyprian and all subsequent tradition have applied to the needs of the spirit and only secondarily to those of the flesh. So it is of "the living Bread come down from Heaven" (John vi,51) that we are first concerned.

This whole section of the Mass, in immediate conjunction with the reception of Christ in Holy Communion, turns upon the theme of peace, and the conflict of evil against peace. Here we are asking, through our great and powerful intercessors, to be delivered from that which is opposed to our peace. That means the absence of sin (interior peace), and the absence of external disturbance. The path to peace, of course, is that of fellowship, of loving association with our fellow men. Here we are gathering the 'fruits' of our Offertory sacrifices.

Our Father, who art in heaven,
hallowed be Thy Name;
Thy kingdom come;
Thy will be done
on earth, as it is in heaven;
give us this day our daily bread;
and forgive us our trespasses,
as we forgive them that trespass against us;
and lead us not into temptation.
R. But deliver us from evil.
P. Amen (Matt. vi,9–13; Luke xi,2–4).   *(Jewish)*
Deliver us, we beseech Thee, O Lord, from all evils, past, present, and to come; and, by the intercession of the blessed and glorious Mary ever Virgin, Mother of God, and of the holy Apostles Peter and Paul, and of Andrew, and of all the Saints, mercifully grant us peace in our days; that through the assistance of Thy mercy, we may be always free from sin, and secure from all disturbance. Through the same Jesus Christ Thy Son our Lord, who with Thee and the Holy Ghost liveth and reigneth, God.
P. World without end.
R. Amen.   *(Roman)*

Pax Domini

The breaking of the Bread, preparatory to distributing it, is made to subserve the peace-theme.

P. May the peace of the Lord be always with you.
R. And with thy spirit.

(Jewish)

The unity of Christ's Sacrifice in time and place, and its single hallowing effect on all participants is, in a measure, expressed by this commingling of the Species.

Breaking the Host, he puts a particle into the Chalice, saying:

May this mixture and consecration of the Body and Blood of our Lord Jesus Christ, be to us that receive it effectual to eternal life. Amen.

(Frankish)

Agnus Dei

In Oriental Christianity, what we call the Host was often called simply "the Lamb" (cf. Acts viii,32,33). How natural, then, that they should think of the words of John the Baptist at this juncture (Isa. liii,7,8). It was a pope from the Orient who added this to our Mass.

Bowing, striking his breast, he says:

Lamb of God, who takest away the sins of the world, have mercy on us (John i,29). *Lamb of God, who takest away the sins of the world,* have mercy on us. *Lamb of God, who takest away the sins of the world,* give us Thy peace.

(Greek)

Prayers before Communion

This prayer is now taken as referring primarily to Communion. Originally it referred to the general *kiss of peace*. Innocent III explained the people's kiss as a substitute for the reception of Communion! (*De Alt. Mys.* vi,5.)

Lord, Jesus Christ, who saidst to Thy apostles, *"I leave you peace, I give you My peace"* (John xiv, 27), regard not my sins, but the faith of Thy Church; and grant her that peace and unity which is agreeable to Thy will; who livest and reignest forever and ever. Amen.

(Frankish)

Kiss of Peace

The general kiss of peace, so frequently mentioned in the New

After kissing the altar, the celebrant gives the kiss of peace to the

Testament, was eloquent testimony that Catholics "did not offer their gift at the altar, until they had first been reconciled with their brethren" (Matt. v,23).

In this prayer and in the next, which are both more personal forms of preparation, we have enumerated most of the effects of the Eucharist. Thus we profess our belief that it:

cleanses from all sin,
unites recipient with Christ,
is a means of salvation,
is protection of body and soul,
frees one from all evil,
acts as shield against Satan,
preserves soul unto life everlasting,
will work damnation if unworthily received.

We might most profitably recall here the burning words of Trent on Communion as our bond of union:

"This holy Synod with true fatherly affection, admonishes, exhorts, begs and beseeches, through the bowels of the mercy of our God, that all and each of those who bear the Christian name, would now at length agree and be of one mind in this sign of unity, in this bond of charity, in this symbol of concord" (*Sess.* xiii).

deacon, who in turn gives it to the clergy:
P. *Peace be with you* (John xx,19).
R. And with thy spirit.

Lord Jesus Christ, *Son of the living God* (Matt. xvi,18), who, according to the will of Thy father, hast by Thy death, through the co-operation of the Holy Ghost, given life to the world, deliver me, by this Thy most sacred Body and Blood, from all my iniquities, and from all evils; and make me always adhere to Thy commandments, and never suffer me to be separated from Thee; who with the same God the Father and the Holy Ghost livest and reignest God forever and ever. Amen.

(English)

Let not the participation of Thy Body, O Lord Jesus Christ, which I, though unworthy, presume to receive, turn to my judgment and condemnation; but, through Thy mercy, may it be a safeguard and a remedy both to soul and body; who with God the Father, in the unity of the Holy Ghost, livest and reignest God forever and ever. Amen.

(Spanish [Visigothic])

The Priest's Communion

These words of Psalm 115, here slightly modified, occur again.

Taking the Host in his Hands, he says:
I will take the Bread of Heaven, *and call upon the Name of the Lord* (Ps. cxv,13).

(Italian)

Everyone recognizes that this aspiration applies to the recipient the sentiments of the noble Roman of Capharnaum.

Right after communicating, the priest is enjoined by the Missal "to remain for a little while meditating on the most Blessed Sacrament."

Perhaps at no place in the entire Mass does the sacred text more accurately reflect the psychological emotions of our day than these simple, stirring words. Yet they are words of David of three thousand years ago!

This form parallels that which accompanies the priest's reception of the Species of Bread.

Striking his breast, he says:

Lord, I am not worthy that Thou shouldst enter under my roof; say but the word, and my soul shall be healed (Matt. viii,8). *(Thrice.)*

(Italian)

Receiving the Host, he says:

May the Body of our Lord Jesus Christ preserve my soul to life everlasting. Amen.

(Frankish)

Taking the Chalice, he says:

What return shall I make to the Lord, for all He has given to me? I will take the Chalice of salvation, and call upon the name of the Lord (Ps. cxv,12,13). *Praising I will call upon the Lord, and I shall be safe from my enemies.*

(Italian)

Receiving the Blood of our Saviour, he says:

May the Blood of our Lord Jesus Christ preserve my soul to everlasting life. Amen.

(Italian)

The People's Communion

There is a certain amount of repetition in these forms for the Communion of the people. Viewed strictly from the standpoint of unity, they are not really necessary, since the *Confiteor* at the beginning of the Mass could serve for people as well as for priest as preparatory to Communion.

I confess to almighty God, to blessed Mary ever Virgin, etc.
Behold the Lamb of God, behold Him who taketh away the sins of the world (John i,29). *Lord, I am not worthy that Thou shouldst enter under my roof; say but the word, and my soul shall be healed* (Matt. viii,8). *(Thrice.)*

(Frankish)

The things contrasted in this short prayer, mouth and mind, temporal gift and eternal remedy, remind us again that Catholicism must be *lived* to be effective.

Grant, Lord, that what we have taken with our mouth, we may receive with a pure mind; that of a temporal gift, it may become to us an eternal remedy.

(Frankish)

The expressions in the first person singular would indicate that this form is neither very ancient, nor Roman. On investigation it turns out to be a Visigothic or medieval composition. The thought-content is about the same as in the foregoing form.

May Thy Body, O Lord, which I have received, and Thy Blood which I have drunk, abide in my breast; and grant that no stain of sin may remain in me, who have been fed with this pure and holy Sacrament. Who livest and reignest forever and ever. Amen.

(Spanish)

Communion Anthem

The Communion Anthem is the refrain once sung over and over, between verses of a psalm, at the distribution of Communion. To come singing to Communion, and to recede singing from the celestial Repast may again be as common as it once was.

This is My Body which is being
  given on your behalf,
This cup is the New Covenant
  in My Blood, saith the Lord:
This do ye as often as ye drink thereof,
  in remembrance of Me (I Cor. xi,24,25).

(Roman)

Postcommunion

The Roman form of public thanksgiving after Communion is that collect we call the Postcommunion. Here is where one can best find the Church's basic attitude toward the "fruits" of Communion. Such precision of form is used that only one thought is usually expressed. God is thanked for spiritual nourishment, for soul-health, for a sense of corporate unity. If all have been further incorporated

P. The Lord be with you.
R. And with thy spirit.
       Let us pray.
May the Divine Victim we offered
  and received,
    put new life into us, O Lord,
  that linked with Thee in deathless love,
  we may produce the fruit that dieth not:
  through Jesus Christ, Thy Son,
    our Lord,

into Christ, then they are "Concorporate" with each other!

who liveth and reigneth with Thee,
in the unity of the Holy Ghost, God,
world without end.

R. Amen.

(Roman)

The Mass comes to a rapid ending now. The dismissal echoes a bidding of the Jewish synagogue service.

P. The Lord be with you.
R. And with thy spirit.
P. Go, you are dismissed.
R. Thanks be to God.

(Jewish)

This prayer, now reckoned as part of the Mass, was originally written to supply the celebrant's private devotion with suitable thoughts as he left the altar. It can well afford us now a momentary examination on how worthily we have tried to take part in the celebration of the great Mysteries.

Let the performance of my homage be pleasing to Thee, O Holy Trinity; and grant that the Sacrifice which I, though unworthy, have offered up in the sight of Thy Majesty, may be acceptable to Thee; and, through Thy mercy, be a propitiation for me, and all those for whom it has been offered. Through Christ our Lord. Amen.

(Frankish)

The Blessing

How fruitful if we always recalled how Christ blessed the Apostles as He commissioned them His co-workers!

Blessing the people, he says:
May Almighty God, the Father, Son and Holy Ghost, bless you.
R. Amen.

(Jewish)

The Last Gospel

St. John's Summation. The sublime passage at the head of St. John's Gospel has been held in the highest esteem from the very dawn of Christianity. St. Augustine tells us of a Platonist philosopher (*De Civ. Dei*, x,29) who considered it "fit to be written in letters of gold and set up to be read in the highest

P. The Lord be with you.
R. And with thy spirit.
P. The beginning of the Gospel according to St. John.
R. Glory be to Thee, O Lord.
In the beginning was the Word, and the Word was with God, and the Word was God. He was in the beginning with God. All things

places." Christians used to read this passage to comfort the sick, to strengthen the dying: in short, there were all sorts of practices connected with it in the private devotional lives of the people. A local council at Seligenstadt, Germany, in 1022, complained of a superstitious desire of some to hear this Gospel every day (*Mansi,* xix,398). After priests had begun to recite this passage, as part of their thanksgiving as they left the altar, it was not long before popular devotion found a way to insist on its recital at the altar. The movement seems to have spread from Germany. The custom of reciting this Gospel passage at the end of Mass had become quite common, when it was finally sanctioned by the reformed Mass Book of 1570.

We may be very grateful for its introduction. A more beautiful *summary of the whole work of Redemption,* which the Mass itself renews, does not exist than those golden words:

The Word was God. . . .
In Him was life,
and the life was the light of men. . . .
The light shineth in the darkness,
and the darkness hath not overcome
    it. . . .
To as many as receive Him,
He gave power to become the chil-
    dren of God. . . .

There is no better sentiment in which to come away from the Table of Sacrifice.

were made through Him, and without Him was made nothing that was made. In Him was life, and the life was the light of men; and the light shineth in the darkness, and the darkness hath not overcome it.

There was a man sent from God, whose name was John; he came for witness, to witness concerning the light, that all might believe through him. He was not the light, but was to witness concerning the light.

It was the true light, which enlighteneth every man that cometh into the world. He was in the world and the world was made through Him, and the world knew Him not. He came to what was His, and His own received Him not. But to as many as received Him He gave power to become children of God, to them that believed in His Name, that were begotten not of blood, nor of the will of the flesh, nor of the will of man, but of God.

And the Word was made flesh and dwelt amongst us, and we beheld His glory, glory as of the Only-Begotten of the Father, full of grace and truth (John i,1–14).

R. Thanks be to God.

(German)

Fourteenth-Century Source Material

(One of the Church's most influential women was the unlettered Dominican nun, St. Catherine of Siena [died 1380]: In her dictated DIALOGUE *she speaks as in the person of God the Father.)*

I am their bed and board, and My sweet and loving Word is their food, for they eat the Bread of souls in the Person of this glorious Word, for I give Him to you, that is, His Flesh and Blood, wholly God and wholly man, in the Sacrament of the Altar, by My Goodness, while you are still pilgrims and wayfarers, so that you may not slacken your pace through faintness, or lose the memory of the benefits of the Blood shed for you with so much fire of love. . . . The Holy Spirit serves those souls, for He is the affection of My Charity which ministers to them both gifts and graces. This sweet Servant both fetches and carries to Me their painful but sweetly loving desires, and to them the fruit of the Divine Love, and of their labors, so that they feed on the sweetness of My Charity, so that, as thou seest, I am the Table, and My Son is the Food, and the Holy Spirit proceeding from Me, the Father, and from Him, the Son, is the server . . . (Ch. lxxviii).

By receiving this Sacrament, she [the soul] dwells in Me and I in her, as the fish in the sea, and the sea in the fish — thus do I dwell in the soul, and the soul in Me — the sea pacific . . . (Ch. cxii).

I also say to thee, that as the Mystical Body of the Church now abounds in tribulation, so it shall one day all the more abound in sweetness and consolation, and this shall be its sweetness, the reform produced by good and holy pastors . . . (Ch. xii). [The clergy] are placed in the Mystical Body to feed your souls, administering to you the Blood in the Sacraments which you receive from the Church, their task being to extract the thorns of mortal sin, and to plant in you the seed of grace. They are My laborers in the vine of your soul, grafted upon the Vine of the holy Church. . . . I am the Husbandman who planted the true Vine of My only-begotten Son in the earth of your humanity, so that you, being branches joined to the Vine, may bring forth fruit (Ch. xxiii).

Laboring their own vine, they labor their neighbor's, for they cannot labor one without the other. . . . Remember then that all rational creatures have their own vine indeed, but it is joined directly to their neighbor's vine, so closely that no one can do good or harm to his neighbor, without doing it to himself, and all of you together make up the universal Vine, which is the whole congregation of Christians who are united in the Vine of the Mystical Body of holy Church, from which you draw your life. . . . See, then, that I have placed you all as husbandmen, and now again I invite you to labor, because the world is reaching an evil pass. . . . I wish you then to be true husbandmen, and with great zeal to cultivate souls in the Mystical Body of the Holy Church, and this I say because I wish to do mercy to the world (Ch. xxiv).

*　　*　　*

St. Catherine, acting as a peace envoy, was once set upon by a mob, but they refrained from killing her. "I am right in weeping," she wrote of it, "because I am not worthy that my blood . . . should wall up a stone in the Mystical Body of holy Church."

Topics for Further Discussion:

Exclusion from the Catholic fellowship is expressed as *excommunication*, exclusion from the reception of Communion.

The precept to assist at Mass binds weekly, that to communicate, only yearly: how is such an anomaly to be explained?

"The Eucharist makes men men." — *G. K. Chesterton.*

Two Catholics who "cannot stand" each other, live in the same building and attend the same church. Show how the Eucharist can bridge their antipathy.

A workman out on strike finds himself next to his employer at the Holy Table: Suggest a suitable prayer of thanksgiving for each of them as *addressed to Christ just received into the heart of the other.*

Readings:

F. Boeser, *The Mass-Liturgy* (Milwaukee: Bruce, 1932); "The Communion," etc., pp. 100–141.

F. Cabrol, *The Mass, Its Doctrine, Its History, The Story of the Mass in Pen and Picture* (New York: Kenedy, no date); "Mass of the Faithful," pp. 27–36; *passim.*

A. Goodier, *The Inner Life of the Catholic* (New York: Longmans, Green, 1933); "The Sacrifice of the Mass," pp. 76–92.

C. Grimaud–J. F. Newcomb, *"My" Mass* (New York: Benziger, 1928); "Communion during Mass," pp. 211–230.

J. Kramp, *The Liturgical Sacrifice of the New Law* (St. Louis: Herder, 1926); "The Sacrificial Repast," pp. 159–200.

―――― *Eucharistia, Essays on Eucharistic Liturgy and Devotion* (St. Paul: Lohmann, 1926); "The Sacrificial Banquet of Holy Communion," pp. 69–110.

E. Leen, *The True Vine and Its Branches* (New York: Kenedy, 1938); "The Principle of Unity in the Mystical Body," pp. 78–91.

G. Lefebvre, *Catholic Liturgy, Its Fundamental Principles* (St. Louis: Herder, 1937); "Holy Communion," pp. 77–92.

H. Lucas, *Holy Mass, The Eucharistic Sacrifice and the Roman Liturgy* (St. Louis: Herder, 1914); II, "The *Pater Noster*," etc., pp. 69–86.

N. Maas, *The Treasure of the Liturgy* (Milwaukee: Bruce, 1932); "The Communion," pp. 98–114.

M. S. MacMahon, *Liturgical Catechism, The Church, The Mass, The Year* (Dublin: Gill and Son, 1926); "The Communion," pp. 130–170.

P. Maranget, *The Roman Mass* (St. Louis: Herder, 1928); "The Communion," pp. 74–92.

V. Michel, *The Liturgy of the Church* (New York: Macmillan, 1937); "The Sacrifice-Banquet," pp. 192–209.

T. H. Moore, *Beyond the Altar Rail* (New York: Fordham Univ., 1939); "The Sacrament of Oneness," pp. 77–88; "Beyond the Altar Rail," pp. 97–106.

P. Parsch–F. C. Eckhoff, *The Liturgy of the Mass* (St. Louis: Herder, 1936); pp. 257–318.

M. Perkins, *Speaking of How to Pray* (New York: Sheed & Ward, 1944); "For the Building Up of the Body of Christ," pp. 190–205.

J. de Puniet, *The Mass, Its Origin and History* (London: Burns, Oates and Washbourne, 1931); "The *Pater Noster* and the Fracture," etc., pp. 171–195.

J. Putz, *My Mass* (Ranchi: Cath. Press, 1938); "The Communion," pp. 33–46, etc.

M. Zundel, *The Splendour of the Liturgy* (New York: Sheed and Ward, 1939); "The Liturgy of the Supper," pp. 211–253.

Chapter XV

THE MASS: NEW TIMES, NEW MODES

*If thou bless [God] in spirit [alone],
how shall he that filleth the place of the layman
say the* AMEN *to thy Eucharist?* (I Cor. xiv,16.)

THOSE who are now young may confidently expect to witness in our country a gradual but most profound change in the normal conduct of public worship, and especially of Mass-worship. Those privileged to travel in Europe may even now observe the same change in a much more advanced stage of realization. While with us this matter is still largely in the preparatory stage, and is far more in evidence in the school than in the church, the situation nonetheless definitely challenges those in training for the tasks of tomorrow. Both the goal of the movement and its peculiar urgency in the age in which we live are indicated in these words of Pope Pius XI: "A need of our times is social, or communal, praying, to be voiced under the guidance of the pastors, in enacting the solemn functions of the liturgy. This will be of the greatest assistance in combating the numberless evils which disturb the minds of the faithful, and weaken the faith in our age." The immediate objective of the new mode of public worship is an *active,* as opposed to the long prevalent *passive participation* on the part of the lay worshipers. The present-day necessity for this communal praying was more completely developed by the sovereign Pontiff in an audience to representatives of capital and labor the world over:

1929

You are twice and thrice welcome, while from so many nations far and near you bring Us so worthy a representation of the workers of the entire world. You bring Us a representation actuated by that happy concord and union of employees and employers, and directors and workmen, which is necessary for the advantage of every one. . . .
We have promised to give you something very short and which can put into three words all the eloquence of the *Rerum Novarum* [Leo

211

XIII's *Encyclical on the Condition of Labor*] and of the *Quadragesimo Anno* [*Encyclical on the Reconstruction of the Social Order on Christian Principles*], for whatever the Catholic program of Catholic direction, individual or social needs.

Here are the three words: prayer, action, sacrifice. . . .

Prayer in the first place. . . . Prayer, individual, domestic, public and social, *particularly social*. . . . That is what you need, you, the workers; you, the financiers: you, who underwrite all industry; you, who labor in justice and charity, in fraternity and in peaceful co-operation; in the practice of all virtues, in the respect of all rights and values, and particularly moral values.

1931

Thus, the harmonious cooperation of Catholics of all classes in applying Christian principles to our social ills is what is envisaged as the result of the new mode of communal worship. And since the whole movement is of today and tomorrow, we propose to build this chapter not on the documents of the Catholic past, but on the words of Pope Pius XI, and the American bishops carrying out his directions in our midst.

Active Participation, the Need. Within the lifetime of anyone now in college, and particularly since the *Encyclical on the Christian Education of Youth,* the courses of religious instruction in our Catholic educational system have been, and are still being, overhauled to throw more emphasis on corporate worship, and to illustrate and inculcate active lay participation. The change in *intellectual apprehension* is already a marked one, so that the situation humorously described by Bishop J. F. Busch at the Third Annual Liturgical Day, Saint Cloud, ought soon to be no more: "Too many seem to be satisfied with only an *implicit participation* in the Mass. Like the poor illiterate, who could not memorize the Our Father, but put a copy of it near his bed and said as he retired, 'O Lord, these are my sentiments,' so the attendance of many at Mass is little more than an indifferent or reluctant *Amen.*" How reminiscent of the Apostle's gentle irony:

1929

1931

> I will pray with my spirit,
> I will pray with my understanding *also;*
> I will sing with my spirit,
> I will sing with my understanding *also.*

I Cor. xiv, 15

Progress has been made since Bishop C. D. White (Spokane) addressed the Sixth National Eucharistic Congress in Omaha, 1930, in these words:

> There is lacking among the vast majority of Catholics in our country that active participation in the Mass that the Church so eagerly desires. . . . Not to mention the great number who are little more than spectators during the Mass; not to mention that other class whose prayers are principally for some pressing temporal need, prayers said without any reference to the Mass but merely during the time of Mass — apart from these classes how relatively small, no doubt, the number of our Catholic people is who follow the Mass in an intelligent manner and actually join with the priest in offering the Sacrifice.

"Detached, Silent Spectators?" Clearly, such an elementary intellectual participation in the great communal Act of Mass is an impossible basis for intelligent *active* participation therein. But no less is it clear that even the best *intellectual* appreciation of the true character of Catholic worship, as the homage paid to God *jointly by Christ and His members*, is but the starting point for active and communal participation. One can know a vast amount about participating actively in the Mass, and still hold back in complete detachment, just as one can have advanced mental participation, and yet be as silent as death. Merely knowing what we are to do, here as in every other matter, is no guarantee that we shall make the act of the will and do it. But in view of all that has been said in previous chapters on the necessity of self-oblation in the Mass, it will be enough to add here the short sentence of Pope Pius XI: "The faithful come to Church in order to derive piety from its chief source, *by taking an active part* in the venerated mysteries and the public, solemn prayers of the church." Thus each one's internal homage must flow into the external realm, each one's personal homage must be merged into a communal act, each individual must be, not so much a worshiper, as a conscious co-worshiper with Christ. It was in the face of an almost parallel situation that St. Paul spoke so convincingly:

On Promoting the Liturgy, 1928

> Else if thou bless [God] in spirit [alone],
> how shall he that filleth the place of the layman
> say the *Amen* to thy Eucharist?
> For he knoweth not what thou sayest;
> thy Eucharist is [no doubt] good,
> but thy neighbor is not helped.

I Cor. xiv,16,17
Greek

"It is most important," says Pius XI, "that when the faithful assist at the Sacred Ceremonies . . . they should not be merely *detached and silent spectators,* but . . . they should mingle their voices with the clergy or the choir, as it is prescribed." On Promoting the Liturgy, 1928

Stages on the Road. Between the Holy Father's vision of all worshipers, whose joint homage wells as from

one heart and one soul

Acts iv,32

and the actual state of the case in America, there is a middle ground still to be traversed, which includes these several stages:

General consciousness of participation as lay-priests in Christ;

General participation by use of the Missal;

Articulate participation in low Mass;

Choral participation in the sung Mass;

Frequent, even daily, participation by receiving Communion at Mass. Suppose we make clear by some quotations how surely and orderly, in the United States, our consecrated hierarchy is guiding us toward this most important papal goal.

Lay-Priests All. A primacy of honor wreathes the archiepiscopal throne of Baltimore and Washington, and so it is fitting to give the first word here to its present possessor. Says Archbishop M. J. Curley:

"By Him, and with Him, and in Him" do the laity act. As co-offerers with the great High Priest whose members they are, the faithful partake vitally in the Mass: they offer a real and true Sacrifice together with their Chief; they give glory to the Holy Trinity, united as they are with the Son of God, their Elder Brother.[1]   1928

In a Pastoral to his people of the diocese of Peoria, Bishop J. H. Schlarmann sounds the same note, when he says:

All the faithful, inasmuch as they are true members of the true mystical body of Christ, have a share in His sacerdotal dignity. The Spirit of the Lord adores and prays in them in a manner so exalted and so worthy that St. Paul is at a loss to explain this intimate relation of the soul with its Creator. . . . The worship of Christendom is a *social* worship. . . . Liturgy, then, is the essential and perfect public

[1] C. Grimaud–J. F. Newcomb, *"My" Mass* (New York: Benziger, 1928), Foreword. Quoted with permission.

worship which Christian society, as such, renders to God through Christ.

It was to a national gathering of professional men that Archbishop J. G. Murray of St. Paul spoke as follows:

> The consecration of all the professions to the preservation of life ... is elevated to an infinitely higher plane by companionship with Him ... in the Holy Eucharist that we may ... be more perfectly incorporated in His mystical body and partake in His ministry itself. Not to the clergy, but to the laity St. Paul addressed the exhortation: "Let us exhibit ourselves as the ministers of God." Not to the clergy, but to all the people, did St. Peter exclaim: "You are a royal priesthood." Participation in Christ implies participation in all that He is: Priest, Prophet, and King, even though each of us may not have the vocation or the sacramental authority to function as channels of sacramental grace to others.

Missal-Participation. How eagerly Pope Pius XI welcomed the multiple tokens of the forthcoming change, each of which he greeted as "a new and consoling promise of a not distant return of the great Catholic family to that loving, intelligent participating in the sacred liturgy of the Church." Among such harbingers of better things is the ever growing use of the missal: "The language of the liturgical prayers of the missal," said the late pontiff, "will convey to the faithful an invitation to draw [piety] from the fountains of the spiritual life." It is obvious that if an intimate union between priest and people is to be fostered, they should have the same prayer formulas. The almost bewildering multiplication of American editions of the missal, ranging from the one-Mass *Leaflet Missal* to the complete year-round Mass-book, shows that Americans in vast numbers are joyously heeding the famous injunction ascribed to Pope Pius X, *not to pray at Mass, but to pray the Mass.* In this matter too, episcopal leadership points the way. Thus the auxiliary Bishop of Cleveland, Most Rev. J. A. McFadden, addressing a Catholic Youth group on the apostolate of the Mass, said:

> In the use of the missal the wondrous beauty of the Mass is revealed to you, wonderful thoughts will be given to you to inspire and aid you in your work. In knowing the Mass you will want to assist at it more frequently; and in assisting at Mass, you will want to participate in it more fully by receiving our Lord in Holy Communion.

Margin notes: 1934; II Cor. vi,6; I Pet. ii,9; 1935; 1934; 1934; 1933

Bishop F. J. Tief (Concordia)[2] has frequently urged his people, priests and laity, to offer the Mass in unison, and to this end he urges the laity's use of the missal. "When pastor and people unite in reciting the liturgical prayers of the missal," he once observed sagely, "there will be no room for modern innovations." But if active participation stops at the use of 1936 the missal, Catholics would still be more or less separate worshipers, and altogether silent worshipers. Pius XI felt that it is most important that they be articulate and vocal in communal praying.

Dialogue Mass. In the light of our immediate past a laity vocally participating in Mass worship would seem to be a modern innovation, but as Archbishop J. J. Glennon (St. Louis) once turned it in a felicitous phrase, "This is not an innovation: it is a restoration." It helps us to keep 1925 the right perspective, in looking at this matter, to remember that the *normal* Mass-rite of former days was not low Mass, but high Mass. At high Mass the acting roles, so to speak, are divided between celebrant, deacon, subdeacon, acolytes, choir, and people, in such fixed fashion that the rite cannot be celebrated properly without all of them. The very same principle of *everyone having something to do* at low Mass also is now naturally leading to what is called the Dialogue Mass. This striking mode of Mass-worship has not yet received definitive form but it consists in these two things: the *answering* of the entire group along with the altar-servers in all these ordinarily say, and, second, in addition, *reciting* along with the priest of the *Gloria, Credo, Sanctus, Benedictus, Agnus Dei.* The first of these spheres of lay-activity, the matter of responding with the server, is not something unknown before: the rubrics of the missal even yet reflect that it was once common. In the second characteristic of reciting aloud *with the priest,* the novelty consists in applying to recitation at low Mass the traditional ideal of common partici-pation in the sung Mass. Here, too, the innovation is on the side of restoration.

Emerging from Silence. It has frequently, if cautiously, been sanc-tioned by the Sacred Congregation of Rites, subject to the control of the local bishop, because "the practice, though in itself praiseworthy," may under some circumstances engender disturbance.[3] "Your Eminence has the *full right* prudently to regulate this form of liturgical piety," con-

---

[2]Resigned.
[3]T. L. Bouscaren, *Canon Law Digest* (Milwaukee: Bruce), II, 1937, p. 84.

cludes the letter from the Holy See to the Cardinal Archbishop of Genoa
that we have been citing above. The practice is taking root everywhere
in Christendom. Naturally many American bishops have welcomed it,
so that the Dialogue Mass becomes daily more common, especially in
educational institutions and religious houses. Soon it will be conspicuous
as parochial, communal Mass-worship. "It is a laudable custom, spreading in our day," writes Bishop A. J. Muench (Fargo) in a pastoral letter
to his people, "to have the *Missa Recitata* [Dialogue Mass] in order to
bring the people closer to the altar." Note how this authorization of
Bishop J. A. Duffy (Buffalo) condenses everything into the briefest
compass:

> Our priests are authorized to organize the Dialogue Mass when they
> are sure it will be done correctly, that is, with the uniform and regular
> pronunciation of the Latin words and with careful attention to the
> words of the priest, so as not to delay him.

As a purge of egoism the Dialogue Mass is a most effective medicine.
Some would prefer to go fast, others to go slow, some would prefer
prayers of their own fashioning, or no definite prayers at all. To the demands of the Dialogue Mass may well be applied St. Paul's exhortation:

> Wherefore, my brethren,
> when you come together for the repast,
> *wait for one another.*

I Cor. xi,33

Restoration of Choral Worship. The most far-reaching reform of
Catholic worship now in progress concerns itself with the revival and
restoration of popular choral worship. "In order that the faithful may
more actively participate in the divine worship, the Gregorian Chant, in
that which pertains to the people, should be restored to their use" (Pius
XI). The reform legislation dates back to the dawn of the century, and
in publishing it the venerated Pius X expressed the hope that it would
be met "with that alacrity of will which springs from an intimate persuasion" of its reasonableness. The project has only slowly met with the
desired understanding of the real questions involved, and this is the more
regrettable in that no special musical competence is needed for their
comprehension. The matter is rather a problem in the nature of worship,
than in that of music. No educated Catholic nowadays can afford not to
know what the Church's aim really is. And lacking this knowledge, he

1935

1936

1937

*On Promoting
the Liturgy,
1928*

1903

is not in a position to promote what is unquestionably one of the foremost papal objectives. There is question of two things: of restoring song to the people; and of restoring a definite kind of song, Gregorian Plainsong. It will reward us to pass in briefest survey the perennial principles concerning the use of song as an element of Catholic worship, and that done, we shall see at once why the Church finds in the Gregorian Plainsong the ideal expression of those principles.

The Gregorian Chant has always been regarded as the supreme model of Church music [says Pius X], so that it is fully legitimate to lay down the following rule: *the more closely a composition for Church approaches in its movement, inspiration, and savor the Gregorian form, the more sacred and liturgical it becomes; and the more out of harmony it is with that supreme model, the less worthy is it of the temple.*   1903

What then are the principles linking sacred music and Catholic worship?

For the Ear of God. Music, one of God's choicest gifts to man, is   •
as a second, and higher, faculty of speech, the tongue of man's spirit, a language of emotional self-expression phrased in rhythmic sound. In a way that all know but none can fully express, music speaks directly from soul to soul, and though its message often escapes words, there is not a surer, truer communication of soul with soul than in the medium of the musical art. When this language of music is wedded to man's normal language, and words become an element of the music, we call it song. By common consent of mankind, song is the most exalted expression of emotion, one of the supreme expressions of fellowship. Now, when song becomes an element of worship, as is most fitting and natural, it becomes prayer set to music, becomes homage paid to God, through the exalted channel of purest rhythmic sound. The most elemental of all canons governing sacred music is that it is *addressed to God,* and not to man. To be true to its first law, sacred music must be meant for the ear of God. As such, it must be of man's very best.

"Each Hath His Own Gift." As a true expression of corporate wor-   I Cor. vii,7
ship, ancient Gregorian Plainsong made due and proper provision for the active participation of every worshiper. Thus, the sung dialogue between celebrant and people was cast in monotonic recitation, graced with the simplest cadences. The Epistle and Gospel were also in a monotone slightly inflected with cadences corresponding accurately to the sense pauses or punctuation. In such elements as the Offertory and Communion proces-

sions, the people were supplied with simple, short refrains, while the more capable singers of the choir or *schola* chanted in unison the "new matter," the verses of the Psalm. In the Gradual and, more so, in the Alleluia-verse, all the skill that could be mustered in chorus and solo paid its homage to God in the prolongation of phrases of purest sound, intensest emotion. "He who sings a *Jubilus*," says St. Augustine of this part of the Mass, "needs no words; it is a song of joy without words; it is the voice of a heart dissolved with joy . . . its joy is too great to be put *In Ps.* xcv into words." Thus, the second basic principle of the Church's ideal music is that it provides a musical vehicle suited to every worshiper's talents and capacities. Plainsong was for the plain man, to be complemented by the more expert voices in choral support in unison, or even by solo support. Here was a mode of choral worship in which each had his own gift, and a chance to use it, as

> filled with the Spirit
> speaking to one another in psalms and hymns and
> spiritual songs,
> singing and making melody with your heart
Eph. v,18,19 to the Lord.

Art for Prayer's Sake. The third principle underlying Gregorian Plainsong flows immediately from its character as sung prayer. Prayer, that is, adoration, or thanksgiving, or petition, or contrition of the creature before the Creator, ought never jeopardize its sacred character, even when put to music, by shifting the chief emphasis to the musical setting, instead of keeping it on the *words being prayed.* The musical setting is, therefore, "a complementary part" (Pius X), a secondary element, an elevating, interpreting, "emotionalizing" element, but not the principal factor. "Its principal office is to clothe with suitable melody the liturgical text . . . its proper aim is to *add greater efficacy to the text,* in order 1903 that *through it* the faithful may be the more easily moved" (Pius X). The Gregorian principle of composition made the music subserve the words. Phrased negatively, it meant that there was not the slightest change, inversion, or repetition of the words for musical reasons.

Freedom of the Spirit. One more fundamental principle of Gregorian choral worship must be noted, and it is one that makes it the envy of the modern composer. It is based, namely, not on the artificial and constant recurrence of a *fixed rhythmic unit,* such as the structure of verse, but on the natural, free-flowing rhythm of prose speech. Plain-song, with its naturally inflected recitative, or its melodies following what one might call the natural curve of prose sentences, is music in which, to great degree, "the thought constructs the tune, so that reading for the sense will best bring out the rhythm." In this Plainsong Mass the people's part included the short responses, the *Kyrie*, the *Gloria*, the *Creed*, the *Sanctus*, and *Agnus Dei*. The choir, or *schola*, while supporting the whole and carrying the variable texts of the Introit, Offertory, and Com-munion processions, handled the elaborate Gradual and Alleluia verses.

How Plainsong Was Lost. Gregorian chant was unison singing, but it was sung in octaves by men and children. Part-singing, besides octaves, was beginning to creep in when some singers chanted a fourth below, thus duplicating the melody at a different pitch. This manner of chant encountered harmonic problems, such as the simultaneous sounding of discordant notes. The difficulty was avoided by *keeping one part station-ary for a moment.* This use of simultaneous but different melodies was a turning-point in the whole history of music, leading on to the discovery of concord and the invention of counterpoint, wherein a melody or com-bination of melodies are added as accompaniments to the basic melody. The emphasis had here shifted from the interpretation of the prayer-text to the elaboration of harmonic compositions. The people, unable to sing these elaborations, surrendered to the theater-like pleasure of passive listening. Composers proved false to the principles of choral worship, and choral worship withered. That is the loss the Church would now redress. This, not primarily for the sake of the musical art, but for the sanctification of souls:

> The chief object of Pope Pius X [says Pius XI] . . . was to arouse and foster a Christian spirit in the faithful. . . . Wherever the regulations on this subject have been faithfully observed, the spirit of religion has prospered; the faithful have gained a deeper understand-ing of the sacred liturgy, and have taken part with greater zest in the ceremonies of the Mass, in the singing of the psalms, and in the public prayers.

On Promoting the Liturgy, 1928

"Singing the Mass." In presence of the principles on which the music named after Gregory the Great was built, is there any room for doubting either the supernatural wisdom, or the natural good taste, of Pius X in asking Catholics as a body to repossess themselves of their great cultural heritage? "It was precisely because Pius X knew and loved music that he could so thoroughly differentiate between what was proper and becoming and fitting and that which was none of these things," states Cardinal O'Connell. He says further:

> He [Pius X] foresaw very clearly the little musical revolution that his *Motu Proprio* was sure to cause among the choirmasters. . . . The new regulations, to be sure, were bitterly fought for a while by those who had forgotten the true atmosphere of the divine mysteries. This troubled Pius X not at all and he went forward prudently but firmly in his determination to rid the House of God of a purely paganized art.[4]

True, the bulk of American Catholics have not yet begun to sing their Mass, and perhaps do not even know what the Church intends for them. But on all sides traditional American aggressiveness is making its preparations. Who could have imagined, in 1918, when the Piux X School of Liturgical Music was opened in New York, that a degree-course in Gregorian Plainsong would be inaugurated at Louisiana State University in 1936, or at Duquesne University in 1938? The magnificent gesture of Cardinal G. W. Mundelein in having some 60,000 children sing Mass at the Chicago Eucharistic Congress marked a stage of progress by 1926, and indicated that the restoration of Plainsong is to be by armies of singing children. The annual nation-wide broadcasts of Newark's Legions of Youth, led by their Archbishop, P. J. Walsh, are standing verifications of what Pius X said: "The Gregorian Chant . . . is sweet, soft, easy to learn, and of a beauty so fresh and full of surprises that wherever it has been introduced, it has never failed to excite real enthusiasm in the

1903 youthful singers." There are now dioceses in which the appeal is no longer to the children, but to the young adults. Writes Bishop H. C. Boyle (Pittsburgh):

> It is the will of the Church that congregational singing for the Responses and the Ordinary part of the Mass, as well as for the hymns for the evening services, should be promoted and encouraged. Therefore it will be of great advantage to have well instructed groups of *young men and young women* among the congregation to take the lead
1932 in Church singing.

---

[4] W. O'Connell, *Recollections of Seventy Years* (Boston: Houghton Mifflin, 1934), p. 332: quoted with permission.

A later communication from the same prelate contained the understanding advice, "good will and good conduct are even more necessary than a good voice." Not to multiply quotations, let the case of a diocese be illustrated by two successive utterances on the part of its bishop. In 1931 Archbishop Joseph Schrembs was urging on his people: "The question of the popular singing of the chant is crucial, and it is fundamental of the reform plan that the chant, in its simpler forms, be restored to the use of the people." Presenting his report to Pope Pius XI after the National Eucharistic Congress of 1935, he could write:

> Thousands and thousands of people, far in excess of the number we could possibly have expected, had come to Cleveland. . . . Every note of music sung during the liturgical functions of the Congress was the Church's own music — the Gregorian Chant. There was a choir of 20,000 children, a choir of 20,000 women, and a choir of 60,000 men, a special clerical choir, besides numerous . . . smaller . . . choirs.

Thus "the laity's lost voice" is being recovered in America.

Communion, the Crown. The climax of communal Mass-worship, of course, is communal sharing in that Bread which makes us one body. I Cor. x,17 But this truth is so conspicuous in all current presentations of Catholicism that it is mentioned here merely for completeness' sake. Reference was just made to the Cleveland Eucharistic Congress, and it is fitting that words there addressed to college men and women by Bishop K. J. Alter (Toledo) be recalled:

> The second recommendation to our Catholic college men and women is a *full and complete participation* in the Holy Sacrifice. It is not merely frequent Communion, but frequent Communion in the frequent Mass. Partaking of the Sacrifice has always been regarded as an essential element in establishing a community of worship between priest and people, as well as a union with the Divine Majesty through the intimate joining of the Victim of sacrifice with those who offer it. *Without Holy Communion the Mass lacks completeness and without the Mass, Holy Communion suffers from the same defect.* The two belong together and form thus an integral act of worship which is both public and private in character, and social and individual in its application of grace and spiritual benefit.

As an example of how the new mode of Mass-worship may be carried out, read the account of 85,000 young Catholic workers at Mass, in Paris:

"Night fell on Paris, slowly, and everything was still steeped in light. In the immense stadium—the Parc du Prince — decorated with banners, 85,000 people were assembled — live wheat rippling on the stands, right up to the very top, and over the staircases and platforms. In the middle of the arena, on a high stage, a young speaker, like the celebrant of a new rite, stood up dressed in white. His voice, amplified by a hundred loud-speakers, filled all the air, and every now and again with a perfect rhythm of a powerful cadence, the immense crowd answered his prayer: for a prayer it was, a gigantic prayer, that was being lifted toward heaven by thousands and thousands of voices, and this imprecation left in one's heart the most powerful impression of unity. Each of us experienced to our very depths the joy of being an ant among these thousands of minute white spots in the night, and of breathing in unison with all.

"At the call of the voice, the workers rose. Each delegation of workers had brought the sign of its labor. And each, in a slow offering, came to place it on the central stage, thus constructing a strange and moving altar, showing with admirable symbolism the Christian identification of prayer and work. The miners from the north brought a lump of coal. Those from the east a piece of iron. The furniture-makers brought their plank of wood. There were others who brought stuffs and flowers. From the four points of the horizon the weavers approached the growing altar and, as they came, formed with four long strips of stretched linen a gigantic white cross on the green grass. Finally a slow procession crossed the length of the arena, bearing on many shoulders a cross ten meters long. They were the invalids and their nurses. For suffering is still richer in worth than effort.

"There followed a moment of inexpressible purity. Slowly, in the darkness that was lit up only by thousands of torches encircling the course, the cross was raised on the altar. It was white, clear, triumphant. Meanwhile, pure voices were raised in the poignant silence appealing for a superhuman blessing from her by whom the Saviour of mankind was born. At that moment no one could doubt that once again in history Christian France had rediscovered her mission, the same mission which was evoked in the nave of Notre Dame by the Cardinal Legate, speaking to all France."[5]

---

[5] By Daniel-Rops, *Colosseum*, Dec., 1937; pp. 218, 219: permission of Sheed and Ward.

Summary. One of the most notable features of present-day Catholicism is a reform of public worship, in which passive participation is yielding to active participation in the conscious acting as a member of the Mystical Body, by the use of the missal, the Dialogue Mass, the chanted high Mass, and the frequent, even daily, participation in Mass with the integral crown of Communion.

I ~ te,   mis ~ sa est.

De ~ o   gra ~ ti ~ as.

Fifteenth-Century Source Material

(John Burckard, after years of service as papal master of ceremonies, published in 1502 an ORDER OF THE MASS *from which the rubrics now in force were largely drawn: provisions reflecting the Dialogue Mass that have passed into our Missal are italicized.)*

The Psalm, "Iudica . . ."

The celebrant: "Judge, me, O God . . ."
The server and those present say all or only the alternate verses, and *they respond to the other parts* as indicated below.

Confiteor

[After the celebrant has said the Confiteor], *the Supreme Pontiff,* a cardinal, a legate, a patriarch, and archbishop or a bishop, *and the server and those present,* kneeling, say: "Misereatur . . ."

Kyrie

The celebrant, standing at the center of the altar, with hands joined, says in the same tone of voice (that is, a tone loud enough so that all hearing him can *understand* what is said): "Kyrie, eleison . . ." *If the server, or those present should not make the response,* the celebrant himself says everything.

Receiving the Offerings

If there are any present who wish to make an offering, the celebrant goes to the corner on the Epistle side. Standing with uncovered head and with his left side toward the altar, he removes the maniple from his left forearm, and holding it in his right hand, offers the extremity of it to be kissed by the offerers, saying to each: "May your sacrifice be pleasing to God Almighty," or, "May you receive a hundredfold, and possess life everlasting." After receiving the oblations, the celebrant replaces the maniple on his left forearm, and returns to the center of the altar. . . .

After the Offertory

Then with hands joined before his breast and with downcast eyes, he turns toward the people from right to left, and facing them says in a somewhat louder voice: "Orate, fratres . . ." and continues in silence.

The server and the others present, kneeling, with uncovered heads, *answer,* saying in a low tone, "Suscipiat Dominus . . ."

But should the server and the others present not answer, the celebrant himself says the response in a low voice.

Topics for Further Discussion:

"Resolved, that our zeal be exerted, first, to effect a more active participation of all the faithful in offering this divine Sacrifice; and secondly, to increase among the faithful frequent and daily assistance at this same august Sacrifice." — *Resolutions of Sixth National Eucharistic Congress, Omaha, 1930.*

In the light of the principle of active participation, criticize the current expression, "to hear Mass." What would you substitute for it?

The pedagogical principles, as aside from spiritual reasons, for active participation are these:

Activity is a better teacher than passivity.

An eye and an ear, a voice and a posture are together better than an ear.

External activity both releases and increases internal sentiments.

Joint external activity on the part of the group makes their worship a social, communal act, thus fostering unity.

Criticize the expression: "Good voices are the poorest material for plainsong, because they want to be heard individually."

Is Evelyn Underhill (non-Catholic) correct, when she writes (*Worship,* p. 98): "If we have to choose between extreme cases it is better to stand up and sing, 'Thine for ever, God of love,' surrounded by other Christians of all sorts and sizes, from the Mayor and Corporation to the Brownies and Cubs, than to elude this bracing discipline and murmur the same sentiment in a nice, quiet corner of the church?"

"The recitation of the Rosary, morning prayers, acts of faith, etc., are *good things*. But it is a *better thing* for the people to join their voices with the server and the priest at the altar." — *Cardinal Archbishop Minoretti*, Genoa, 1933.

"Every effort that is made to bring the Catholic people really to participate in the liturgical worship of the Church is a service of inestimable value to the cause of Christ." — *Bishop E. V. O'Hara* (Great Falls, now Kansas City), 1936.

Readings:

Catholic Church Music, Legislation of Pius X, Benedict XV, and Pius XI (London: Burns, Oates and Washbourne, 1933); *passim*.

The Chant of the Church (Collegeville: Liturgical Press, 1930); "The Reform of the Church Music," Mrs. Justine B. Ward, pp. 3–22. Pamphlet.

W. Douglas, *Church Music in History and Practice* (New York: Scribner, 1937); "Foundation Principles of Church Music," pp. 3–30.

G. Ellard, *The Mystical Body and the American Bishops* (St. Louis: Queen's Work, 1939), pp. 78–97.

—— *Men at Work at Worship* (New York: Longmans, 1940), "The Worker Gets a Voice," pp. 131–145; "Open- or Closed-Shop Choirs," pp. 146–167.

—— *The Dialog Mass* (New York: Longmans, 1942), pp. 126, 127, a partial list of American colleges using the Dialog Mass: *passim*.

J. Fitzsimons–P. McGuire, *Restoring All Things* (New York: Sheed and Ward, 1938); G. Lefebvre, "Catholic Action and the Liturgy," pp. 16–50.

J. Kearney, *The Meaning of the Mass* (London: Burns, Oates and Washbourne, 1936); "The Mass Is Our Sacrifice," pp. 128–166.

V. Michel, *The Liturgy of the Church* (New York: Macmillan, 1937); "The Liturgical Chant," pp. 316–340.

National Liturgical Week, 1940 (Newark: Benedictine Liturgical Conference, 1941).

A. Robertson, *The Interpretation of Plainchant* (London: Oxford Press, 1937); "General Survey," pp. 1–9; *passim*.

R. R. Terry, *The Music of the Roman Rite* (London: Burns, Oates and Washbourne, 1931). Choirmaster's manual.

Textbooks:

A Benedictine of Stanbrook, *A Grammar of Plainsong* (Liverpool: Rushworth & Dreaper, ed. 1934).

D. Johner, *A New School of Gregorian Chant* (New York: Pustet, 1925).

Pocket Manuals:

Monks of St. John's Abbey, *Parish Kyriale* (Collegeville: Liturgical Press, 1935).

Mass of the Angels (Collegeville: Liturgical Press, 1938).

M. B. Hellriegel, *Our High Mass* (St. Louis: Queen's Work, 1930).

Chapter XVI

PRAYING WITH CHRIST

> *In psalms, hymns, and spiritual*
> *canticles*
> *sing . . . to God by His grace* (Col.
> iii,16).

THE paramount position of sacrifice in worship has been consistently stressed in these pages. Thus far nothing has been said
about the worship of corporate prayer. Obviously, since sacrifice
is the crowning act of corporate prayer, a public prayer-in-action, as it
were, it necessarily rests upon a broad and deep foundation of corporate
prayer. In the realm of Christian worship the Divine Sacrifice of the
Mass is as a sun, around which daily revolve, like so many planets, the
seven Hour Prayers of the day and the three Prayer Watches of the
night. Besides these regular satellites in our worship of prayer, there are
stars of all magnitudes and orbits, the innumerable and widely varying
services held in the churches throughout the year. These services are
public, and consequently fairly well known to us, but with the unseen,
systematic prayer-world of the Divine Office, as it is called, it is highly
desirable to make fuller acquaintance. For, to say nothing at all of its
breadth and depth and orderly beauty, we have the very personal reason
that it *belongs to us.* In the abbeys and monasteries of Christendom,
monks and nuns by the thousand are engaged by day and by night in
chanting the *Opus Dei,* the Church's official praises of the Most High:
They form with Christ at the throne of the Father the voice of the
Mystical Body. Their austere worship of prayer belongs to the whole
Body, and *thus to ourselves as well.*

Mass in Cycle of Prayer. Besides the religious, men and women,
who perform the Office publicly in choir, *all priests,* as everyone knows,
recite the Office privately every day, just as they are privileged to offer
the Sacrifice daily. In this private recitation of the Office it is not easy

for the laity to see how the *Mass has daily a definite position* in the prayer cycle, of which it forms the great climax. Where Christians have the opportunity to assist at the Office rendered in public, they notice how the Mass occurs now after this Hour, and now after that, according to the rules as fixed as the phases of the moon.

Evening to Evening. As a rule, our *prayer-day begins at sundown,* when the Office called Vespers, or Evensong, inaugurates the worship of the day. Somewhat later, at nightfall, there is the Office called Compline, short prayers said before retiring to rest. To pray during the quiet of the night is another one of those natural promptings of the religious impulse, and was found widely among the pagan and Jewish religions of the past. It will be recalled that the early Christians held such nocturnal services for prayer and instruction, to which the Sacrifice might or might not be added. These ancient vigils, as they were called, live on in the three Night Watches of our office of *Matins,* which is now followed directly by Mass only once in the year. The midnight Mass of Christmas canonically follows immediately after Matins. On all other days this Office is followed by the joyous service of praise called *Lauds,* "which hail the rising sun as the image of Christ triumphant." When certain Masses of Requiem are celebrated, they follow upon the next Hour, called *Prime.* On all Sundays and feast days of higher rank, technically known as doubles and semidoubles, Mass follows upon the office of *Terce;* while on those of lower rank, known as simples, Mass comes after the hour of *Sext.* On penitential days, as in Lent, it is only after *None* that the Sacrifice is offered. In many ways Mass and Office are interrelated. Here let mention be made of only three: the Office of the day reviews the life of the saint in whose honor Mass is being celebrated; it provides a homily on the Gospel of the Mass; and it re-echoes hour after hour the Collect of the Mass.

These "Hours" Mostly Jewish. Although many details of the origin of the Divine Office are lost in the impenetrable mists of history, there seems no reason for doubting that the framework of the Christian *prayer-day,* as sketched above, is part of our *inheritance* from Israel. That the Night Watches, or Matins, are continuations of the nocturnal vigils connected with the Mass of the Catechumens, itself an adaptation of Synagogue worship, seems quite clear. Evensong and the morning Lauds are mentioned even in the meager records of the first century, and they would be natural continuations of the domestic prayers of the Jews. Even the custom of praying at the third, and sixth, and ninth hours has direct parallels in Israelitic worship. At those hours in the morning and afternoon sacrifices were offered at Jerusalem as trumpets sounded the call to prayer. This, it should be noted, was private prayer, but performed at these times. It was while the Apostles were in prayer at the *third* hour that the Pentecostal Spirit descended upon them; it was while Peter prayed at the *sixth* hour that he received the important vision about admitting Gentiles to the Brotherhood; and as Peter and John entered the Temple precincts to pray at the *ninth* hour they cured the man born lame.

Acts ii,15

Acts x,9

Acts iii,1

Tradition Becomes Christian. The first-century treatise, *The Teaching of the Twelve Apostles,* is silent as to the specific hours of prayer during the day, merely bidding all recite the *Our Father* three times daily. In the next century, Tertullian speaks of the third, sixth, and ninth hours as set times of private prayer. In the early third century, Hippolytus, in the *Apostolic Tradition,* shows how the Romans observed these prayer-pauses throughout the day:

viii,3

> If thou art in thy house, pray at the third hour, and glorify God; and if elsewhere, and that hour be come, pray in thy heart to God; because at that hour they stripped Christ and nailed Him to the Cross. . . . Pray at the sixth hour, for at that hour . . . the day was divided and darkness came; and they shall pray at that hour a strong prayer. . . . And at the ninth hour he shall be long in prayer with glorifying. . . .

Other prayers mentioned by Hippolytus for the faithful were at midnight, on rising in the morning, and at the supper hour. All these were private, except the last named, which was social, and linked with an evening meal in common at the beautiful service known as the Lighting of the Lamps.

Roman Office Popular throughout West. Thus, even from Apostolic times the Christians' daily prayers, whether public or private, were arranged in a rhythmic sequence extending throughout the day and night. Now, it was not long before there were numberless persons of both sexes consecrated by vow to the special service of God, and so this whole realm of prayer was speedily *organized into public, social*

Day unto day
declareth the message.
Night unto night
revealeth the knowledge.
(Ps. XVIII - 3)

worship. The full complement of the seven Day-Hours, as we have them
now, and the three Night Watches, existed in approximately their present
modes as early as the fifth century. How this worship of social prayer
spread throughout the West with the expanding frontiers of Christen-

dom is the history of the illustrious Benedictine Order, whose founder had written in his *Rule:*

Ps. cxviii,164   The prophet says: "Seven times a day do I praise Thee"; and we observe this sacred number in the seven services of the day; that is, matins, prime, terce, sext, nones, vespers, and completorium; for the hours of the daytime are plainly intended here, since the same prophet provides for the nocturnal vigils,[1] when he says in another place: "At Ps. cxviii,62   midnight I will rise and give thanks unto Thee." We should therefore praise the Creator for His righteous judgments at the aforesaid times: matins, prime, terce, sext, nones, vespers, and completorium; and at night we should rise and give thanks unto Him.

"Men of One Book." As soon as one asks *what* prayers were said by the primitive Church, or the early Middle Ages, the answer is everywhere and always "The Psalms: the Psalms and Christian hymns." Psalm means in the Greek a *chant,* and the word was always used to designate the collection of one hundred and fifty prayer-poems of Holy Writ. These had been the substance of both private and public prayer among the Jews, and, as such, were used by Christ and the Apostles from childhood. Naturally they passed into the prayer-life of the Church, and they remain to this day the major portion of the Church's fixed prayer. Since the great break with tradition at the time of the Reformation, the laity of today can hardly be said to know the Psalms. And yet as far as fixed formulas of prayer were concerned, *Christians* for fifteen hundred years *were men of this one book.*

Prayer-Poems Set to Music. In the form of rhythmic, parallel units of thought, couched in the language of poetry, the Psalms are the classic example of natural, direct converse with God. His Greatness, Goodness, and Mercy are nowhere better contrasted with man's many needs of body and soul, and with his sinfulness. Human hopes and fears, joys and sorrows, love of God and flight itself from that very love are most perfectly expressed in these inspired songs. Age after age has heaped encomiums on the Psalter, so that a vast literature has grown up in its praise. That these poetic prayers of the chosen people of old have not lost their appeal for our modern mentality may be illustrated by a quotation from the late Dom Cabrol, a contemporary. He says:

---

[1] What Benedict called **vigils are** now called Matins, and what he designated as **Matins we** now call Lauds.

Study, then, this book. Are you sad? It weeps with you. Are you full of joy? You will find in it songs of rejoicing. Are you sinking under the burden of your sins? It will lend you words to express your sorrow and repentance. If your soul is in doubt, if you have felt the emptiness of all human things, it will hold up to your gaze the hope of Heaven. . . . If your soul in the presence of God feels like barren ground, from which no prayer can spring, open this book; it will teach you how to pray.

Sung in Fields and Vineyards. St. Ambrose said of the Psalms that they are suitable for all, and loved by pious souls in every age. "We find in them," he goes on, "instruction as well as beautiful poetry. We *sing them to enjoy the latter* and we study them to profit by the former." He here touches a note well worth our attention. The Christians sang the Psalms for very enjoyment. Even apart from the public assemblies, in which the Psalms were sung together, these prayer-songs rose spontaneously to the lips. St. Paula, a Roman matron and friend of St. Jerome, related how in her day, "The farmer at his plough used to sing the *alleluia;* the sweating harvester lightened his labor with the singing of the Psalms; the vintager wielding the curved pruning knife chanted some snatch of Davidic poetry." David's measures echoing over hill and dale *Ep. 46,12* filled the pagans with wonder, and Eusebius, the historian of the persecutions, relates how this holy enthusiasm of the Christians brought the pagans in shoals to their assemblies. Here the beauty of the Christian rites further won them.   *H. E. X,iii*

Sung at Common Worship. The part played by these chants in the conversion of Augustine has been told a thousand times. In the period of indecision, prior to his surrender to grace, Augustine could sit unmoved even through sermons of St. Ambrose pleading in such words:

In Christ, then, are all things. Christ is everything to us. If thou hast wounds to be healed, He is thy *physician;* if fever scorcheth thee, He is a *fountain;* wouldst thou punish evil doing, He is *justice;* dost thou need help, He is *strength;* dost thou fear death, He is *life;* dost thou long for Heaven, He is the *way;* dost thou flee from darkness, He is *light;* dost thou hunger, He is *food.*   *De Virg. I,6*

But when the people rose to chant the Psalms, Augustine's stubborn heart melted quite within him. Looking back upon that time even years afterward, he would write in his *Confessions:*

How I have cried, my God, over the hymns and canticles when the sweet sound of the music of Thy Church thrilled my soul! As the music flowed into my ears, and Thy truth trickled into my heart, the tide of devotion swelled high within me, and the tears ran down, and there *IX,6* was gladness in those tears.

Testimony of Newman. The Office, too, was a milestone in the conversion of a modern Augustine, Cardinal Newman. He narrates how profoundly moved he was, while still an Anglican, on making the acquaintance of "that most wonderful and most attractive monument of *Apol. II* the devotion of the saints." Elsewhere, and still an Anglican, he wrote:

> There is so much excellence and beauty in the services of the Breviary, that, were it skillfully set before the Protestant by Roman controversialists as the book of devotions received in their Communion, *Tracts, 75* it would undoubtedly raise a prejudice in their favor.

The Holy Church in Prayer. It would be pleasantly instructive here to open one or other of the four volumes of the breviary and quote this Psalm or that, or read together some of the hymns ("private psalms" they were once called) of Ambrose, or Damasus, or Sedulius, or Fortunatus, or Gregory the Great among the ancients, Thomas Aquinas among the Schoolmen, or Robert Bellarmine among the moderns. But instead, let us turn to the *social aspect of this worship of prayer*. The priest with breviary in hand, the monks and nuns in choir, are the voice of the Church at prayer. Pope Pius XI took occasion to describe it thus:

> What a spectacle for Heaven and earth is not the Church in prayer! For centuries without interruption, from midnight to midnight, is repeated on earth the divine psalmody of the inspired canticles; there is no hour of the day that is not hallowed by its special liturgy; there is no stage of life great or small that has not its part in the thanksgiving, praise, supplication, and reparation of the common prayer of *Ency. on Repara-* the Mystical Body of Christ, which is the Church.
> *tion, 1932*

In lines, every word of which is charged with historic significance, the same supreme pontiff sketched the incomparable teaching role of this corporate prayer:

> These general supplications . . . were at one time made both day and night in the presence of great bodies of the faithful. And it is remarkable how much from earliest times those noble songs . . .

contributed to fostering piety among the people. For especially in the ancient basilicas, where bishop, clergy, and people *joined alternately* in singing the divine praises, liturgical chants were of no little avail, as history records, in *winning a great many of the barbarians* to Christian worship and civilization. In the Christian temples the opponents of Catholicity *learned* more deeply the *dogma of the communion of saints;* wherefore the Emperor Valens, an Arian, before the majesty of the divine mystery as performed by St. Basil, was seized with strange stupor and fainted; and at Milan St. Ambrose was charged by heretics with *charming the multitudes by his liturgical chants;* and Augustine, greatly impressed by these, decided to embrace the faith of Christ. Later on, into the churches, where *all the citizens formed* themselves into *a great choir,* came *artisans, builders, sculptors,* and even *students of letters* who *were embued through the liturgy* with that knowledge of theological matters, which today shines forth so clearly and which we admire in those remarkable monuments of the Middle Ages.

On Promoting the Liturgy, 1928

Corporate Prayer and Economic Ills. History supplies irrefutable arguments for proving the adage, "Let the law of praying confirm the law of believing." The part prayer ought to play as the solvent of current economic ills is likewise sketched by Pius XI in the words:

Prayer will remove the fundamental cause of present-day difficulties which We have mentioned above — that is, the insatiable greed for earthly goods. The man who prays looks above to the goods of Heaven whereon he meditates and which he desires; his whole being is plunged in the contemplation of the marvelous order established by God, which knows not the frenzy of success and does not lose itself in futile competitions of ever increasing speed; and thus, automatically, as it were, will be re-established that equilibrium between work and rest, whose entire absence from society today is responsible for grave dangers to life, physical, economic, and moral. If therefore those, who through the excessive production of manufactured articles have fallen into unemployment and poverty make up their minds to give the proper time to prayer, there is no doubt that work and production would soon return to reasonable limits and that the conflict which now divides humanity into two great camps struggling for transient interests would be changed into a noble and peaceful contest for goods heavenly and eternal. . . .

Nothing remains for Us therefore save to invite this poor world that has shed so much blood, has dug so many graves, has destroyed so many works, has deprived so many men of bread and labor — nothing else remains for Us, We say, but to invite it in the loving words of the sacred liturgy: "Be thou converted to the Lord thy God."

Ency. on Reparation, 1932

Christ Praying for Us. There is a further consideration in the social aspect of this Christian prayer. The Divine Office is not only the voice of the Church on earth, but of the Church in heaven, *the voice of the Sole-Begotten,* in whom the Father is well pleased, adoring, praising, interceding, and making amends before the Most High for Himself-in-us and for us-in-Himself. Thinking of this endless mediation of Christ, St. Augustine, in commenting on the Eighty-Fifth Psalm, penned one of his most beautiful pages. It deserves quotation at length.

No greater gift could God possibly bestow upon mankind than the gift of His Word by whom He made all things, constituting Him their Head, and conforming them with Him as members, so that He should be at once Son of God and Son of Man, one God with the Father, one Man with men.

Thus when we address God in prayer we do not separate His Son from Him; and when the Body of the Son (the Church) prays, it does not separate itself from its Head; and He Himself becomes the *Saviour of His Body,* our Lord Jesus Christ, the Son of God, who prays for us, and prays in us, and is prayed to by us; He prays for us as our Priest; He prays in us as our Head; He is prayed to by us as our God. Let us then recognize our utterances in Him, and His utterance in us. . . .

Eph. v,23

Let our mind, however, rouse itself, and be awake in its faith, and see that He whom it was contemplating just now *in the form of God,* has also taken *the form of a servant and humbled Himself,* and hanging on the Cross has willed to make His own those words of the Psalmist, *My God, My God, why hast Thou forsaken Me?* He is prayed to, therefore, in the form of God; He prays in the form of a servant; there as Creator, here as the created, assuming without change the created nature that He was to change, and making us one man with Himself, Head and Body.

Phil. ii,7,8

Ps. xxi,2

We pray, then, to Him, through Him, in Him; we speak with Him, and He speaks with us: we speak in Him, and He speaks in us the prayer of this Psalm, which is entitled *A prayer of David,* because our Lord according to the flesh is the son of David, while according to His Godhead He is the Lord of David. . . .

Let none then, when he hears the words of this Psalm, say, "It is not Christ that speaks," or again, "It is not I that speak." Nay, if he recognizes himself in the Body of Christ, let him say both *"Christ speaks and I speak."*

Speaking with Christ. This joint speaking to God of Christ and Christians goes on whether we advert to it or not. But it is in keeping with the growing consciousness of the Mystical Body and all it connotes, that the *laity are* nowadays *learning* to speak in the Church's Hour-Prayers with the speaking Christ. The movement, thus far, is not visible in any large way in America, but even now it becomes commoner year by year for the faithful to assist at Vespers and *to make their own* the Hour-Prayers of *Prime* and *Compline*. By way of illustrating a page from this great prayer book of the ages, Compline for Sundays is set out below. The prayer is not very different now from what it was fifteen hundred years ago.

COMPLINE FOR SUNDAYS

Pray, Father, bless us.
Pr. May the Lord Almighty grant us a quiet night and a perfect end.
Ch. Amen.

Short Lesson

Brethren, be ye sober and watch. Your adversary the devil goeth about like a roaring lion, seeking whom he may devour. Whom withstand ye, steadfast in the faith. And do Thou, O Lord, have mercy on us.   I Pet. v,8,9
Ch. Thanks be to God.
Pr. Our help is in the Name of the Lord,
Ch. Who made heaven and earth.
Our Father, *silently.*

After the Our Father, the Priest says the "Confiteor" and the congregation answers:

Ch. May the Almighty God have mercy on you, and forgive you your sins, and bring you to everlasting life.
Pr. Amen.

The congregation then makes the same confession:

Ch. I confess to Almighty God, to blessed Mary ever virgin, to blessed Michael the Archangel, to blessed John the Baptist, to the holy Apostles Peter and Paul, and to all the saints, and to you, father, that I have sinned exceedingly, by thought, word and act, *through my fault, through my fault, through my most grievous fault.* Therefore I beseech the blessed Mary ever virgin, blessed Michael the Archangel, blessed John the Baptist, the holy Apostles Peter and Paul, and all the saints, and you, father, to pray to the Lord our God for me.

The Priest answers:

May Almighty God have mercy on you and forgive you your sins and bring you to everlasting life.

Ch. Amen.

Pr. May the Almighty and Merciful Lord grant you forgiveness absolution, and remission of your sins.

Ch. Amen.

Pr. Convert us, O Lord of our salvation.

Ch. And turn away Thine anger from us.

Pr. O Lord, make speed to help me.

Ch. O Lord, make haste to succor me.

Glory be to the Father, and to the Son, and to the Holy Ghost.

As it was in the beginning, is now, and ever shall be. World without end.

Amen.

Antiphon: Have mercy.

Psalm IV

When I call on Him, my just God heareth me.
When I was straitened, Thou didst set me at large,
Be gracious to me, and hear my prayer.

Ye children of men, how long will ye be of hardened heart?
Why love ye the futile; and seek after the false?

Know ye that the Lord hath wondrously favored His worshiper.
The Lord doth hear me when I invoke Him.

Be angry [with me, if ye will]; but sin not.
What ye plan in your hearts repent of on your couches.

Offer a due sacrifice, and put your trust in the Lord.

Many are they who say: Who will give us to see good fortune?
Shown forth upon us is the light of Thy face, O Lord.
Thou givest joy to my heart,

Greater than doth the produce of corn and wine and oil, when these
abound.

In peace I will lay me down, and sleep forthwith.
For Thou, O Lord, makest me abide in calm security.

Glory be to the Father.

Psalm XC

He that dwelleth in the shelter of the Most High,
He that abideth in the shadow of Saddai,
saith to the Lord: My protector art Thou,
My refuge, my God in whom I trust.

For He rescueth thee from the hunter's snare,
And from the word that destroyeth:
With His pinions He shieldeth thee;
Under His wings thou art secure;
His truth guardeth thee like a shield.
Thou shalt not fear the terrors of night,
Nor the arrow that flieth by day
Nor the plague that creepeth abroad in the darkness,
Nor the demon's attack at the noontide.
If thousands fall at thy right hand,
Yet will [the evil] not reach unto thee;
But with thine eyes thou shalt see,
Shalt see the doom meted out to sinners.

For Thou, O Lord, art my refuge.

Thou hast chosen the Most High as thy refuge:
No evil shall come unto thee;
No plague shall draw nigh to thy tent;
For to His angels He hath given thee in trust
To keep thee in all thy ways:
In their hands they shall bear thee up,
Lest thou dash thy foot 'gainst a stone.
On snakes and adders thou shalt tread,
The lion and the dragon thou shalt trample on.

Because he trusted in Me I will help him;
I will guard him, for he knoweth My Name:

He calleth to Me, and I hear him;
In time of need I am with him;
I rescue him and make him great;
With fullness of days I will sate him;
I will make him see My salvation.

Glory be to the Father.

Psalm CXXXIII

Praise ye the name of the Lord,
　All ye servants of the Lord,
　　Ye who stand in the House of the Lord,
In the courts of the House of our God!

In the night raise your hands towards the Sanctuary,
　And praise ye the Lord.

"May the Lord bless thee from Sion,
　He who made heaven and earth!"

Glory be to the Father.
　Antiphon: Have mercy on me, O Lord, and grant my prayer.

Hymn

Now that the daylight fades away,
　By all Thy grace and love,
Thee, Maker of the world, we pray
　To watch our bed above.

Let dreams depart and phantoms fly,
　The offspring of the night,
Keep us, like shrines, beneath Thine eye,
　Pure in our foe's despite.

This grace on Thy redeemed confer,
　Father, co-equal Son,
And Holy Ghost, the Comforter,
　Eternal Three in One.
　　　　　　　Amen.[2]

---

[2]Translation by J. H. Newman.

Little Chapter

Thou art in the midst of us, O Lord, and over us Thy Holy Name is called: do not desert us, O Lord, our God. *Jer. xiv,9*

Ch. Thanks be to God.

V. Into Thy hands, O Lord, I commend my spirit.

R. Into Thy hands, O Lord, I commend my spirit.

V. Thou hast redeemed us, O Lord, the God of truth.

R. I commend my spirit.

V. Glory be to the Father, and to the Son, and to the Holy Ghost.

R. Into Thy hands, O Lord, I commend my spirit.

Antiphon: Keep us safe.

The Song of Simeon

Luke ii,29–32

Now dost Thou dismiss Thy servant, O Lord, according to Thy word
    in peace:

For mine eyes have seen Thy Salvation,

That Thou hast prepared before the face of all peoples,

To be a Light for the enlightening of the Gentiles, and to the glory of
    Thy people, Israel.

Glory be to the Father.

Antiphon: Keep us safe, O Lord, while we wake, and guard us while we sleep; that our waking be with Christ, and our repose in peace.

Pr. The Lord be with you.

Ch. And with thy spirit.

Let Us Pray

Visit, we beseech Thee, O Lord, this dwelling place, and drive far from it all the deceits of the Enemy: let Thy Holy Angels dwell herein to keep us in peace, and may Thy blessing be ever upon us. Through Jesus Christ our Lord, who with Thee in the unity of the Holy Ghost liveth and reigneth God, world without end.

Ch. Amen.

Pr. The Lord be with you.

Ch. And with thy spirit.

Pr. Let us bless the Lord.

Ch. Thanks be to God.

The Blessing

May the Almighty and Merciful Lord bless and guard us, the Father the Son, and the Holy Spirit.

Ch. Amen.

At the end of Compline is sung one of the great hymns in honor of our Lady, according to the season of the year. From Trinity Sunday to Advent is sung:

Hail, holy Queen, Mother of mercy, our life, our sweetness and our hope. To thee do we cry, poor banished children of Eve. To thee do we send up our sighs, mourning and weeping in this valley of tears. Turn then, most gracious Advocate, thine eyes of mercy toward us, and after this our exile, show unto us the blessed fruit of thy womb, Jesus. O clement, O loving, O sweet Virgin Mary.

V. Pray for us, O holy Mother of God;

R. That we may be made worthy of the promises of Christ.

Let Us Pray

Almighty, everlasting God, who with the cooperation of the Holy Ghost, didst prepare the body and the soul of the glorious Virgin Mary to become a habitation meet for Thy Son; grant that, as we rejoice in her commemoration, we may, by her loving intercession, be delivered from present evils and from everlasting death. Through the same Christ our Lord. Amen.

Last of all is said:

V. May the divine assistance remain always with us.

R. Amen.

And the *Our Father*, the *Hail Mary*, and the *Creed*, said silently.

Summary. Besides the worship of sacrifice, the Church through certain designated members, performs an unceasing office of prayer wherein through the divinely inspired poetry of the Psalms and hymns and other sacred writings, she voices the praise, adoration, and reverence of the Divine Majesty. This prayer is distributed over the seven Day Hours and three Night Watches. Its importance lies in the fact that is the prayer of the whole Church, the prayer, therefore, of Christ praying with and for His members. An encouraging sign of our times is the growing interest of the laity in the Divine Office, the *Opus Dei*.

Sixteenth-Century Source Material

(The Divine Office, when attacked by the heresiarchs of the sixteenth century, was eloquently defended by St. Robert Bellarmine in his monumental BOOK OF THE CONTROVERSIES. *He says in part.)*

These prayers and praises are called the Divine Office, since in them is contained our duty toward God, to pray to and to praise whom is the office of Christians, and especially of those who are called clerics and monks. Thus God says by Isaias:

> My house shall be called the house of prayer for all the nations.   lvi,7

This is to be taken, not primarily of the material structure, that is, the temples and oratories, but especially of the mystical dwelling-place of God, which is ourselves. For herein lies the difference between Christians and all other peoples: the latter, ignorant of original sin and the corruption and weakness of human nature, trust to their own industry and efforts, whereas Christians rely in all things on the divine assistance, have recourse to God in prayer, and implore His aid and mercy, so that the Church cannot be more briefly defined than as the house of prayer. Although the office of praying by way of petition is something passing, and will not last longer than man's [earthly] pilgrimage, the office of praising God will last forever, according to the words of the Psalmist:

> Blessed are they that dwell in Thy house, O Lord;
> they shall praise Thee forever and ever.   Ps. lxxxiii,5

If one were to ask for a definition of the Divine Office, let this be given: *The Divine Office is a definite method of publicly praising God and entreating Him, mentally and vocally at the same time, instituted by competent ecclesiastical authority.*

First, we say *"a definite method,"* for not any and every praying to God and praising God is the Divine Office, but a certain definite order of psalms, hymns and prayers, which all who are obligated to recite the Divine Office must follow.

Secondly, we say *"publicly,"* because the Divine Office is recited by public and sacred ministers, publicly, in the name of the whole Church, for the common and public weal. That is why, even when it is said by one man and in a private residence, one does not omit such forms as "The

Lord be with you," "Let us pray," "Let us bless the Lord," and the like. These are addressed to the whole Church, and in the name of the same Church he answers himself, "And with thy spirit," "Thanks be to God," and so forth.

Thirdly, we say *"a method of praising and beseeching,"* because the Office of which we speak entails these two obligations, blessing God for benefits received, petitioning Him for things to be received. In this the Office of the Church Militant differs from that of the Church Triumphant, which, when it shall exult in all its members after the Judgment Day, will contain only the praises of God.

In the fourth place, we say "[a method of praising . . .] *God,"* for the whole Office is properly offered to God alone. This is the sacrifice of the lips, of which we read in the Forty-Ninth Psalm:

xlix, 23   The sacrifice of praise shall glorify me.

Nor should it disturb us that one Office is called "of the Saints," another "of the dead," a third "of the season," and so on. The one is called "of the Saints," when it is offered to God in memory of the Saints, and when God is praised in His Saints, just as another is called "of the dead," when we entreat God therein to grant refreshment and rest to the dead. Finally, whether the Office be designated as "of the dead," or in whatever way, the psalms, hymns, Collects, and other parts of the Office are always directed to God.

Fifthly, we say *"mentally and vocally at the same time,"* because the form of the Office, of human institution, necessarily demands an external act. Hence he would not satisfy his obligation who, praying to and praising God mentally only, and not with his voice, did not pronounce all the words completely and distinctly.

Finally, the definition includes *"instituted by competent ecclesiastical authority."* For no one can prescribe a definite norm of prayer, except the one in authority. . . . Pope Gregory VII, in a General Council prescribed the number of the Psalms and Lessons, as is seen in the canon. . . . — *De Controv.* III: *De Bon. Oper.* X.

Topics for Further Discussion:

Explain the laity's loss of interest in the Psalms and the Office generally.

The additional sense of solidarity in praising God in the very words used on earth by Christ and by so many millions of Christians.

That no history of literature in any Christian country can overlook the treasures of the breviary.

In former times, when few could read or write, people learned the Latin Psalms, and sang them with delight.

In European countries simplified editions of the Breviary have begun to be used widely within late years.

In England a Magnificat Society of laity is organized in groups of eight members, who divide among themselves the several Hours of the Divine Office.

In the United States, within the past few years, social-minded adults, study clubs, student organizations, sodalities, and the like, have linked themselves together into a League of the Divine Office, and corporately recite on occasion some part of the Divine Office.

Readings:

P. Batiffol, *History of the Roman Breviary* (New York: Longmans, Green, 1912); "The Genesis of the Canonical Hours," pp. 1–29.

J. Baudot, *The Breviary, Its History and Contents* (St. Louis: Herder, 1929); *passim.*

F. Cabrol, "Breviary," "Matins," "Lauds," "Vespers," etc., *CE.*

—— *Liturgical Prayer, Its History and Spirit* (New York: Kenedy, 1922); "Forms of Prayer Used in Antiquity," pp. 32–42.

G. Ellard, *Men at Work at Worship* (New York: Longmans, 1940), "After Hours and Office Hours," pp. 255–272.

R. Hoornaert, *The Breviary and the Laity* (Collegeville: Liturgical Press, 1936); *passim.*

V. Michel, *The Liturgy of the Church* (New York: Macmillan, 1937); "The Divine Office," pp. 274–293; "The Daily Cycle of Praise," pp. 294–315.

M. Perkins, *At Your Ease in the Catholic Church* (New York: Sheed and Ward, 1938), " On Time With the Church," pp. 133–141.

J. A. Rickaby, *Readings from St. Augustine on the Psalms* (New York: Benziger, 1925); *passim.*

E. I. Watkin, *The Catholic Centre* (New York: Sheed and Ward, 1939), "Adoration," pp. 227–247.

Text translations:
Full Breviary:

J. Bute, *The Roman Breviary* (4 v.) (London-Edinburgh: Blackwood, 1908).

Nuns of Stanbrook, *The Roman Breviary* (4 v.) (London: Burns, Oates and Washbourne, 1936, 1937).

Day Hours:

Nuns of Stanbrook, *The Day Hours of the Church, The Liturgy of the Layfolk* (London: Burns, Oates and Washbourne, 1921).

Prime:

The Hour of Prime (Collegeville: Liturgical Press, 1935).

C. C. Martindale, *Morning Prayers from the Liturgy* (London: CTS).

Vespers:

A. Fortescue, *Vespers for Sundays* (London: CTS).

Compline:

D. Attwater, *Into Thy Hands*, Compline for entire week (Collegeville: Liturgical Press).

C. C. Martindale, *Compline for Sundays and Festivals* (London: CTS).

Chapter XVII

A CHRISTIAN BECAUSE CHRIST-ED

Unless a man be born anew
of water and of Spirit
he cannot enter into the Kingdom of
Heaven (John iii,5).

IT HAS been the theme of all the preceding chapters of this book that Christians lead a super-life, living in a Christocentric sphere, where they share by communication in the life and prerogatives of Christ. Attention was especially focused on the supreme function of sacrificial worship, wherein, as participants of the priesthood of Christ, all Christians have important roles to play. It will now be necessary to broaden the scope of inquiry, and study the whole cultual aspect of Christian life. At least all the more important elements in this divinely instituted scheme for the fullest and most adequate human existence must be examined in purpose and function. First and foremost it is essential to see by what means we were initiated into Christianity, how we were ingrafted into the Mystical Body of Christ. Belief in Christ's doctrine, even the most self-sacrificing surrender in living the doctrines of Christianity, do not suffice to make a Christian. We are Christians because we have been "reborn" in sacramental baptism. The word *christen* meant literally to make Christian, and this was done by baptism, but that basic meaning having worn smooth with long usage, modern writers speak of baptism as the act by which we are Christ-ed.

Purification by Water. "Baptism" etymologically means being *dipped* or plunged *into water*. As a natural religious rite it means submitting to a ceremonial washing, or cleansing, at the hands of another. It is thus an exterior act which of itself expresses a consciousness of guilt, a voluntary surrender of self in order to be purged of the guilt, and bodily cleansing in token of interior purification. It is seen to be an eminently fitting sign to express the most conspicuous features of Christian initiation. As such it was deliberately chosen by Christ.

Sacramental Institution. At the opening of His public ministry, Christ went out to where John the Baptist was preaching penance and this natural baptism as a confession of guilt. John was quite clear and insistent in his preaching that *his* baptism could not directly remit sin, but was merely a token of contrition in the faith of the Mightier One to come. By receiving on His own sinless members the *natural baptism* of penance, Christ wished to *consecrate* this cleansing ablution by giving it the *sacramental efficacy* of spiritual regeneration. It will be seen from St. Matthew's account how each of the Three Divine Persons singly and distinctly concur in instituting sacramental baptism.

> Then cometh Jesus
>   from Galilee to the Jordan
>   unto John, to be baptized by him.
>
> And John was for hindering Him, and said,
>   "It is I
>   who need to be baptized by Thee,
> and comest Thou to me?"
>
> But Jesus answered and said to him,
>   "Let it be so at this time;
>   for so it becometh us to fulfill all justness."
>
> Then he letteth Him come.
>
> And Jesus, having been baptized,
> came up straightway from the water,
> and behold,
> the heavens were opened,
> and he saw the Spirit of God descend as a dove
> coming upon Him.
>
> And behold,
>   a voice from the heavens, saying,
>   "This is My beloved Son,
>   in whom I am well pleased."   Matt. iii,13–17

The New Birth. The rite thus solemnly ordained Christ explained by calling it rebirth, a second birth, a birth of water and the Holy Spirit.

Laver of Rebirth

Unless a man be born anew
   of water and of Spirit,
he cannot enter into the Kingdom of Heaven.

That which has come into being from the flesh
   is flesh.

That which has come into being from the Spirit
   is spirit.

So do not be astonished that I have said to thee,   John iii,5–7,
   "You must be reborn."   tr. by C.C.
                                              Martindale

When Christ sent the twelve Apostles through Galilee, and later the seventy-two disciples, to preach and heal, St. John narrates how they baptized. These temporary commissions had their culmination in the final apostolic investiture: John iii,22–26; iv,1,2

All power in Heaven and earth
   hath been given Me.
Go ye, therefore, make disciples of all nations,
   baptizing them
   in the name of the Father
   and of the Son
   and of the Holy Spirit:
teaching them to observe all things I have commanded you:
   and behold, I am with you all days,
   unto the consummation of the world.   Matt. xxviii,18–20

On the day of Pentecost, when the throngs ask of Peter, "What are we to do?" he answers,

Repent ye, and be baptized,
   every one of you,
   in the name of Jesus Christ
   unto the forgiveness of your sins;
and ye shall receive the gift of the Holy Spirit.   Acts ii,37,38

From that day onward baptism has been the Christian's initiation, his *supernatural* birthday, his entrance into the circle of God's adopted children, and his incorporation into the Mystical Body of Christ. The great St. Athanasius sums up all we have said in a few sentences:

It is clear that the descent of the Holy Spirit upon Him at the

Jordan was for our sake, because He bears our body. It was not He derived the advantage of it, but we who through Him have been sanctified. We shared in His anointing in such wise that one could say of us:

> Know you not that you are the temple of God,
> and that the Spirit of God dwelleth in you?

I Cor. iii,16

When the Saviour, then, purified Himself in the Jordan, it was we in Him and through Him that were purified. And when He received the Spirit it was we who through Him received it.

Cont. Arianos, xlvi

"Rising to New Life." St. Paul's favorite concept of baptism links it with Christ's death and *resurrection from the tomb*. To understand his language, we must recall that the sacrament was normally administered by immersing the candidate into water and then drawing him out of the water. Being *plunged beneath the water* reminded Paul of Christ's going down into the tomb; the rising from the water suggested Christ's glorious victory over death, all the more so since the baptismal waters had all their efficacy from the very fact of Christ's death and resurrection. So the natural man with his sins descended into the water as to a tomb to die to self and to sin, and the sinless Christian arose therefrom to walk in newness of life:

> Know ye not,
> that as many of us as were baptized unto Christ Jesus,
> we were baptized unto his death?
> We were buried therefore with Him
> through his baptism unto death,
> that as Christ was raised from the dead,
> through the glory of the Father,
> so we also should walk in newness of life.

Rom. vi,3–5

Citizen of Grace-World. "Rebirth" gives a depth of meaning which the Scriptures and the Fathers could never exhaust in numberless explanations. In the words of Christ to Nicodemus, there is a delicate play on words no translation can render; the word ἄνωθεν, rendered "anew," can equally well mean "from above." The new birth from on high implies not only the complete cleansing from all sin, but the entrance into the supernatural life by being implanted into Christ: for all of us,

whether Jews or Greeks,

whether slaves or free,
were baptized into one body. . . .
Now you are [together] the body of Christ,
and severally His members.   I Cor. xii,12,27

And all these members, as those of God's adopted sons, are "sealed
against the day of redemption" by the mark of the Holy Spirit. Once   Eph. i,14; iv,30
baptized, therefore, always a Christian; the supernatural life here imparted may be killed, but once given this testimonial seal of adoption,
there is no process of "unbaptism." This son of God may go astray and
be lost, but unto God the son has been born, and son he remains forever.

Oath of Allegiance. Baptism was the first element of Christianity
to be called by the Latin word *sacramentum*. This term had meant a
solemn, sacred oath, such as the *sacramentum militare,* by which soldiers
consecrated themselves and swore fidelity to the military calling. Baptism
was called sacrament, or oath, because it involved on the part of the
neophyte *an irrevocable undertaking henceforth to serve under the standard of Christ.* How this secondary aspect of baptismal initiation came to
designate the whole process becomes clear if we reflect that in Greco-
Roman paganism the vilest sins, lying, stealing, impurity, and the like,
had been, so to say, deified by being linked with some special god or
goddess. The sinful actions had become, as it were, acts of worship to
the false divinity in question. Thus the neophyte, who wished to embrace
Christianity, had to be taught that baptism entailed forswearing all these
depravities, these false gods, and swearing undying allegiance to a God
of infinite sanctity.

"Resurrection" on Easter Morning. The Christian teachings had
to be slowly unfolded, and assimilated, and to a great extent lived for a
fairly long period (three years as a rule), before a catechumen was
considered fit for baptism. The baptism itself was *administered in the
night preceding Easter Day,* so the neophytes would rise to the new life
at the moment Christ rose from the tomb. The Lenten season was given
up to a final, intensive training of the Catechumens, and was marked by
periodic public scrutinies, or examinations, as the baptismal night drew
near. To heighten the psychological impressions of the great act of
initiation, the rites of the sacrament itself, at a time when the Mass had
hardly passed beyond the simplicity of the Supper Chamber, had taken
on a wealth of symbolic richness and elaboration.

Ancient Rites Preserved. The present rites of infant baptism, which are also used in the United States for adults, are a shortened form of an eighth-century ritual: many parts are much older; thus the celebrated questions of renouncing Satan, and his works, and his pomps, were already traditional when Tertullian wrote at the end of the second century. No part of the whole of our worship so truly preserves ancient forms unchanged as this baptismal ritual. In the rites reproduced on page 253 every prayer is word for word from the eighth-century redaction, barring two minor exceptions to be mentioned.

THE RITE OF BAPTISM[1]

The first part of the rite (1–5) reproduces in outline the ceremonies of enrolling a catechumen. It could take place at any time. The candidates were closely questioned as to their motive, status, and occupation. If this last was one connected with pagan worship, or entailing great risks of apostasy, the candidate had to arrange to find a new one. On being accepted by the Church, the candidate was enrolled as a catechumen of the lowest grade, a "hearer" of the Church's teaching.

This and all the exorcisms of the rite are designed to free the baptismal candidate from the power of Satan. If the candidate were an infant, he was subjected to Satan because of original sin; if an adult, still more subject because of evil inclinations, past sins, and the consequent enslavement of the will.

The sign of the cross, at once the symbol of Christ's triumph and the Christian's strength, is solemnly traced upon the candidate that he may become "a temple of God" as one "destined to be born anew."

Text

Reception of the Catechumen. Time, by appointment; place, at door or vestibule of church.

1. *Priest:* N, what dost thou ask of the Church of God?
Answer: Faith.
Priest: To what doth faith bring thee?
Answer: Life everlasting.
Priest: If then thou wilt enter into life, keep the commandments. Thou shalt love the Lord thy God with thy whole heart, and with thy whole soul, and with thy whole mind; and thy neighbor as thyself.

2. **The priest breathes gently upon the face of the child, and says once (to each if there are more than one):**

Depart from him (*change personal pronouns according to sex*), thou unclean spirit, and give place to the Holy Ghost the Paraclete.

3. **The priest makes the sign of the cross with his thumb upon the forehead and the breast of the child, saying:**

Receive the sign of the cross upon thy *forehead* and upon thy *heart;* take unto thee the faith of the heavenly commandments, and be thou such in thy ways that thou mayest *be henceforth fit to be a temple of God.*

---

[1]The translation is by Reverend R. E. Power, *The Gift of Life,* reproduced by courtesy of The Liturgical Press.

Let us pray.

GRACIOUSLY hear our prayers, we beseech Thee, O Lord, and protect by Thy unfailing might this soul of Thy choice, N, now marked with the sign of our Lord's holy Cross, that holding to his first knowledge of Thy infinite perfection, he may deserve, by keeping Thy commandments, to come to the glory *destined for those who are born anew:* Through Christ our Lord. Amen.

4. The priest lays his hand upon the head of the child (or of each), and afterwards holding the hand extended, he says (in the plural for more than one):

The laying on of hands is always one of the Church's most solemn rites. Here it is an act of appropriation: she acknowledges the candidate as her own, places a protecting hand upon him, and commends him meanwhile to God as one now "signed with the seal of God's Wisdom," the cross.

Let us pray.

ALMIGHTY, everlasting God, Father of our Lord Jesus Christ, deign to look with favor upon Thy servant N, whom Thou hast been pleased to call to the beginnings of faith. Heal him of all blindness of heart; sunder all the snares of the enemy in which he has been entangled; open to him, O Lord, the gate of Thy fatherly love, that *signed with the seal of Thy wisdom,* he may be free from the corruption of all wicked desires, and under the blessed influence of Thy commandments *may he serve Thee gladly in Thy Church,* advancing in perfection from day to day: Through the same Christ our Lord. Amen.

Salt was for the ancients the universal instrument of purification

5. The priest blesses salt, which, once blessed, may be used at any

and preservation. Salt is here blessed, and put upon the tongue of the candidate in order to give expression to the Church's desire that he be preserved from the corruption of sin, and given a relish for heavenly doctrine.

With this giving of blessed salt, a rite which was repeated over and over during the catechumenate, the enrolling of the catechumen was terminated.

time thereafter for the same purpose, in which case the following prayer is omitted.

Blessing of the Salt

I purge thee of evil, creature of salt, in the name of God the Father Almighty, and in the charity of our Lord Jesus Christ, and in the power of the Holy Ghost. I purge thee of evil by the living God, the true God, the holy God, by God who hath provided thee for the well-being of mankind, and commanded that thou be consecrated by His servants for those who come unto the life of faith, so that in the name of the Holy Trinity, *thou mayest be made a means of spiritual aid to drive the enemy away.* We therefore implore Thee, O Lord our God, to make holy with Thy sanctification and to bless with Thy blessing, this creature of salt, *that it may become to all who receive it, an effective remedy,* working ever within them; in the name of the same Jesus Christ our Lord, who shall come to judge the living and the dead and the world by fire. Amen.

The priest puts a little of the blessed salt into the mouth of the child, saying (to each):

N, receive the salt of wisdom; may it be unto thee an earnest of God's favor unto life everlasting. Amen.
Priest: Peace be with thee.
Answer: And with thy spirit.
After that the priest says (plural for more than one):

Let us pray.

O GOD of our fathers, Source of all truth, most humbly we pray Thee, of Thy goodness, to look with favor upon Thy servant N, and permit not that he, who now tastes this first morsel of salt, should hunger any more, but rather may he abound in heavenly food, that he may be always fervent of spirit, joyful in hope, always honoring Thy holy Name. Lead him to the font of the new and better birth, that as one of Thy faithful he may deserve to win the everlasting reward which Thou has promised: Through Christ our Lord. Amen.

The rites which follow next (6–7) recall the first great "scrutiny" of the Wednesday after the third Sunday of Lent. The catechumens, now advanced to the rank of "petitioners" for baptism, were being instructed daily and subjected to rigid examinations. Typical elements of the ceremonial part of these scrutinies are here preserved, a repetition of the exorcism, a renewed signing with the cross, and a reiteration of the Church's maternal solicitude as portrayed in the laying on of hands, and an earnest prayer on behalf of the neophytes.

6. *Priest:* I bid thee begone, unclean spirit, in the name of the Father, and of the Son, and of the Holy Ghost; that thou depart and keep far from this servant of God, N, for He commands thee, accursed demon, who trod the waves under foot and extended a helping hand to Peter about to sink. Therefore, accursed fiend, acknowledge thy doom and give honor to the living and true God, give honor to Jesus Christ, His Son, and to the Holy Ghost, and keep far from this servant of God, because Jesus Christ our Lord and God has been pleased to call him to His holy grace and blessing, even to the font of baptism. *(The priest signs the child [or each] saying): And this sign of the holy cross, which we trace upon his forehead, do thou,*

accursed fiend, *never dare to violate:* Through Christ our Lord. Amen.

7. Continuing, the priest lays his hand upon the head of the child (or of each), and then holding the hand extended, he says (in the plural for more than one):

Let us pray.

HOLY Lord, Father almighty, eternal God, author of the light of truth, I earnestly call down upon this Thy servant Thy eternal and all-holy love, that Thou wouldst *be pleased to guide him with the light of Thy wisdom.* Make him pure and holy, *give him skill to learn the truth,* that having been deemed worthy of the grace of Thy baptism, he may persevere in firm hope, right purpose, and holy doctrine: Through Christ our Lord. Amen.

The rites thus far considered are nowadays performed at the door of the church, within the vestibule.

Admittance to the Holy Place and Progress to the Font

The next rites (8-10) enshrine what remains of the most beautiful of the ancient Roman initiation forms. This was the "Great Scrutiny," called also "The Opening of the Ears." This took place on Wednesday of the fourth week of Lent, in the great basilica at St. Paul's tomb.

The final sifting of the catechumens had now been made, and the chosen ones were henceforth known as the "elect." After the Gradual of the Mass on this day, four deacons entered in cere-

8. The priest places the end of the stole, which hangs from his left shoulder, upon the child (the first, if there are more than one) and leads him into the church, saying:
N, enter into the temple of God, that thou mayest *have part with Christ,* unto life everlasting. Amen.

9. After they have entered the church, the priest, leading the way to the font, says aloud, together with the sponsors, the Apostles' Creed and the Lord's Prayer.

I BELIEVE in God the Father almighty, Creator of heaven and

monious fashion, carrying Gospel books, which were deposited on the four corners of the altar. Whereupon a short discourse characterized each gospel in turn, and a deacon chanted its opening passage. Thereupon the *Creed,* which it was forbidden to write, was recited for the catechumens, and then in turn recited *by* the catechumens. Lastly the *Our Father* was recited and explained clause by clause.

The final selection of the catechumens is mirrored in our rites now by the admission at this point to the baptistry. The "giving" and the "giving back" of the *Creed* and *Our Father* are indicated by their recital in common on the way to the baptistry.

The short bidding to enter the church (8) is of medieval composition.

On the morning we call Holy Saturday, took place a ceremonial examination, which, too, is reflected still in our rites. There was first the definitive exorcism of the Evil One (11–13), "that he keep far from this creature of God's making," (soon to be) "a temple of the living God."

Ancient pagan Romans used

earth. And in Jesus Christ, His only Son, our Lord, who was conceived by the Holy Ghost, born of the Virgin Mary, suffered under Pontius Pilate, was crucified, died and was buried. He descended into hell, the third day He rose again from the dead. He ascended into heaven, and sitteth at the right hand of God the Father almighty; from thence He shall come to judge the living and the dead. I believe in the Holy Ghost, the Holy Catholic Church, the communion of saints, the forgiveness of sins, the resurrection of the body, and life everlasting. Amen.

10. OUR Father, who art in heaven, hallowed be Thy name. Thy Kingdom come. Thy will be done on earth, as it is in heaven. Give us this day our daily bread. And forgive us our trespasses, as we forgive them that trespass against us. And lead us not into temptation, but deliver us from evil. Amen.

11.   Final Preparation

Place: at entrance of baptistry
Then before entering the baptistry, with his back to the gate of the baptistry, the priest says:

I bid thee begone, unclean spirit, if any remain, in the name of God the Father almighty, and in the name of Jesus Christ, His Son, our Lord and Judge, and in the power of the Holy Ghost, that you keep saliva as an instrument of diabolic exorcism; ancient Christian Romans remembered how on occasions Christ had used it in His healing, as, for instance, on that occasion in the Decapolis, when they brought Him one deaf and dumb: "He thrust His fingers into the man's ears, and touched his tongue with spittle. And looking up to heaven, He sighed, and saith to him: 'Ephpheta, that is, Be thou opened!' And straightway the man's ears were opened, and the bond of his tongue was loosened" (Mark vii,32–36).

Re-enacting this ceremony in its entirety was liable to give some offense, and hence, as St. Ambrose explains, "For the sake of propriety, the nostrils are touched instead of the tongue."

The solemn forswearing of Satan (13), was followed formerly by a solemn swearing of allegiance to Christ. Even though the ceremonial oath has disappeared, this remains the last and most formal step the neophyte can take in entering the service of Christ. The real incorporation is effected by Christ.

Enrolled as a soldier, the neophyte is anointed with oil for the contest with the world, even as athletes used to strengthen their bodies with anointing.

far from this creature of God's making, N, whom our Lord has been pleased to call to His holy temple, *that he also might be made a temple of the living God*, and that the Holy Ghost might dwell within him: Through the same Christ our Lord, who shall come to judge the living and the dead, and the world by fire. Amen.

12. The priest takes a little saliva on his thumb, and touches the ears and the nostrils of the child (or each) saying (while he touches the ears):

Ephpheta, which is, Be thou opened.

Then touching the nostrils, he says:

Unto the odor of sweetness. But thou, spirit of evil, begone; for the judgment of God is at hand.

13. The priest now questions the one to be baptized (or each), as follows:

N, dost thou renounce satan?
Answer: I do renounce him.
Priest: And all his works?
Answer: I do renounce them.
Priest: And all his pomps?
Answer: I do renounce them.

14. The priest dips his thumb in the Oil of Catechumens, and anoints the child (each) on the breast and between the shoulders in the form of a cross, saying once (to each):

I anoint thee with the oil of salvation in Christ Jesus our Lord, that thou mayest have life everlasting. Amen.

The priest wipes his thumb and the anointed places with cotton wadding, or other such thing.

The final act of the neophyte's initiation now begins. The time was as near as possible to the momentous hour wherein Christ "rose again for our justification" (Rom. iv,25); the place was the celebrated baptistry of the Lateran Basilica.

15. The Baptism

Place: at the fountain.

Standing in the same place, outside the railing or grille, he takes off the violet stole, and puts on a white one. Then he enters the baptistry, as do also the sponsors with the child. The priest, at the font, interrogates again the one to be baptized, the sponsors answering for a little child.

Priest: N, dost thou believe in God the Father almighty, Creator of heaven and earth?
Answer: I do believe.
Priest: Dost thou believe in Jesus Christ, His only Son, our Lord, who was born and who suffered for us?
Answer: I do believe.
Priest: Dost thou believe also in the Holy Ghost, the holy Catholic Church, the communion of saints, the forgiveness of sins, the resurrection of the body, and life everlasting?
Answer: I do believe.

Then the priest says (to each):

N, wilt thou be baptized?
Answer: I will.

Grouped before the bishop, the candidates make a final profession of faith, then one by one they are led down several steps into the saving laver, to be immersed in mystic death to self and to sin, to rise as ingrafted members of the Mystical Body. "It is no longer I that live; it is Christ that liveth in me" (Gal. ii,20); this is not only the ardent cry of a St. Paul; it is the act of faith of every Christian.

16. Then the godfather, or godmother, or both if there are two sponsors, holding the child (touching an adult), the priest takes baptismal water in a small vessel or pitcher, and pours it three times upon the head of the child in the form of a cross, say-

ing at the same time, only once, distinctly and attentively:

The essential form of baptism is contained in this short formula. This is all that is said by a lay person in administering this sacrament in an emergency.

N, I baptize thee in the name of the Father (*pouring the first time*), and of the Son (*pouring the second time*), and of the Holy Ghost (*pouring the third time*).

Where there is a custom of baptizing by immersion, the priest takes the child, and being careful that it come to no harm, he immerses it three times, using the same words as above.

Royal Unction of the Lord's Adopted

In ancient times the new members of Christ were confirmed immediately after baptism. So, after being clothed with new and snow-white garments, they were led before the bishop that he might impart the plenitude of the Holy Spirit. This anointing with chrism here preserved in our rite is a distant reminder of the former anointing of the confirmation.

17. Then the priest dips his thumb in the holy chrism, and anoints the child (each) on the crown of the head, in the form of a cross, saying:

MAY God almighty, the Father of our Lord Jesus Christ, *who has given thee a new life by water and the Holy Ghost,* and granted thee remission of all sins, may He anoint thee with the chrism of salvation in the same Christ Jesus our Lord, unto life everlasting. Amen.
Priest: Peace be to thee.
Answer: And with thy spirit.

Bestowal of Symbolic Gifts

In lieu of the new robes formerly given to the baptized as they emerged from the font, the Church now gives a veil by way of preserving this beautiful bit of symbolism. This prayer form is of medieval Gallican origin.

18. Having wiped his thumb and the anointed place, and laid a linen cloth upon the head of the child, in lieu of a white garment, he says (to each):

Receive this white garment, which mayest thou wear without stain before the judgment seat of our Lord

Jesus Christ, that thou mayest have life everlasting. Amen.

19. The priest gives to the baptized (or to the sponsor) a lighted candle, saying (to each):

Receive this burning light, and without fail be true to thy baptism; keep the commandments of God, that when our Lord come to claim His own, thou mayest be worthy to greet Him with all the saints in the heavenly court, and live forever and ever. Amen.

It was with burning torches held aloft that the "newborn from the dead" here marched into the basilica, singing: "I will go unto the altar of God," for their first Holy Mass and Communion in the dawn of Easter morning. To betoken the joy and sweetness of the hour they were at the holy table given to partake of milk and honey.

The Dismissal in Peace

20. Last of all, he says (plural for more than one):

N, go in peace and may the Lord be with thee. Amen.

The rite above described is to be used also when a deacon baptizes solemnly by special permission, but the salt and the water must have been blessed by a priest.

Summary. Such are the baptismal rites at present as of old. They are so redolent of chaste joy, unbounded hope and trust, that they disclose for us, with a vividness that is extraordinary, the wickedness of sin, the wonder of its effacement, this miracle of the New Birth by which we are made sons of the Most High.

Seventeenth-Century Source Material

(Louis Bourdaloue, S.J. (1632–1704), "the king of preachers and preacher of kings," was one of the greatest lights of the Christian pulpit: he is speaking of our duties toward the Church.)

The Church is a body, I mean a mystical body and a moral one. This body has a Head, who is Jesus Christ, and He has members, and these are the faithful. So the Apostle St. Paul teaches us in various passages, but especially in his *Epistle to the Ephesians,* where he speaks as follows in reference to Jesus Christ:

> "He [God] hath subjected all things beneath His feet," Ps. viii,6
> and hath given Him for supreme Head to the Church,
>   which is His body,
> the fulness of Him who is wholly fulfilled in all. Eph. i,22,23

As if the great Apostle should say: My brethren, we make but one body with Jesus Christ and in Jesus Christ. The assembly of all the faithful, united to Jesus Christ by faith, behold the body of the Church: But the faithful themselves taken separately and considered each one individually, behold the members of the Church. The more the members grow and increase in strength, the more the body deriveth fullness and acquisition of strength: and even the Head Himself receives additional perfection in His quality as Head in the measure in which the body, by the union of its members, strengthens and perfects itself. And this character, our being not only children of the Church, but members of the Church, this is one of the most beautiful titles in which we may glory before God and in respect to God. As members of the Church we belong in a special way to Jesus Christ, since in virtue of the Baptism we have received, and by which we were engrafted into the body of the Church, we have contracted a very close and intimate relationship with Jesus Christ.

Topics for Further Discussion:

The disposition of Providence whereby anyone, even a non-Catholic, can validly baptize.

Since faith and contrition are absolute requisites for adult baptism, the justification of the practice of infant baptism.

The purpose, requisites, and duties of a sponsor at baptism.

The three modes of baptism, by immersion (whole or partial), by infusion (pouring), and by sprinkling.

The use in case of urgent necessity of water mixed with foreign matter, tea, etc.

Readings:

A. d'Alès, *Baptism and Confirmation* (St. Louis: Herder, 1929).
F. X. Doyle, *The Wonderful Sacraments* (New York: Benziger, 1924); "Baptism," pp. 53–89.
W. H. Fanning, "Baptism," *CE.*
C. Grimaud–J. F. Newcomb, *One Only Christ* (New York: Benziger, 1939); " 'Our' Deification," pp. 99–107.

F. C. Kolbe, *The Four Mysteries of the Faith* (New York: Longmans, Green, 1926); "The Third Mystery as Divine Sonship," pp. 71–77.

C. Lattey, *Six Sacraments, Papers Read at the Summer School of Catholic Studies, Cambridge, 1929* (St. Louis: Herder, 1930); "Baptism," pp. 73–110.

C. Marmion, *Christ the Life of the Soul* (St. Louis: Herder, 1923); "Baptism," pp. 152–168.

J. P. Murphy, *The Sacrament of Baptism*, TF, 22.

M. Perkins, *Speaking of How to Pray* (New York: Sheed & Ward, 1944); "The Mighty Working of His Power," pp. 79–104.

R. Plus, *Baptism and Confirmation* (London: Burns, Oates and Washbourne, 1930).

W. F. Robison, *The Seven-Fold Gift* (St. Louis: Herder, 1922); "The Gate of Life," pp. 1–30.

Chapter XVIII

"RADIOACTIVE" CATHOLICS

*Be strengthened powerfully
through the Spirit
in the inward man* (Eph.
iii,16).

ADULT Catholics of our day, and especially college-trained Catholics, are expected by the Holy See to be Christianizing as well as Christian souls. Addressing Catholic collegians of Italy, Pope Pius XI spoke of them as co-apostles, centers radiating beneficent activity even as "radioactive focuses" ceaselessly raying forth Christlike influence. It may strike the modern ear as something of a surprise, not to say anticlimax, to hear the same pontiff say that the zeal and the inexhaustible dynamism needed for such an apostolate is a legacy of the sacrament of confirmation. "If one consider well," writes the Holy Father, "it will be seen that the very sacraments of Baptism and Confirmation impose — among other *obligations* — this Apostolate of Catholic Action. . . . Through *Confirmation* we become soldiers of Christ. A soldier must labor and fight not so much for himself as for others." Nor does it escape the Holy Father that this link with confirmation strikes us as novel. In fact the official Italian *Manual of Catholic Action* elaborates this very idea:

To Cardinal Cerejeira, 1934

Confirmation could well be called the Sacrament of Catholic Action. But the dogmatic truths, from which the duty of Apostolate comes forth as a practical corollary, are but little known, little meditated by Christians. In them, too often, the Catholic sense is lacking, and the noble instinct of Apostolate. *Catholic Action must therefore especially study this Sacrament.*[1]

[1] L. Civardi, *A Manual of Catholic Action* (New York: Sheed and Ward, 1936), p. 68; quoted with permission.

"The liturgy, well and lovingly understood," continues the papal spokesman in the passage quoted, "gives great help herein." Following such pointed suggestions, alert Catholics the world over are now reappraising the abiding gifts and graces they received in childhood on the day of their confirmation. Is this sacrament making us "radioactive focuses" of the Catholic way of living?

Supernatural Coming of Age. Baptism alone excepted, no one incident of childhood can compare with the reception of confirmation as far as the supernatural life is concerned. No matter how young or how old one may be when he receives this sacrament, it is confirmation that marks the passage from supernatural childhood to *supernatural maturity.* Confirmation is the Catholic's coming of age, attaining his majority, with the strength, the personal *and social* rights and duties of an adult. St. Thomas phrases this with his customary clarity in saying: "The Sacrament of Confirmation confers the fulness of the Holy Spirit in view of the spiritual vigor that befits the adult man. Now man, when adult, begins to communicate his actions to others, whereas at first he lived only to himself." The same idea is set out more fully in another luminous passage of the *Summa:*

S.T. III. Q. lxxii, a.2

> Just as Baptism is a spiritual regeneration unto Christian life, so also is Confirmation a certain spiritual growth bringing man to perfect spiritual age. But it is evident, from a comparison with the life of the body, that the action which is proper to man immediately after birth, is different from the action which is proper to him when he has come to perfect age. And therefore by the sacrament of Confirmation man is given a spiritual power in respect of sacred actions other than those in respect of which he receives power at Baptism. For in Baptism he receives *power to do those things which pertain to his own salvation,* forasmuch as he lives to himself: whereas *in Confirmation he receives power to do those things which pertain to spiritual combat with enemies of the Faith.*

Ibid., a.5

Since we have been confirmed, we are no longer children in the supernatural order, but men. Let us then, with the help of the liturgy, scrutinize this testimonial of our maturity as citizens in the City of God.

Twofold Sign. To begin with the external *sign* of the sacrament, or perhaps one should say "signs," for there are two external features here, the one an anointing with oil, the other a laying on of hands. Both are

Seal of the gift of the Spirit

elemental ritual acts to be met often in natural religions as well as in the revealed religions of Judaism and Christianity.

Anointing. In the Orient the household uses of *oil* were surprisingly varied: in the kitchen it was in constant demand in preparing the foods; in the dining room it was a condiment; in the bath it was the basis of all soaps, unguents, and perfumes (the liberal use of which was a recognized token of joy); in the sickroom it was the instrument of healing; in the reception room it was used to anoint the heads of guests; throughout the whole house it was burned in the lamps. How natural that it should enter conspicuously into the rites of religion, and should have been used in a solemn anointing of kings and prophets and priests! In another connection mention was made of the fact that in Jewish speech one appointed by God for certain special works was by that very fact called "anointed," and that the word *Messiah* is literally rendered "The Anointed One." If *Christians* (the *anointed*) were to become incorporated into Christ (the Anointed), was it not under the circumstances almost inevitable that an anointing with perfumed oil should become an official sign thereof?

This root meaning of "Christian" as "anointed" was sometimes made a matter of taunt against the Church. Thus, about the year 180, we find Theophilus, Bishop of Antioch (where the name originated) defending the name as follows:

> When you laugh at me, calling me a Christian, you do not know what you are saying. First, that which is anointed is sweet and serviceable, and ought not to be laughed at. What ship can be serviceable and seaworthy, unless it be first anointed? Or what tower or house is sightly or serviceable when it has not been anointed? What man, on entering into this life, or when contending in the games, is not anointed with oil? What work can be comely and sightly if it be not anointed and polished? Then even the air and all that is under heaven is, in a kind of way, anointed with light and spirit, and do you not wish to be anointed with the oil of God? We therefore are called Christians on this account, because we are anointed with the oil of God.

Apol. ad Autol.
I,12

Laying On of Hands. Similarly the laying on of hands was a religious rite carrying men's thoughts back through immemorial years, as for instance, to the dying Jacob blessing his sons. Jews would recall how with this solemn act was invested the ministry of the Synagogue. Early Christian neophytes from non-Jewish circles would more readily recall how Christ had laid His hands on the sick in healing, and how this was the usual ceremony of ordination in the *Acts*. This, too, was an appropriate sign to betoken the grant of full and perfect manhood in the supernatural life, and so it is associated with the sacrament of confirmation.

Divine Guest Received. One of the first of the many names by which this sacrament has been known was "Conferring the Holy Ghost." This was a technical term having a definite and circumscribed meaning. "Have you received the Holy Ghost?" conveyed the same idea as our words, "Have you been confirmed?" Now, what is the reality expressed in those words, "conferring the Holy Ghost"? First of all, let us recall momentarily whom we are speaking of as being conferred on us in confirmation. The Holy Ghost is the Third Person of the Triune God, equal from all eternity to the Father and the Son, but distinguished from Father and Son by reason of the proper manner in which He possesses the Divine Nature. God the Father is the first divine Person; God the Son is the second divine Person, begotten eternally of the Father by an act of intellectual generation; God the Holy Ghost is the third divine Person, who proceeds eternally from the Father and the Son as the term of their mutual love. The Holy Spirit, of His very nature, is an outpouring and overflowing of divine life and love and holiness: He is, as it were, God's love personified! Of old God had promised by the prophets that He should pour out His Spirit upon all flesh, and Christ clarified this ancient promise by foretelling His part in its fulfillment:

> I send the promise of My Father upon you;
>> but stay you in the city
> until you be endued with power from on high.   Luke xxiv,49

> I will ask the Father
>> and He shall give you
>> another Advocate,
> that He may abide with you forever.   John xiv,16

On Pentecost the mighty wind and the visible tongues of fire were reserved for those in the upper chamber, but the lifegiving Spirit was for all: "We are all given to drink of the one Spirit." The Advocate and Helper abides, a permanent Guest, in each of us as in a temple, to be the glad assurance of our divine sonship, to help us pray, to be to the Father, as a *Pledge*, or Hostage one might almost say in all wonder and reverence.   I Cor. xii,13 I Cor. iii,16 Rom. viii,16 Rom. viii,26 II Cor. i,22

Effects of Sacrament. Two *consequences* of the reception of confirmation are of very special importance: that we thereby share in a higher degree than at baptism in the general priesthood of Christ, and that it gives us a solemn assurance that we *have the strength* to maintain the supernatural life within us, despite all the temptations and storms of life.

Lay Priesthood. It is said in another connection that all Christians share in the priesthood of Christ according to the graduated characters they receive at baptism, at confirmation, and at holy orders. "In a sacramental character," says St. Thomas, *"Christ's faithful have a share in the priesthood of Christ,* in the sense that as Christ has the full power of a spiritual priesthood, so the faithful are likened to Him by sharing a certain spiritual *power* with regard to the sacraments and to things pertaining to divine worship." Baptism is the lowest degree of this participation; it gives the baptized such a share in Christ's priestly functions as minor children have in the actions of a parent. It is a chiefly *passive* sharing. *Confirmation* advances the Christian to the status of an adult with the right and duty of *actively* sharing as co-workers with Christ in His priestly functions, as St. Thomas has it, especially "in those things which pertain to the spiritual combat with the enemies of the Faith." The confirmation *character* is the soul's permanent consecration and deputation for the multiple engagements of social Catholicism. Our duty thus becomes clear, once we realize our abiding capacity, through this character, to be "radioactive" Catholics, bodying forth the Light which is come for the life of the world.

S.T. III. Q. lxiii, a.5

Ibid., Q. lxxii, a.5

Christ-Strong in the Spirit. If the Christian is early called upon to wage battle for his faith and for his salvation, he is in confirmation given the strength to wield the arms of light, and confront danger confidently, knowing that "the Spirit . . . beareth up our weakness." The Christian possesses permanent sacramental powers because "the anointing . . . received from Him abideth." This Christian attitude of humble trust and confidence has nothing of the arrogant error of those who think they are predestined to heaven no matter what they may do. Rather the Christian realizes his own abiding capacity to ruin everything, but knows, too, that as long as he has good will, he will be strengthened, so that

Rom. viii,26

I John ii,27

> temptation will not come upon him
> but such as he can bear;
> and God is faithful
> and will not suffer you to be tempted
> beyond your strength.

I Cor. x,13 Confirmation is the Christian's supernatural life assurance.

Apostolic Practice. The Gospels do not tell us when or how Christ *instituted* this sacrament, but the *Acts* show as clearly as could be desired, the *practice of the apostolic Church*. There was the instance of the evangelization of Samaria by the deacon Philip. He had preached and had begun the initiation of the believers with baptism. Later on the Apostles (the highest grade of the priesthood) came to complete the work by conferring the Holy Ghost. As St. Luke narrates:

> But when they believed
> Philip's preaching of the gospel
> of the kingdom of God
> and of the name of Jesus Christ,
> they were baptized, both men and women. . . .
>
> Now when the Apostles in Jerusalem
> heard that Samaria had accepted the word of God,
> they sent to them Peter and John,
> who went down and prayed for them,
> that they might receive the Holy Spirit;
> for as yet He was fallen upon none of them,
> but they had *only* been baptized
> in the name of the Lord Jesus.
> *Then they laid their hands upon them,*
> *and they received the Holy Spirit.*
> But when Simon saw
> that the Spirit was given
> through the laying on of the Apostles' hands . . .

Acts viii,12–19

Paul at Ephesus. Some twenty years later, on landing at Ephesus, St. Paul encountered a group of twelve people, who were earnest disciples of Christ. Paul took them for baptized Christians, and asked, as a routine matter:

> "Did ye receive the Holy Spirit when ye believed?"
> But they answered,
> "Nay, we have not even heard
> Whether there be a Holy Spirit."

> And he said: "What baptism, then, did ye reccive?"
> They said: "The baptism of John [the Baptist]."

> Then Paul said:
> "John baptized with **a baptism of repentance,**

> telling the people that they were to believe
> in Him who was to come after him,
> that is, in Jesus."

> Upon hearing this
> they were baptized
> in the name of the Lord Jesus;
> *and when Paul laid his hands on them,*
> *the Holy Spirit came upon them,*
> and they spoke in tongues and prophesied.

Acts xix,2–7

Time of Administration. Since confirmation presupposes and complements *baptism*, the procedure of Paul on this occasion of confirming the neophytes immediately after baptizing them was the normal one in Christian antiquity. Even after infant baptism had become the rule, the Church still kept for a time the custom of confirming infants. This usage is still retained in the Oriental churches, and has not entirely disappeared in the West. There is no doctrinal difficulty involved in the practice, since the conferring of adult *supernatural* standing in no wise depends upon natural age, but the Church came gradually to prefer that this sacrament should be administered *when it is needed;* namely, when the child begins to use his rational faculties (Canon 788), and so must begin to fight for the preservation of the great gift of supernatural life he possesses as a Christian. The Church still regards as ideal that the sacraments be received in the ancient order, baptism, confirmation, Holy Eucharist, but only when this does not entail any delay in admitting the child to eat at the Sacred Table.

The instructive rite of confirmation follows:

THE RITE OF CONFIRMATION[2]

This introductory versicle admirably expresses the purpose of the sacrament of confirmation. It and the subsequent verses have formed part of the rite since the Middle Ages.

Those who are to be confirmed kneel with hands joined before the bishop, who, standing with hands joined, says:

Versicle: May the Holy Ghost come upon you, and may the power of the Most High keep you from sin.
Response: Amen.
V. Our help is in the name of the Lord.
R. Who made heaven and earth.
V. Lord, hear my prayer.
R. And let my cry come unto Thee.
V. The Lord be with you.
R. And with thy spirit.

Then with hands extended above those who are to be confirmed, he says:

Let us pray.

This beautiful prayer, the solemnity of which is heightened by the fourfold "Amen," is the oldest part of the text of this rite. It is contained in a ritual tradition ascribed to Pope Gelasius (492–496). The description of the "sevenfold Spirit" is a citation from the Messianic prophecy of Isaias, of about 800 B.C.:

And the Spirit of the Lord shall
    rest on Him,
  the Spirit of wisdom and under-
    standing,
  the Spirit of counsel and of
    fortitude,

ALMIGHTY, everlasting God, who hast deigned to bring these Thy servants to a new life by water and the Holy Ghost and hast granted them remission of all their sins, send forth upon them Thy sevenfold Spirit of Holiness, the Paraclete from heaven.
R. Amen.
The Spirit of wisdom and of understanding.
R. Amen.
The Spirit of counsel and of fortitude.
R. Amen.

---

[2]The translation is by Reverend R. E. Power, *The Seal of the Spirit*, reproduced by courtesy of The Liturgical Press.

the Spirit of knowledge and of godliness,

And He shall be filled with the Spirit of the fear of the Lord. (Isa. xi,23.)

It will be noted that this ancient prayer catches up and elaborates the seventh token of the Spirit, according to Isaias, and links it with a solemn sign of the cross. In olden times, when confirmation was administered immediately after baptism, priests or other attendants could help in anointing the sense organs and other parts of the body, but the signing of the forehead with chrism was reserved to the bishop. This is the specific confirmation anointing.

The words here said by the bishop express the final taking possession of the candidate by the power of Christ's cross, and the strengthening that is being imparted. The precise formula was not fixed by Christ, and this one was not adopted as final in the Western Church until the Middle Ages. Older forms abounded in the ritual books. The oldest Roman form we know comes from St. Hippolytus (225): "*I anoint you with holy oil in the Lord the Father Almighty, and Christ Jesus and the Holy Ghost.*" In the ritual of Pope Gelasius (492–496) the form was simply: "*The seal of Christ unto life everlasting,*" which closely resembles that still used in the Oriental churches.

The Spirit of knowledge and of piety.
R. Amen.

FILL them with the Spirit of Thy fear, and graciously seal them with the sign of the cross unto life everlasting, through the same Jesus Christ, Thy Son, our Lord, who liveth and reigneth with Thee, in the unity of the same Holy Ghost, God through all eternity.
R. Amen.

Then the bishop confirms them as they kneel in order; first the boys and the men, then the girls and the women. In each case, he is told the name to be taken in confirmation and, dipping the tip of his thumb in the holy chrism, he confirms the person as follows:

N, I seal thee with the sign of the ✠ cross, and I confirm thee with the chrism of salvation, in the name of the Father, ✠ and of the Son, ✠ and of the Holy ✠ Ghost.
R. Amen.

Before beginning to say these words, the bishop lays his right hand upon the head of the one to be confirmed, and as he says "of the cross," he makes the sign of the cross with the holy chrism

The slight blow on the cheek, now usually explained as a reminder that those confirmed must be ready to suffer all things for their Faith, is a ceremonial adaptation of the embrace and kiss originally given adult converts. The rite became a fatherly pat on the cheek when the candidates were normally children. The old salutation remains, *"Peace!"*

These two prayers, and the intervening versicles, eloquently express the idea that the Spirit of God now inhabits the Christian heart as in a temple, but a frail and imperfect temple, one needing always to be perfected. As long as the sovereignty of free will remains, it is possible to reject God and the supernatural order. Even in that case, because of the character, as St. Chrysostom says, "We may be recognized as deserters" (In I Cor. ii,1). St. Ambrose dwells upon the more consoling truth: "We are sealed by the Spirit that we may be able to keep within the splendor and likeness of Him and His grace . . . *that the Holy Ghost may express in us a picture of His heavenly likeness.*"

Let us listen to a Pentecost sermon by St. Augustine: "The Apostle says, 'One body, one spirit.' Listen, members of that body! The body is made up of many members and one spirit quickens them all. Behold, by the spirit of a man, by which I myself am a man, I hold

upon the forehead. Continuing, he makes the sign of the cross over the person at the name of each of the three divine persons.

Then he strikes the confirmed lightly upon the cheek, saying:

Peace be with thee.

An attending priest removes the holy chrism from the forehead with cotton batting, which is afterwards burned.

After washing his hands, the bishop reads the Antiphon:

PRESERVE, O God, what Thou hast wrought in us, from out Thy holy temple which is in Jerusalem. Glory be to the Father and to the Son and to the Holy Ghost. As it was in the beginning, is now, and ever shall be, world without end. Amen.

Then turning to the altar, with hands joined he says:

V. Show unto us, O Lord, Thy mercy.

R. And grant us Thy salvation.

V. Lord, hear my prayer.

R. And let my cry come unto Thee.

V. The Lord be with you.

R. And with thy spirit.

together all the members; I command them to move; I direct the eyes to see, the ears to hear, the tongue to speak, the hands to work, the feet to walk. The offices of the members are divided severally, but one spirit holds all in one. . . . What our spirit — that is, our soul — is to our members, that the Holy Ghost is to the members of Christ, to the body of Christ, which is the Church. Therefore the Apostle, when he had spoken of the one body, lest we should suppose it to be a dead body, says 'There is one body.' I ask: 'Is this body alive?' It is alive. Whence? From the one Spirit. 'There is one Spirit'" (*Sermon 267*).

Two final blessings complete the ceremony. The last of these is justly cherished for its Scriptural language, its depth of feeling, and its venerable antiquity.

Let us pray.

O GOD, who didst give the Holy Ghost to Thy Apostles, and didst will that He should be given through them and their successors to the rest of the faithful, look with favor upon our lowly ministration, and grant that the same Holy Spirit, coming upon those whose foreheads we have anointed with the sacred Chrism and sealed with the sign of the holy cross, may graciously consecrate their hearts as a temple of His glory by dwelling within them: Thou who with the Father and the same Holy Ghost, livest and reignest, God through all eternity.
R. Amen.

Then the bishop says:
Behold, thus shall everyone be blessed that feareth the Lord.
Turning to those who have been confirmed, and making the sign of the cross over them, he blesses them as follows:

THE Lord bless you out of Sion, that you may see the blessings of Jerusalem all the days of your life and may have life everlasting.
R. Amen.

Summary. Confirmation is a sacrament, in which, through anointing and the imposition of hands, the Christian initiation is completed in the conferring of the Holy Ghost; it advances the Christian to adult standing in the Church, and associates him with the highest grade of the priesthood of the laity; it is named from its distinctive characteristic of imparting spiritual strength and confident assurance in God.

Eighteenth-Century Source Material

(Long before 1784, when John Carroll became Vicar-Apostolic and Bishop, the position of American colonists, permanently "deprived of the Sacrament of Confirmation," was most acutely felt.)

Now, coming to the rich and populous provinces of *New England* and *New York* one may find many a Catholic here and there, but they have no opportunity of practicing their religion as no priest visits them, and if we are to judge of the future from the present conditions of the inhabitants, there is not much likelihood that Catholic priests will be permitted to enter these provinces. . . .

Among the old possessions of Great Britain on the continent of America, the only colonies in which priests are permanently located are the provinces of *Maryland* and *Pennsylvania*. In the latter, the Catholic Religion was formerly tolerated by law. In *Maryland*, the laws are opposed to it, as in England; however these laws are rarely put into execution and usually there is a sort of tacit toleration.

It is claimed in *Maryland* there must be around sixteen thousand Catholics, of whom about half approach the sacraments. To take care of these there are twelve missionaries of the Society of Jesus.

The number of Catholics in *Pennsylvania* is between six and seven thousand. They have a public church in Philadelphia, which is the capital of the province. They are ministered to by four priests likewise Jesuits. . . .

There are besides some Catholics in *Virginia*, on the confines of *Maryland*, and in those parts of *New Jersey* which border on *Pennsylvania*. But they have no priests permanently residing among them, their spiritual wants being administered to by missionaries from the two provinces above mentioned. As to *Carolina* and *Georgia*, it is impossible to say whether there are any Catholics there or not. One thing is certain, there are no priests in those provinces.

Florida, a province ceded by Spain in the same Treaty of **Paris,** already mentioned, is almost a wilderness, but the few Catholics who have remained there are allowed the freedom of practicing the Catholic religion in the same manner as the inhabitants of Canada.

Louisiana, or the province of *Mississippi,* which formerly belonged to the French, has for the most part been ceded to the English by the same Treaty, that is, up to the Mississippi River, which gives the province its name. The same freedom of worship has been granted in favor of the Catholic inhabitants, of whom there must be a considerable number. But as to how they are taken care of spiritually the writer has no information whatever. . . .

The great distances of these provinces from his residence [in London] hinders him [the Vicar-Apostolic] from visiting them personally. And therefore he cannot have the information necessary to know abuses and to correct them; *he cannot administer the Sacrament of Confirmation to those faithful who remain totally deprived of this spiritual aid;* he cannot furnish them with priests. . . .

If the Sacred Congregation, moved by these considerations . . . considers it meet to create a Vicar-Apostolic over the other English colonies and islands, it seems that the city of Philadelphia in Pennsylvania would be the place best suited for him to reside in. . . . — *Bishop Richard Challoner,* Vicar-Apostolic of London, to Rome, about 1763. (Quoted from Guilday's *Life and Times of John Carroll* by permission of the Encyclopedia Press.)

Topics for Further Discussion:

That priests by delegation can validly confirm.
Circumstances attending the consecration of the chrism.
Purpose and function of sponsors at confirmation.
The confirmation of infants.
The appropriateness of the Western practice in conferring confirmation at the beginning of adolescence.

Readings:

A. d'Alès, *Baptism and Confirmation* (St. Louis: Herder, 1929).
F. X. Doyle, *The Wonderful Sacraments* (New York: Benziger, 1924); "Confirmation," pp. 90–109.
F. C. Kolbe, *The Sacrament of Confirmation,* TF, 23.
M. Laros, *Confirmation in the Modern World* (New York: Sheed and Ward, 1938); "The Sacrament of Personality," pp. 17–34; "The Sacrament of Catholic Action," pp. 89–114.
C. Lattey, *Six Sacraments, Papers Read at the Summer School of Catholic*

Studies, Cambridge, 1929 (St. Louis: Herder, 1930); Canon George, "Confirmation," pp. 111–130.

M. Perkins, *Speaking of How to Pray* (New York: Sheed & Ward, 1944); "The Oil of Gladness," pp. 105–116.

R. Plus, *Baptism and Confirmation* (London: Burns, Oates and Washbourne, 1930).

W. F. Robison, *The Seven-Fold Gift* (St. Louis: Herder, 1922); "The Soldier's Signing," pp. 31–63.

T. B. Scannell, "Confirmation," *CE*.

Chapter XIX

OUR SUPERSUBSTANTIAL BREAD — EMMANUEL

Give us each day our daily bread
(Luke xi,3).

CONSIDERATION of the Holy Eucharist thus far in this book has been limited to the aspect of *Sacrifice*. There is another important realm of Eucharistic truth, that in which this Trust is commonly designated the *Blessed Sacrament*. The Eucharist is both Sacrifice and Sacrament. Like every *sacrifice*, it enables man to approach God by means of a symbolic gift; like the other *sacraments* the Eucharist enables God to approach man, so to speak, by imparting ever new measures of that God-life which we call sanctifying grace. Above all other sacrifices, the Eucharist stands in unapproachable pre-eminence, the fulfillment of what they merely prefigured. And above the other sacraments, the Eucharist enjoys a parallel superiority, for whereas all the sacraments are channels of Christ's grace, this contains and confers Christ, the very fountainhead of grace, Himself. In fact, the multiple relations of the Sacrament of the Eucharist to the other sacraments seemed to the *Catechism of the Council of Trent* to afford the key to the knowledge of the full truth about the limitless riches it contains. That book suggests:

As, however, no language can convey an adequate idea of its utility and fruits, pastors must be content to treat of one or two points, in order to show what an abundance and profusion of all goods are contained in those sacred mysteries.

This they will in some degree accomplish, if, having explained the efficacy and nature of all the Sacraments, they *compare the Eucharist to a fountain, the other Sacraments to rivulets*. For the Holy Eucharist is truly and necessarily to be called the fountain of all graces, containing, as it does, after an admirable manner, the fountain itself of celestial gifts and graces, and the author of all the Sacraments, Christ,

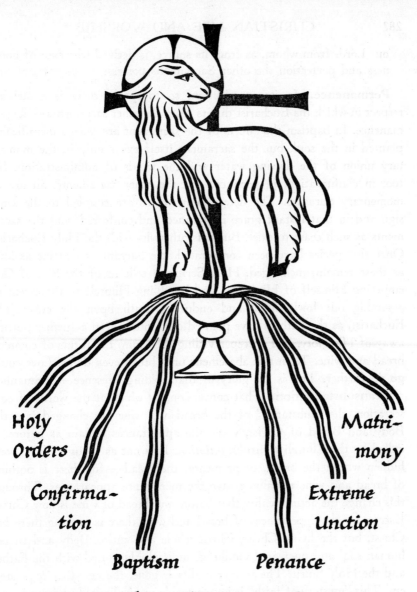

Holy
Orders

Confirma-
tion

Baptism

Matri-
mony

Extreme
Unction

Penance

Compare the Eucharist to a fountain,
the other Sacraments to rivulets.
(Catechism of Trent)

our Lord, from whom, as from its source, is derived whatever of goodness and perfection the other Sacraments possess.

Permanence. In its constitution, so to speak, there is a striking respect in which the Eucharist differs from the other sacraments — its permanence. In baptism the effects of the sacrament are indeed ineradicably planted in the soul, but the sacrament itself exists only in the momentary union of the flowing water and the words of administration. So, too, in confirmation, in penance, and the other sacraments, all are of momentary duration. The determining words are coupled to the sense sign and in that instant grace is signified and conferred, and the sacraments as such cease to exist. But it is otherwise with the Holy Eucharist. Once the species have been consecrated, the Sacrament remains as long as these remain unchanged. Holy Scripture tells us of the Son of God emptying Himself of His glory, and humbling Himself to the extent of assuming our lowly flesh, and enduring death upon the cross. The Eucharist, as the Fathers have pointed out, entails even a further putting away of His glory, and a deeper veiling even unto the forms of common bread and wine. Than this abasement unto bread even divine Love could go no further. This is the glory of that abiding Presence — Emmanuel.

Transubstantiation. That conversion, by which at the words of consecration, the "substance" of the bread and wine are changed into the Body and Blood of Christ, while the appearances remain as before, is called by the Church *transubstantiation*. It is not as though Christ were hidden within the bread, or permeates the bread — for there is nothing of bread and wine remaining save the mere sense appearances. Through this change the actual reality that before was bread or wine is now Christ. Except for the appearances of bread and wine there is nothing there *but* Christ, but the living Christ, Christ whole and entire, Body and Blood, human soul and uncreated Godhead, indissolubly united with the Father and the Holy Spirit. The former reality is gone, the new Reality is present. This "mystery of faith" is impenetrable to our limited understanding. The twentieth-century child (or adult) is taught this great truth of the Eucharist in substantially the same words and phrases as are found in the oldest catechism we have, that of St. Cyril of Jerusalem, of about 347. He wrote:

> In the figure of the bread is given to thee the Body, and in the figure of wine the Blood, so that when thou receivest the Body and Blood of

Christ, thou mayest become of one body and blood with Him; for *thus we are become Christ-bearers (Christophoroi)*, when His Body and His Blood are distributed in our members.

What appears to be bread is not bread, although it seems thus to the taste, but is the Body of Christ. . . . At Cana in Galilee He once changed water into wine which is akin to Blood; and shall we not believe Him when He changes wine into Blood?   *Cat.* **xxii**

Two Uses Enjoined. Concerning this Sacrament, by which Christ has committed Himself to our keeping, we have two commands from divine authority, "Do this in memory of Me," and "Take ye and eat." These two uses, *Sacrifice* and *Communion*, coincide fairly well in actual practice, since Communion is designed primarily as a means of imparting to man the return-graces won by the Sacrifice. So inseparably is the Return-Gift connected with the Gift, that without the Communion of at least the priest there is no *integral* Sacrifice. That this truth was once much more commonly appreciated by the vast multitude of the faithful than it is at the present day may, perhaps, be shown by the popular terms with which Communion was referred to. Formerly the common term in the English language for Communion was "Housel," which means etymologically "Oblation," or "Sacrifice." In our own times we speak of the Host and are surprised to learn that for those who first used the term, "Host" (*hostia*) meant sacrificial victim.

Development Brought Other Uses. Christ once compared His Kingdom to a grain of mustard seed, the smallest of seeds when sown, but capable of becoming a tree of stately proportions. And what has been said by way of incidental illustration in the preceding chapters amply illustrates how the offices of Christian worship have undergone a silent but ceaseless development ever since the Pentecostal bath of fire. Just as the great *dogmas* themselves gradually disclosed, and still disclose, their fullest depths and beauties, so the *devotional life* of the Church has become constantly richer by the never-ending blossoming of Catholic piety. In this slow, expansive process, which one cannot observe from day to day, it may even be said that each succeeding age comes into possession of a deeper and fuller Christianity. On looking back one wonders how former ages got along without what we now find so necessary.

A "Thing" and a "Person." In the history of Eucharistic development *an explicitly conscious devotion* to the Real Presence was reserved for the period beginning roughly with the second Christian millennium. No fact is more essential in any historic study touching the Holy Eucharist than this, because this fact gradually brought about such a new reverence for the Holy Eucharist as to effect far-reaching changes in

the *uses* made of it. Of course there was always an implicit realization of, and embryonic devotion to, the Real Presence, but when this passed into the realm of the actual consciousness, the Eucharist, as it were, changed in our estimation of It and attitude toward It from a *thing*, a very holy thing, the holiest of all things, the Body of the Lord, into a *Person*.

Where once people thought it fit and proper to carry the Blessed Sacrament on their persons for safety on embarking on a sea voyage, or to hoist It to the tips of their battle standards, and so plunge into the fray, the newer attitude brought it about that the Eucharist was elevated at Mass, was enthroned upon the altar, was visited, was *prayed to*, in fine, was adored as God. Instead of the Eucharist being wrapped in scarfs and carried on a sea voyage, as formerly, the Eucharistic Lord was now borne in solemn state to bless the vessels by His Presence before sailing.

Still less was the Eucharist now allowed to be kept in little boxes in private dwellings, but instead the families gayly adorned the homes on Corpus Christi Day with whatever of homely finery they possessed, that so their homage might be evidenced as the King was borne through the streets. It can be seen at a glance what a turning point in the history of Christian piety was marked when the full implications of the worship of the Real Presence were realized.

Spread of New Attitude. In the first ages of the Church, whatever *nonsacrificial* uses of the Blessed Eucharist developed (and they were many), these followed by close analogy the two revealed sacrificial ones, Gift and Food. The Eucharist was above all else a *means* to be used in serving God and sanctifying oneself. But it happened that the newer attitude took its rise precisely at a time when, as the *Catechism of the Council of Trent* informs us, people were often accustomed to put off the actual reception of Communion for years at a time. The then existing "Eucharistic void," so to speak, in everyday life caused the new point of view to grow and spread all the more readily. The hunger and thirst, that were not being slaked at the Table of the Lord, were being sated by the very Presence of the Beloved, in visiting and bringing gifts to the Prisoner in the Tabernacle, by attending as a courtier whenever He went through the streets, in uniting with the other villagers to sing His praises and beg His benediction before nightfall, and in other such pious practices. The elevation in the Mass, the tabernacle on the altar, the repository of Holy Thursday, the Corpus Christi processions, the Exposition of Holy Hour, of Forty Hours, our familiar evening Benediction — even the hastiest recollection of what these things mean for us is enough to show what an immeasurable enriching of Christian life has resulted from direct Eucharistic adoration.

Returning to Tradition. But the Church above all else has the trust to be true to her past, to

> guard the good deposit
> through the Holy Spirit
> who dwelleth in us.   II Tim. i,14

Thus it is that, while preserving all the gains of the newer aspect of Eucharistic piety, she is wisely and gradually leading us back once more to the more sacrificial outlook of the more distant past. A modern theologian summed up all we have been saying in the words: "The first ten centuries knew predominantly the *means* aspect of the Blessed Eucharist, the second ten, the *Person* aspect; the day is now dawning when Christians shall simultaneously possess both aspects of this matchless truth."

Personal Values for Super-Life. "The effect of the Sacrament [of the Eucharist]," says St. Thomas, "corresponds to what is done externally in its administration." What is done externally is a social serving of Food. And when directing the modern mind to the older point of view regarding the frequent reception of the Eucharist, Pope Pius X took pains to restate clearly the primary purpose of Communion:

> The desire of Jesus Christ, and of the Church, that *all Christians should daily approach this holy banquet* is based chiefly on this, that Christians united to God through the Sacrament should derive therefrom the *strength* to conquer concupiscence, and should wash away light faults of daily occurrence, and should forestall more serious ones to which human frailty is exposed. The chief thing here is not to safeguard honor and reverence to [our] Lord, [as the Jansenists had taught].

Dec. 20, 1905

This food for the super-life is set before Christians at the conclusion of their social worship of Sacrifice. St. Paul calls the Communion Table "the Supper of the Lord."

I Cor. xi,20

The notable circumstance that the Eucharistic Food, instead of being transmuted into human flesh and blood, as ordinary bodily nourishment, has the singular faculty of itself transmuting men, little by little, into Christs, has been commented upon times without number. Pope Urban IV, who was a contemporary of St. Thomas (thirteenth century), has expressed this thought with classic beauty:

> This Bread is eaten, but not transmuted; it is nowise changed into the consumer, but if it be worthily received, the recipient becomes like to it. This transmutation is brought about by the *streaming in upon us* of the spirit and *life* of Christ. As a result "Christ liveth in us"; our thoughts, our senses and impulses, our will and activity *assume a resemblance* to the hidden Life of the Eucharistic Saviour, and become divine.

Bull, *Transiturus*

S.T. III. Q. lxxix, a.1

St. Thomas describes this primary effect of the reception of the Eucharist under four terms: nutriment, growth, repair, and delight. By this last he means a certain sense of spiritual exhilaration and a consequent attraction toward God's goodness and sanctity.

Measure of Christ-Life. The good that food does one only commences after eating, when the food begins to be assimilated into living tissue. And the food value of the same diet, taken in the same quantities, remains within narrow limits a constant quantity. But what is the measure of the new Christ-life imparted in Communion? This does *not* remain a constant, but is capable of indefinite expansion and increase, since it corresponds to the *use* that is made of the graces already given. The life value of tomorrow's Communion will depend upon the use being made every hour of today in *living* by the Christ-life given in this morning's Communion.

Today and Tomorrow and the Eucharist. Men and women now everywhere face the threat of a revolution that was characterized by Pope Pius XI as nothing less than relapse into barbarism. "This modern revolution," said this pontiff, "it may be said, has actually broken out, or threatens everywhere, and it exceeds in amplitude and violence anything yet experienced in the preceding persecutions launched against the Church. *Entire peoples find themselves in danger of falling back into a barbarism* worse than that which oppressed the greater part of the world at the coming of the Redeemer." Serenely the Church plans for the future, knowing that she is deathless as long as the world shall run. She will meet the danger by emphasizing the relation of the Eucharist to social solidarity. "To those who read the history of the Church with a discerning eye," explains Archbishop E. A. Mooney (Detroit), "it is clear that each succeeding age has seen insistence instinctively placed on some application of Christian doctrine which meets the special needs of that age. Our own age, with its significant experiments in social solidarity, is witnessing a providential concentration of Christian thought on the doctrine of the Church as the Mystical Body of Christ, and on some of the obvious social implications of that doctrine. . . . It is the one Christ living and working in us. Christ so identifies Himself with the individual members of the Church that our thought of Him would be utterly one-sided and incomplete if it were to consider Him without reference to them. We are members then of one another and of Christ who is our Head. . . . The Holy Eucharist is, to use a phrase which the Fathers of the Church loved, the prime ordinary means of effecting

On Atheistic Communism, 1937

our incorporation with Christ; but St. Paul would have us remember that it is the means of our incorporation with Christ as Head of His Mystical Body, the Church, through which in every age the power of Christ functions in the world, through which the divine work which 1935 Christ came to do, is carried on among men."

Summary. The Eucharist is a sacrament (solemnly promised at Capharnaum and instituted at the Last Supper), wherein the Body and Blood of Christ are made present by the power of the words of consecration, under the species or appearances of bread and wine. The Real Presence endures as long as the species remain unconsumed. Besides the divinely appointed uses of the Eucharist in the Christian Sacrifice (as Gift and as Return-Gift), Christian piety has discovered various others, the chief of which is Eucharistic adoration. By its reception as Communion the Holy Eucharist provides the chief channel of God's grace to the individual, and is the chief token of Christian fellowship. As such it is the aspect of Eucharistic doctrine that is particularly emphasized at present.

THE RITE OF HOLY EUCHARIST ADMINISTERED AS VIATICUM[1]

When the priest enters the sickroom he says:

V. Peace be to this house.
R. And to all who dwell therein.

Having put the Blessed Sacrament upon a linen corporal on a table, and genuflecting before It, the priest sprinkles the sick person and the bed with holy water, saying:

Thou shalt sprinkle me, O Lord, with hyssop, and I shall be cleansed: Thou shalt wash me, and I shall be made whiter than snow.
Have mercy upon me, O Lord, according to Thy great mercy.
Glory be to the Father, and to the Son, and to the Holy Ghost.
As it was in the beginning, is now, and ever shall be, world without end. Amen.
Thou shalt sprinkle me: *as above, down to* snow.
V. Our help is in the name of the Lord.
R. Who made heaven and earth.
V. O Lord, grant my prayer.

---

[1]Reproduced with permission from *The Last Sacraments and Prayers for the Dying,* with notes by C. C. Martindale, London, CTS.

R. And let my cry come unto Thee.
V. The Lord be with you.
R. And with thy spirit.

Let us pray.

Hear our prayer, O holy Lord, Father Almighty, everlasting God; and deign to send Thy holy angel from heaven, to guard, cherish, protect, visit, and defend all who dwell in this house, through Christ, our Lord.
R. Amen.

Thereupon he inquires concerning the sick person's need or desire of confessing before receiving Viaticum. Then the Confiteor (I confess) is recited either by the sick person, or by someone in his stead, and the priest shall say:

May the Almighty God have mercy on thee, and dismissing thy sins, bring thee through into everlasting life. Amen.

May the Almighty and Merciful Lord grant thee indulgence, absolution, and remission of all thy sins. Amen.

Having made a genuflection he holds up the Blessed Sacrament so that the sick person can see It, saying:

Behold the Lamb of God; behold Him who taketh away the sins of the world.

He adds in the accustomed manner "Domine non sum dignus," "O Lord, I am not worthy," and gives Holy Communion to the sick person, saying:

Receive, brother (or sister) the viaticum of the Body of our Lord, Jesus Christ, that He may protect thee from the malicious foe, and bring thee safe into everlasting life. Amen.

Then the priest washes his fingers in a little water, and wipes them; in due time this water will be thrown into the fire. Then he says:

V. The Lord be with you.
R. And with thy spirit.

Let us pray.

O Holy Lord, Father Almighty, Eternal God, we earnestly beseech Thee that the Body of our Lord Jesus Christ, that our brother (sister) has received, may avail him (her) as an eternal remedy both for body and for soul, who liveth and reigneth with Thee, in the unity of the Holy Spirit, God world without end.
R. Amen.

If a particle of the Blessed Sacrament be left, the priest blesses the sick person with It, in silence. Else, he blesses him as usual, saying:

The blessing of God Almighty, Father, Son, and Holy Ghost descend on thee and remain forever.

R. Amen.

Nineteenth-Century Source Material

(John Henry Newman, one of the greatest modern champions of Catholicism, writes of Christ and the Eucharist.)

He left His Father's courts, He was manifested, He spake; and His voice went out into all lands. He has taken to Himself His great power and reigned; and, whereas an enemy is the god and tyrant of this world, as Adam made it, so, as far as He occupies it, does He restore it to His Father. Henceforth He is the one principle of life in all His servants, who are but His organs. The Jewish Church looked toward Him; the Christian speaks and acts from Him. What is prior to Him is dark, but all that comes after Him is illuminated. The Church, before His manifestation, offered to Him material elements "which perish with the using"; but now He has sent His Spirit to fill such elements with Himself, and to make them living and availing sacrifices to the Father. Figures have become means of grace, shadows are substances, types are Sacraments in Him. What before were decent ordinances and pious observances, have now not only a meaning but a virtue. Water could but wash the Body in the way of nature; but now it acts toward the cleansing of the soul. "Wine which maketh glad the heart of man," and "bread which strengthens man's heart," nay, the "oil which maketh him a cheerful countenance," henceforth are more than means of animal life, and savor of Him. Hands raised in blessing, the accents of the voice of man, which before could but symbolize the yearnings of human nature, or avail for lower benefits, have now become the "unutterable intercessions" of the Spirit, and the touch, and the breath of the Incarnate Son. The Church has become His body, her priests His delegates, her people His members.

This is what Christ has done by His coming; but observe, *while* He did all this for His Church, He claimed all He did *as* His own. Henceforth whatever is done is His doing, and it is called what it is. As He is the unseen Source, so must He be acknowledged as the Agent, the present Object of worship and thanksgiving in all that is done; and His instruments are not even so much as instruments, but only the outward lineaments of Him. All is superseded by Him, and transmuted into Him. Before He came there were many masters, but henceforth only One; before He came many Fathers, but He is the One Father of the coming age, as the Prophet styles Him; before He came, all to whom the word of God came were called gods, but He is the One God manifested in the flesh; before He came, there were many angelic appearances with the name of God on them, but now the great Angel of the Covenant is alone to be worshiped; before He came, there were many priests who had infirmity, offering sacrifices year by year continually, but now there is but One High Priest, "who is set on the right hand of the throne of the majesty in the heavens, a minister of the sanctuary, and of the true tabernacle, which the Lord pitched, and not man"; before, there were innumerable sacrifices of bulls and calves which could never perfect the worshipers, now One Immaculate Lamb who taketh away the sin of the world; before, there were judges, kings, and rulers of various ranks, but now there is but One King of kings, and Lord of lords, in His kingdom. . . . There were mediators many, and prophets many, and atonements many. But now all is superseded by One, in whom all offices merge, who has absorbed into Himself all principality, power, might, and dominion, and every name that is named; who has put His holy and fearful Name upon all, who is in and through all things, and without whom nothing is good. He is the sole self-existing principle in the Christian Church, and everything else is but a portion or declaration of Him. Not that now, as then, we may not speak of prophets, and rulers, and priests, and sacrifices, and altars, and saints, and that in a far higher and more spiritual sense than before, but that they are not any of them such of themselves; it is not they, but the grace of God that is in them. There is under the Gospel but One proper Priest, Prophet, and King, Altar Sacrifice, and House of God. Unity is its characteristic sacrament, all grace flows from One Head, and all life circulates in the members of One Body. — Quoted from *A Newman Synthesis*, by permission of Sheed and Ward.

Topics for Further Discussion:

The "matter" of the Eucharist, bread (originally leavened, now unleavened in the Western Church) made from pure wheat flour, and pure grape wine.

The former custom of communicating infants after Baptism with a few drops of the Precious Blood.

Inconveniences attending Communion under both species.

In "offering up" Communion for another, one renders God the same adoration and thanksgiving as in any Communion, and personally receives the sacramental grace (increase of Christ-life), while some of the petitionary and satisfactory values are diverted to the person for whom the Communion is offered.

"The best preparation for receiving our Lord tomorrow is to receive Him today."

The reception of Communion as a divine precept.

That Christ is truly received even by persons in mortal sin.

"Every hour is good for Mass-serving." — *St. John Berchmans.*

Readings:

T. E. Bridgett, *A History of the Holy Eucharist in Great Britain* (London: Burns, Oates and Washbourne, 1908); "The Eucharist in the Life of the People," pp. 217–292.

P. Claudel, *Ways and Crossways* (New York: Sheed and Ward, 1933); "The Physics of the Eucharist," pp. 55–71.

J. C. Hedley, *The Holy Eucharist* (New York: Longmans, Green, 1907); "Apparent Absence of *Cultus* of the Holy Eucharist in the First Thousand Years of the Christian Era," pp. 253–271.

J. Kramp, *Eucharistia, Essays on Eucharistic Liturgy and Devotion* (St. Paul: Lohmann, 1926); "The History of Eucharistic Adoration," pp. 111–157.

E. Leen, *The True Vine and the Branches* (New York: Kenedy, 1938); "The Bread of Life," pp. 92–107.

C. Marmion, *Christ the Life of the Soul* (St. Louis: Herder, 1923); "Panis Vitae," pp. 279–304.

R. Plus, *The Eucharist* (London: Burns, Oates and Washbourne, 1931).

J. Pohle, "Eucharist, the Blessed, as a Sacrament," *CE.*

Seventh National Eucharistic Congress (Cleveland, 1936); E. A. Smith, Address "Communionism and Communism," pp. 229–233.

G. D. Smith, *The Sacrament of the Eucharist*, TF, 25.

H. Thurston, "Benediction," *The Month*, 97, 98 (1901), pp. 587–597, 58–69, 186–193, 264–276; "Our English Benediction Service," 106 (1905), pp. 394–404.

A. Vonier, *A Key to the Doctrine of the Eucharist* (New York: Benziger, 1925); "Transubstantiation," pp. 176–192.

Ninth Eucharistic Congress, Westminster, 1908 (London: Sands, 1909); H. Thurston, "Benediction of the Blessed Sacrament," pp. 452–463.

Chapter XX

THE FATHER OF THE PRODIGAL

If any one have sinned,
we have an Advocate with the Father;
Jesus Christ, the Just
(I John ii,1).

ONE of the reproaches most frequently flung at Christ in His public life was His consorting with sinners. It was a scandal to the religious leaders of the day that He came not to call just Matt. ix men, but sinners, that He conversed with the Samaritan woman, that John iv He dined with Zachaeus, spared the woman taken in adultery, and John viii allowed another woman of ill fame to bathe His sacred feet with her tears. He was, moreover, charged with blasphemy when He claimed to Luke vii remit sin. Matt. ix

Luke xix

"The Friend of Sinners." The attitude then taken toward Christ has been throughout the centuries consistently taken against His Church. What Catholic has not heard the taunt: "Your Church is the friend of the criminal, the lawless, the sinner!" To which the Church serenely responds that the disciple is not above the Master, that her mission is Matt. x,24 precisely to seek out and reclaim what was lost, to bring back to super- Luke xv,4 natural life that which was dead, that she must be ready to forgive those Luke xv,28 who sin against her, not to seven times, but up to seventy times seven. Matt. xviii The Catholic Church is unique among religious bodies now and always, as the whole world knows, in that she provides a regularly constituted ministry of sacramental forgiveness. Something over sixteen hundred years ago, at the very height of the Diocletian persecution, one of the Church's champions made the claim:

But because all the separated heretical assemblies call themselves Christians, and think that theirs is the Catholic Church, you ought to know that that is the Catholic Church where there is confession and repentance, which soundly cures the sins and wounds to which weak- Lactantius, *De* ness of the flesh is heir. *div. Inst.* ix, xxx

293

Christ is in God

reconciling

the world

unto Himself

So was Catholicism characterized in the Roman Empire, and so is it characterized in our world of today, as attested by the great modern apologist, Mr. Chesterton:

> When people ask me, or indeed anybody else, "Why did you join the Church of Rome?" the first essential answer, if it is partly an elliptical answer, is, "To get rid of my sins." For there is no other religious system that does *really* profess to get rid of people's sins. . . . The Sacrament of Penance gives a new life, and reconciles man to all living. . . . The gift is given at a price, and is conditioned by a confession. In other words, the name of the price is Truth, which may be called Reality; but it is facing the reality about oneself.[1]

How indeed could the Christian religion be constituted without this saving sacrament? Christ came that through His death we might have supernatural life and strength and effectiveness in actual solidarity with Him.

> If, then, any man be in Christ,
> he is a new creature:
> the former things have passed away:
> Behold, all things are made new!

> But all things are of God,
> who hath reconciled us to Himself through Christ
> and hath given us the ministry of reconciliation:
> God . . . was reconciling the world to Himself in Christ.   II Cor. v,17–19

A Needed Remedy. This atonement with Him is effected by baptism, and lasts *as long as man does not break it by a serious and deliberate violation of God's law.* Such violations, of which St. Paul enumerates as types, impurity, idolatry, drunkenness, serious stealing and cheating, are I Cor. vi,10 *mortal,* are fatal; that is, they kill the supernatural life within, rendering the subject quite incapable of normal supernatural activity. Then what? Are these souls without further refuge? The weakness of our perverted natures, and the blindness to supernatural things, so characteristic of mankind, were known to God, and would be reckoned with in any economy of salvation that *could* be generally workable. In His ministry Christ worked miracles to prove that He personally had power to remit sin, Matt. ix and He more than once promised to Peter and the other Apostles that Mark xvii

---

[1] *Autobiography of G. K. Chesterton* (New York: Sheed and Ward, 1936), pp. 340, 342; quoted with permission.

Matt. xviii   He would confer on them the exercise of a like power in His name.
Then, on the very day on which "He arose from the dead for our justi-

Rom. iv,25   fication," He conferred the great boon of the sacrament of penance on
His Church.

> "Peace be to you.
> As the Father hath sent Me,
> I also send you."

> When He had said this,
> He breathed on them:
> and He saith to them:

> "Receive ye the Holy Ghost.
> Whose sins ye shall forgive,
> they are forgiven them:
> and whose sins ye shall retain,
> they are retained."

John xx,21,22

How Used by Apostles. When the religious rebels of the sixteenth
century questioned the traditional interpretation of this passage, as
referring to the institution of the sacrament of penance, the Council of
Trent anathematized them for it. The power here given the Apostles,

Acts v   they *fearlessly exercised*. Peter judged Ananias and Saphira; Paul excom-

I Cor. v;   municated and later pardoned an incestuous Corinthian; he bade

II Cor. ii   Timothy, "those who sin, rebuke in the sight of all"; James addressed

I Tim. v   Christians with the energetic words:

> Make clean your hands,
> ye sinners,

James iv   and hallow your hearts,

while the tenderness of John's disposition moved him to phrase similar
counsels in the terms:

> If we say that we have no sin,
> we deceive ourselves,
> and the truth is not in us.
> If we confess our sins,
> He is faithful and just,
> so as to forgive us our sins,

I John i,8,9   and cleanse us from all iniquity.

If there is one thing clear from the New Testament, it is the infallible Church's conviction of her power to loose and bind the bonds of sin.

Variation in Usage. The Church was *conscious of her sacramental power* of remitting sin (provided the penitent was properly disposed) from Pentecost onwards; yet it is equally true that *her manner of exercising that power* has undergone great changes in the course of time. Our familiar habits of weekly or monthly confession were unknown in antiquity. Rather, as far as the meager records of the time tell the whole story, penance was administered quite differently then. Certain parts of the sacramental ritual or process, which are now strictly private, were then often, if not always, public, and semisocial, in appearance as well as character. Whether the actual confession of sins was private or public, the expression of contrition usually had to be made in public, and the satisfaction, or the "penance" as we call it, was usually public, with the absolution deferred until this satisfaction had been performed before the entire community. The absolution itself was usually administered in public. When we read in *The Teaching of the Twelve Apostles* (of about the year 80): "On the Lord's Day . . . come together, break bread and celebrate the Eucharist, *after confessing your transgressions,* that your Sacrifice may be pure," it is not clear whether this refers to private confession, or to a public confession of guilt couched in more or less general terms, after the manner of our *Confiteor* at the opening of Mass. This latter is, in the light of later custom, more probable.

Before the second century had run its full course, there is clear testimony that *for grievous sins* the organization of public penance was already far developed. (For minor transgressions, sacramental absolution was not needed, but could be had of the bishop on application.) Of the usages connected with the remission of serious sins we can learn much from Tertullian's picture of it. This was written at the very dawn of the third century, and shortly before that ardent spirit was carried away by ultrarigorism against the very system he here describes.

This act . . . of confessing our sins to the Lord, not indeed as if He were ignorant of them, but because thereby a *satisfaction* is made for them; repentance, too, is born of confession, and by repentance God is appeased. And so confession becomes a disciplinary act of great humiliation and prostration to the penitent; it regulates the *dress,* the *food;* it enjoins sackcloth, and subdues the spirit with anguish; it bids a man alter his life, and weep over his past sins; it restricts meat and drink to the greatest simplicity possible; it nourishes prayer by *fasting;* it inculcates groans and tears and invocations of the Lord God day and night, and teaches the penitent *to cast himself at the feet of the presbyters,* and to fall on his knees *before the beloved of God,* and to beg of all the *brethren to intercede on his behalf.* . . .

On Penance, c.ix

The body cannot rejoice in the injury of one of its members; all must grieve together and jointly strive for its cure. The Church is in one as well as in the other, and the Church is Christ. When, therefore, you prostrate yourself before the knees of your brethren you are touching Christ, you entreat Christ.

c.x

Early Strictness Mitigated. In the great persecutions of the third century, and the opening years of the fourth, there were many *Christians who fell away* at the hour of trial. Now *apostasy* was one of the mortal sins for which the full rigors of public penance was prescribed by tradition. But the persecutions soon spent themselves, and the "fair-weather Christians" came back in such numbers as to make the *application of the old rules impracticable.* Disputes arose as how the situation was to be handled. The rigorists were for excluding the "lapsed" for good and all, or at least, until the hour of death. The milder spirits, the popes in the van, adopted what seemed to the other party scandalously lax standards, so much so, in fact, that Tertullian and many others preferred to cut themselves off from the Church that stooped to welcome apostates back.

Public Penance in the East. These controversies focused attention on the whole matter of penitential administration, and helped to spread milder ways, but the system as a whole remained on the same basis. When a man had committed one or more of the graver sins, he had to make the fault known to the bishop, or his representative. So much was done as a rule, in private unless the matter was so notorious that it could not be hidden. The bishop then appointed the culprit to one or other class of penitents, and enjoined a regime of mortification and self-denial which our modern outlook finds almost unbelievably strict. The penitents were (in the East) grouped into "mourners," "kneelers," "hearers," and "bystanders." These terms designated definite degrees of exclusion from participation in common worship. The *mourners* were forbidden even the entrance to the church: stationed outside in sackcloth and squalor they petitioned the prayers of those who entered. *Hearers* could, indeed

IMPOSING PUBLIC PENANCE

Miniature in an old pontifical. (Reproduced from Thurston's *Lent and Holy Week,* by courtesy of Burns, Oates and Washbourne.)

enter the Church, and remain as long as the catechumens, but they were forbidden to raise their voices in the common prayers. This was allowed the *kneelers,* who, as the second highest class of penitents, knelt in an appointed place and received an imposition of hands before dismissal. *Bystanders* mingled freely with the faithful and were allowed to be present at the Sacrifice, but not to take part in the gift-procession or the Communion. Besides these public exercises of humility and submission, definite fasts, abstinences, almsgiving, prohibitions to bathe, and the like,

EXPELLING THE PENITENTS

Miniature in an old pontifical. (Reproduced from Thurston's *Lent and Holy Week,* by courtesy of Burns, Oates and Washbourne.)

were part of the regime. The general absolution, or reconciliation as it was called, took place on Holy Thursday, so that the entire community could celebrate the Easter solemnities together.

At Rome. The system just described was that of the Orient. A facile writer from Constantinople, Sozomen, having witnessed the Roman penitential discipline about 450, gives this description of it:

> In the churches of Rome the place of those who are in penance is very conspicuous: they stand with downcast eyes and the seeming of mourners. *When the service is concluded,* not being allowed to take part in what is allowed to the initiated alone, with wailing and lamentations they *prostrate themselves* on the ground. The bishop, weeping, comes towards them, and prostrates himself with cries for mercy. Then the bishop first rises and permits those prostrate to rise, and, having said a prayer in fitting fashion over the repentant sinners, dismisses them.
>
> Freely each does penance by fasting, abstention from bathing, abstinence, or whatever is appointed him, and so waits for the time allotted by the bishop. When the appointed day is at hand, he is absolved from his offenses like a debtor that has paid his debt, and he has his place among the people restored to him.

Hist. Eccles. vii,16

In the Lenten weekday Masses we have preserved, in the *Prayer Over the People,* the petition mentioned above as being said with so much ardor at the end of the daily Mass at Rome.

Gradual Transition to Modern Practice. As the Christian centuries unrolled, this *penitential discipline* gradually underwent progressive *mitigation.* At first the rigorous satisfactions demanded began to be commuted to much easier ones; still later, the private features of the rite were enlarged to include what had been heretofore, as a rule, public; lastly, the reconciliation, or *absolution,* was given at the *time of the confession,* on the promise that the satisfaction, "penance" we should say, would be performed as enjoined. The blessed ashes put on our foreheads on the first day of Lent are the one relic surviving of the old regime of public penance. Thus while the acts of both priest and penitent remained substantially the same, the external circumstances attending them came gradually to bear little resemblance to the rigors of an earlier and more robust age. Latterly, the full role of this sacrament of penance in the day-by-day work of character building, the "putting on of Christ," becoming ever clearer, our frequent confession became linked with the daily Sacrifice and Communion in the scheme of the full Christian lives possible in our days.

A Sacramental Judgment. One reason we have dwelt upon these old customs is that they illustrate the nature and character of the several parts of this sacrament better than the more compendious rites of today. "If any one say," declared the Council of Trent, "that the sacramental absolution of the priest is not a *judicial* act . . . let him be anathema [excommunicated]." The acts of the presiding cleric, bishop, or priest as the case may be, under the old regime, assigning a very definite term and measure of penance, overseeing its fulfillment, and then publicly absolving — these were more apt to strike an observer as actions of a judge on the bench than absolution privately and straightway given to all applicants suitably disposed, on their acceptance of a trivial "penance," which seems to bear no comparison to the gravity of the faults committed. But a momentary reflection will show that, as things are at present, all the *judicial* elements are preserved intact. Even now, the priest absolving a penitent judicially acquits him, as it were, of the sins, and this only after he has judged the penitent to be properly disposed.

Sess. xiv, 1551

Jurisdiction. One of the essentials of this Sacrament seldom understood by the laity is its relation to what is called jurisdiction. Election or appointment confers on a judge in civil life the power of officially interpreting the law, but only in such cases as are referred to him in a court by the State. Holy orders gives the priest once and for all the power of binding and loosing sins, but the priest must be assigned to a tribunal in a given diocese before he can exercise that power. This assigning of a priest to a diocesan tribunal is called a grant of jurisdiction (over sinners); again, such a priest is said to have faculties to absolve sinners applying to his tribunal. This jurisdiction, stemming primarily from Christ's grant to Peter, comes to the priest through the bishop of the diocese. Thus, every confession, far from being a purely personal matter in an obscure corner, represents a cross section of authority exercised by the Church's entire hierarchical structure: Christ–pope–bishop–priest–penitent. In his ringing *Encyclical on the Priesthood,* Pope Pius XI says in this connection:

These words [of absolution] fall, it is true, from the lips of one, who, in his turn, must needs beg the same words of absolution from another priest. This does not debase the merciful gift; but makes it, rather, appear greater: since beyond the weak creature is seen more clearly the hand of God through whose power is wrought this wonder. As an illustrious layman has written, treating with rare competence of spiritual things: ". . . when a priest, groaning in spirit at his own unworthiness and at the loftiness of his office, places his consecrated hands upon our heads; when, humiliated at finding himself the dispenser of the Blood of the Covenant; each time amazed as he pronounces the words that give life; when a sinner has absolved a sinner; we, who rise from our knees before him, feel we have done nothing debasing. . . . We have been at the feet of a man who represented Jesus Christ . . . we have been there to receive the dignity of free men and of sons of God."

The Catholic Priesthood, December, 1935

Self-Accusation. The act from which the whole rite is nowadays popularly denominated, *confession, follows logically from the judicial character* of the power of absolving, as well as from the *medicinal nature* of the sacrament. In regard to this latter, the same Council of Trent aptly quotes a line from St. Jerome: "If the invalid shrink from disclosing his wound to the physician, the latter does not heal that of which he remains ignorant." Regarding the judicial examination to be made by the priest, it is clear that no presiding judge can give a ruling, or verdict, or pardon, until the case has been presented to him. This confession must be, as far as circumstances permit, the full record of the case. There is question here of good will, rather than of absolute, objective integrity of confession. Forgetfulness, ignorance, the affliction of dumbness, the inability then and there to speak the language of the only confessor available, even in emergencies, the lack of time, these render absolute integrity impossible but do not invalidate the confession.

In Eccl. Com. **x,11** *Sess.* xiv, 1551

Salutary Sorrow. A more important element, in fact the *most important part* of the whole process, is *sorrow,* or contrition for sin. This means, as everyone knows, detestation and sorrow of heart for sin committed, together with a determination to sin no more. There can be no question of pardon without this. Catholics are often charged with holding that the mere telling of sins in confession is enough to wipe them out, and that afterwards one can return without qualm to the former habits of sin. The most elementary idea of God's justice and sanctity, to say nothing of the constant teaching of the Church, should show how groundless is this charge. If this resolve to sin now no more spring from the love of God and the knowledge that sin outrages His loving kindness, this contrition itself will obtain the pardon of sin, but there remains the obligation of submitting serious sins to the tribunal of penance. Less perfect, but still supernatural, sorrow for sin is sufficient to obtain sacramental forgiveness.

The Function of the "Penance." The role of satisfaction, or the function of the "penance" assigned by the confessor, is in danger of being underestimated in our present usage. Yet it is so important that a penitent cannot be absolved until he has *accepted* the penance enjoined. This is essentially something done as a display of good will, something done personally to expiate the past, and to foreshadow amendment for the future. This satisfaction is to be viewed in its relationship toward God, toward Christ, and toward the fellow members of the Mystical Body. As considered in reference to God, this penance is an acknowledgment that, while the loving mercy of God has condoned the guilt of sin, and its eternal punishment, still His justice demands the restoration of good order by the acceptance of some temporal punishment. As regards Christ, the penance reminds us that the Atonement was primarily a work of satisfaction, and that the members are called upon

> to make up in [their] flesh
> what is lacking of the sufferings of Christ.   Col. i,24

In this connection one should not forget that it is through our Mediator that the modicum of penance here prescribed to us actually has *sacramental efficacy*. The relation of my penance to the entire Mystical Body rests on the principle that the *prayers* and *merits of the Church as a whole* are an important factor in paying this satisfaction to God's justice. St. Pacian, in explaining sacramental absolution of the individual, writes in this strain: "It is obtained by all the faithful." St. Ambrose exhorts the sinner to ask for public penance "so that Christ will intercede for thee, . . . so that the Church pray for thee, so that the entire people weep for thee." There is, in fact, a close cooperation of the entire Christian body in the purification of the sinner, and thus Christ's gift to His Church involves the work of the Mystic Christ as well as that of the Head. In paying our tiny mite of a few Our Fathers and Hail Marys we are in reality drawing a sight draft on the boundless merits of the Mystical Body, Head and members. It is in these terms that the Council of Trent speaks of our "penance":

Rom. v,10
II Cor. iii,5
Rom. viii,17

Phil. iv,13

I Cor. i,31
Cf. Acts xvii,28
Luke iii,8

Sess. xiv, 1551

Whilst we thus, by making satisfaction, suffer for our sins, we are made conformable to Jesus Christ, who satisfied for our sins, from whom all our sufficiency is; having also thereby a most sure pledge that, if we suffer with Him, we shall also be glorified with Him.

But neither is this satisfaction, which we discharge for our sins, so our own as not to be *through Jesus Christ*. For we who can do nothing of ourselves, as of ourselves, can do all things, He cooperating, who strengthens us. Thus, man who has not wherein to glory, but all our glorying is in Christ: in whom we live; in whom we merit, in whom we satisfy; bringing forth fruits worthy of penance, which from Him have their efficacy; by Him are offered to the Father; and through Him are accepted by the Father.

In marked contrast to the severity of by-gone ages, we see and experience the beneficent operation of the great *fund of merit* in the Church, won by Christ, His most blessed Mother, and the saints, upon which we are privileged to draw so easily *by means of indulgences*.

THE RITE OF SACRAMENTAL ABSOLUTION

This prayer and the next are in reality deprecatory forms of absolution, a wish formally expressed that God will grant the remission of sin. Historians are of the opinion that the original forms of verbal absolution were expressed in this deprecatory manner.

The absolution here passes to the direct, indicative mood. The raising of the right hand of the priest is a formal laying on of hands. The oldest absolution ritual we have (about 280) prescribes: "And while the whole people prays over him, *lay hand upon him,* and suffer him henceforth to be in the Church" (*Didascalia,* vii).

This prayer illustrates the multiple relation of the penance, that it is a satisfaction to God, that it has its prime value through the mediation of Christ's death, and through the participation of the merits of the Virgin Mary and the whole Mystical Body.

When the priest wishes to absolve the penitent, after a suitable penance has been imposed and accepted, he says:

May God almighty have mercy on thee, and forgive thee thy sins, and bring thee to life everlasting. Amen.

Then with the right hand raised toward the penitent, he says:

May the almighty and merciful Lord grant thee pardon, absolution, and remission of all thy sins. Amen.

MAY our Lord Jesus Christ absolve thee; and I by His authority absolve thee from every bond of excommunication and interdict, as far as I am able, and thou hast need. Moreover, I absolve thee of thy sins, in the name of the Father, and of the Son, and of the Holy Ghost. Amen.

May the passion of our Lord Jesus Christ, the merits of the blessed Virgin Mary and of all the saints, whatever good thou mayest do and whatever evil thou mayest have to endure, profit thee unto the remission of sins, increase of grace, and glory in the life without end. Amen.

For any good reason the above prayers may be omitted except

that beginning "May our Lord Jesus Christ," etc.

Should any danger of death be imminent, the priest may say briefly:

I absolve thee of all censures and sins in the name of the Father, and of the Son, and of the Holy Ghost. Amen.

Summary. Penance is a sacrament instituted by Christ to restore supernatural life and effectiveness to Christians who have committed mortal sins after baptism. The several acts of the penitent — contrition, confession, and satisfaction — and those of the priest — absolution and counsel — are found in the modern as well as in the ancient forms of administration.

Twentieth-Century Source Material

(Since St. Francis de Sales [died 1622], perhaps no Catholic has been so influential in his writings as Columba Marmion, O.S.B. [died 1923]: This extract[1] on penance in Christ is from CHRIST, THE LIFE OF THE SOUL.)

I Cor. xv,31   "I die daily." Those are St. Paul's words; but if he died daily, it was that he might the better live the life of Christ.

And in speaking of his sufferings, he wrote those words that appear so strange and are of such profound depth:

> I . . . make up in my flesh
> what is lacking to the sufferings of Christ,
> on behalf of His [mystical] body,
Col. i,24   > which is the Church.

Is there then something wanting to the sufferings, to the satisfactions of Christ? Certainly not. Their value is infinite. Christ's sufferings are the sufferings of the Man-God who substituted Himself for us. Nothing is wanting to the perfection and plenitude of these sufferings; they were more than sufficient to redeem us all.

> *He Himself* is a propitiation for our sins . . .
I John ii,2   > also for the *whole* world.

---

[1]Quoted by permission of Herder Co.

Then why does St. Paul speak of "filling up" these sufferings?

St. Augustine gives us the reply. The whole Christ, he says, is formed by the Church united to her Chief, and by the members (which we are), united to the Head (which is Christ). Christ, the Head of this mystical body, has suffered; the great expiation was that of Jesus; the members, if they wish to remain worthy of the Head, must in their turn bring their share of suffering and renunciation:

> The sufferings were indeed filled up, but in the Head: there remained the sufferings of Christ in His body: well, you are His body and members. *In Ps. lxxxvii,5*

Contemplate Christ Jesus on His way to Calvary, laden with His cross; He falls under the weight of this burden. If He willed, His divinity would sustain His humanity; but He does not will it. Why? Because, in order to expiate sin, He wills to feel in His innocent flesh the burden of sin. But the Jews fear He will not live to reach the place of crucifixion; they therefore constrain Simon the Cyrenean to help to carry His cross, and Jesus accepts his help.

Simon, in this, represents us all; as members of Christ's mystical body, we must help Jesus to bear His cross. It is a sure sign we belong to Him, if following Him, we deny ourselves and take up our cross:

> If any one will come after Me,
> let him deny himself,
> and take up his cross daily,
> and follow Me. *Luke ix,23*

Here is to be found the secret of the voluntary mortifications of faithful souls, privileged souls, holy souls — those mortifications that afflict and macerate the body as well as those that repress even the lawful desires of the mind. Such souls have doubtless expiated their own sins, but love constrains them to expiate for those members of Christ's body who offend their Chief so that the vigor, beauty, and splendor of this mystical body may not be diminished. If we truly love Christ, we shall, following the counsel of a prudent director, generously take our share of these voluntary mortifications which will make us less unworthy members of a crucified Head. Was it not this that St. Paul sought? Did he not write that he had suffered the loss of all things so that he might be admitted to the fellowship of Christ's sufferings and be made conformable to His death?

That so I may know Him . . .
what [the] fellowship in His sufferings,
and become one with Him in His death.

Phil. iii,10

Topics for Further Discussion:

The vast difference in kind between mortal and venial sin.

Matt. iii;
Mark i

Confession as a purely natural, psychological need, e.g., of the Jewish crowds moved to repentance by the Baptist.

The medieval ascetical practice of confessing to laymen in the lack of a priest at a moment of grave danger.

The amount of sanctifying grace *restored* by sacramental absolution.

That the pope cannot, outside of the sacrament of penance, remit sin, either his own or others'.

"The confession of faults . . . in some form or other is to be found among all races" (Cf. Karrer, *Religions of Mankind*, p. 90).

Readings:

F. X. Doyle, *The Wonderful Sacraments* (New York: Benziger, 1924); "Penance," pp. 153–177.

L. W. Geddes–H. Thurston, *The Catholic Church and Confession*, Calvert Series (New York: Macmillan, 1928).

E. J. Hanna, "Penance," *CE*.

H. Harrington, *The Sacrament of Penance*, TF, 27.

J. C. Heenan, *Priest and Penitent* (New York: Sheed and Ward, 1938); "The Confessor's Point of View," pp. 73–85; *passim*.

C. Lattey, *Six Sacraments, Papers Read at the Summer School of Catholic Studies, Cambridge, 1929* (St. Louis: Herder, 1930); F. Cabrol, "Penance," pp. 131–162.

C. Marmion, *Christ the Life of the Soul* (St. Louis: Herder, 1923); "The Sacrament and Virtue of Penance," pp. 187–211.

M. Perkins, *Speaking of How to Pray* (New York: Sheed & Ward, 1944); "According to the Riches of His Grace," pp. 140–155.

R. Plus, *The Ideal of Reparation* (London: Burns, Oates and Washbourne, 1926).

W. F. Robison, *The Seven-Fold Gift* (St. Louis: Herder, 1922); "The Second Hope for Salvation," pp. 64–96.

Chapter **XXI**

A MYSTICAL BODY IN MINIATURE

The husband is the head of the wife,
as Christ too is head of the Church . . .
the mystery here is great
(Eph. v,22–32).

THE correct attitude toward Christian marriage is strikingly expressed by a contemporary French writer in the words: "If anyone wants to understand marriage, he must first understand Christ." The superhuman dignity and the inherent sacredness of marriage, as an institution of an all-wise Creator, have always been clear to sane human reason. These convictions, as Pope Leo XIII said, were as if stamped and written on human nature itself. But it was not until Christ had restored the pristine concept of marriage in its purity, and until St. Paul completed the revelation by informing us that marriage is a symbol, or likeness, "a foreshadowing" (Leo XIII), of the Incarnation of Christ and His union with the Church, that the full beauty and effulgence of the divine plan burst upon man. By marriage there is established in each family, as it were, a mystical body in miniature. Let us read this page of the Glad Tidings at the start:

> Wives [be subject], to your husbands
>   as to the Lord,
> because the husband is the head of the wife,
>   as Christ too is Head of the Church,
>   Himself being the Saviour of the body.

> Well, then, as the Church is subject to Christ,
> so also should wives be to their husbands in everything.

> Husbands, love your wives,
>   as Christ also loved the Church
>   and gave Himself up for her sake,

that He might sanctify her,
purifying her in the bath of water by means of the word,
that He might present her to Himself a glorious Church,
not having spot or wrinkle or any such thing,
but holy and without blemish.

Even thus ought husbands love their wives
as their own bodies.

He that loveth his own wife loveth himself.

Surely no man ever hateth his own flesh;
nay, he doth nourish and cherish it,
even as Christ the Church;
because we are members of His body.

For this shall man leave father and mother,
and shall cleave to his wife,
Gen. ii,24   and the two shall come to be one flesh.

The mystery here is great —
Eph. v,22–32   I mean in reference to Christ and the Church.

Like Union of Natures in Christ. In marriage, then, Christian or
non-Christian, we have an institution planned and established by God
to symbolize and illustrate the union between divinity and humanity
effected for our sanctification in the Person of Christ. These are not
mere flourishes of rhetoric, but ennobling truths for our enlightenment
and happiness. That is why one must say that to comprehend marriage
fully, one must know Christ. Let us study this parallel which divine
revelation teaches us exists between a family and the Mystical Body.

A Fountain-Head of Life. All *life*, whatsoever it be, comes from
God. All created life is owing to that infinite *Act of Love* whereby the
Goodness of God diffuses itself. There is within the Holy Trinity the
intellectual generation of the Son and the eternal procession, *through
Love*, of the Holy Spirit: outside, or overflowing beyond the Trinity,
there is that temporal outpouring love we call the creation and conserva-
tion and provident guidance of the universe. God foreknew that in the
fullness of time He should send forth His Sole-Begotten Son wedded
to human flesh to restore *supernatural life* to fallen humanity. This
unique, indissoluble, and life-giving union of Godhead and manhood we
call the Incarnation. From the outset God wished to foreshadow this

Like Christ's Wedding with the Church

ineffable mystery and at the same time He wished to associate man, the lord of the visible world, as closely as possible with Himself in the selfsame Act of Love from which life flows. Therefore He made man male and female, and bade the two become one flesh in a union nothing can dissolve, to cooperate with Himself in propagating life.

Life as Basis for Super-Life. But the union of Godhead and humanity does not end at the Incarnation; in a sense explained in a former chapter it extends itself in the Church to *all Christians* who become *incorporated* therein. Thence exists that mysterious, invisible flow of supernatural life from the Head to the last and the least of the members day after day, year after year, century after century, until the end of time. Similarly in marriage God has appointed that man and woman, as long as the world shall last, shall have His gracious commission to work with Him in diffusing natural life. In the Mystical Body men are endlessly reborn to grace; in marriage men are endlessly born *for* grace.

Man and Woman and God. In the Mystical Body, besides the Person of Christ, and His mystic Bride, the Church, there is Another, God Himself: so in marriage, besides the man and woman, there is the *Third Partner, God.* This is that inherent dignity and sanctity of the very nature of marriage, which has led men everywhere to surround it with sacred, religious rites. That marriage cannot derive from nature alone either its end or its means is forcibly shown by Dr. Karl Adam, a celebrated German professor of theology. "Its principal end," he says, "the generation of children, cannot be attained unless God, the Creator of the spirit, intervene in the paternal function and complete it by the creation of the soul. By that very fact, marriage, even in its natural reality, overflows the confines of this world, and surpasses the forces of this world. From that point of view alone, every marriage is a mystery. Then consider its interior structure. We find there is a sensible, corporeal side, and a moral, spiritual side. Inasmuch as it is placed in the sphere of the senses, marriage is in danger of losing itself by sinking into animality. It must cry for help from above to escape from the preponderance of the corporeal element. On its moral and spiritual side, it is more than a simple alliance of mind and heart; it implies the mutual self-surrender of two persons destined to be welded together in one flesh, a thing which is done in all security only with the Divine good pleasure." The mystery here is great; it is the ever-abiding presence of the Third Partner of the marriage union.

Wedlock Sacramentalized. The foregoing paragraphs viewed marriage as it was first given to man, when God, as Tertullian put it, "after taking the female from the male, recombined in wedlock the two bodies taken from the selfsame substance." But the primal contract of permanent and mutual self-surrender, which constitutes the essence of marriage, demanded of its very nature an exclusive and indissoluble bond. If it gave high privileges, it entailed severe and inescapable obligations. The rights of the Third Partner are inalienable, and must be respected whatever be the cost. Therefore, it was decreed that in the New Dispensation God's helps would be proportionately generous. Hence it is that there can now be *no marriage contract* between Christian man and maiden which is *not* at the same time one of *Christ's sacraments,* an efficacious sign of grace which "sanctifies both man and wife." As life in the Mystical Body is a complete *supernaturalizing* of the character of human existence, so Christian marriage as a sacrament means a complete supernaturalizing of the character of family life.

To His Wife, iii

Council of Trent

Permanent Title to Grace. The married state, to which the vast majority of Christians are called, is God's great school of sanctification. Therein all entrants, thanks to the *abiding character* of the sacramental helps for the work at hand, have an *absolute title to all the graces* they shall need for the faithful performance of their duties as long as life shall last. In that truly "epoch-making document," Pope Pius XI's *Encyclical on Christian Marriage,* our Holy Father followed St. Augustine in likening this permanent help to the effects of baptism and holy orders, and said:

> [The faithful at marriage] open up for themselves a treasure of sacramental grace from which they draw supernatural power for the fulfilling of their rights and duties faithfully, holily, perseveringly even unto death. Hence this sacrament *not only increases sanctifying grace,* the permanent principle of the supernatural life, *but also adds* particular gifts, dispositions, *seeds of grace,* by elevating and perfecting the natural powers in such a way that the parties are assisted not only in understanding but in knowing intimately, in adhering to firmly, in willing effectively, and in successfully putting into practice those things which pertain to the marriage state, its aims and duties, *giving them, in fine, right to the actual assistance of grace, whensoever they need it for fulfilling the duties of their state.*

1930

But the same great pontiff bespeaks the need of cooperating with grace, else "the grace of matrimony will remain . . . an unused talent . . . unless the spouses exercise these supernatural powers and cultivate and *develop the seeds of grace they have received.*" St. Thomas speaks in the same strain in a beautiful passage: "And because the *Sacraments effect what they represent,* we must believe that grace is bestowed by this Sacrament upon persons marrying, to enable them to have their part in the union of Christ with His Church; and this aid is very necessary for them, that in their application to fleshly and carnal things, they may not be separated from Christ and the Church."

Cont. Gent. iv,78

Helpmates in Love. One more point of comparison between marriage and the Mystical Body. The Church, as Christ's Bride, is subject to Him, but at the same time, is a queen with her own wide sphere of regal and maternal prerogatives. If the wife in marriage is subject to the husband, this does not in any way infringe her womanly dignity as wife and mother and companion. It means, as Pope Pius XI says: "In this body which is the family, the heart [must not] be separated from the head. . . . For if the man is the head, *the woman is the heart,* and as he occupies the chief place in ruling, *so she may and ought to claim for herself the chief place in love.*" It is of such a Christian marriage that Tertullian gives us the classical picture, in words addressed to his own wife:

> Who can tell the happiness of that marriage which is brought about by the Church, confirmed by the Oblation [Mass], sealed with the benediction which the angels proclaim, ratified by the Heavenly Father? Henceforth between the two there is but one flesh and one spirit. They pray together, they prostrate together, they fast at the same time, they instruct each other, exhort and support each other. Together they go to Church, they take their place side by side at the banquet of God, they are united in trial, in persecution, and in joy. They sing Psalms and hymns together, each striving to excel the other in singing the praises of God. To them may Christ send His peace. Whenever two are united there He is also present.

To His Wife,
ii, ix

THE MARRIAGE RITE AS WITH THE NUPTIAL MASS[1]

As marriage is pre-eminently a social function, it is but natural that its religious rites should be affected by local social usages. The customs and rites of the Roman Ritual are but Christianized adaptations of the religious type of pre-Christian Roman marriage. In the Middle Ages these simple rites were overlaid with local customs, but these have once more disappeared, as not consonant with modern tastes.

These questions and answers, which give formal expression to the marriage consent, and actually constitute the contract, are from the pre-Christian Roman rite of betrothal, or promise of future marriage.

The joining of the right hands was a natural marriage rite of both East and West in pre-Christian times. In ancient art husbands and wives are often represented together with their right hands clasped.

The Sacramental Contract

The parish priest, or other priest appointed to witness and bless the marriage, being properly vested and attended, goes to the altar. Those who are to be married come, with at least two witnesses, and kneeling before the officiating priest, answer clearly his inquiry as to their consent. The priest first asks the bridegroom, who kneels at the right of the bride:

N., wilt thou take N. here present, for thy lawful wife according to the rite of our holy Mother, the Church?

The bridegroom answers:

I will.

Then the priest asks the bride in the same manner:

N., wilt thou take N. here present, for thy lawful husband according to the rite of our holy Mother, the Church?

To which she answers:

I will.

After they have thus expressed their consent, the priest bids them join their hands and pledge faith to one another, after the following form:

I, N.N., take thee N.N., for my lawful wife (husband), to have and to hold from this day forward, for better, for worse, for richer, for

---

[1]The translation is by Reverend R. E. Power, *Marriage in Christ,* reproduced by courtesy of The Liturgical Press.

The formula is not to be understood as if the priest were the minister of the sacrament — the contracting parties themselves are co-ministers — but as a testimonial on the part of the Church's official witness.

The marriage ring, too, comes down from pre-Christian times. Tertullian mentions it as a symbol of fidelity; St. Clement of Alexandria speaks of it as a seal of the mistress of the house.

poorer, in sickness and in health, till death do us part.

With their hands still joined, the priest pronounces over them these words:

I unite you in marriage, in the name of the Father, and of the Son, and of the Holy Ghost. Amen.

Then he sprinkles them with holy water, after which he proceeds to bless the ring.

V. Our help is in the name of the Lord.
R. Who made heaven and earth.
V. Lord, hear my prayer.
R. And let my cry come unto Thee.
V. The Lord be with you.
R. And with thy spirit.

Let us pray.

BLESS, O Lord, this ring, upon which we invoke a blessing in Thy name; that she who is to wear it, being true to her husband in all things, may abide in peace according to Thy will, and live with him always in well-requited affection: Through Christ our Lord. Amen.

The priest sprinkles the ring with holy water and gives it to the bridegroom who places it on the ring finger of the bride's left hand, while he says:

With this ring I thee wed, and I plight unto thee my troth.

The priest then says:

IN THE name of the Father, and of the Son, and of the Holy Ghost. Amen.

The bridal veil, again, is a marriage emblem of general occurrence. Tertullian speaks of it as worn by women from the time of the engagement onward. St. Ambrose speaks of marriage as being sanctified by the benediction and the *priestly veil,* which words may indicate that it was put on the bride by the priest. The oldest Roman ritual we have calls marriage the *Nuptial Veiling,* and St. Gregory's Mass Book calls it *The Veiling of Brides.*

The bridal wreath is also of the Greco-Roman world — except that then one was worn by the groom as well: St. Chrysostom and others speak of it.

This prayer is found in the oldest marriage ritual of the West: it dates back to the fifth century at the latest.

A good illustration of how ancient religious rites were symbols to be fulfilled in Christian worship is the fact that a bloody sacrifice with the taking of auspices was a part of the pagan marriage ritual.

Continuing, the priest says:

V. Preserve, O Lord, what Thou hast wrought in us.

R. From out Thy holy temple, which is in Jerusalem.

Lord, have mercy on us. Christ have mercy on us. Lord, have mercy on us. Our Father, etc.

V. And lead us not into temptation.

R. But deliver us from evil.

V. Save Thy servants.

R. Who hope in Thee, my God.

V. Send them help from Thy holy place, O Lord.

R. And out of Sion defend them.

V. Be unto them, O Lord, a tower of strength.

R. From the face of the enemy.

V. Lord, hear my prayer.

R. And let my cry come unto Thee.

V. The Lord be with you.

R. And with thy spirit.

Continuing, the priest says:

Let us pray.

LOOK with favor, we beseech Thee, O Lord, upon these Thy servants and deign to watch over the provision of Thy wisdom for the increase of the human race, that those who are made one according to Thy will, may be safeguarded by Thy protection: Through Christ our Lord. Amen.

Hereupon, if the nuptials are to be solemnly blessed, the parish priest shall celebrate the Nuptial Mass as given in the Missal, being careful to observe all therein prescribed.

In keeping with this rubric, there are local divergencies in the rites of marriage from country to country, but these are tending now to disappear.

This celebrated blessing of the bride, which follows so closely upon the Canon of the Mass, is the fifth-century (or older) Roman blessing, with a slightly more modern addition at the end. The first and older portion is a succinct little treatise on the nature of Christian marriage; the second part holds up to the bride the encouragement of so many saintly mothers.

This blessing can be received but once in a lifetime.

Moreover, whenever there are other laudable customs and ceremonies attaching to the celebration of marriage, it is fitting to retain them.

After the Pater Noster, the priest, standing at the epistle side and turning to face the married couple, who kneel at the altar step, reads over them the following prayers:

Let us pray.

HEARKEN with favor, O Lord, to our pleading, and deign to watch over the provision of Thy wisdom for the increase of the human race, that the union which has Thee for its author, may have Thee also for its unfailing protector: Through Jesus Christ, Thy Son, our Lord, etc.

Let us pray.

O GOD, who of nothing didst create all things by Thy all-powerful will; who in giving order to the world's beginning, didst bestow upon man, as a being made to the image of God, woman to be his inseparable helpmate, in such manner that from the flesh of the man the body of the woman should take its beginning, thus teaching that what was so united in origin, it would never be lawful to put asunder; *O God who hast made marriage sacred by a significance so sublime that in the nuptial contract Thou wast pleased to foreshow the mystical union of Christ and the Church;* **O God, by whom husband and wife** are made one, and the union ordained so in the beginning is enriched with that blessing which neither the punishment of original sin nor the curse of the deluge availed to abolish; look with favor upon this Thy servant who now, upon entering the holy state of marriage, humbly seeks the help of Thy protection. May the yoke that is upon her be one of love and of peace; spotless and true be her married life in Christ; may she follow always the saintly models of her sex; may she be dear to her husband as Rachel was; wise as Rebecca; long-lived and faithful as Sara; may the author of man's downfall have no place in her through deeds of his prompting; may she adhere in all things to the rule of faith and the precepts of Thy law; loyal to her plighted troth, may she abhor all unlawful advances; may she gain strength from the practice of virtue, may her demeanor befit her state, and her modesty inspire respect; may she be apt in the knowledge of heavenly truth, favored with offspring, upright and incorruptible; may she come at last to the peace of the blessed and the glory of heaven above; and may they both see their children's children unto the third and the fourth generation, and come at length to a happy old age: Through the same Jesus Christ, Thy Son, our Lord, etc.

Before blessing the congrega-

This blessing, of Gallican origin, is modeled upon Jewish blessings of the Old Testament. It fittingly expresses the wishes of mother Church for her newly married children.

tion, the priest turns toward the newly married couple and says:

MAY the God of Abraham, the God of Isaac, the God of Jacob be with you, and may He fulfill unto you His blessing; that you may see your children's children unto the third and the fourth generation, and thereafter enjoy forever eternal life, with the help of Jesus Christ our Lord, who with the Father and the Holy Ghost, lives and reigns, God through all eternity. Amen.

Summary. Divine revelation teaches us that Christian marriage is a sign or symbol of the Mystical Body of Christ. In origin, both come from God; in structure, both are one and indissoluble; in proximate end, both have for purpose the diffusion of life; in means, both consist in a love of mutual self-surrender; in goal, finally, both tend to God and eternal happiness, by effecting man's sanctification. The Fathers of the Church recalling how the first woman was taken from the side of the first man, often speak of the Church, Christ's Bride, as having issued from the wound of the lance as He hung upon the cross. This language has even found place in the solemn doctrinal declarations of an ecumenical council, that of Vienne (1311–1312): "[Christ] having yielded up His Spirit, bore it that His side should be opened with a lance, that in the mingled flow of blood and water thence there might be formed the sole and spotless and virginal mother, the holy Church, the Spouse of Christ, just as from the side of the first man in his sleep Eve was taken and fashioned for his wife." Thus, to know marriage, one must know Christ, for the marriage of Christians is a mystical body in miniature.

Twentieth-Century Source Material

(An indefatigable apologist of our day, Father Martindale, in his booklet, WEDLOCK.)

Nothing Christian is understood save within the all-covering doctrine of our incorporation into Christ, so that Marriage itself, within Christianity, must not on any account be thought of in the very least merely as the most faithful of non-Christian monogamists think of it, but as one of many means whereby Christ fills us with His life, and draws us deeper into His own. . . .

Let us recall again what Marriage, by the law of nature, that is, God's will working itself out in creation and in man in particular, is meant to be. It is a free contract made between two human wills, the wills of a man and a woman promising to live together, and with no one else, and till one or the other dies. The object of this contract is primarily the pro-creation of children and the furtherance of the race: the inspiration of the contract should be mutual love and trust. . . .

But now Catholic doctrine teaches that our Lord not only preserves all this — so that the very substance of Christian marriage is a free per-manent contract between two, but raises this so that it becomes a Sacra-ment. Christ does not give Grace merely on the occasion of this contract being made, or because it is made, but through and by means of it. Hence it is strictly true to say that the two Christians who make the contract, by that very fact administer each other the Marriage Sacrament. They are its ministers, not the priest. The Church, in the person of her priest, stands by and blesses, and is glad in the Sacrament that she witnesses; but her priest is not its Minister. The bride and bridegroom are that. So that *the very first and infinitely best wedding gift that they make to one another is Grace* — grace in the divinest sense, such as is freely given by means of every Sacrament and by Christ Himself, and grace directed precisely toward making the married life well and truly livable to the end. . . .

For Sacraments *do* what they *symbolize*. Here you have two human persons becoming "unto one flesh." That, in the long run, symbolizes the union of Christ with His entire Church, His Bride. Today we are thinking of an individual transaction, and Marriage is meant to sym-bolize directly and to effect the deeper union of those who contract it with Christ, and, we may add, looking deeper still, to symbolize the union of the divine with the human nature in our Lord Himself, though this cannot be made more than it is. The eternal Son of God for love of us took up our human nature and so united it with His own divine nature that there is now *one Christ,* one Person, human and divine. Christ catches up each one of us who wills, and so unites him with Him-self that they make "one Spirit," one mystical wedded Person. Numerically we are not one and the same with Christ, any more than bride and bridegroom cease to be two human individuals. But we do become mystically wedded to Him, and each soul has the right to see itself, if it wills, as the Bride of Christ. Hence Christian Marriage, in which two become "unto one flesh," is the most perfect human symbol of that wedlock between each living Christian soul "in grace" and its Redeemer, and this, in its turn, is the intended reproduction, on that level, of the Incarnation. — Quoted by permission of Sheed and Ward.

Topics for Further Discussion:

"The basis of a happy wedlock and the ruin of an unhappy one is prepared and set in the souls of boys and girls during the period of childhood and adolescence." — *Pius XI.*

The right of the Church to establish and define nullifying impediments to the marriage of Christians.

The purpose of banns.

Famous attempts to force the Church to grant divorces: Philip II of France and Pope Innocent III; Henry VIII of England and Pope Paul III; Napoleon I and Pope Pius VII.

Eugenics is scientifically unsound; enforced sterilization, morally wrong.

Readings:

F. X. Doyle, *The Wonderful Sacraments* (New York: Benziger, 1924); "Marriage," pp. 215–247.

G. H. Joyce, *Christian Marriage, A Doctrinal and Historical Study, Heythrop Theological Series* (New York: Sheed and Ward, 1933).

C. Lattey, *Six Sacraments, Papers Read at the Summer School of Catholic Studies, Cambridge, 1929* (St. Louis: Herder, 1930); G. H. Joyce, "Matrimony, Dogmatic Theology," pp. 225–241; E. J. Mahoney, "Matrimony, Moral Theology," pp. 242–257.

A. Lehmkuhl, "Marriage, Sacrament of," *CE.*

E. J. Mahoney, *Christian Marriage,* TF, 30.

Pope Leo XIII, *Great Encyclical Letters of Pope Leo XIII* (New York: Benziger, 1903); "Christian Marriage" (*Arcanum divinae*), p. 58.

M. Perkins, *Speaking of How to Pray* (New York: Sheed & Ward, 1944); "The Sacrament of Matrimony," pp. 129–139.

Pope Pius XI, *Encyclical on Christian Marriage* (New York: America Press, 1931).

W. F. Robison, *The Seven-Fold Gift* (St. Louis: Herder, 1922); "The Consecration of Love," pp. 194–225.

M. Schlüter–Hermkes–E. R. Smothers, *The Family* (New York: America Press, 1938; pamphlet), *passim.*

H. Thurston, "Marriage, Ritual of," *CE.*

S. Undset, *Stages on the Road* (New York: Knopf, 1934); "Reply to a Parish Priest."

A. Vermeersch, *What Is Marriage?* (New York: America Press, 1931.)

Chapter XXII

OTHER CHRISTS

As ministers of Christ,
and stewards of the mysteries of God,
so let men account us
(I Cor. iv,1).

AS THE sacrament of matrimony through natural parenthood
provides for the natural life of Christians, that of holy orders
secures the diffusion of the supernatural life of the Mystical
Body. Both sacraments have a markedly social character. Neither is
necessary for the salvation of any individual; each in its own way is
indispensable for the life of the Church as a body. Marriage cooperates
with God in a *creative* act, and is therefore intrinsically holy: the priesthood enables man to cooperate with Christ in the *redemptive* and *sanctifying* process from birth until death, and hence is of incomparable holiness
and dignity. The whole of the Christian religion is priestly through and
through, since it is merely an extension of, and sharing in, the essentially
priestly character of the Mediator. Those baptized and those confirmed,
as we have seen, share in the lower degrees of the extension to man of
the priestly character and powers of Christ, but the baptized and the
confirmed revere the immeasurably higher rank and powers of those in
holy orders. The laity share in the *internal* priesthood of Christ, to adopt
the language of the *Catechism of the Council of Trent,* whereas the
recipients of holy orders share also in the *external* priesthood. To quote:

Regarding the internal priesthood, all the faithful are said to be
priests, once they have been washed in the saving waters of Baptism.
Especially is this name given to the just who have the Spirit of God,
and who, by the help of divine grace, have been made living members
of the great High-Priest, Jesus Christ; for, enlightened by faith which
is inflamed by charity, they offer up spiritual sacrifices to God on the
altar of their hearts. . . .

The external priesthood, on the contrary, does not pertain to the faithful at large, but only to certain men who have been ordained and consecrated to God by the lawful imposition of hands and by the solemn ceremonies of holy Church, and who are thereby devoted to a particular sacred ministry.

II, c. vii, Q. xxii

Dignity of Priesthood. Such persons are called by Holy Writ "ministers" (that is "servants"), "stewards of the mysteries of God," "*ambassadors* on Christ's behalf," "yea, God's *fellow workers*," whose duty it is to live the Christian life that they "may present every man perfect in Christ Jesus." They are thus called to the august duty of acting as Christ's agents and representatives. Their work is threefold: they carry on Christ's high function of teaching, and Christ's governing function in the Church, but both of these for the sake of their third duty, that of *sanctifying* the members of the Mystical Body. No one can govern well beyond the measure of his own self-government. No one can effectively teach moral lessons beyond the measure in which he lives them. And although the sanctifying effects of the sacraments are not nullified by the sins or sinfulness of their minister, still, taking things in the large, one may say that none but a holy priest will be able "to present every man perfect in Christ Jesus." While there will be occasional lapses in even the highest positions (there is frailty wherever there is flesh and blood), still the *office* of the priesthood is one of the highest holiness, and the priesthood is the Catholic's pride and joy. No one has expressed the Catholic's attitude toward priests better than St. Francis of Assisi, who out of humility declined to be numbered among them. In his *Testament* he writes:

Col. i,28

The Lord gave, and still gives me, such faith in priests who live according to the form of the holy Roman Church, *because of their clerical character,* that if they should persecute me, I would still have recourse to them. And if I were as wise as Solomon and should find a poor priest in this world, I would not preach against his will in his church. And I wish to fear, love, and honor all priests as my lords. I am unwilling to think of sins in them, because I discern in them the Son of God, and they are my lords. And on this account I wish to perceive in this world nothing of the most high Son of God except His most holy Body and His most holy Blood which they receive in the sacraments, and they alone administer to others.

c.III

The ideal of the priesthood is enshrined in the expression *Alter*

See whose ministry is confided to you.
(Pontifical)

Christus, "another Christ," and despite all shortcomings the distinction of priests before the world is that they do possess what Pope Pius X called "that priceless blessing, a *sense of Christ.*" St. Thomas, who postulated no ordinary holiness, but excelling virtue in the cleric, was merely recording Catholic tradition when he wrote that "each minister of the Church is, in some respect, a copy of Christ," and Pope Pius XI interprets this saying as follows: "The priest, as is said with good reason, is indeed 'another Christ'; for, in some way, he is himself a continuation of Christ."

S.T. III. Supp.
Q. xl,a.4

Encyclical, On
the Priesthood

What hath the Lord not placed in my hand [mused St. Charles Borromeo, Archbishop of Milan], when He hath placed there His Only-Begotten, co-equal and co-eternal Son? In my hand He hath placed all His treasures, His sacraments and graces: he hath placed there souls, His dearest possessions . . . : in my hand He hath placed Heaven, which I can open and shut to others.

So it is that priests "watch over our souls, as men who have to render an account."

Heb. xiii,17

Institution of Sacrament. When and under what circumstances was this sacrament instituted? This is an instructive question. "If anyone say that by the words: '*Do this in commemoration of Me,*' Christ did not constitute *and ordain* the Apostles priests, so that they and other priests might offer His Body and Blood, let him be anathema"; the Council of Trent thus answers our question in clearly formulating the age-old belief of Catholics. In other words, as has often been pointed out, by the very fact of establishing the Christian Sacrifice, and commanding its offering, Christ constituted and ordained the Apostles priests. The Apostles were ordained in a sort of super-sacramental manner: the Sacrifice itself brought the priesthood with it. This circumstance is illuminating, as showing the intimate relationship between the priest and his chief function, to offer sacrifice:

Sess. xxii, 1562

Every high priest,
taken from among men,
is ordained . . .
that he may offer up both gifts and sacrifices.

Heb. v,1

Ordination by Imposition of Hands. Christ could (and did) ordain the Apostles priests in this special manner, but for all that He fixed that the mode of initiation for other priests should be the ancient, solemn *rite of laying on of hands.* From Pentecostal days onward this sacrament in its several degrees of diaconate, priesthood, and episcopacy, has been conferred with prayer and a solemn imposition of hands. In the course of time the ordination ritual in the West became enriched with a vast and manifold symbolic ceremonial, during which the vestments and insignia of office are solemnly presented to the candidate. This ceremonial is reverently preserved, but the real essence of the rite remains, as of old, in the laying on of hands.

There is something very special about this ordination imposition of hands. It is not merely an *ordination* rite, that is, the imparting of sacramental powers, but it connotes an election, a calling, a choice on the part of God. *"Clergy"* is a Greek word meaning choice, allotment, portion; the clergy in a special manner are the Lord's choice and portion:

> Ye have not chosen Me,
> but I have chosen you.

In turn God becomes the chosen lot and portion of the clergy themselves: as one is being enrolled in the clerical state, he repeats with joy in the words of King David:

John xv,16

> The Lord is the portion of my cup,
> and mine inheritance.
> Thou art He
> who restorest mine inheritance to me.

Ps. xv,5

Function Seen in Primitive Names. Concerning this same matter of names, one may learn other worth-while lessons by scrutinizing those connected with this sacrament. There is first that of the sacrament itself, *holy order* or *holy orders,* to designate collectively the several ranks or grades of the Christian ministry. The *"deacons"* are so called from a Greek word meaning "servants": the first capacity in which we find deacons in the New Testament is that of serving the common table of the Christian community of Jerusalem. Besides administering all that pertained to the temporal needs of the Christians, they assisted the Apostles in various functions, even that of preaching. It was for his success in preaching that St. Stephen, the protomartyr, won his crown. *"Priests"* or *"presbyters,"* again, are words from the Greek meaning "elders." Even now in ordaining young Levites for the altar, the bishop prays: "May they prove themselves *elders* by the gravity of their conduct and the strictness of their lives; that meditating on Thy law day and night, they may believe what they read, teach what they believe, and practice what they preach." Our word *"bishop"* is a rendering of a Greek word meaning "overseer," or watcher, or superintendent. The Fathers in their homilies often dwell on the truth expressed in that word, that they are set up by God to "watch over" the Christian flock.

Minor Orders. In the chapel of the seminary of the Archdiocese of Chicago the sanctuary is raised four steps above the nave. These four steps are marked respectively with the Latin equivalents of *"Door-keeper," "Exorcist," "Reader,"* and *"Acolyte,"* names which designate the so-called minor orders of the Western Church. As the administrative functions of the early deacons increased, these duties were distributed among inferior assistants, so that gradually there grew up this definite sequence of minor orders. Later on, owing to changes in the manner of administering Church charities, and Church rites, these lower orders fell into desuetude, and for the most part the orders themselves disappeared at Rome. Meanwhile, however, they had been introduced into Gaul, and it was from thence that they returned later on to Rome and were adopted there once more. They remain as ceremonial stages in the promotion of clerics. In the East there is only one minor order, that of Reader, who still enjoys his ancient and important function of chanting the Lessons, other than the Gospel ones, at holy Mass.

Major Orders. Again, the same seminary chapel at Mundelein illustrates the *major orders* in that the altar is set three steps above the sanctuary, and this time the gradations bear the equivalents of *"Sub-deacon," "Deacon,"* and *"Priest."* Whether the subdiaconate is really a grade of the sacrament, or merely the last step in the approach to it, is a question on which theologians are not agreed. There is no room for doubt, however, that the diaconate is a divinely instituted grade of the ministry and that its reception is a true sacrament, imprinting a seal or character on the soul. As ecclesiastical life is now organized, deacons are seminarians and have no administrative duties, but by Canon Law their proper functions still include the administration of Holy Communion and baptism (both by delegation).

Priest and Bishop. The *priesthood* is of two grades, that of simple priests and that of bishops. The chief and most important function of the priest is to offer the Sacrifice, and in this matter, as St. Thomas says, "the Pope's power is no greater than that of a simple priest." But priest and bishop possess this power in different ways: the priest has it and can use it himself, the bishop, besides using it, can *impart* it to others. Therein lies the chief difference between these two grades of the priesthood. Thereby Christ provides not alone for the celebration of the Sacrifice but for the perpetuation of those heralds and ambassadors He singled out to be with Him, and work with Him, and to carry His message to the uttermost parts of the earth.   Acts i,8

Distinction as Related to Eucharist. St. Thomas, the prince of theologians, has an interesting passage in the *Summa* wherein he derives the distinction of all the grades of holy orders from their separate relationships to the Holy Eucharist. The *episcopacy,* treated elsewhere, is alone not included in this engaging little essay:

> The distinction of Orders is derived from their relation to the Eucharist. For the power of Order is directed either to the consecration of the Eucharist itself, or to some ministry in connection with this sacrament of the Eucharist. If in the former way, then it is the order of *priests.* . . . The cooperation of the ministers is directed either to the sacrament itself, or to the recipients. If the former this happens in three ways. For in the first place there is the ministry whereby the minister cooperates with the priest in the sacrament itself, *by dispensing,* but not by consecrating . . . and this belongs to the *deacon.* . . . Secondly, there is the ministry directed to the disposal of the sacramental matter in the sacred vessels of the sacrament; and this belongs to *subdeacons.* . . . Thirdly, there is the ministry directed to the proffering of the sacramental matter, and this belongs to the *acolyte.* . . . The ministry directed to the *preparation of the recipients* can be exercised only over the unclean, since those who are clean are already apt for receiving the sacraments. Now the unclean are of three kinds, according to Dionysius. For some are absolute unbelievers and unwilling to believe; and these must be altogether debarred from beholding divine things and from the assembly of the faithful; this belongs to the *doorkeepers.* Some, however, are willing to believe, but are not as yet instructed, namely catechumens, and to the instruction of such persons the Order of *readers* is directed. . . . But some are believers and instructed, yet lie under an impediment through the power of the devil, namely, those who are possessed; and to this ministry the Order of *exorcists* is directed.   S.T. III. *Supp.* Q. xxxvii,a.2

Ordination Rites. The length of the rites of ordination makes it impossible to reproduce them here. But even if space requirements did not preclude this, it would no doubt be more profitable to single out for comment some of the more characteristic features of the ritual of episcopal consecration and priestly ordination. Originally these similar promotions had an almost identical rite, a prayer said while imposing hands on the candidate. Throughout the centuries, both rites have grown in complexity, but along remarkably parallel lines. The greatest difference now is that three bishops are required to consecrate a new bishop, while only one is needed to ordain a priest. The most imposing ceremonies are here enumerated in opposite columns. With these lists before one, reference will be facilitated.

Priestly Ordination

1. Presentation of candidate.
2. Litany of Saints.
3. Laying on of hands.
4. Investiture with stole and folded chasuble.
5. Anointing of hands.
6. Presentation with bread and wine.
7. Offertory gift: one lighted candle.
8. Concelebration of Mass.
9. New priest given nonconsecrated wine after Communion.
10. Investiture with full chasuble.
11. Oath of homage and obedience.

Episcopal Consecration

1. Presentation of candidate: reading of papal mandate, examination, profession of faith.
2. Litany of Saints.
3. Laying on of hands.
4. Investiture with Gospels.
5. Anointing of head and hands.
6. Investiture with staff and ring.
7. Offertory gifts: two lighted candles, two loaves of bread, two barrels of wine.
8. Concelebration of Mass.
9. Communion under both Species.
10. Investiture with miter and gloves.
11. Enthronization.

The People's "Veto." Ordination was always a function to which as much *publicity* was given as possible. Some sort of public examination of the candidates and the willingness of the people to accept them as their spiritual leaders is one of the conditions attaching to ordination rites. The examination of the bishop-elect now includes, besides his solemn presentation, the reading of the papal mandate, a formal catechizing, and a public profession of faith. At the ordination of priests the candidates are solemnly presented, and their worthiness then attested by the archdeacon. Then, as a relic of times long past, the bishop bids the people "to freely disclose whatever be known of their conduct and morals." The bidding then goes on:

> Let your assent to their ordination be given because of their merit, rather than through any partiality to them. If anyone, therefore, has anything against them, let him come forward and declare it in God's name and for God's sake; but let him be mindful of his own condition.

Penitential Preparation. It was only *after fasting and prayer* that the early Christians at Antioch "imposed hands on Saul [Paul] and Barnabas"; following this example ordinations have traditionally been Acts xiii,2 conferred only after fasting and strict penitential exercises. From the end of the fifth century, in the Latin churches, the ordination of priests was restricted to the Saturdays of the Ember weeks: for the consecration of bishops a Sunday was chosen (because the Holy Ghost came down upon the Apostles on a Sunday), but even in this case a certain penitential mien marks the beginning of the rites. In the impressive Litany of the Saints intercessions are sent up to all the members of the Mystical Body in glory on behalf of the ordination candidates.

"A Priest Forever." The *imposing of hands* is the august sacramental rite. Of the effects of the imparting of "the Holy and Quickening Spirit," St. Gregory of Nyssa, a brother of St. Basil, wrote in the fourth century:

> The same power of the Word renders the priest venerable and honorable, singled out, by this consecration bestowed on him, from his fellowship with the generality of man. While but yesterday he was one of the multitude, one of the people, he is suddenly rendered a guide, a president, a teacher of righteousness, an instructor in hidden mysteries.

Orat. in Bap. Christi

When the imposing of hands is finished, the sacramental character has been imposed.

Anointing with oil as an ordination rite probably originated with the

Visigoths of Spain, who, about the same time that they revived the Old Testament rites of anointing their kings, also began to anoint the hands of priests at ordination. Later the Franks brought in the anointing of the bishop's hands and then of the bishop's head.

Investiture with Insignia. The many ceremonial investitures which now characterize the ordination ritual are also probably due to an impulse first given by the Visigoths. At any rate the conferring of the stole as an emblem of the priestly office is first found among them. This led to manifold imitation. At this point in the present rites a new priest is clothed with stole and folded chasuble while a new bishop is solemnly given a pastoral staff and ring.

Interesting relics of the one-time *gift-procession* survive in the ordination Mass. But, whereas the priest presents merely a lighted candle, the new bishop offers two such candles, and two loaves of bread, and two small barrels of wine. At the solemn rites of canonization, at a papal Mass, in addition to the gifts just enumerated, the Pope's offering also includes two live doves.

Concelebration. By concelebration of the ordination Mass is meant the simultaneous consecration of the *same* sacrificial elements by the officiating bishop and the ordination candidates. This is another very ancient feature here preserved. At both episcopal consecration and priestly ordination the Mass is concelebrated. The new bishop celebrates partly on a side altar and partly at the main altar with the consecrating prelate. The new priest concelebrates as he kneels before the altar at which the bishop offers the Sacrifice. While we often speak of a new priest's first Mass as being a day or so after ordination, strictly speaking his first Mass is in immediate conjunction with the ordination itself. This is one of the most impressive elements of the ordination rites.

Formerly, as we know, all normally communicated under both sacramental Species. When this was in process of disappearing, the laity often communicated under the Species of Bread and were then given a sip of *nonconsecrated wine.* Both these stages of ceremonial development are mirrored in the ordination ceremonies, for the new bishop communicates under both Species, while the new priest, after communicating under the one Species of Bread, partakes of a chalice of nonconsecrated wine.

At the end of the Mass there is a final investiture. The new priest is robed in the full chasuble, and then pays filial homage to the bishop.

This last little rite preserves for us the *feudal swearing of fealty* to the suzerain. The bishop this time receives his miter and gloves, and is then solemnly enthroned on his episcopal chair.

Summary. Holy orders is a sacrament of three degrees which elevates a layman to the highest communicated grade of the priesthood of Christ, thereby empowering the recipient to administer the sacraments and whatever pertains to the government of the Church according to the degree in which one has received the sacrament. Like baptism and confirmation it imparts an abiding character. It is administered by a bishop with prayer and imposition of hands on a baptized Christian of the male sex.

Twentieth-Century Source Material

(Pope Pius XI, on the priest's relations to the Mystical Body, in the Encyclical Letter, THE CATHOLIC PRIESTHOOD, *1935.)*

Besides this power over the real [here used in the sense of "Sacramental"] Body of Christ, the priest has received other powers, august and sublime, over His Mystical Body. There is no need, My Venerable Brethren, to enlarge upon the beautiful doctrine of the Mystical Body of Christ, a doctrine so dear to St. Paul; this beautiful doctrine that shows us the Person of the Word-made-Flesh in union with all His brethren. For from Him to them comes a supernatural influence, so that they, with Him as Head, form a single Body of which they are the members. Now a priest is appointed

> dispenser of the mysteries of God   I Cor. iv,1

for the benefit of the members of the Mystical Body of Christ; since he is the ordinary minister of nearly all the Sacraments — those channels through which the grace of the Saviour flows for the good of humanity. The Christian, at almost every important stage of his mortal career, finds at his side the priest with power received from God, in the act of communicating or increasing that grace which is the supernatural life of his soul.

Scarcely is he born before the priest, baptizing him, brings him by a new birth to a more noble and precious life, and makes him a son of God and of the Church of Jesus Christ. To strengthen him to fight bravely in spiritual combats, a priest invested with special dignity makes him a soldier of Christ by holy chrism. Then, as soon as he is able to recognize and value the Bread of Angels, the priest gives It to him, the living and life-giving Food come down from Heaven. If he fall, the priest raises him up again in the name of God, and reconciles him to God with the Sacrament of Penance. Again, if he is called by God to found a family and to collaborate with Him in the transmission of human life throughout the world, thus increasing the number of the faithful on earth and, thereafter, the ranks of the elect in Heaven, the priest is there to bless his espousals and unblemished love; and when, finally, arrived at the portals of eternity, the Christian feels the need of strength and courage before presenting himself at the tribunal of the Divine Judge, the priest with the holy oils anoints the failing members of the sick or dying Christian, and reconsecrates and comforts him.

Thus the priest accompanies the Christian throughout the pilgrimage of this life to the gates of Heaven. He accompanies the body to its resting place in the grave with rites and prayers of immortal hope. And even beyond the threshold of eternity he follows the soul to aid it with Christian suffrages, if need there be of further purification and alleviation. Thus, from the cradle to the grave the priest is ever beside the faithful, a guide, a solace, a minister of salvation and dispenser of grace and blessing.

Topics for Further Discussion:

The appropriateness of celibacy for the clerical state.
The exclusion of woman from sacramental ministry.
"No loyalty to the Church where disloyalty to the clergy."
The papal condemnation of Anglican Orders. (Cf. "Anglican Orders," CE.)
The relationship of the priest and bishop to the physical Body and the Mystical Body of Christ.
"Not every priest is a saint, but every saint is a priest." In what sense is this true?

Readings:

Pius XI, Encyclical on the Catholic Priesthood (New York: The Catholic Mind, xxxiv, 1936); pp. 41–79.
H. Ahaus, "Orders, Holy," CE.
O. Cohausz, The Priest and Saint Paul (New York: Benziger, 1927); passim.
C. Cronin, The Christian Priesthood, TF, 29.
F. X. Doyle, The Wonderful Sacraments (New York: Benziger, 1924); "Holy Orders," pp. 195–215.
P. A. Kelly, The Romance of a Priest (New York: Kenedy, 1927); passim.
F. C. Kolbe, The Four Mysteries of the Faith (New York: Longmans, Green, 1926); "The Sacraments of Growth," pp. 146–155.

C. Lattey, *Six Sacraments, Papers Read at the Summer School of Catholic Studies, Cambridge, 1929* (St. Louis: Herder, 1930); B. Grimley, "Holy Orders," pp. 163–224.

H. E. Manning, *The Eternal Priesthood* (London: Burns, Oates and Washbourne, 1924); *passim*.

W. F. Robison, *The Seven-Fold Gift* (St. Louis: Herder, 1922); "The Source of Sacred Power," pp. 162–193.

A. G. Schmidt, *The Ceremonies of Ordination to the Priesthood* (Chicago: Loyola Press, 1917). Full English translation of ordination rite.

Chapter XXIII

THE HAND OF THE HEALER

He bound up his wounds,
pouring thereon oil
(Luke x,34).

FROM the very dawn of reason we are taught to pray daily, and many times daily, for special helps "at the hour of our death." For even apart from the fear and natural shrinking at the prospect of departing from life, there is the supernatural aspect of that situation, the all-importance of which cannot be overestimated. For weal or woe, eternity is decided by the dispositions of the will at the hour of death, and Christians have always felt that the archenemy of Christ attacks with "artillery, foot and horse" in what is called the final agony, that is, the supreme struggle for victory. This belief is so described by the Council of Trent:

> Although our enemy seeks and seizes throughout our lives occasions to destroy our souls, still there is no time at which he more strenuously puts forth all the efforts of his cunning to ruin us utterly, and, if he can, shake our confidence in the divine mercy, than when he sees that end of life is imminent.

Now, the loving kindness of God, which, as well as His Wisdom,

reacheth from end to end mightily,
and disposeth all things sweetly,

Wisd. viii,1

has provided special sacramental help for all the other normal and abnormal crises in the Christian life. It was not to be expected that the hour of death, so uniquely critical above every other hour of existence, should be left without its proper sacramental aid. Nor was it. The *crisis of serious illness,* and the collapse of the approach of death, are *provided with a sacrament* wonderfully suited to its proper function; namely, to heal the last wounds of sin, and impart strength and courage at the end.

The customary lucidity of St. Thomas shows to excellent advantage when he treats of the nature and purpose of this sacrament:

> By dispensation of divine justice, the sickness of the soul, which is sin, sometimes passes to the body. Such bodily sickness is sometimes conducive to the health of the soul, where it is borne humbly and patiently and as a penance whereby one may make satisfaction for sin. Sometimes, again, sickness injures spiritual well-being by hindering the exercise of virtues. It was fitting, therefore, to have a spiritual remedy, applicable to sin precisely in this connection of bodily sickness being a consequence of sin. By its spiritual remedy bodily sickness is some-times cured, when it is expedient for salvation.

Cont. Gent. V, iv,73

The Oil of Healing. The therapeutic use of oil is as old as the world, and remains fairly common even nowadays in the form of salves and ungents, and the like. In the domestic life of the Orient this use of oil was a very conspicuous one, and is reflected many times in Holy Writ. When Isaias in a vision foresaw the Redeemer's sufferings, he said:

> From the sole of the foot unto the top of the head,
>   there is no soundness therein:
> wounds and bruises and swelling sores:
>   they are not bound up, nor dressed,
>   nor fomented with oil.

Isa. i,6

Of the story of the Good Samaritan, as told by Christ, we recall how he "bound up his wounds, pouring thereon oil." Again, one remembers, Luke x,34 that when Christ sent the Twelve to preach the advent of the Kingdom of God, in the second year of the public ministry, the account of their labors is summed up as follows:

> And they went forth and preached repentance,
>   and cast out many devils,
> and anointed many sick with oil, and healed them.

Mark vi,12–13

Homely Healing Becomes Sacrament. In Christ's day and long afterwards, anointing with oil in time of sickness was a commonplace household remedy. Nothing could be more appropriate to become the external *sign* of the special sacramental graces with which Christ wished to strengthen the soul in time of sickness than this same, everyday anoint-

God, Physician of souls and bodies, heal thy servant.

ing. Let it not be thought that, because the anointing of the sick was elevated to the dignity of a sacrament, the ordinary, household, non-sacramental anointing was discontinued. Far from it; it continued to play a prominent part in the lives of Christians. But to return to the consideration of the sacrament known as the last anointing.

Compared with Confirmation. The young child at the dawn of its rational life is anointed in token of strengthening in confirmation: before

the last battle the aged warrior is anointed in token of strengthening in
extreme unction. In the identical action what different outlooks! The
former is the joyous application of the oil of the athlete; the latter, the
soothing, softening, penetrating oil of the physician.

Institution Promulgated. The time and place of the *institution* of
this sacrament have not been revealed to us; but for the rest, St. James,
the brother (a Semitic equivalent for "cousin") of Christ, gives us ample
details of its *nature, rite,* and *effects* in the passage:

Is any one among you sick?	*(Subject)*
Let him call in the priests of the Church,	*(Minister)*
and let them pray over him,	*(Rite)*
anointing him with oil in the name of the Lord.	*(Rite)*
And the prayer of faith shall save the sick man,	*(Effect)*
and the Lord shall raise him up	*(Effect)*
And if he have committed sins	*(Conditional effect)*
he shall be forgiven.	

Jas. v,14–15

Reserved to Seriously Sick. The first circumstance that stands out
emphatically in this passage is that this is *a sacrament for the sick.* The
original Greek of James makes it clear that a serious, or dangerous,
sickness is meant. Therefore the Church has always understood that she
is not at liberty to give this sacrament to one, even in imminent danger
of death, but as yet in sound health, as soldiers going into battle, or a
criminal about to be executed. On the other hand, the Church urges it
upon one sick with a serious illness, although in no apparent danger of a
speedy death, as in the case of a consumptive patient, who may well live
for months, or eventually recover. The sacrament is intended to give
special helps in the crisis of a serious sickness, whether the latter prove
fatal or not. The sacrament may be received as often as the sick person
falls into a fresh danger of death, even in the course of the same illness,
when after rallying from danger, he suffers a relapse.

Former Variety in Rites. Some have thought that, since St. James
speaks of *priests in the plural number,* the sacrament must be administered
by several of them together; and, indeed, in both East and West, the Last
Anointing was often so administered. But the Church has taken care to
prevent the notion from gaining ground that it *must* be administered in
this multiple fashion. Such a view, in fact, would really put the sacrament out of reach of most people. **The Church interprets St. James'**

expression as referring to priests as a body or group, much as we speak of the clergy.

The *rite* of this sacrament was probably determined by Christ *only in the general terms* recorded by the Apostle, that there should be an anointing accompanied by prayer. Now these two elements could be combined in a limitless variety of ways. Neither did the Church see fit until almost modern times to prescribe detailed forms. Thus there is no sacramental ritual with a more diversified and interesting history than extreme unction. Something of the former ritual diversity will be indicated below in our survey of the present rites.

Twofold Effects. Let us pass to the important question of the proper effects of the last anointing. A glance at St. James' text shows that he indicates, as following upon the anointing, two effects, or classes of effects, the former unconditionally, the latter conditionally: "the Lord shall raise him up" and "*if* he have committed sin, he shall be forgiven." Let us take up these effects, or classes of effects (for each has a twofold nature), in the order in which the Apostle gives them.

How Soul Is Strengthened. The "*raising up*" here promised means, if the Greek words are closely scrutinized, "*an awakening,* a resuscitation, a stirring up, bringing to life from torpor or dullness." Who does not know that sickness, grave sickness, by lowering the vitality, induces "lethargy, exhaustion, inability to concentrate, stupor, even illusions, and hence extreme difficulty in prayer when prayer is the great necessity"? Under such circumstances it is much harder to make the most fruitful use of ordinary means of grace, and in particular, the ordinary means of setting one's conscience in order, the sacrament of penance. Last anointing was called by the Fathers and Schoolmen, and the Council of Trent sanctions and perpetuates the name, "the complement of penance." It must then *complete,* as it were, the sick man's reception of penance, fill up what perchance was lacking to it, and even go further than the latter could go under the circumstances by way of putting the soul in final readiness to meet God face to face. This the sacrament does by supernaturally stirring up, waking up, invigorating, and strengthening the soul for the needs of the hour. From this it becomes clear why this sacrament cannot be given to those who are not sick. The ordinary means suffice for them. It also becomes clear why it cannot be administered to another class, those, namely, who are too young to have committed any sin. Infants before arriving at the use of reason cannot hinder by sin the flow of Christ-life within them, and so neither ordinary nor extraordinary means are needed to preserve their measure of divine life intact.

Bodily Healing at Times. The healing effects of the sacrament *need not be limited* to soul-healing. The Church teaches that, "*sometimes, when it is expedient for the salvation of the soul*" (Trent), God uses this sacrament to restore the sick to health. Without invoking or excluding miraculous effects, this is readiest understood as follows: the renewed vigor of soul, the calmness and self-possession, "that immunity from disorder," which St. Thomas called the principal effect of the sacrament, combines so forcibly with the bodily strength in resisting disease, that restoration to health is facilitated.

S.T. III Supp. Q. xxxii,a.2

Remission of Grave Sin. The remission of sin, *if* there be such in the soul of the recipient, is also mentioned by St. James as an effect of this sacrament. How and in what degree does the last anointing remit sin? As far as *mortal* sins are concerned, which after all are the only ones that slay the Christ-life, extreme unction is *not* a substitute for the reception of penance. If the sick person is physically able to show repentance in some manner, whether this be complete self-accusation or not, he is absolved before being anointed. Therefore the normal condition of the soul at the reception of last anointing is that of freedom from mortal sin. If, however, a sick person, in the state of mortal sin, be no longer capable of any form of confession, as, for instance, in a comatose state, and have previously conceived at least imperfect contrition for his sins, last anointing makes up for the impossibility of penance, and directly remits mortal sins. Here one sees the ingenuous limits to which divine love can go in providing channels of grace for wayward and willful man.

Remnants of Sin Removed. Venial *sins,* and the *temporal punishment* due to remitted sins, mortal and venial, these are remitted according to the measure of the recipient's contrition. The scope of the remission is limited only by the disposition of the recipient, not by the generosity of the Giver. The Church's traditional teaching in this matter is that, given the proper dispositions on the part of the recipient, that is, a sincere detestation of *all* sin, this sacrament *prepares the soul for immediate entrance into the glory of heaven.* "This sacrament is the last remedy that the Church can give, since it is an immediate preparation

S.T. III, 2. 29, a1; 2. 65, a7

for glory," says the Angelic Doctor, and similarly in another context:

Cont. Gent. iv,73 "This sacrament . . . leaves nothing in him . . . to hinder his reception into glory." These same views are taught by SS. Albert the Great and Bonaventure, Duns Scotus, Durandus, and many others. But since, as in the familiar case of a plenary indulgence, the recipient may fulfill the conditions to a greater or less degree, and thus receive greater or less remission of punishment, so, too, in the last anointing, the patient is not offered a magical means of escape from purgatory, or from the consequences of a misspent life.

Extreme unction does give, to sum up, sacramental grace, fresh vigor, assurance of help to the end, and confidence in a merciful welcome at the portals of God's Country.

Names of Sacrament. Before perusing the present rites of the sacrament, let us recall that the common names for it now are *survivals* from a large field. In the West this sacrament was variously denominated "Holy Oil," "Holy Oil of the Sick," "Anointing with Holy Oil," "Chrism," "The Office of Anointing," "Imposition of Hands upon the Sick," "The Sacrament of the Departing," and the like. *"Extreme unction"* is recorded as early as the ninth century, but became common only some five hundred years later. In the Orient this sacrament was sometimes called *Heptapapdum* (*Office of the Seven Priests*), or more commonly, as at present, *Euchelaion* (Prayer-Unction).

THE RITE OF LAST ANOINTING[1]

The rite is here set out according to the norms of the Roman Ritual, although as a general rule in this country extreme unction is administered immediately after the patient has confessed and received Communion in the form of Viaticum, that is, provision for the journey. In that case the priest omits the prayers 1–3, and begins at number 4.

A wealth of picturesque ceremonial usage formerly attached to the administration of extreme unction. Its functional relation to penance was brought out by associating it immediately with that sacrament, instead, as in our present rites, of having it follow the reception of Viaticum. The sacrament was often, especially in monastic institutions, administered by three, or five, or seven priests,

A. Entry and Blessing of Room

On arriving at the place where the sick person lies, the priest enters the room and says:

1. Peace be to this house.

Response. And to all that dwell therein.

2. Then after placing the oil on a table, being vested in a surplice and violet stole, the priest presents the crucifix to be piously kissed by the sick man; whereupon he sprinkles him, the room, and the bystanders with holy water in the form of a cross, saying: Asperges, as given below.

Antiphon: Sprinkle me, O Lord, with hyssop, and I shall be cleansed; wash me, and I shall be made whiter than snow. *Ps. 50:* Have mercy on me, O God, according to the greatness of Thy mercy. Glory be to the Father, etc. Sprinkle me, O Lord, *repeated as above.*

3. If the sick person wishes to go to confession, let the priest hear him and give absolution. Then let him console the patient with edifying words, and if time permit, briefly remind him of the force and efficacy of this sacrament; let him comfort the soul as need be, and lift it up to a firm hope of life eternal.

Afterwards he says:

4. *V.* Our help is in the Name of the Lord.

---

[1]The translation of the prayers is by Reverend R. E. Power, *God's Healing,* reproduced by courtesy of The Liturgical Press.

who approached the sick chamber in procession. Their entry, and the hallowing of the sickroom, has left little trace in our present rites, but the ancient prayers surviving (4–7) are considerable. Among the features that have now disappeared from this part of the rite are: the incensing of the bed chamber, the sprinkling of the room with ashes in token of penance, laying the sick person on a penitential hair-cloth, and the like. These are clearly reminiscent of the rites of reconciliation after public penance.

These prayers (5–7) are very old forms, coming down from the ninth century at the latest. They seem to be of Gallican origin. In tenor and content they are properly prayers for the entry of the clerics come to administer the sacrament.

R. Who made heaven and earth.
V. Lord, hear my prayer.
R. And let my cry come unto thee.
V. The Lord be with you.
R. And with thy spirit.

Let us pray.

5. MAY there enter this house, O Lord Jesus Christ, with our unworthy coming, unending happiness, heaven-sent prosperity, joy undisturbed, practical kindness, and unfailing health; may every approach of the demons to this place be turned to flight; may the Angels of peace come hither, and harmful discord of whatever sort depart from this house. Glorify Thy holy Name, O Lord, in our regard and bless what we are about to do; show forth Thy power through our coming here, unworthy though we be; Thou who art holy and gracious, and abidest with the Father and the Holy Ghost through all eternity. Amen.

6. LET us pray to our Lord Jesus Christ, and beg of Him to bestow His blessing abundantly upon this dwelling place and

all who make their abode in it. May He give them a good Angel as a guardian, and make them devoted to His service, that they may take to heart the grandeur of His law. May He keep far from them all that might work evil against them; may He deliver them from all anxiety and distress, and protect them from all harm in this their dwelling place; who with the Father and the Holy Ghost, etc.

Let us pray.

7. HOLY Lord, Father almighty, eternal God, graciously hear us, and deign to send Thy holy Angel from heaven to watch over, encourage, protect, abide with, and defend all who have their home in this habitation: Through Christ our Lord. Amen.
8. The foregoing prayers may be omitted in whole or in part, if urgency demand. Then the Confiteor ("I confess") having been said in Latin or the vernacular, the priest gives the general absolution.

I CONFESS to almighty God, to blessed Mary ever Virgin, to blessed Michael the Archangel, to blessed John the Baptist, to the holy Apostles Peter and Paul, to all the saints, and to you, Father, that I have sinned exceedingly in thought, word and deed; through my fault, through my fault, through my most grievous fault. Therefore I beseech blessed Mary ever Virgin, blessed Michael the

In the recitation of the *Confiteor* at this point is preserved a relic of the rites of penance, which sacrament was formerly, as was said, administered at this point. The injunction to the bystanders to recite the seven Penitential Psalms and the Litany of the Saints during the unction reflect conditions when the actual anointing was much more elaborate than at present.

This prayer is a modification of an ancient form of reconciliation or absolution. It will be noted how the laying on of hands is spoken of as a rite indicative and effective of the remission of sin.

Archangel, blessed John the Baptist, the holy Apostles Peter and Paul, all the saints, and you, Father, to pray to the Lord our God for me.

MAY God almighty have mercy on thee, and forgive thee thy sins, and bring thee to life everlasting. Amen.

Then with the right hand raised toward the penitent, he says:

MAY the almighty and merciful Lord grant thee pardon, absolution, and remission of all thy sins. Amen.

Then, before beginning to anoint the sick person, let the priest admonish the bystanders to pray for him, as by reciting the seven Penitential Psalms, and the Litany of the Saints, or other suitable prayers, while he administers the anointing.

9. Extending his hand over the head of the sick person, the priest says:

IN THE Name of the Father, and of the Son, and of the Holy Ghost, may all power of the devil against thee be at an end, through the imposition of our hands and through the invocation of the holy and glorious Virgin Mary, Mother of God, of her most worthy Spouse, St. Joseph, and of all the holy Angels, Archangels, Patriarchs, Prophets, Apostles, Martyrs, Confessors, Virgins, and all the other saints. Amen.

There is beautiful symbolism in the present manner of anointing the sense organs, and the hands and feet. Sin does not attach to the body, but to the soul; but the successive hallowing of the members *through which* the soul has committed sin is eminently fitting.

A great variety of usage lies behind the present simple and touching rite. Anointings were once multiplied to include "almost every member of the body" (old ritual), with a very special one reserved for the spot "where the pain was greatest."

In the same way the words spoken at anointing lacked a prescribed formulation until the sixteenth century. Our present formulae are found in scattered books as early as the tenth century, but they made their way to exclusive usage very slowly.

The present form of this sacrament in the Eastern Church, a form which the Catholic Church recognizes as valid, is: *"Holy Father, Physician of souls and bodies, heal this Thy servant from the infirmities of body and soul which hold him."* Comparison of this with our present form brings out the interesting fact that one emphasizes only the healing properties, while the other expresses only the remission of sin. But these ideas really coalesce, as was seen above.

10. Having moistened his thumb with the Holy Oil, he anoints in turn the eyes, the ears, the nostrils, the mouth, the hands and the feet — each and all with the sign of the cross — saying for each unction:

THROUGH this holy unction and His most tender mercy, may the Lord forgive thee whatever sin thou hast committed by the sense of sight — *changing the name of the bodily power at the end of the repeated form, according to the natural function of the part anointed* — of hearing, of smell, of taste and the power of speech, of touch, by the power of motion. Amen.

For any serious reason, the anointing of the feet may be omitted.

If a member or organ be mutilated, let the part adjoining be anointed, keeping the words unchanged.

The hands of a priest are to be anointed not on the palm but on the back, because the palm has been anointed in ordination.

In any case of extreme urgency, it is enough that the forehead be anointed, with the following form:

THROUGH this holy unction may the Lord forgive thee whatever sin thou hast committed. Amen.

11. The anointing finished, the priest rubs his thumb with a bit of bread, and washes and wipes his hands. This ablution water and the bread are later to be thrown into the fire. The priest says:

Lord, have mercy on us. Christ, have mercy on us. Lord, have mercy on us. Our Father, etc. (*the body of the prayer in a subdued voice*).

V. And lead us not into temptation.

R. But deliver us from evil.

V. Save Thy servant.

R. Who puts his trust in Thee, my God.

V. Send him help from the holy place.

R. And from Sion come to his defense.

V. Be Thou to him, O Lord, a tower of strength.

R. Against the face of the enemy.

V. Let not the enemy prevail against him.

R. Nor the wicked one have power to hurt him.

V. Lord, hear my prayer.

R. And let my cry come unto Thee.

V. The Lord be with you.

R. And with thy spirit.

Let us pray.

These petitions illustrate in their origin the source of most of the shorter prayers of our Christian forefathers; these versicles are one and all taken from the Psalms, the inspired prayer-poems of the Chosen People. There is no phase of the religious aspirations of the human heart that the Psalter does not express with classic perfection. That is why in more Christian times they formed the great, common prayer-book of the entire Church.

The three prayers with which these sacramental rites are brought to an end are likewise venerable monuments of the Christian past. The first two are found in extant manuscripts of the ninth century,

12. O LORD GOD, who through St. James Thy Apostle hast said: *Is any man sick among you? let him call in the priests of the Church, and let them pray over him, anointing him with*

the third may be still older. It will be noted that they recapitulate the thoughts of the celebrated passage of St. James on extreme unction, and enshrine in forceful eloquence the resourceful and inexhaustible love of Christ and the Church for every Christian soul.

oil in the Name of the Lord; and the prayer of faith shall save the sick man, and the Lord will raise him up; and if he be in sins they shall be forgiven him; cure, we beseech Thee, O our Redeemer, by the grace of the Holy Ghost, the ailments of this Thy sick servant; *heal his wounds; forgive his sins; relieve him of all miseries of body and mind;* and graciously bless him with perfect health within and without, that being made well again by the gift of Thy goodness, he may be able to take up anew the duties of his state in life: Thou who with the Father and the same Holy Ghost, livest and reignest God, through all eternity. Amen.

Let us pray.

14. LOOK with favor, we beseech Thee, O Lord, upon N, Thy servant, failing from bodily weakness, and refresh the soul which Thou hast created, that being corrected by Thy chastisement, he may find himself cured by Thy healing: Through Christ our Lord. Amen.

Let us pray.

14. HOLY Lord, Father almighty, eternal God, who by pouring forth the favor of Thy blessing upon our ailing bodies, dost care with endless bounty for the work of Thy hands; graciously hearken to us who call upon Thy holy Name, and having freed Thy servant from sickness and granted

him good health, do Thou lift him up by Thy right hand, sustain him by Thy saving help, defend him by Thy might, and restore him to Thy holy Church with every advantage that could be wished for: Through Christ our Lord. Amen.

Twentieth-Century Source Material

(Gloomy rigorism associated with Purgatory is an excrescence on the ancient traditions, to which modern authors are redirecting our attention, as Professor Bartmann in his book, PURGATORY, A BOOK OF CHRISTIAN COMFORT.)

In Purgatory the virtue of faith remains active and operative, just as it was on earth, and by it the soul knows many things that contribute immensely to its happiness. Faith embraces and includes the whole mystery of our Redemption. . . . Why should not then the Souls in Purgatory experience something of this joy, even more abundantly than God's children on earth? All the more as Christ is the glorious mystical Head of the Souls in Purgatory, as of all those whom faith and charity unite to Him? So we say: these souls are even more intimately connected with the Head of the Church, Christ, than when they were on earth, for no temptation, no doubt, can shake their immovable faith; it cannot be affected by the jeers of freethinkers or the scorn of atheists; on the contrary, the torch of faith burns brightly, clearly, and steadily within the souls that people this mysterious land. The blessed bond of a common faith unites them in a blissful union to Christ and all the other spirits. The best thing about the faith is that, according to St. Paul,

Eph. iii,16   by it Christ dwells in our hearts . . .

To the essential joys of Purgatory and such as are common to all spirits, particular or personal ones may be added. "Every day is a holy day for a soul that tries to bring its will into perfect harmony with God's will." If that is so, then every day in Purgatory is a holy day, for apart from those in heaven, there are no souls more closely united to God's will than those in Purgatory. To these uninterrupted holy days may be added the great anniversaries of our redemption which the Church observes on earth. Since we are all members of one and the same body, whether we be on earth, in Purgatory, or in heaven, we share in all the joys of the whole mystical body of Christ. So we may surely suppose that the splendour of the great festivals which we celebrate here on earth spreads its radiance even as far as Purgatory. It is against our principles to indulge the imagination — the dogma of Purgatory is far too serious and important for that; but the idea that the whole invisible world, insofar as it is peopled by the children of the kingdom of heaven, joins in the celebration of the festivals which the Church of this world observes in honor of Christ, its Head and its Saviour, rests on such solid ground that it cannot simply be brushed aside. Now all our festivals are festivals of grace, and where grace illumines a soul, joy also bursts forth, irrespectively of the point that it may have reached on the road to salvation. . . . And the theme of its song of victory is suggested by St. Paul when he says: "I know in whom I have believed." Every fresh arrival *II Tim. i,12* in Purgatory enters with these feelings of joy and gratitude. Notwithstanding the delay he had to bear with, he knows that in essence and substance his redemption is complete and perfect. . . . There the soul no longer cherishes many hopes: it retains but one, all the others having forsaken it at its entrance into the next world:

> Looking for the blessed hope
> and the manifestation of the glory
> of our great God and Saviour Jesus Christ. *Tit. ii,13*

— Quoted by permission of Burns, Oates & Washbourne.

Topics for Further Discussion:

A frequent difference of time ranging from a half hour to two hours or so, between the moment of apparent death and actual death, and the consequent duty with respect to last anointing.

Neglect to inform a sick person of the gravity of the illness, an omission with probably eternal consequences.

Last anointing *before* a major surgical operation.

Circumstances under which extreme unction is the only means of salvation.

The frustration of extreme unction by impenitence.

Readings:

J. P. Arendzen, *Extreme Unction*, TF, 28.

B. Bartmann, *Purgatory, A Book of Christian Comfort* (London: Burns, Oates and Washbourne, 1936); "Is It Possible to Avoid Purgatory," pp. 204–227.

F. X. Doyle, *The Wonderful Sacraments* (New York: Benziger, 1924); "Extreme Unction," pp. 178–194.

J. B. Ferreres, *Death Real and Apparent* (St. Louis: Herder, 1906); *passim.*

A. J. Kilker, *Extreme Unction* (St. Louis: Herder, 1927).

C. Lattey, *Six Sacraments, Papers Read at the Summer School of Catholic Studies, Cambridge, 1929* (St. Louis: Herder, 1930); L. W. Geddes, "Extreme Unction," pp. 258–282.

————, *Man and Eternity, Papers Read at Summer School of Catholic Studies, Cambridge, 1936* (London: Burns, Oates and Washbourne, 1937); W. J. O'Donovan, "Death from a Medical Point of View," pp. 72–88.

M. Perkins, *Speaking of How to Pray* (New York: Sheed & Ward, 1944); "Anointing for Glory," pp. 117–123.

W. F. Robison, *The Seven-Fold Gift* (St. Louis: Herder, 1922); "Health or Help," pp. 131–161.

R. H. J. Steuart, *The Inward Vision* (New York: Longmans, Green, 1932); "Dies Irae," pp. 139–147.

P. J. Toner, "Extreme Unction," *CE*.

Chapter XXIV

FROM LIFE TO LARGER LIFE

Touching them that sleep . . .
Grieve not even as the rest
who have no hope (I Thess. iv,13).

THE acid test of man's attitude toward life is his attitude toward death. This silent leveler is often called "God's most eloquent messenger"; undoubtedly death speaks a language all understand. His ceaseless visitations bring it about that, whereas the adolescent and the young number kin and friends mostly among the living, the mature and the aging count *theirs* among the dead. Death takes no holiday. Ever and again we are called to assist at the last, sad rites for some departed friend, so that it gradually becomes borne in upon us that still sharper partings will cut off those nearest and dearest to us on earth. For each individual one of life's chief tasks is to learn to die. Sorrow and grief at bereavement are as natural to man as the bonds of love they sever. Just as natural, too, is the desire to show reverential honor to the departed by investing interment with special religious rites. From immemorial years these two reactions in the presence of death have been reckoned as universal human promptings. They attend the biers of civilized and savage, of Hebrew and Hindu, of the Christless and the Christian. But Christianity hallows and tempers both the sorrow of separation and the dutiful piety of obsequies, for we are not like those "who have no hope."

Pagan's Views on Death. It was a mark of the *degeneration of the ancient pagan religions* that the primitive and reverent customs of burial had gradually given way, by the time Christianity appeared, to the desecration of the funeral *pyre*. But it is really not surprising, in the light of the pagan's utter hopelessness before death, as proclaimed by numberless sepulchral inscriptions along the great highways, that the inhuman and degrading practice of cremation had been adopted quite generally. For what was death in the eyes, let us say, of a Roman of the

Interior of a Pagan Columbarium
or "Dovecote"

After cremation of the bodies, the ashes were deposited in the small wall niches,
which were sealed with tile or marble, and the spot then marked for identification.
(Based on illustration in Lanciani's *Pagan and Christian Rome*,
courtesy Houghton Mifflin Co.)

time of Augustus? With one voice his poets called it *night:* Virgil and
Horace, Ovid and Catullus find no fitter phrase for it than "everlasting
night," "perpetual night," "black night." His philosophers echoed, it is
true, mankind's traditional yearnings for immortality, but in such hollow
tones that many, high and low alike, substituted for a belief in the life
beyond "a search for the great Perhaps." Romans of every rank set upon
their tombs such memorials as these:

INTO NOTHING FROM NOTHING HOW QUICKLY WE GO

or the following:

ONCE WE WERE NOT, NOW WE ARE AS WE WERE

or that reckless sentiment so freely used as to be understood when only
the initials of the words were engraved:

I WAS NOT, I WAS, I AM NOT, I CARE NOT

Curses and Blasphemy. Often these pithy messages from the grave
express merely bewilderment as in this puzzling admission:

I LIVED AS I LIKED, BUT WHY I DIED, I KNOW NOT

But frequently the bitterness of death becomes a curse against fate, or
against God. "Curse the harshness of my lot" begs a boy of ten from
his narrow tomb, a tone which is intensified in the passionate blasphemy
of a young woman:

I LIFT MY HANDS AGAINST GOD, WHO TOOK ME AWAY, THOUGH I HAD
DONE NO HARM, AT THE AGE OF TWENTY

Christian "Cities of the Dead." It is a good instance of the contrasts always afforded by Christianity to the spirit of the world that only
a few steps could separate such pagan tombs along the roadside from the
entrances to *Christian burial chambers* where all was vastly different.
Here, amid lively, light-hearted, frescoed scenes of garden and grove,
the elaborate vaulted rooms and galleries breathe peace in the presence
of sorrow, life in the presence of death, and a simple, joyous love following the departed ones now "called from darkness into God's wondrous
light." The Christian calls his *necropolis* a "cemetery," which means a   I Pet. ii,10
sleeping-place, a new word, coined, it seems, by him, and one that

Euseb. H. E. vii,13 puzzled the pagans. Thus, the last edicts of persecution speak of "Christians worshiping in those spots called 'sleeping-places.'"

At First Protected by Law. Although, as the edict just quoted would indicate, the Christian burial places were, in the last persecutions, outlawed and violated, before that they had been *protected and shielded by law* for generations. Even the mangled bodies of the martyrs put to death as outlaws could be reverently caught up, and clothed in fine raiment, and openly carried with flowers and lights and incense and singing to the Christian burial places, whether these were in the open fields, or in the private subterranean vaults of the wealthy members of the community. Thus the burial of St. Cyprian was a spectacle to the entire city of Carthage. Whether in the fields, then, or in the catacombs, as the case might be, the bodies once incorporated into the Mystical Body were reverently laid to rest. The inscriptions on these tombs were such simple, touching messages as these:

IN PEACE

LIVE IN GOD

GOD REFRESH THY SOUL

PEACE BE YOURS IN GOD

MARCIAN SLEEPS IN PEACE

FARE THEE WELL IN CHRIST

PEACE FROM THE BRETHREN

FAREWELL TO THEE IN CHRIST

FAREWELL MY BELOVED IN PEACE

HAPPY FLORENTIUS LITTLE LAMB OF GOD

VICTOR DWELLS IN PEACE AND IN CHRIST

Christians' Views on Death. Here we are in the presence of a radically different attitude toward death, the *Christian attitude,* that of II Tim. i,12 those who *know in whom they have believed,* and who cherish firm hope of life eternal with God. The very air of the Christian sleeping-place is sanctified, because charged with this expectation of a larger, truer life in the unveiled vision of God's Majesty.

Pagan Rites Christianized. Tertullian, who wrote at the end of the second century, tells us of the custom of meeting annually at the graves of the dead to celebrate the Christian Sacrifice. This was a Christianizing of an older, pagan banqueting practice, as was mentioned on page

103. In like manner, *nearly all the other common usages* attending Christian burial today are *adaptations* from the pagan customs of early Christian times. In Tertullian's day it was still reckoned an undesirable relic of paganism that flowers, and wreaths in particular, were strewn upon coffin and grave, but by St. Jerome's time this beautiful custom was accepted without question. Jerome writes to his friend Pammachius: "Husbands spread violets, roses, lilies and purple blossoms on the graves of their wives, and so assuage the sorrow of their hearts in these offices." *Epis. 26 ad Pam.*

The great historian of the early persecutions, Eusebius, speaks of the zealous care with which the bodies were *cleansed,* and anointed with sweet-smelling spices, and *wrapped* in white linen cloths. All of which reminds one forcibly of the Gospel story of the burial of Christ. Of St. Cecilia and other famous martyrs it is known they were interred in regal cloth-of-gold. St. Cyprian, in the middle of the third century, gently scolded his flock that at funerals they wore *"black garments of mourning, whereas the departed have already put on the shining raiment"* *De Mort. xx* of glory. But the wearing of black persisted, and later on even conquered the Church, since it is now found in the sacred vestments and the hangings of altar and bier. St. Jerome contrasts the howling of the heathen funeral procession with the comforting *psalms* as sung by the Christians. The funeral *processions,* held as a rule in the evening, reminded St. John Chrysostom, of Constantinople, of an escort of honor, because of the torches carried, the waving of palm branches, the smoking censer, and oft-echoing cries of *Alleluia.*

Consolation amid Sorrow. Some of the most precious pages of St. Augustine's great letter to God, his *Confessions,* narrate the circumstances of the passing of his saintly mother, Monica. She had said as the end drew near: "Lay this body anywhere; let not the care for that in any way disquiet you. This only I request that you should remember me at the Lord's altar, wherever you be."[1] Augustine relates at what great cost he was able to refrain from weeping then, and "when the sacrificial price of our redemption was being offered for her," and again during the prayers at the grave. Of his tears shed later in private the memory came back to him more than ten years after as he wrote the *Confessions,* and he says of them quite unashamed: "And now let who will judge me as

---

[1] At this time Augustine had no thought of becoming a priest; the expression refers to the custom of a public remembrance of the dead made during Mass.

The Papal Crypt
in the Catacomb of Callistus

he will, and if he find sin therein that I wept for my mother and
for such a mother, let him not deride me, but rather if he be of large
charity, let him weep himself for my sins and ask pardon of Christ
for me."   *Conf. ix,12*

St. Monica died at Ostia near Rome in the summer of 387. From a
far-distant quarter, Syria, in the Christian Orient, we have of about that
same date summary directions concerning Christian burial:

> In the funerals of your dead [we read in a work called the *Constitu-
> tions of the Apostles*] lead them forth with psalms, if they were faith-
> ful in the Lord. . . . Offer the acceptable Eucharist, the anti-type
> of the royal Body of Christ in your churches [for them], and in your
> cemeteries. . . . Assemble in the cemeteries, reading the Sacred
> Scriptures and singing psalms for the martyrs . . . and for all the
> saints [i.e., all departed Christians] . . . and for your brethren.   *Con. Apos. vi,32*

Larger Life Beyond. Enough has been said to make it clear that
our customary offices toward the dead come down to us from remotest
times, and sanctified by the sorrows and resignation of all the Christian
centuries. It should also be doubly clear that in these rites the Church
seeks to give eloquent, if tempered, expression to the genuine human
sorrow of the occasion, together with an expression of her *unshakable
faith in the fuller life* beyond the grave. If she says in one breath, "Weep   *Eccles. xxii,10*
for the dead," she adds in the next, "Weep *but little* for the dead, for   *Eccles. xxii,11*
he is at rest." Excessive sorrow, warns St. Cyprian, is like denying the
faith, and gives the Gentiles a chance to say "that we mourn for those   *De Mort. xx*
who, we say, are alive with God, as if they were extinct and lost." The
faith we profess is couched in those matchless phrases spoken near the
grave of Lazarus:

> I am the Resurrection and the Life;
> he that believeth in Me, even if he die, shall live,
> and whosoever liveth and believeth in Me,
> he shall never die.   *John xi,25*

So well had St. Paul plumbed the meaning of these words that he could
fearlessly say:

> Christ shall be glorified in this body of mine,
> whether by its life or by its death.
> For with me to live is Christ, *and to die is gain*.   *Phil. i,20–21*

The last line of the quotation was graven on his tomb at Rome.

Resurrection of the Body through Christ. St. Paul's converts at Corinth engaged in his absence in endless disputes about the resurrection from the dead, that of Christ, and their own. His mode of answering their questions links our own resurrection to Christ's in such a way that there is, after all, only *one* resurrection from the dead. It is wholly in virtue of the Christian's solidarity with Christ that he is to rise again:

> But, in truth, Christ *is* risen from the dead,
>   the first fruits of them that sleep.
> For since by a man [came] death,
> by a man also [cometh] resurrection from the dead.
>   For as in Adam all die,
> so in Christ shall all be made to live.
>   But each in his own order:
>   Christ the first fruits,
> then they that are Christ's [shall rise] at His coming.

I Cor. xv,20–24

This calm assurance Paul never tired of repeating. Let two other short citations complete our investigation of his thought in this matter. To the same Corinthians he wrote at a later date:

> For we know that He who raised up the Lord Jesus
>   will raise us up also with Jesus
> and place us along with [the just].

II Cor. iv,14

Speaking to the Romans, Paul attributes the resurrection to the indwelling of the Holy Spirit:

> If the Spirit of Him who raised Jesus from the dead
>   dwelleth within you,
> then He who raised up Jesus from the dead
> will also bring to life your mortal bodies
> through His Spirit who dwelleth within you.

Rom. viii,11

In short the resurrection of the Head has merited that of the members, and is the pattern thereof.

Since the abundant consolations the Church's Burial Ritual can afford will one day *be needed to comfort us* in bereavement, it well repays one to peruse these rites betimes. Below are set out extracts typical of the entire service.

EXTRACTS FROM THE RITES OF CHRISTIAN BURIAL

A. Procession to the Altar

The priest, in the house of the deceased, or, in this country, more commonly at the door of the church, sprinkles the corpse with holy water and recites Psalm CXXIX:

Out of the depths I cry to Thee, Lord,
O Lord, hearken to my voice!
Let Thine ears give heed to my plaintive cry!

If Thou, Lord, shouldst retain sin,
O Lord, who could stand?

But with Thee is forgiveness,
And because of Thy Law I trust in Thee, Lord.

I wait for Yahweh, my soul waiteth,
And for His word I look eagerly.

My soul hopeth for the Lord
More than watchers for the morning.

Wait, O Israel, for Yahweh!
For with the Lord is loving kindness and plenteous redemption.

He will ransom Israel
From all its sin.

The corpse is brought to the altar, the symbol of the Heavenly City, where God and His Christ, surrounded by saints and angels, await the coming of the just. To this high assemblage the Church now addresses her petition:

Come to his (her) assistance, all ye saints of God; meet him (her), all ye angels of the Lord, receiving his (her) soul, suffering it in the sight of the Most High.

May Christ receive thee, who hath called thee, and may the angels conduct thee to Abraham's bosom.

Receiving his (her) soul, offering it in the sight of the Most High.

Eternal rest give to him (her), O Lord. And let perpetual light shine upon him (her);

Offering it in the sight of the Most High.

If the Office of the Dead is to be said, it follows here.

B. Mass for the Dead

Many minor peculiarities characterize a Mass for the Dead, or Mass of Requiem, as it is called. In general these are all indications of an extreme antiquity. These Mass-formularies were among the very first to develop, and spread rapidly. Once they had become well known, popular attachment resisted further change.

Among the proper parts of the funeral Mass are:

Collect

O God, whose *property it is always to have mercy and to spare,* we humbly present our prayers to Thee in behalf of the soul of Thy servant N, which Thou hast this day called out of the world: beseeching Thee not to deliver it into the hands of the enemy, nor to forget it forever, but command it to be received by the holy angels, and to be carried into Paradise; that, as it hoped and believed in Thee, it may not undergo the pains of hell, but may obtain everlasting joys. Through Jesus Christ, Thy Son, our Lord, etc.

Epistle

We would not have you ignorant,
brethren,
touching them that sleep,
that you grieve not,
even as the rest *who have not hope.*
For, as we believe that Jesus died and rose again,
God will likewise bring with Jesus
those who have fallen asleep through Him.
For this we tell you as the Lord's word,
that we who live,
who survive unto the Lord's coming,
shall not precede them that are fallen asleep.
For the Lord Himself at a signal —
the voice of an archangel and the trumpet of God —
shall come down from heaven;
and the dead in Christ shall rise first.
Thereupon we the living, who remain,
shall together with them
be caught up in the clouds
to meet the Lord in the air,
and thus *we shall be ever with the Lord.*
I Thess. iv,12–17   Comfort ye one another, therefore, with these words.

Gospel

At that time: Martha said to Jesus,
  "Lord, hadst Thou been here,
  my brother had not died;
  and even now I know
  that whatsoever Thou shalt ask of God,
  God will give Thee."

  Jesus saith to her,
  "Thy brother shall rise again."

  Martha saith to Him,
 "I know that he shall rise again at the resurrection,
  on the last day."

  Jesus said to her,
  "I am the Resurrection and the Life;
 he that believeth in Me, even if he die, shall live,
  and whosoever liveth and believeth in Me,
  he shall never die.
  Believest thou this?"

   She saith to Him,
  "Yea, Lord, I have believed
 that Thou art the Christ, the Son of God,
  that cometh into the world."   John xi,21–27

At the Offering

Have mercy, O Lord, we beseech Thee, on the soul of Thy servant, N, *for which we offer this Victim of praise,* humbly beseeching Thy Majesty that by this service of loving atonement he (she) may deserve to attain everlasting rest. Through Jesus Christ, etc.

After the Communion

Grant, we beseech Thee, Almighty God, that the soul of Thy servant, which today hath departed this world, *being purified and freed from sins by this Sacrifice,* may obtain both forgiveness and eternal rest. Through Jesus Christ, etc.

C. The Final Absolution

At the end of the Mass, the priest lays aside the maniple and chasuble, and puts on a black cope. Then standing at the foot of the corpse, he once more solemnly intercedes for the complete freeing of the soul from all penalties due to sin.

Enter not into judgment, O Lord, with Thy servant, for in Thy sight shall no man be justified, unless by Thee is granted to him the remission of all his sins. Let not, then, we beseech Thee, the sentence of Thy judgment fall heavily upon him (her) whom the true supplication of Christian faith commends to Thee; but by the assistance of Thy grace may he (she) be worthy to escape the judgment of Thy vengeance, who whilst he (she) lived was signed with the sign of the Holy Trinity: Thou who livest and reignest forever and ever. Amen.

D. Order of Burial

It is especially in the concluding section of these rites that the reverence for the dignity of a Christian's body is given expression. To this end the body is not interred until its last resting place has been blessed. Blessing the grave the priest says:

O God, by whose mercy the souls of the faithful find rest, vouchsafe to bless this grave, and depute Thy holy angel to guard it: and absolve from every bond of sin the souls of those whose bodies are herein interred, that in Thee they may forever rejoice with Thy saints. Through Christ our Lord. Amen.

Christ's promise of resurrection through Himself is then sung as an antiphon before and after the joyous hymn "Benedictus" [cf. Luke i,68–79], Zachary's song of thanksgiving at the approach of man's redemption. These sentiments of supernatural happiness should fill the Christian mind as it turns away from the grave. God's mercies are hymned that the fruits of redemption have been applied in last and fullest measure to the soul now entering upon the life of glory.

Summary. The universal sanctifying power of Christianity hallows and assuages man's natural sorrow in bereavement. While tenderly allowing the expression of genuine grief, the Church gently turns her funerary rites into a magnificent profession of faith in the Christian's destiny of sharing the God-life forever, and the further promise of the resurrection of the body through the merits of and after the pattern of Christ's own resurrection.

If it be
   in [view of] this life alone
   that we have set our hopes in Christ,
we are more to be pitied
   than all [other] men.

I Cor. xv,19

Twentieth-Century Source Material

(In Gertrude von Le Fort's HYMNS TO THE CHURCH, *done into English by Mrs. Winthrop Chandler, the Mystical Body finds exquisite treatment: the volume closes with the lines here cited):*

The Last Things: IV

But when once the Great End of all mysteries shall begin,

When the Hidden One shall blaze forth in terrible storms of unfettered love,

When His home-call shall rend the welkin like a tempest and the wasted desire of His creation shall shout for joy,

When the bodies of the stars burst into flame and out of their ashes light shall rise delivered,

When the heavy dykes of matter break and open all the sluices of the invisible,

When decades of centuries sweep back like eagles, and embattled aeons come home to eternity,

When the vessels of speech shall be shattered, and torrents of the never-uttered shall burst forth,

When the loneliest souls are washed up into the light, and see there what they never knew about themselves;

Then will the Revealed One raise my head, and before His sight all my veils will rise in flames,

And I shall lie there like a naked mirror in the presence of all worlds.

And the stars shall find in me their praises, and the ages will find in me their eternity, and the souls will find in me their divinity.

And God will recognize in me His love.

And henceforth my head shall wear no other veil than the dazzling light of Him who is my Judge.

And the world will be lost in this veil of light.

And the veil shall be called mercy, and mercy shall be called infinite.

And the infinite shall be called blessedness. Amen.

— Quoted by permission of Sheed and Ward.

Topics for Further Discussion:

The Church's refusal of funeral services to such as order their bodies cremated (Canon 1240).

The attendance of Catholics at non-Catholic funeral services.

The Protestant rejection of prayers for the departed.

The sending of "Mass cards" instead of elaborate floral pieces.

The custom of having anniversary Masses celebrated for departed relatives, etc.

The series of thirty so-called Gregorian Masses.

The medieval fancy of a cessation of purgatorial suffering on Sunday.

"Heaven is *not* heaven, is not a place of happiness, *except* to the holy." — *Newman*.

The word *purgatory* does not occur in the liturgy.

Page through the Missal and note for how many regular occasions Masses of Requiem are provided, and that there are some *twenty* sets of prayers for such Masses appropriate to a wide variety of circumstances.

"Life is so short it seems God's greatest joke on man." — *St. Catherine of Siena*.

Texts of the Funeral Rites:

Mass for the Dead and the Burial Service (London: CTS).

Mass on the Day of Burial (St. Paul: The Leaflet Missal, 1931).

Masses for the Dead (Milwaukee: Bruce, 1932).

The Funeral Mass and Burial Service for Adults (Collegeville: Liturgical Press, 1929).

Readings:

J. P. Arendzen, *The Church Triumphant*, TF, 35.

B. Bartmann, *Purgatory, A Book of Christian Comfort* (London: Burns, Oates and Washbourne, 1936); "The Psychology of the Hereafter," pp. 47–52; "Purgatory in the Church of the Fathers," pp. 88–107; *passim*.

F. Cabrol, *Liturgical Prayer, Its History and Spirit* (New York: Kenedy, 1922); "Death," pp. 296–307.

C. Grimaud–J. F. Newcomb, *One Only Christ* (New York: Benziger, 1939); " 'Our' Death in Christ," pp. 209–219; " 'Our' Resurrection," pp. 220–233; *passim*.

C. Lattey, ed., *Man and Eternity, Papers Read at the Summer School of Catholic Studies, Cambridge, 1936* (London: Burns, Oates and Washbourne, 1937); F. Moncrieff, "Purgatory and Indulgences," pp. 161–200.

C. Marmion, *Christ, the Life of the Soul* (St. Louis: Herder, 1923); "Coheredes Christi," pp. 388–402.

J. McCann, *The Resurrection of the Body*, TF, 34.

J. B. McLaughlin, *Purgatory or The Church Suffering*, TF, 32.

F. J. Sheed, *A Map of Life* (New York: Sheed and Ward, 1933); "Heaven," pp. 140–144.

H. Thurston, "Burial, Christian," *CE*.

A. Vonier, *Death and Judgment*, TF, 31.

Chapter XXV

EMANCIPATING AND ENLISTING CREATION

Creation itself shall be freed
from its slavery to corruption . . .
unto the freedom . . .
of the children of God (Rom. viii,21).

WHEN will America have a Catholic culture? Or, when, at least, will American Catholics produce a complete and consistent Catholic culture for themselves in America? It is not a flippant play on assonances to reply that this will be when we allow the aura of our cult to permeate out to the utmost periphery of our living, or when we allow our Catholicism to be catholic in the sense of all-embracing. "Christianity, as no other religion," says Father Karrer, "evokes life in its entire extent and fulness, accepting it to bless it. It regards nothing that exists as contemptible or insignificant. *The entire creation is God's.* But for that very reason the universe is not the sum-total of being; 'all things are not the All,' — the belief that they are must ultimately lead to despair or stoical resignation. 'God has entered nature to deify nature.' "[1]

Graduated Dependence. All created things have been created for God, but all are not for God in the same way. The several orders of creation have subordinated relationships toward the First Cause. Irrational creatures subserve man, man subserves Christ, Christ subserves God. "All things are yours," says St. Paul, "and ye are Christ's, and Christ is God's." The close relationship between Christ and irrational nature is emphatically repeated in several passages of the same Apostle, nowhere with greater beauty than in *Colossians:*

I Cor. iii,22

> Now He [Christ] is the Image of the unseen God,
> first-born before every creature.

---

[1] O. Karrer, *The Religions of Mankind* (New York: Sheed and Ward, 1936), p. 214.

367

For *in Him* were created all things in heaven and on earth,
   things seen and things unseen,
whether thrones or dominations or principalities or powers —
   all creation is through Him and unto Him.
   And Himself is prior to all,
and in Him all things hold together.
   He again is the Head of the body, the Church:
it is He who is the beginning, the first-born from the dead,
   so that among all He Himself may stand first.
   For in Him it hath pleased [the Father]
   that all fullness should dwell,
and through Him to reconcile all things to Himself.

Col. i,15–20

Creation at Large Enslaved. Now, one of the minor tragedies consequent upon the primal fall of man was that it *upset and unbalanced* this divinely planned subordination and movement of *irrational nature* toward its End and Author. Since the unseeing and unreasoning homage of the lower orders is rendered God *by assisting man* in paying his meed of homage, when man refused to serve the Creator, lower nature also, as St. Paul puts it, was thereby made subject to vanity, enslaved, like man, beneath the yoke of sin. Man indeed was redeemed from *his* subjection to vanity by Christ's death, but the full emancipation of nature at large from *its* servitude will come only at the end of time:

   Yea, creation with eager straining
awaiteth the manifestation of the children of God.
   For creation was made subject to vanity —
not of its own will, but by reason of him who subjected it —
   yet with hope that creation itself shall be freed
   from its slavery to corruption
unto the freedom of the glory of the children of God.
For we know that all creation doth groan and travail together

Rom. viii,19–22   unto this hour.

Progressive Emancipation. How is nature, thus groaning in enslavement, to use the Apostle's strong language, to be set free? The full and *complete manumission* will come only at "the manifestation of the children of God," that is, at the end of time. But a partial and *progressive liberation* of these enslaved creatures has been going forward in the Church ever since Christ walked the earth in His mortality. It is this idea, with its consequent important bearings on the full Christian life, that is sketched in this chapter. Another sidelight of the Christian's dignity is afforded by examining how the Church liberates and employs the innate, upward tendency of nature toward the spiritual and moral realm, toward inclusion among those things which are brought under the sole scepter of Christ.

Channels of Christ-Life. To start with, one sees how Christ Himself *liberated* and *enlisted certain elemental creatures* by making them channels of His sacramental graces. The water, which now has power to cleanse from original and personal sin, is surely freed from its primal subjection to vanity, and given patents of high nobility among all lower creatures. All water is now in a sense holy water. Likewise the oil, through the sacramental instrumentality of which unfailing strength and assurance are communicated in turn to the adolescent and the dying Christian, is sacred, set apart, and once more fulfills its real destiny of serving God in serving man. The simplest, commonest foodstuffs, bread and wine, are lifted to an unimaginable plane of nobility, when in obeying the transubstantiating Hand of God, their accidents permit us to have a visible Sacrifice and a visible Real Presence. Simple human actions, too, can thus be quickened to the divine touch, and carry the life of God to man. The mutual marriage contract of a man and woman, the ceremonial imposition of hands, and the acts of confession and contrition, all of these are ennobled and enlisted in Christ's "homely" processes of sanctification.

Making Nature Sacramental. Outside the scope of the seven sacraments, which are the work of Christ Himself, the *Church* has been inspired *to emancipate* a vast and indeterminate number of creatures, *sacramentals* as she calls them, and enlist them in her service of God. Thus, in the single act of erecting a building for her worship, the Church has shown countless ways of hallowing and dedicating to *her* use, and thus directly to Christ's use, myriad objects of irrational nature. The stone and brick of the towering structure, the arches, the vaultings, the columns and capitals — are all ennobled by being built into a house of God. The gleaming marbles of the sacrificial altar, or of the Communion table, or of the statuary, the glowing colors of the glasswork, the wrought iron and brass, the tapestries and veils and linens and vestments, the carved crucifix, the jeweled chalices and monstrance — do not all these unthinking objects here subserve their highest possible function by being given a voice in the sweeping oratorio of praise, which a church building is? The poetry of majestic ritual and the strains of noble chant, the fragrance of flowers, the gleaming tapers, the silver-tongued bells, the fuming thurible, the tossing of banners, the palm branches of triumph, the ashes of penance, the black shroud of the cata-falque — all these natural objects the Church has known how to eman-cipate and recruit as aids to sanctity, as subsidiary channels of Christ-life, as strands of "the cords of Adam."

Osee xi,4

But a devout Christian, after all, passes but a small part of the sum total of his life within a church. The long hours of the day are spent in office or factory or market or clinic or court; the precious joys of family life are limited for the most part to the sphere of the home. The scenes of one's occupation and the focal point of the home, both these are of incalculable importance in determining man's life, and therefore in deter-mining the quality of the *Christian life*. Consequently the Church is solicitous that her members should leave nothing undone that might well be done toward emancipating and enlisting as sacramentals the thousand and one natural objects that surround one at home or at work. The munificent hand of the Church is willing and anxious to bless and elevate *all* that pertains to the surroundings of the Christian. Conversely, an enlightened and appreciative use of this power of the Church is a token of the genuine Christian spirit.

Homage and Not Superstition. Before considering in any detail the wealth or variety of the sacramentals, with which Mother Church would surround the Christian life from morning until night, it is well to understand their real value, and to vindicate them clearly from the realm of superstition. Wherein differs the act of a Catholic in putting a blessed medal of St. Christopher on his automobile, let us say, and the act of a savage bushman tying a crooked horn to the axle of his rude cart? The latter, we say, is superstition, while the former is not. But why not? The external action performed may be quite similar in either case. In the case of the crooked horn as a talisman against mishap to the cart, we have a deliberate attempt *to supplement the efficaciousness of prayer* by a means in itself insufficient, but conceived as endowed with religious power. That is superstition. But the medal, by reason of its being blessed by the Church, derives an efficacy from the Church's inter-

cessory powers with God. By the Church's act the medal is embodied
into the grace-system, in a real, if subsidiary, way; the medal becomes a
radiating-point of God's special relationships with man in His Son. The
medal is in God's sight a sign of redemption, invoking in the only Name
under Heaven whereby man must be saved a special blessing, which is   Acts iv,12
another way to say a special Providence of God. Then, too, the medal
is a sign for ourselves, and a reminder of the pious sentiments with which
we commended the automobile and its use to God, through the mediation
in this case of St. Christopher (Christ-bearer), in the knowledge that
God's graces and blessings *are attracted by the continuance of such
sentiments.* Sacramentals great or small thus differ from sacraments in
this, that the efficacy of the sacramentals depends more upon the sentiments of those using them, than in the case of the sacraments. Again,
if one is typing on a machine, say, that has been blessed, he is just as
likely to misspell words or strike the keys in the wrong order as if sitting
at a machine not so blessed. (The example is chosen quite at random,
but the Ritual does provide a blessing for typewriters.) But the knowledge that the machine in the first case has been blessed and dedicated
to God will awake in the user, *if he knows and adverts to the fact,* a
certain sense of reverence as in dealing with something sacred, and of
God's assisting presence, or man's destiny. However fleeting or instanta-
neous, or even inchoative, these acts may be, they are seeds of faith and
hope and love, and so assist man in referring his work to God even
though deficient in orthography. By multiplying around us these minor
agencies of grace, man is assisted in carrying out the Apostle's injunction:

> Whether you eat or drink or do aught [besides],
> do all for the glory of God.   I Cor. x,31

Hallowing the Home. In what manifold ways may not the blessings
of the Church bring a sanctifying influence into the intimacies of life?
Suppose one begins by grouping some of the forms of benediction that
concern individuals and family life. First of all the *home* or *apartment*
is the object of several blessings. The dwelling is sprinkled with lustral
water, as God is besought "to send an angel from heaven to guard,
cherish, shield, and defend all who live in this home." Another form
for the blessing of the home implores of God that through His blessing
it may become "a home of health, chastity, self-conquest, virtue . . .

goodness . . . and thankfulness to God the Father, Son, and Holy Ghost." In some Catholic countries, as in Italy, for instance, the custom obtains of having all the homes blessed yearly on Easter Eve. There is another type of quasi-blessing of the Christian home (and *this* is more common among us), the presence in the home of sacred images, crucifixes, statuettes, and religious pictures from the inexhaustible treasury of Christian art.

Mother and Children. The home, of course, exists only for those who dwell in it, and the Church's solicitude in first instance concerns these living members of Christ. The pregnancy of a mother is blessed with beautiful prayers that recall how the Body of Christ was formed through the overshadowing of the Holy Spirit. We are familiar with the blessing of a mother after delivery, a blessing we call in an old phrase "the churching of women." This blessing is desired by every Christian mother, because it brings her into touch with Mary's Purification. The newborn infant's blessing embodies a beautiful prayer addressed to Christ, "the Son of the living God, born before all ages, but who wished to be born an infant in the fullness of time." In a similar strain, "the merciful Lord and consoler of the faithful" is reminded in a blessing for the sick how He once visited and cheered and cured the mother-in-law of Simon Peter. Part of this exquisite formulary is:

> May the Lord Jesus Christ be with thee, to defend thee; within thee, to preserve thee; before thee, to guide thee; behind thee, to protect thee; and above thee, to bless thee.

Common Household Objects. This solicitude for the sick suggests benedictions for the wine of the sickroom, as well as for bandages and medicines and foodstuffs. Mention of these may serve to introduce us to blessings for household objects. At the blessing of the fire, or fireplace, whether this be the old-fashioned hearthstone, or the modern range, the thought of God as "the Light unfailing" is emphasized. Many of the major household objects are or may be recipients of special blessings. Suppose we single out the radio by reason of its paramount possibilities in advancing or hindering "the growth in Christ." The Church would by all means have so important an instrumentality ennobled and enlisted on the side of Christ. She says in blessing it:

> O God, who walkest on the wings of the wind, and who alone dost

wonderful works; grant, that as by the power implanted in this metal Thou dost bring quicker than the lightning-flash absent things hither, and dost speed things present hence away; so we, taught by new inventions, and supported by Thy grace, may be able more easily and quickly to come to Thee. Through Jesus our Lord. Amen.[2]

Blessing of Automobile. Closely resembling the radio, in its capacity for affecting the Christian life, is the automobile. The blessing for this is well suited to impress upon those who have it employed those sentiments spoken of above, which insure God's benediction and special protection. No day passes but that the press abounds in accounts of automobile fatalities, and everyone knows that the use of an automobile, so helpful in every way, is nevertheless attended by constant and serious dangers. In her blessing for an automobile the Church recalls with a certain solemnity how the immeasurable treasure of faith in Christ came to the Ethiopian man as he was riding in his chariot, and goes on to beg of God that His guiding Hand and His grace may attend this car through all paths and turnings of life.

Acts viii,27

The Airplane. All remember how a small and frail monoplane carried an intrepid American youth in solitary flight across the broad Atlantic. Where Colonel Lindbergh succeeded, many others have failed before and since, at the cost of their lives. But despite these disasters, flying itself goes steadily forward, until the full measure of man's mastery over the air will have been gained. Therefore the Church has prepared a blessing for airships, the first prayer of which is rendered:

O God, who dost all things for Thyself, and hast ordained all the elements of this world for the service of mankind; bless, we beseech Thee, this airship; so that, every evil and danger being far removed, it may promote a wider spreading of the praise and glory of Thy Name, and a more prompt dispatching of human affairs, and that it may foster in the souls of all using it heavenly desires. Through Christ our Lord. Amen.

A second prayer here begs God's blessings on all flyers who commit themselves to Mary's protection, and a third begs for them an angel companion from God on all such journeys.

Blessings for the City. The benedictions just mentioned bring one

---

[2]This form, originally framed for telegraph instruments, is used also for radios.

beyond the home, and out into the world of business. Here, too, the Church would have the sanctification of her presence become ever more prominent. She provides blessings for mills and factories, shops and ships as well as for all manner of agencies more directly social or communal, such as dynamos, telegraph lines, fire-fighting apparatus, ambulances, railway lines and equipment. Printing presses, libraries, archives, schools — all can be enlisted into the corps of the sacramentals, by specially appointed forms of benediction. Just as a city dweller is never far from a church, he need seldom find himself in a place where the hallowing touch of the Church's blessing has not been felt or may not reach.

And for the Country. The vast numbers of Christians engaged in occupations rural or pastoral are not left unprovided for in the Church's armory of blessings. The farm lands themselves are the object of frequent dedications to God; the seed, the sown fields, the ripening crops, the first fruits, the harvest, all are commended to the dominion of Him who alone giveth the increase. The swarming bees, the poultry, the herds and flocks — these, too, may be dedicated to God by prepared and appropriate formulae. Draft animals, man's invaluable servants, are a matter of special concern. Their stable may be placed under heaven's special protection with a prayer that commemorates how "the ox knew its Master and the ass the manger of its Lord" that winter night when there was no room in the inn. Does the farm possess a well, or a pond? In either case, this must have a benediction. Is a bridge building? It will be sprinkled with holy water, while God is asked to depute His angels to protect and defend it, and all who pass over it.

"The Middle Ages Were Ignorant." Of course, a skeptic could point out that much of the value set upon the Church's multiple blessings in ages gone by was due to popular ignorance of the physical sciences. There is truth in the fact that having the modern home protected by a lightning rod is felt to afford that assurance of safety formerly attached to a form of benediction. But when the fullest measure of man's mastery over nature is in every "scientific" way employed, the truest science still proclaims that we are insignificant creatures before the All Mighty. We do well, by the Church's special blessings, and by a thousand informal acts of dedication of our own, to increase and intensify the influence of Christ on the environment, physical and social, in which we live.

Summary. Thus, in whatever place or calling the individual Christian

may live, the solicitude of the Church, whose wisdom is not from hence, unwearyingly furnishes him with many minor instrumentalities of sanctification. She seeks thereby to liberate and enlist and bring under the headship of Christ a creation that groans to be freed from its slavery
Rom. viii,20   to corruption. In particular, the Christian should thus envisage all the primary objects of his work and pleasure, his home, office, factory, and instruments of trade. The *rationale* of this attitude is expressed by St. Paul thus:

> Everything God hath created is good,
> and nothing is to be rejected,
> so it be received with thanksgiving,
I Tim. iv,4   > for it is sanctified by the word of God and by prayer.

Twentieth-Century Source Material

(Few heralds of religion in our day bear comparison with Father Karl Adam of Tübingen; the passage cited is from his great book, THE SPIRIT OF CATHOLICISM.*)*

And in order that the rhythm of social life may be made harmonious by religious and sacramental concords, the Church approves innumerable confraternities and sodalities, confraternity altars and banners and feasts, in which religious effort aims at a specially intimate and lofty community expression. And to that extent it may be rightly said that Catholicism is the "religion of exalted moments." From out of the infinite abundance of its wealth it is constantly, as the hours pass, bringing new gems and new treasures to light, and these give a constantly new stimulus to the faithful and enrich them and do not suffer their interest to flag. So Niebergall describes the Church as a "mistress of joy to her children." The life and activity of the Church are irradiated with innocent joy, serene brightness, devout gladness. "Gothic architecture," said the Protestant Dean Lechler, "is at home only where the Mass bell rings." And he justly adds: "Without the worship of Catholicism neither Raphael, nor Fra Angelico, neither Hubert Van Eyck, nor the younger Holbein, nor yet Lorenzo Ghiberti, Veit Stoss and Peter Vischer, would have produced the marvellous achievements of their art and endowed the churches of God on earth with a wealth of sacred beauty which will remain a treasure for all time." I am not sure that this intimate connection of Christian art with the Holy Eucharist, of the cathedral with the

Tabernacle, is generally recognized. Catholic churches, whether of ancient or modern times, with all their wealth of beauty, are eucharistitc creations. They have sprung from a living faith in the sacramental Presence of our Lord. And where this faith has departed they lose their deepest meaning and are left without the idea which created and inspired them. They are beautiful but dead, bodies without a soul.

Much more might be said to show how the Church, in her sacramental work for souls, embraces also the inanimate creation, consecrating the altar stone, consecrating also the church's bells. We might speak of her Rogation Days whereon she blesses the produce of the fields, and tell how on Corpus Christi Day she carries the Blessed Sacrament out into the spring-time. The whole of nature, the flowers of the field, the wax of the bee, the ears of corn, salt and incense, gold, precious stones and simple linen — there is nothing which she does not bring into the service of the sacred Mystery, and bid them speak of It with their thousand tongues. Under her hands all nature becomes a "Lift up your hearts" (*Sursum Corda*) and a "Bless ye the Lord" (*Benedicite Domino*). "Everywhere," says Niebergall, "she makes men see the Holy and she fills the whole environment of her adherents with its charm and radiance." And where the Church herself is not active, there her children are at work. With hands that are rude and humble, but with eyes shining with the light of faith, they erect their sacred images and crucifixes in fields and by mountain paths, and carry the light and consecration of the divine up to the soaring peak and down to the foaming torrent. Amid a Catholic folk and in a Catholic land — there statues of our Lady stand by the roadside, there the Angelus bell is heard, there men still greet one another with the words, "Praised be Jesus Christ."

*   *   *

We have endeavored to estimate in a few brief sentences the Church's sacramental and mystical action in the formation of the *homo sanctus,* the saint. We have seen that she is able both comprehensively and profoundly, with realistic force and with psychological insight, to bring God's grace down to men, and amid the dust and turmoil of everyday life to make the All Holy visible amidst innumerable candles. . . .

— By permission of Macmillan Company.

Topics for Further Discussion:

"Neither is there any other nation . . . that hath gods so nigh them." Deut. iv,7.

"Christians do not hold that the divine Presence must of necessity follow mystic elements and forms of words . . . but that [it] accompanies a calm and Godlike disposition." — *Synesius, a fifth-century bishop.*

Your description of the ideal Christian atmosphere in a factory or store; in a newspaper or magazine office.

That Christian symbolism affords a richer, and truer, conception of the world.

"The liturgy is creation, redeemed and at prayer, because it is the Church at prayer." — *Guardini.*

Readings:

F. Cabrol, *Liturgical Prayer, Its History and Spirit* (New York: Kenedy, 1922); "Sanctification of Places and Things," pp. 203–244.

A. Fortescue, "Ritual *(Rituale Romanum),*" CE.

A. Gasquet, *Sacramentals and Some Catholic Practices* (St. Paul: Lohmann, 1924); "The Sign of the Cross," pp. 24–30; "Blessings and Consecrations," pp. 39–43; "Images," pp. 44–52, etc.

R. Guardini, *Sacred Signs* (New York: Benziger, 1931); Introduction, pp. ix–xiv; "The Sign of the Cross," pp. 3–4; "Holy Water," pp. 35–38; "Blessing," pp. 69–72; "Sacred Space," pp. 73–76; "Sacred Hours," pp. 81–90, etc.

—— *The Church and the Catholic* (New York: Sheed and Ward, 1935); "The Awakening of the Church in the Soul," pp. 28–31.

O. Karrer, *The Religions of Mankind* (New York: Sheed and Ward, 1936); "Christianity Is the Religion of Wholeness," pp. 211–221.

G. Lefebvre, *Catholic Liturgy, Its Fundamental Principles* (St. Louis: Herder, 1937); "The Sacramentals," pp. 105–117.

N. Maas, *The Treasure of the Liturgy* (Milwaukee: Bruce, 1932); "The Sacramentals," pp. 115–210.

V. Michel, *The Liturgy of the Church* (New York: Macmillan, 1937); "The Sacramentals," pp. 253–273.

Rituale Romanum, Table of Contents.

P. T. Weller, *Roman Ritual,* Blessings (Milwaukee: Bruce, 1946); *passim.*

Chapter XXVI

CHRISTOCRACY THROUGH LITURGY

A glorious Church . . .
holy and without blemish
(Eph. v,27).

GOD does not exist for man, but man exists for God. In a sense nonetheless true, if not so palpably obvious, Christ does not exist for Christians, but Christians exist for Christ. Thus far in this course prominence has been given to the ideas of the supernatural life through incorporation into Christ, and the offices of corporate worship and the sacraments as so many channels of fuller participation in this super-life. The Christian life thus viewed is found to be one of incomparable dignity and nobility by reason of this most intimate association with, and participation in, the life of the God-Man. But our primary concern thus far has been with the question: What is the Church's function in *my* regard? What does the Church do for *me*? Bluntly stating the question in this egocentric way shows how one-sided our view of the Christian life has been, and the singular importance of the proper corrective at this point needs no further exposition.

It behooves us to ask fairly, what are the fruits of the Christian life? If the Christian life is livable, it should produce fruits of personal sanctification through the operation of the immanent, supernatural principle of grace, and fruits of social sanctification, through the measure of the Christian's beneficent influence on those around him. Though growth in grace is not directly measurable, its consequences are so clear there is no mistaking them: "By their fruits ye shall know them." Matt. vii,16

Finding One's Place. Instead of asking, then, what the Church does for me, the question ought to be approached from the other side, and phrased in some such way as this: "Now that I am incorporated into the Church, the Mystical Body of Christ, and live by its super-life, *what is my function in the Church,* what is *my* contribution to the well-being and activity of the Church?" I, even I, am an integral part of the mystic Christ, and as such I have my own proper functions to perform. I must see to it, in the first instance, that I be a sound, a serviceable, smooth-functioning, cooperative unit, that the whole Body be not hindered and lamed on my account.

If one member suffereth,
all the members suffer therewith;

I Cor. xii,26

to the measure in which I fall short, in that measure will the glory of Christ be forever incomplete in me. Christ, who appointed some as Apostles, some as evangelists, some as shepherds and teachers, has ingrafted me into this vast, living Vine of Christ-life, that I may contribute my special fruitfulness to the whole. Definite tasks are envisaged for me in the great work to be done before

we all attain to the unity of the faith
and of the full knowledge of the Son of God,
to the perfect man,
to the full measure of the stature of Christ.

Eph. iv,13

The Work to Be Done. To make Christianity as a whole, humanity as a whole, a faultless reproduction of Himself, is Christ's great task, one to be fully achieved only at the end of time. But, meanwhile, as the myriad gems of the mosaic, each Christian must be separately formed and fashioned and fitted into *his* place in the whole. The Master-Worker is ever at His work, and each one of us, while being ourselves further fashioned in His hand, is at the same time a tool for the fashioning of others.

For we are His handiwork,
created in Christ Jesus for good works,
which God hath prepared beforehand
that therein we may walk.

Eph. ii,10

This fact of cooperating with the Master-Worker gives the Christian life, in unparalleled grandeur, its richness, its joyous creativeness, the gripping enthusiasm of an artist at work shaping Christ in himself and others. Life is given a new and matchless purpose by adoption into the Mystical Body,

that they who live
may no longer live to themselves,
but to Him who died for them
and was raised from the dead.   II Cor. v,14

Solidarity in God vs. Godless Solidarity. Let us consider the up-to-dateness of this Catholic Action on the foundation of the Mystical Body. "A Catholicism with a traditional sociology," observes Gurian in a recent work, "is of little use in a world as it is today." And even before the beginning of this century the centrifugal forces of "post-Christian" civilization had clearly indicated the catastrophe toward which they were bearing us. Reaction, even violent reaction, was inevitable, if civilization was to endure. The Fathers of the Vatican Council (1870) were deliberating, under the guidance of the Spirit of Love, on the doctrine of the Mystical Body as the divine magnet to repolarize, reintegrate, consolidate modern living: "In order that it should be held before the faithful and deeply rooted in their minds, this most excellent concept of the Church . . . *can never be sufficiently emphasized.*" But the sudden outbreak of *Mansi, 51, 539* war dispersed the Council before that consultation was completed. Meanwhile gospellers of materialist and godless communism saw in hatred and class war the means with which to arrest the march of events and win through to a solidarity, dehumanized and de-souled, it is true, but a solidarity. The two programs are diametrically opposed: the clash of conflict will ring throughout the world.

"The Old Order Changeth." From that time forward the Church has ever more insistently spoken the social language of the Mystical Body. Pius X framed the Church's whole program in the words of an almost untranslatable passage from *Ephesians,* about the integration of all men under Christ's headship,

a dispensation to be realized in the fullness of time,
to bring all things [as] to a head in Christ.   Eph. i,10

Pius XI, throughout his long pontificate, emphatically reiterated the same evangel. "The hypostatic union of Christ," he once phrased it, " . . . brings back and puts before us the image of that unity by which our Redeemer wishes His Mystical Body, the Church, to be distinguished. . . . *The personal unity of Christ exists as the divine examplar with which He wishes the structure of society to conform.*" In the greatest of *Light of Truth, 1931* his messages, *On the Reconstruction of the Social Order on Christian Principles,* the pontiff twice appeals to the doctrine of the Mystical Body. In the first of these passages he affirms of the social order, as reformed by functional groups from just natural principles, that it will *bear comparison* with the divinely revealed society of the Mystical Body; that it will be, namely, a quasi-mystical body built on the natural plane. Farther on, in treating of the realization of this new order of things, he says that the *intimate conviction* of membership in the Mystical Body of Christ is a prerequisite to the upbuilding of the new social order:

> Then only will it be possible to unite all in a harmonious striving for the common good, when all sections of society have the intimate conviction that they are members of a single family and children of the same heavenly Father, and further, that they are one body in Christ and members each of the other.

Rom. xii,5, Douay

We are fitted to help build a new social order only when we are thoroughly Mystical Body-minded.

"Communication of Christ-Life." The layman is called upon, even obliged, to work on this vast undertaking, by the very fact of his own membership in the Mystical Body. "The very sacraments of Baptism and Confirmation *impose* . . . this apostolate of Catholic Action . . . since through [them] we become members of the Church, or of the Mystical Body of Christ, and among the members of this body . . . there must be solidarity of interests and reciprocal communication of life."

Pius XI, 1934

"Now from this Pauline visualization of the Church there follow certain inevitable conclusions," argues Archbishop J. F. Rummel in addressing the National Council of Catholic Women. "The first is the necessity of solidarity among its members, involving mutual dependence and mutual responsibility. No member can subsist alone and no member can repudiate a definite sense of proportionate responsibilities for the welfare of others or for the perfection of the whole body. There is no room for individualism in the Mystical Body. Individualism shrivels up men's souls and robs them of the glorious opportunity of sharing in the full life of the Church and enjoying the exhilarating sensation of passing forward the stream of life blood and energy to other members of the 1935 Mystical Body." The picture the Archbishop here paints is the current

Pope Pius XI

pattern of American Catholicism in its social relationships, as one or other further quotation may illustrate. "In an age when men seem to have lost the appreciation of Christianity as a divine life," wrote Archbishop J. G. Murray in 1936, " . . . it seems providential that the Mystical Body has become the basis for the spiritual reconstruction of society." Archbishop S. A. Stritch handed on the same message when addressing a gigantic Catholic Action rally in Milwaukee, 1937:

Saint Paul expresses this social unity with the metaphor of the Mystical

Body of Christ in which we all are members, each doing his own function for the welfare of the whole. *Here we have a formula for which men these days are groping.* We may say that the exaggerated and unfortunate systems proposed are a very part of the groping.

Corporate Worship, Corporate Working. This grounding of society, as it were, on the exemplar of the Mystical Body, the upbuilding of an order of things on the principles, the preferences, and the love of Christ, a program to which the ringing name of Christocracy has been given, how is it to be done? or how is it to be *begun?* The answer is phrased with limpid clearness in a recent utterance of the Cardinal Archbishop of Quebec, Rodrigue Villeneuve, in addressing himself to Catholics in the United States:

> In our day, when every effort is being made to instil a religious spirit in society, it would be a lamentable mistake to give predominant place, above liturgy, to various organizations and pious works, whose supernatural efficacy depends entirely on how much they are imbued with a liturgical sense. And therefore, among the many activities of Catholic Action, the liturgical apostolate should be given the first place.[1]

The Apostolic Delegate, the Holy Father's personal representative in the United States, Archbishop Giovanni Cicognani, in 1934 analyzed the papal program of Catholic Action as comprising:

1. A striving after personal sanctification;
2. More frequent *participation in public worship;*
3. Applying the *zeal thereby aroused* to Christian reform;
4. Through channels of hierarchic guidance.

Some months later, addressing the Catholic Charities Conference, in Peoria, Archbishop Cicognani gave us a masterly exposition of the relations between corporate worship and Catholic social action. He says in part:

> The Holy Sacrifice of the Mass, and Holy Communion, which is an integral part of that Sacrifice, are the only true life that we possess. Upon that nourishment depend both the entire life of the individual Christian and the corporate life of the Church in the body of her faithful here on earth. The Christian has no life of his own. . . .
> From the beginning of the Church even to this day it is in the

---

[1] Cf. *Liturgical Arts,* XI (1937), 1, p. 6.

Eucharist that God makes Himself known: that God and man meet. . . . In earliest times, the clergy and faithful were comparatively few in number. Only one Mass was celebrated in each church. Bread and wine were offered by the faithful for the Holy Sacrifice; and every one brought gifts to be distributed later to the clergy and to the poor. This offering was considered obligatory, for it was held necessary to provide for all the needy of the Christian community. The rich and poor met alike as brothers of Christ. . . . They knew themselves to be incorporated into Our Lord: and as He made Himself one with them and gave Himself for all, so they would fire the world with love and, by His Gospel, make themselves one with another.[2]

Lay Liturgists, Lay Workers. And the laity, the Catholic Actionists, so to speak, how are they reacting to the papal and episcopal leadership? Shall we mention the *Liturgy Manual* of the National Catholic Alumni Federation? It is the belief of this body of lay leaders that in fostering corporate worship they have an "opportunity to engage in an essential form of Catholic Action more important in its ultimate consequences than any . . . merely economic and material plan." With similar direct- 1935 ness the National Council of Catholic Women voiced their corporate program "for the extension of the Mystic Body of Christ," to encourage the nation-wide adoption of courses in worship and plainsong by all Catholic colleges and high schools, and to second eagerly all efforts to promote active lay participation in worship. The Catholic youth move- 1936 ment, as led by the Sodality of the Blessed Virgin, has for several years subscribed to Father Lord's statement: "We may almost say that devotion to the Mass and the appreciation of Catholic Liturgy are at the very basis of Catholic Action." Note the significant resolutions passed by the 1932 Catholic college men and women at the Cleveland Eucharistic Congress of 1935:

"*Resolved:* 1. That the University and College Men and Women become active leaders of Catholic Action;

"2. That the students and graduates attend daily Mass;

"3. That Catholic men and women participate regularly in the Holy Sacrifice by receiving Holy Communion;

"4. That the Liturgical Movement be encouraged and promoted by the University and College students;

---

[2] A. G. Cicognani, *Addresses and Sermons* (New York: Benziger, 1938), pp. 197 sqq.; quoted by permission.

"5. That the students and graduates foster a greater appreciation of public worship or communal prayer."

Sociology and Catholic Action. A phenomenon no one can fail to take into account in any survey of our current Catholic life is the *Catholic Worker* group. Dorothy Day, converted Communist, and editor of the paper of that name, has dedicated the movement to "bringing the doctrine of the Mystical Body to the man in the street," and in this effort she has stated she considers nothing more serviceable than the liturgy.

1934

Bishop J. H. Schlarmann (Peoria) not long ago called liturgy "the finest possible course in Sociology and Catholic Action." Indeed, corporate worship is nowadays serving as a bridge, leading those interested in worship into sociology and sociologists into the sphere of corporate worship. Note this neat juxtaposition: there appeared almost simultaneously two books, *Christian Social Reconstruction*[3] by Dom Virgil Michel, O.S.B., and *Fire on the Earth*[4] by Paul Hanley Furfey. Well, the former book, which is the most systematic American commentary on the great encyclical on reconstruction, is by the late editor of *Orate Fratres,* our leading *liturgical* review; the latter work, by an author of years' standing in *sociology,* becomes a book in praise of the liturgical movement, which the author characterizes as "the rallying point for those who are enthusiastic about the new social charity." "Catholic Action will be successful in its efforts only in proportion as the liturgy is grasped and lived by its promoters," is the theme running through Confrey's *Catholic Action, a Text-Book for Colleges and Study Clubs.*[5] Even the sociologies being written for high-school use focus attention on the motivation of corporate worship and the Mystical Body, as clearly evidenced by Confrey's *Social Studies*[6] and, to a less extent, Ross' *Rudiments of Sociology.*[7]

Gal. iii,29

"All One Person." The whole realm of social, including racial, economic, and religio-political activity of American Catholicism is being grounded on the notion of this endless upbuilding of Christ's Mystical Body. One sector of the far-flung line that is winning singularly beneficent victories is that of racial relationships, based on the recognition and application of the truth that

---

[3] Milwaukee: Bruce, 1937.
[4] New York: Macmillan, 1936, p. 53.
[5] New York: Benziger, 1935, p. 47.
[6] New York: Benziger, 1934.
[7] Milwaukee: Bruce, 1934.

> there is not Gentile and Jew . . .
> barbarian, Scythian,
> slave, freeman,
> but Christ is all and in all.   Col. iii,10,11

Again, to a generation of laymen that had grown impersonally business-like and "efficient" in institutionalized charity, are being recalled the salutary lessons of *The Saints and Social Work*, and the motives of a personal love of the poor set before us once again: "To love our neighbor is to love God; for He is part of the Mystical Body of Christ. Too often we regard the words of our Lord,

> As long as ye did it to one of these, My least brethren,
> ye did it to Me,   Matt. xxv,40

as a mere metaphor, whereas these words are really an accurate expression of the consequences of the union of the poor with Christ in the Mystical Body."[8]

A Glorious Church, a Glorious Land. This Church, the Mystical Eph. v,27 Body as growing up in our own land, is the Church of yesterday, that of the pioneers and missionaries adventuring for Christ on the frontiers of each age's expanding civilization. It is, moreover, the Church of the Middle Ages, of the catacombs, of the Apostles. The Christ that won the love of Paul on the road to Damascus long ago is the same that inflamed St. Ambrose and St. Augustine. Benedict of Nursia knew no other, nor Francis of Assisi, nor Dominic, nor Xavier, nor Vincent de Paul. The martyrs Agnes and Cecilia flung away their lives for the same Lover of Men who captured the affections of Scholastica, Clare and Catherine, Theresa of Avila, and Thérèse of Lisieux. In the narrow rounds of collegiate duties, or in the wider schools of life, the Christian of the twentieth century is called upon in turn to collaborate with the same peerless Leader in making himself and all others, as far as possible, flawless copies and expressions of Christ. The motivating force now is that same love of Christ which Cyprian described long ago in the last lines of his treatise *That Idols Are Not Gods:*

> It is with Christ that we journey, and we walk with our steps in His footprints: He it is who is our Guide and the burning Flame which

---

[8] M. E. Walsh, *The Saints and Social Work* (Silver Spring, Md.: Preservation of the Faith Press, 1937), p. 3.

illumines our paths; Pioneer of Salvation, He it is who draws us toward heaven, toward the Father, and promises success to those who seek in faith. We shall one day be that which He is in glory, if by faithful imitation of His example, we become true Christians, other Christs.[9]

Toward this country, land of our birth, fed in its traditions so largely on the "post-Christian" gospel, and threatened with paroxysms of accumulated poison, what is our obligation in bringing America under the saving and unifying headship of Christ? Bishop O'Hara (Kansas City) once put the question thus in a pastoral to his flock:

> It is reported that on Saturday evening, November 13th, of this year [1937], 3,000 Communists at Madison Square Garden in New York, with clenched fists raised in the Communist salute, "pledged their complete devotion to the Leninist struggle for socialism, for a Soviet America." These represent in America the forces which within the past eighteen months have destroyed or desecrated every church or altar under the power of loyalist Spain. As against their spirit of class hatred we shall gather in the spirit of Him who said: "Love your enemies, and do good to them that hate you." As against materialist atheism, we shall strive to serve God "in spirit and truth." As against a Soviet America, or any other form of dictatorship, we shall pray God for the perpetuation of the spirit of traditional American democracy, and for a renewal of a Christian sense of social justice and social charity. The Sacramental Presence of Jesus Christ on our altars is the symbol and cause of the unity of the Christian people who form the Mystical Body of Christ.

Matt. v,44
John iv,24

The Church is ready for the rescue; we must march with it, conscious of our Christing at baptism, our Christ-strength from confirmation, fed Christ-ful in the daily Eucharist; the call is to us armies of Christocrats recruited in our corporate worship. America's manhood in homes and schools and factories, in council chambers, legislative halls and executive mansions, Christocracy must reach, permeate, consolidate.

Summary. Action corresponds to being, as the axiom runs. The Catholic is embodied in a holy, corporate mode of being. To this state corresponds the duty nowadays called Catholic Action, which, motivated by corporate worship, corporately works out the peaceful revolution of bringing modern life under the headship of Christ.

---

[9]The translation is quoted from C. Marmion, *Christ, the Life of the Soul.*

Twentieth-Century Source Material

(One of the keenest observers of the present scene is Christopher Dawson, from whose book, RELIGION IN THE MODERN STATE, *we quote.)*

It is often objected that Christianity fails to find a remedy for our modern difficulties and that it has no clear-cut solutions for the political and economic problems of the present age. And this is in a sense true, inasmuch as it is not the business of Christianity to solve political and social problems except insofar as these problems become moral or religious. There is no Christian economic system that can be compared with the Capitalistic system or with the Communist economics. There is not even a Christian State in the absolute sense, there are only States that are more or less Christian and all more or less different from one another.

This is not to say, as Protestants used to say, that religion is a matter for the individual conscience and not a social matter at all. Christianity is anti-individualistic — as anti-individualistic as Communism itself. It is not merely a social religion, it is in its very essence a society, and it is only in the life of this One Body that the individual human being can attain his true end. But this society is not a State or an economic organization. It is the society of the world to come, the Bride of God, and the Mystical Body of Christ. Consequently Christian sociology is also theology. It is the theory of this divine society through which and through which alone the true destiny of the human race can be realized. All other societies are partial and relative ones — they exist to serve the temporary needs of humanity and to organize and protect the natural foundations on which the supernatural structure of the one absolute society is built up. As soon as they make themselves the absolute ends of human life they become *counter-churches,* representative of that City of Man which to the end of time makes war upon the City of God. — Quoted by permission of Sheed and Ward.

Topics for Further Discussion:

"There is no time or place better suited for the education of youth in Catholic Action than the schools and colleges." — *Pius XI* to Brazilian Hierarchy, 1936.

" 'Two things equal to a third are equal to each other.' . . . Incorporated into Christ, we are concorporated with each other." — *Bishop R. A. Kearney* (Auxiliary, Brooklyn), 1935.

"Once the Christian feels . . . the joy of incorporation into the Mystical

Body . . . then almost spontaneously . . . he will strive to impart the blessing he has received." — *Bishop J. A. Duffy* (Buffalo), 1935.

"Catholic peoples are wont to help one another mutually . . . practising the law of charity and brotherhood which joins us all in one Mystical Body of Christ." — Opening words, *Letter of Spanish Bishops,* 1937.

Readings:

Pope Pius XI, *On the Reconstruction of the Social Order on Christian Principles,* edit. *Catholic Mind,* June 8, 1931.

——— *On Atheistic Communism,* edit. *Catholic Mind,* April 22, 1937.

——— *The Present Position of the Catholic Church in the German Empire,* edit. *Catholic Mind,* May 8, 1937.

B. Confrey, *Catholic Action, A Text-Book for Colleges and High Schools* (New York: Benziger, 1935); "On What Is Catholic Action Based?" pp. 46–68; *passim.*

L. Civardi, *A Manual of Catholic Action* (New York: Sheed and Ward, 1936); A. G. Cicognani, Preface, pp. xvii–xxiii; *passim.*

R. J. S. Hoffman, *Restoration* (New York: Sheed and Ward, 1934); "Restoration and the Great Adventure," pp. 181–205.

J. LaFarge, *Interracial Justice* (New York: America Press, 1937); "A Catholic Interracial Program," pp. 172–187.

O. von Nell-Breuning, *Reorganization of Social Economy* (Milwaukee: Bruce, 1937; enl. ed.); "The Mystical Body of Christ," pp. 253, 254; "The Well-Springs of Love," pp. 339, 340.

J. F. T. Prince, *Creative Revolution* (Milwaukee: Bruce, 1937); "Catholic Revolution," pp. 98, 99.

F. Stratmann, O.P., *The Church and War* (New York: Sheed and Ward, 1928); "The Mystical Body of Christ," pp. 17–30; "War and the Mystical Body," pp. 31–46.

M. Ward, *Insurrection vs. Resurrection* (New York: Sheed and Ward, 1937); "Epilogue," pp. 538–551.

Chapter XXVII

IN RETROSPECT

*Whose is the adoption and the glory . . .
and the liturgy and the promises*
(Rom. ix,4).

B Y PRESENTING Catholicism from the point of view of its worship, this book has sought to give the reader a clearer realization of his or her position in the Christian scheme of life. This point of view is inspirational; for, in the very fact of having been baptized, Catholics are absorbed in a super-world, endowed with super-life, become in a real sense, super-men. In exploring these truths the mind is lifted to hitherto unsuspected heights, which afford the vision of new wonders in man's own nature, in the Church, and in the eternal kingship of Christ. Indeed, it may be said that even a glimpse is had of the enchanting beauties of the eternal mansions of God.

Lifted Up in Christ. A deep sense of how much human nature is ennobled by being elevated to the divine life in and through Christ should be one of the most abiding and transcendent lessons of this study. Another most important conviction, which should be built into the Catholic's everyday consciousness as a result of this course, is a sense of fellowship, of corporate being, so to speak, with Christ and His members. Christian *worship* is social and corporate, that of the members with the Head: "No man goeth to the Father save through Me"; Christian *work* is likewise corporate, that of the members with the Head: "Without Me ye can do nothing." When these truths are pondered, and their vital consequences little by little drawn out in the diversities of life, they should produce a twofold modification of one's appreciation of Christianity. Toward Christ a new bond is formed in the deepened knowledge of His mediatorial character, and in the realization of a sharing in His life and eternal priesthood. Respecting the neighbor, there is a far loftier estimate

John xiv,6

John xv,5

391

of social obligations toward actual or potential fellow members of the Mystical Body. Contact with religion in its holiest rites, sacrifice, and sacraments has its enduring gains from the unifying concepts of Christ-life and Christ-work. In fine, in the light of the new knowledge, a synthesis results in which the close-knit solidarity of all things under the scepter of Christ is perceived as never before.

From the first page onward our never-failing Scriptural guide has been the Apostle of the Gentiles, from whose inspired writings have been drawn all our proofs. He now furnishes us with the apt phrases set out above, in which we can sum up, and, as it were, outline the leading ideas of the whole book.

No Longer I That Live. After a preparatory comparison of the "catechism religion" of childhood with maturer understanding of the same, we began with the stupendous fact that the Christian through Christ, the second Adam, has been lifted up by *adoption* into the family of God. We are made to share, as St. Peter puts it, in the very nature of God. We are made *to live,* to return to the language of St. Paul, *with the life of Christ* living within us. In fact, in the eyes of God, all other life save this co-life with Christ is as death. We who were formerly dead in sin have been *brought to life in Christ.* Commenting on those words, "It is no longer I that live; it is Christ that liveth in me," an English author writes:

Gal. ii,20

> As if he [Paul] would say (for he is speaking only of the life of grace), I have life in the eyes of God only so far as the life that I have is the life of Christ, only insofar as I *am* Christ. God looks for Christ in me, and I am alive — I am what He created me to be — in proportion as He sees Christ in me.[1]

A comparison of the new life acquired in Christ with the old integrity lost in Adam led us to estimate more truly, if still inadequately,

> what is the breadth and length and height and depth —
> to know the charity of Christ that surpasseth knowledge,
> *that ye be filled unto all the fulness of God.*

Col. iii,19

Ye Did It to Me. As a further step, the contemplation of Christianity as a Christocentric universe proves to be a theme rich in abiding values.

---

[1] R. H. J. Steuart, *The Inward Vision* (New York: Longmans, Green, 1933), pp. 56, 57.

What consequences may not follow from the general realization of the truth that to be a Christian means to be one with Christ? What a many-sided revelation of Christianity as a whole, of my place in that union, and of the endless *social implications* of this living solidarity!

> Herein there is not gentile and Jew . . .
> barbarian, Scythian, slave, freeman,
>   but Christ is all and in all.   Col. iii,11

Once upon a time the living of this truth had such direct and transforming effects on Christians everywhere and in all their mutual associations, that the world in amazement cried: "See how these Christians love one another!" To such an extent nowadays "has the love of many grown cold," that a scoffing cynic parodies the ancient tribute, "See how *these* Matt. xxiv,12 Christians tear one another!" In the widespread disillusionment and dis-belief of our age, Catholicism will flourish and extend its beneficent influence only in proportion as it renews itself in this sense of social union and love. It is a sad commentary on the needs of the age that the motto of the present Pope should have to read: "In justice there is peace."

Corporate Worship a Dictate of Nature. It is profitable at times to give oneself an account of ideas so long taken for granted that they are as it were relegated to the storerooms of the subconscious mind. In this way the *concept of worship* was re-examined early in the course. It was seen to be one of those primal impulses of human nature, as native to man as the air we breathe, and as necessary. It belongs to the very creaturehood of man, so to speak, to "seek after God," to adore Him Acts xvii,27 as the Creator, to thank Him as our Benefactor, to petition Him as Father, and to appease Him as Judge. These spontaneous motions of the mind and heart are voiced in external acts of worship (called in their ensemble liturgy), and quite naturally they tend to become public and social. "There can be no religion," says St. Augustine, "there can be no Contra Faustum, religion true or false, without external ceremonial." xix,11

Priestly Mediation. What characterizes Christian worship in con-trast to all others is its manner of approach toward God. The pagan and the Jew go direct to God; the Catholic approaches Him only *through a*

> *Mediator* standing between God and man,
> himself a man, Jesus Christ.   I Tim. ii,5

Instead of being an intermediary who interposes Himself between God and man, Christ is found to be a real and vital connecting bond, linking the human with the divine.

> Amen, Amen, I say to you:
> ye shall see the Heaven opened
> and angels of God ascending and descending
> upon the Son of Man.

John i,51

To Preserve, Not to Destroy. How admirably Christianity in its worship *hallows* and *purifies* and *preserves* all that is good in man's native religious impulses was seen in broad outline. From the dawn of recorded history man was everywhere seen to seek to set up permanent relationships between himself and the Creator. To this end he organized social and public worship, set up priesthoods, devised elaborate rituals, composed fixed prayers, and instituted all the other offices of religion. He early explored the many possible ways of expressing devotion through varieties of vocalization, of posture, through the use of natural symbols, and in the manifold creation of sacred art-forms. Further, he felt prompted to consecrate to God all the crises of natural life, birth, adolescence, marriage, sickness, death, interment, with religious usages proper to each case. Lastly, he sought to sanctify the ebb and flow of time by observing annual and seasonal religious commemorations of various kinds. By common consent men were agreed that the *paramount expression of the religious sentiment* is the public giving to God of a gift in token of personal and social dedication to Him, and this act is called *sacrifice.* To this natural groping toward God, how eminently Christianity is the all-satisfying solution! Its hierarchical priesthood, its inexhaustible wealth of ceremonial, its almost limitless use of nature and art in its worship, its sevenfold sacramental system — all are utilized in lending adornment and beauty to its crowning excellence, the day-by-day re-enactment of the Christian Sacrifice, which is no other than the supreme Oblation by which the race was ransomed.

"Do This in Memory of Me." The august rites of this *Christian Sacrifice* naturally bulked large in the preceding chapters. Thus, we saw how these were carried out in primitive Christianity, and in the early Middle Ages. This is another valuable aspect of human and Christian solidarity. In Christ, and only "in Him all things hold together." The

Col. i,17

analysis of the Christian's sacrificial calendar showed us the function of this detailed unfolding and commentary on the life of Christ in the upbuilding of a Christian character. In the case of Christ, the Christian theory of life is presented as the Way and the Truth and the Life: in the case of the perfect Christians, the Blessed Virgin Mary and the saints, the theory is shown as reduced to practice. This endless procession of Christ-in-His-brethren walking before us in triumph, little by little engenders an unwavering conviction that we, too, have been

> fitted for our portion
> of the inheritance
> of the saints in light.   Col. i,12

Our Eucharistic Age. The vicissitudes of twenty centuries have brought, as we saw, certain *changes in Christian piety* in relation to even such a central mystery as the Holy Eucharist. Thus, while in the fullest possession of a sacrificial consciousness, the earlier Christians regarded the Eucharist chiefly as a *means* of sacrifice and of personal union with God through the actual reception of Communion. This attitude having been in a measure obscured by historical developments, a new attitude of adoration and worship of the Eucharist itself, of the Eucharist as an *end*, one might say, came largely to occupy the center of Christian piety. In the earlier period the Eucharist made the Sacrifice possible, and was the bond of union with Christ and among the members of the Mystical Body; but there was lacking all that wealth of conscious devotion directed to the Real Presence. In subsequent ages Christ in the Eucharist was reserved in tabernacles, was visited and adored and borne in processions; but Christ as the food and drink of the Father's Table had but a rare opportunity to delight men with His sweetness. Our cursory survey of the guiding factors in these developments awakened a sense of gratitude in us, that it is our good fortune to live in the twentieth century. We are entering upon an age which preserves the gains of the worship of the Real Presence, and is learning to combine them with the ancient sense of fellowship in sacrificial oblation and sacrificial banquet. Additional grounds for gratitude were seen on surveying the reforms now in quiet progress for the fuller and more intimate participation of the laity in the sublimest offices of worship.

Fountains of Life. The study of the *sacraments* was approached by

way of the respective *rites of administration*. This method of approach
was found to yield new and deeper knowledge of these *life-giving streams*.
"The Sacraments," says Archbishop Goodier, "to him who believes in
the indwelling of Jesus Christ, are very much more than the mere ceremonial which is seen from without. They are the ingrafting into the body,
they are the joints of the limbs; they are the channels through which the
blood of Jesus Christ flows down into the members."[2] Abundantly providing for every necessity of life and tenderly anticipating every wish,
the sacraments lift us to the plane whereon the divine life is communicated
to us

> through His power
> which is at work in us,

and the Apostle has it,

> He [God] is able to accomplish
> far beyond all that we ask or understand.   Eph. iii,20

Even in the recreant

> where sin hath been multiplied,
> grace hath abounded yet more.   Rom. v,2

These great sacramental graces the Christian knows he can obtain *only*
in the sacraments. Therefore he "frequents," as he says, the sacraments
as the most manifest evidence of the practice of his religion.

Christocrats. The force of the Christ-life within produces in its
gradual unfolding a sense of strength, an exigency of motion and activity,
an impelling desire to use these faculties for Christ-work. This is the
Christian life in operation, to *"work out* our salvation," our own and   Phil. ii,12
our neighbor's. This means, above all else, allowing Christ to dominate
our lives, to have full sway over our thoughts, aspirations, and activities.
St. Paul called this "making the life of Jesus manifest in our bodies."   II Cor. iv,10
And the timely bearing of all this in the reconstruction of the social
order now being undertaken was reviewed in words of Pius XI and of
our own American bishops.

There, in a word, is the immediate term of the Christian life, Christ,

> the Alpha and the Omega
> the Beginning and the End.   Apoc. xxi,6

---

[2] A. Goodier, *The Inner Life of the Catholic* (New York: Longmans, Green, 1933),
p. 53.

Christians in the world, no less than those called to the sublime consecration of the priesthood or cloister, are Christ's soldiers, His ambassadors, His collaborators, His members in which He is to reach
Eph. i,23 fulfillment.

Christ within you, your hope of glory,
Col. i,28   Him we proclaim.

This fellowship, in which each one "is rooted and built up in Him," we
call our holy Mother, the Church, and Catholics love her with a filial love.

Conscience, it is true, demands that we yield the Church obedience, but
love anticipates conscience by prompt and ready service. Salvation, indeed, requires allegiance to the Church unto death, but fellowship inspires
a sense of responsibility and of common interests and active leadership
for the cause of Christ. "This is the very definition of a Christian," says
Cardinal Newman, "one who looks for Christ; not who looks for gain
or distinction, or power, or pleasure, or comfort, but who looks for the
Saviour, the Lord Jesus Christ."

I count all things loss
by reason of the excellence of the knowledge of Christ.
For His sake I have suffered the loss of all things
and count them but refuse
in order that I may gain Christ
and be found in Him . . .
so that I may know Him,
what the power of His resurrection,
what fellowship in His sufferings,
and become one with Him in His death,
in the hope that I may attain to the resurrection from the dead . . .
Phil. iii,9–14   to attain the reward of God's heavenly call in Christ Jesus.

Outline of Course

"Whose is the adoption"
Chapters I to III
Adult Catholicism; the Mystical Body, Super-nature, or grace.

"and the liturgy"
Chapters IV to XXV
Christ's Priesthood; natural impulse to worship; this, as elevated by

Christ; worship as a social bond; the ecclesiastical year; the altar and vestments; a papal Mass in the early Middle Ages; the relation of the frequency of Communion to the general sacrificial consciousness; historical and ritual study of the present Roman Mass; modern modes of active lay participation in worship; the Breviary: the seven sacraments in relation to Christ-life in the Mystical Body; the Christian's "falling asleep"; sacramentals.

"and the promises"
Chapters XXVI, XXVII
    Christ-work, and its rewards; summary.

Twentieth-Century Source Material

(Monsignor Fulton J. Sheen is an eloquent herald of the doctrines this book propounds: with his permission we conclude by quoting):

. . . Communism, as it has been defined, is not peculiar to Russia alone. We see there the mobilization of souls under an *economic* disguise where one hundred and sixty millions of God's creatures destined for eternal Life are dehumanized and reduced to the state of ants, whose sole business in life is to build up the great ant-hill of the Classless Class; we see it in Mexico with a *political* disguise where treason is synonymous with the worship of the Crucified; we see in with a *racial* mask in Germany where the State would crush the religion of Him who rose from the dead, and would return to the barbarism of gods who are still rotting in their graves. In all three instances men are bludgeoned into living their lives without God; they are beaten and hammered into the new pattern of the collective, where barbarism filters through the sieve of the State and where the gods of economics are supreme. . . .

Because Communism does insist on the social and communal it can never be opposed by any system of ideas, or by any loud shouting about rugged individualism; it can be stopped only by something social and communal. Because it mobilizes souls for economic ends and crushes the spiritual element in man, it can only be stopped by some force which mobilizes souls for eternal ends and preserves the honor of a man. In a word, Communism can be met only by that historical form of Christianity which has been excluded from Western Civilization for 300 years and which is now returning from exile, namely the Church. . . .

What is the Mystical Body of Christ which alone can save the soul of civilization? The Mystical Body of Christ is the Church. In order to understand its role in the world let it be recalled that when Our Blessed Lord was born of the Virgin Mother over 1,900 years ago, under the floor of the world in the village of Bethlehem, the political, economic and social conditions of His time were very much like our own. Politically there was militarism with practically the whole world under the eagle of Rome; economically there was heavy taxation. Hence the burning question: Was it lawful to pay tribute to Caesar? Socially there was a legalism, an externalism, a Pharisaism, or what we call Puritanism.

The interesting and instructive fact is, that He who set out to regenerate a world said nothing whatever about militarism, about finances, about economics; He said nothing about armaments; He even said nothing about the horrors of war. And yet He did something for all these things. How? Not by making religion a purely individual affair, for how could a million men love God without loving one another, since things that are equal to the same thing are equal to each other. Rather did He lay plans to infuse the world with a new society, a new kingdom, a new organism which would be the social prolongation and extension of the Divine Life He brought to earth. . . .

As He took a human body from the womb of His Blessed Mother, overshadowed by the Holy Spirit, so now He took His Mystical Body or the Church from the womb of humanity, overshadowed by that same Holy Spirit. Through this Body, Christ at the right hand of the Father, continues to do the same three things He did with His physical body, namely, to teach, govern and to sanctify. . . .

The Eucharist is the lymph of the Mystical Body. Like a mighty river it swells and sweeps through the Church in every part of the world, breaking its secret of salvation to every individual Catholic, whispering its wondrous message of love for the healing of wounds to this one, dipping the chalice of its wine for the increase of joy to that one, thus making them all one because nourished by the same Bread. Such is the meaning of the words of St. Paul: "WE, being many, are one body, for we all partake of one Bread." What a beautiful foundation for the social order, for international peace, for brotherly love, for we are all one in Christ Jesus Our Lord! . . .

The Communion rail is, for that reason, the greatest Democracy on the face of the earth; it is even a greater Leveller than Death, for there the distinction between the rich and poor, the learned and unlearned, disappears; there the millionaire must take the paten from the common laborer; the employer must kneel at the same board as the employee; the University Professor must eat the same Bread as the simple Irish woman who knows only how to tell her beads. The dividing wall between nationalities is broken down and rebuilt into that spiritual Kingdom where all are one, because One Lord, one Faith, one Baptism, one Bread. Every prayer is said in the great context of that brotherhood, where every selfish act of the rich and every envious deed of the poor, is envisaged as a hindrance to the unity of that Body. Hence we say if you want to be a real Communist then be a communicant and bring your hearts to the anvil of Divine Life, and have them all forged into unity by the Eucharistic Flames of the Sacred Heart, where we call one another, not the atomic name of "Comrade" but the spiritual name of "Brother."

Do you say that the Eucharist as a solution for world troubles is too idealistic; do you condemn it because it is impractical? Certainly it is impractical, but that is precisely why it will succeed. . . . There is only one way left to effect social and economic reconstruction, and that is by spiritual and moral regeneration through the Eucharist and the Sacrifice of the Mass.

That is the impractical way Our Lord chose to redeem and transform the world. Extremely impractical it was to put down economical and political justices by dying on a cross, which was the first Mass; impractical indeed it was to win a victory over the hardened hearts of men by going down to defeat; impractical indeed it was to save a selfish world by the Love which ended in the Sacrifice of the Cross. . . .

SELECT BIBLIOGRAPHY

(On which supplementary reading and term papers may be based)

K. Adam, *Christ Our Brother* (New York: Macmillan, 1931).

———— *The Spirit of Catholicism* (New York: Macmillan, 1936).

A. d'Alès, *Baptism and Confirmation,* Catholic Library of Religious Knowledge (St. Louis: Herder, 1929).

J. Baudot, *The Breviary, Its History and Contents,* Catholic Library of Religious Knowledge (St. Louis: Herder, 1929).

J. M. Bover, *Three Studies from St. Paul* (London: Burns, Oates & Washbourne, 1931).

P. Bussard, *The Vernacular Missal in Religious Education* (Washington: Catholic University, 1937).

P. Bussard–F. M. Kirsch, *The Meaning of the Mass* (New York: Kenedy, 1942).

F. Cabrol, *The Books of the Latin Liturgy,* Catholic Library of Religious Knowledge (St. Louis: Herder, 1932).

———— *Liturgical Prayer, Its History and Spirit* (New York: Kenedy, 1922).

———— *The Mass, Its Doctrine, Its History, The Story of the Mass in Pen and Picture* (New York: Kenedy, no date).

———— *The Prayer of the Early Christians* (New York: Benziger, 1930).

———— *The Mass of the Western Rites* (St. Louis: Herder, 1934).

———— *The Year's Liturgy* (London: Burns, Oates & Washbourne, Vol. I, 1938).

A. J. Clarke, *The Mass: From Shadows to the Truth* (London: Burns, Oates & Washbourne, 1943).

P. Claudel, *Ways and Crossways* (New York: Sheed and Ward, 1933).

H. E. Collins, *The Church Edifice and Its Appointments* (Philadelphia: Dolphin, 1936).

M. C. D'Arcy, *The Mass and The Redemption* (London: Burns, Oates & Washbourne, 1926).

M. C. D'Arcy, V. Huby, L. de Grandmaison, P. Rousselot, *The Life of the Church* (New York: Sheed and Ward, 1932).

C. Dawson, *Religion and the Modern State* (New York: Sheed and Ward, 1935).

**B. Dix, *The Shape of the Liturgy* (Dacre: Westminster Press, 1944).

**W. Douglas, *Church Music in History and Practice* (New York: Scribner, 1937).

L. Duchesne, *Christian Worship, Its Origin and Evolution* (New York: Macmillan, 1923).

J. Duperray, *Christ in the Christian Life* (New York: Longmans, Green, 1927).

G. Ellard, S.J., *Men at Work at Worship* (New York: Longmans, Green, 1940).

—— *The Dialog Mass* (New York: Longmans, Green, 1942).

J. Fitzsimons–P. McGuire, *Restoring All Things: A Guide to Catholic Action* (New York: Sheed and Ward, 1938).

L. W. Geddes–H. Thurston, *The Catholic Church and Confession*, Calvert Series (New York: Macmillan, 1928).

A. Goodier, *The Inner Life of the Catholic* (New York: Longmans, Green, 1933).

L. de Grandmaison, *Personal Religion* (St. Louis: Herder, 1929).

C. Grimaud–J. F. Newcomb, *"My" Mass* (New York: Benziger, 1928).

—— *One Only Christ* (New York: Benziger, 1939).

J. C. Grunden, *The Mystical Christ* (St. Louis: Herder, 1936).

R. Guardini, *The Church and The Catholic* (New York: Sheed and Ward, 1935).

**A. G. Herbert, *Liturgy and Society* (London: Faber & Faber, 1935).

J. Jungman, *Liturgical Worship* (New York: Pustet, 1941).

O. Karrer, *Religions of Mankind* (New York: Sheed and Ward, 1936).

J. Kearney, *The Meaning of the Mass* (London: Burns, Oates & Washbourne, 1936).

J. Kramp, *Eucharistia, Essays on Eucharistic Liturgy and Devotion* (St. Paul: Lohmann, 1926).

—— *The Liturgical Sacrifice of the New Law* (St. Louis: Herder, 1926).

M. Laros, *Confirmation in the Modern World* (New York: Sheed and Ward, 1938).

**Books marked with a double asterisk (**) are outstanding works in this field by non-Catholic authors.

C. Lattey, *St. Paul and His Teaching, Aberdeen Lectures* (St. Louis: Herder, 1930).

—— *Paul* (Milwaukee: Bruce, 1939).

E. Leen, *The Holy Ghost* (New York: Sheed and Ward, 1937).

—— *The True Vine and Its Branches* (New York: Kenedy, 1938).

D. A. Lord, *Our Part in the Mystical Body* (St. Louis: Queen's Work, 1935).

F. F. Mahoney, *Branches of the Vine* (Milwaukee: Bruce, 1936).

C. Marmion, *Our Way and Our Life* (St. Louis: Herder, 1927).

—— *Christ, the Life of the Soul* (St. Louis: Herder, 1923).

C. C. Martindale, *The Mind of the Missal* (London: Sheed and Ward, 1929).

—— *The Words of the Missal* (London: Sheed and Ward, 1932).

E. Masure, *The Christian Sacrifice* (London: Burns, Oates & Washbourne, 1944).

E. Mersch–J. R. Kelly, *The Whole Christ* (Milwaukee: Bruce, 1938).

V. Michel, *The Liturgy of the Church* (New York: Macmillan, 1937).

T. H. Moore, *Beyond the Altar Rail* (New York: Fordham University, 1939).

National Liturgical Week, 1940 (Newark: Benedictine Liturgical Conference, 1941).

J. E. O'Mahony, *Where Dwellest Thou?* (St. Louis: Herder, 1937).

M. Perkins, *At Your Ease in the Catholic Church* (New York: Sheed and Ward, 1938).

R. Plus, *God Within Us* (New York: Kenedy, 1924).

—— *In Christ Jesus* (New York: Benziger, 1923).

F. Prat, *St. Paul* (New York: Benziger, 1929).

J. de Puniet, *The Mass, Its Origin and History* (London: Burns, Oates & Washbourne, 1931).

J. Putz, *My Mass* (Ranchi: Catholic Press, 1938).

J. A. Rickaby, *The Ecclesiastical Year* (New York: Wagner, 1927).

A. Roulin, *Vestments and Vesture* (St. Louis: Herder, 1931).

St. Thomas Aquinas, *On the Blessed Sacrament and the Mass*, translated with Notes by F. O'Neill (London: Pepler & Sewell, 1935).

F. J. Sheed, *A Map of Life* (New York: Sheed and Ward, 1933).

M. de la Taille, *The Mystery of Faith, An Outline* (New York: Sheed and Ward, 1930).

———— *The Mystery of Faith:* Book One (New York: Sheed & Ward, 1940).

A. Tanquerey, *The Spiritual Life* (Tournai: Desclée, 1930).

A. Thorold, *The Mass and the Life of Prayer* (New York: Sheed and Ward, 1939).

H. Thurston, *Lent and Holy Week* (New York: Longmans, Green, 1904).

"The Treasury of the Faith" Series (New York: Macmillan).

**E. Underhill, *Worship* (New York: Harper, 1937).

G. Webb, *The Liturgical Altar* (London: Burns, Oates & Washbourne, revised edition, 1939).

T. Wesseling, *Liturgy and Life* (New York: Longmans, Green, 1938).

M. Zundel, *The Splendour of the Liturgy* (New York: Sheed and Ward, 1939).

Pamphlet publications of The Liturgical Press, Collegeville, Minn.; in particular:

L. Beauduin, *Liturgy, The Life of the Church.*

W. Busch, *The Mass-Drama.*

E. Caronti, *The Spirit of the Liturgy.*

V. Michel, *My Sacrifice and Yours.*

P. Parsch–W. Busch, *Study of the Mass.*

The Holy Sacrifice of the Mass: A Text for Religious Discussion Clubs (Paterson: St. Anthony Press, 1940).

INDEX

Abercius, 90

Acclamations, 107

Acts of Apostles, 3

Adam, Karl, 24, 312; *Christ Our Brother*, 54, 139, 152; *St. Augustine*, 26; *The Son of God*, 11; *The Spirit of Catholicism*, 26, 376, 377

Adam, old, new, 30, 31

Adoption, sonship of, 9

Adoptionism, heresy, 170

Adoration, element of worship, 58

Aesop's *Fables*, 16

Agape, 81

Agnes, St., 387

Albert the Great, St., 183, 342

Almsgiving in Mystical Body, 38, 39

Altar, basic motion of, 62; Christian, 109–121; free-standing, 123; house of, 111; medieval developments, 115; pagan, converted (*illustr.*), 62; position of priest at, 112; relics upon, 114; represents God, 111; tabernacle introduced, 115, 116; table type, 111, 112; table type (*illustr.*), 110

Alter, K. J., 223

Alumni Federation, Nat. Cath. *Liturgy Manual*, 385

Ambrose, St., 162, 189, 233, 234, 235, 259, 275, 303, 317, 387; on daily Communion, 141; *Sacrament of the Incarnation*, 11

Angilbert, St., *Ritual* of, 106

Anointing, last, *see* Extreme Unction

Ante-Mass, alleluia anthem, 167; and synagogue service, 153–158; as in Roman Missal, 156, 157; Collect Prayer, 165, 166; *Confiteor*, 162; Creed, 169; *Gloria*, 164, 165; Gospel, 168, 169; Gradual, 167; growth of, chants, 156, 157; Introit, 164; *Kyrie*, 164; Lesson, Scripture, 166; (Mass of Catechumens), 153–172; Mediatorial prayer of, 166; Ordinary of, 1 Part, 161–170; prayers for all classes, 158, 159; service of prayer and instruction, 159; Synagogue, service described, 158

Arendzen, J. P., *The Church Triumphant*, 366; *Extreme Unction*, 351

Arnault, A., *On Frequent Communion*, 149

Atchley, C. F., *Ordo Romanus Primus*, 136

Athanasius, St., 165, 249

Atonement, 31

Attwater, D., *Into Thy Hands*, 245

Augustine, St., 8; Blessed Virgin and Mystical Body, 17; *City of God*, on worship, 124, 125; 'greatly impressed' by chants (Pius XI), 235; introduced Offertory anthem at Mass, 192; love distinguishes a Christian, 92; on 'Amen,' 190; on bishop's throne, 111; on chasuble, 118; on Christ's mediation, 45; on Christ's place in public prayer, 236; on Communion as union, 132; on Communion in Mystical Body, 64, 65; on Confirmation and Mystical Body, 275, 276; on daily Communion, 141; on Eucharist as 'Life,' 197; on 'filling up' Christ's sufferings, 307; on frequent (daily) Communion, 148; on Gospel of St. John, 206, 207; on joy of choral worship, 220; on lay priesthood, 50; on martyrs' feasts, 104; on Mass as thank-offering, 174; on members of Mystical Body at Mass, 183; on need of ceremonial, 68, 393; on need of religion, 57; on sacrifice of Christians in Mass, 76; on secrecy surrounding Eucharist, 173; on sorrow at mother's death, 357; on unifying function of Communion, 199; wept at Psalm-singing (*Conf.*), 234

Baptism, 246–262; administered by Apostles, 249; and Mystical Body, 23; and new life (St. Paul), 250; birth into Mystical Body, 71; called by Christ a birth, 247, 248; incorporation into Mystical Body, 246; infant form used for adults (U. S.), 252; institution of Sacrament, 247; laver of rebirth (*illustr.*), 248; literally a dipping, 246; oath, 251; of crowds on Pentecost, 249; on Easter Morning, 251; rite of, 253–262; rite, anointing with chrism, 261; rite, enrolling a catechumen, 253–256; rite, exorcisms, 256; rite, "Great Scrutiny," 257, 258; rite, saliva, meaning of, 258; rite, salt, meaning of, 254–256

407

Bartmann, B., *Purgatory*, 350, 351, 366
Basil, St., 235, 331
Basilica, ancient (*illustr.*), 83; Roman, floor plan of, 129
Batiffol, P., *History of the Roman Breviary*, 245
Baudot, J., *The Breviary*, 245
Benedict of Nursia, St., 387; *Rule* of, 232
Benson, R. H., *Christ in the Church*, 11
Berulle, P., de, Card., 11
Bishop, E., *Liturgica Historica*, 123, 136
Blessed Virgin Mary, 395; called a priest, 53; Mother of Mystical Body, 17; Sodality, *see* Sodality of Blessed Virgin
Blessing of people, how introduced into Mass, 207
Boeser, F., *The Mass-Liturgy*, 172, 192, 209
Bonaventure, St., on frequent Communion, 145
Boniface, St., 122
Bourdaloue, L., 262, 263
Bouscaren, T. L., *Canon Law Digest*, II, 217
Boyle, H. C., 222, 223
Bread (and wine), elements of sacrifice, 75
Bread, daily, Eucharistic in Mystical Body, 72
Breviary, *see* Divine Office
Bridgett, T. E., *History of the Holy Eucharist in Great Britain, A*, 171, 292
Burckard, John, *Order of the Mass*, 225, 226
Busch, J. F., 213
Bute, J., *The Roman Breviary*, 245

Cabrol, F., 232, 233; *Liturgical Prayer*, 92, 108, 245, 366, 378; *The Mass*, 92, 172, 192, 209; *The Prayer of the Early Christians*, 92, 108; *The Year's Liturgy*, I, 108
Callistus, Catacomb of, 358
Calvary, Mount and Mass, 175–176
Canada, 277; Martyrs, 105
Capuchins, 146
Carolina, colony, 277
Carroll, John, 277
Catechism of the Council of Trent, The, 323; on frequent (daily) Communion, 148; on need of seven sacraments, 74; on rarity of Communion in past ages, 285; on relation of Holy Eucharist to other sacraments, 280, 281
Catherine of Siena, St., 146, 366; *Dialogue*, 208–209
Catholic Action, and Confirmation (Pius

XI), 265; in current sociology, 386; springs from Mystical Body (Pius XI), 382
Catholic Women, Nat. Council of, 382, 385
Catholic Worker, The, 386
Catholicism, "Adult," 1–10
Catullus, 355
Cecilia, St., 357, 387
Cerejeira, E. G., 265
Ceremonial, natural, Catholicized, 68; natural need of, 60
Challon, R., 277, 278
Chant, Gregorian, allows all to participate, 219, 220; at Chicago Euch. Congress, 222; at Cleveland Euch. Congress, 223; courses at Duquesne University, 222; courses at Louisiana State University, 222; fostered by Archbishop T. J. Walsh, 222; fostered by Bishop H. C. Boyle, 222; how lost, 221; open rhythm of, 220; the Church's supreme norm of music, 219; to be sung by congregations (Pius XI), 218
Charlemagne, 170
Charles Borromeo, St., 326
Chesterton, G. K., 92, 209; *Autobiography of*, 295
Choral worship, addressed to God, not men, 219; aim of modern papacy, 218, 219; is prayer in song, 220
"Christ," adjective, noun, 11
Christocracy, 379–388; Mystical Body basis of (Vatican Council), 381
Christocrats, 397
Christopher, St., 370
Church, Christ's work a, 13
Ciborium (Canopy), 112
Cicero, 17
Cicognani, A. G., 384; *Addresses and Sermons*, 385
Civardi, L., *A Manual of Catholic Action*, 265, 390
Clare, St., 387
Claudel, P., *Ways and Crossways*, 292
Clement I, 88; *Letter of*, 10, 11
Clement II, 86; *Epistle*, on Mystical Body, 40
Clement of Alexandria, St., 316
Cleveland, Eucharistic Congress (1935), 223; collegiate resolutions, 385
Cohausz, O., *The Priest and St. Paul*, 334
Collins, H. E., *The Church Edifice and Its Appointments*, 123
Communion, holy, effects of, in primitive

Church, 84–90; as Return-Gift, 196–197; cementing function (*illustr.*), 198; "Communion Catholics," 196; 'concorporates' Mystical Body, 199; frequency in relation to Offertory procession (*chart*), 142; frequency of, restored, 116; frequent reception in sixteenth century, 146; in New Testament, 80, 81, 84; integral part of layman's Mass (Bishop Alter), 223; integrated with sacrifice, 196–197; intrinsic relation to sacrifice, 194–197; "Mass Catholics," 196; Missal prayers before and after, 202, 203; origin of Paschal 'obligation,' 144; rarity of reception in Middle Ages, 144, 145; received daily, 138; received in homes, 138; St. Bonaventure on frequent reception, 145; St. Thomas on frequent reception, 145; Scriptural names for, 196, 197; social effects of, 79–91; symbol of union of Mystical Body, 80; ultimate meaning, purpose, 197, 199

Communism, Msgr. F. J. Sheen on Mystical Body and, 399–401

Communists, 388

Confirmation, 265–277; administered (*illustr.*), 267; administered at Ephesus by St. Paul, 271, 272; administered at Samaria by Philip, 271; and Catholic Action (Pius XI), 265; and Mystical Body, 23; and priesthood of laity, 270; and the Mystical Body (St. Aug.), 275, 276; anointing, 267, 268; as supernatural maturity, 266; 'Christian' meant 'anointed,' 268; effects of, 270, 271; laying on of hands, 268, 269; rite, anointing, 274; rite, blow on cheek, 275; rites of, 273–276; sacramental signs, 266, 267; strengthening in Mystical Body, 71; time of administering, 272

Confrey, B., *Catholic Action*, 386, 390; *Social Studies*, 386

Conscience, Egyptian, pagan, 66

Constantine, 112

Constantinople, Council of, 170

Constitution of the Apostles, The, 359

Contrition, Babylonian, pagan, 66; element of worship, 59, 60

Corinth, Church of, 10

Corpus Christi, Feast of, 116

Cram, R. A., 172

Creed, Apostles', 7, 107

Creed, Athanasian, 107

Creed of Constantinople, 107

Cronin, C., *The Christian Priesthood*, 334

Cult, Catholic, only full worship, 67; Catholic scope of, 67–76; nature, analysis, 55–64

Curley, M. J., 215

Cuthbert, Fr., *God and the Supernatural*, 78

Cyprian, St., 150, 151, 190, 201, 357, 359; letter of, 38, 39; *That Idols are not Gods*, 387, 388

Cyril of Alexandria, St., 76

Cyril of Jerusalem, St., 104; *Catechetical Instructions*, 139, 140, 282, 283

d'Ales, A., *Baptism and Confirmation*, 263, 278

Damasus, St., 234

Damian, Peter, Mass and Mystical Body, 151, 152

Daniel-Rops, 224

D'Arcy, M. C., *Jesus Christ Priest and Redeemer*, 54; *The Life of the Church*, 8, 11; *The Mass and the Redemption*, 54

Dawson, C., *Religion in the Modern State*, 389

Day, Dorothy, 386

Death, apparent, and Extreme Unction, 351; burial, offices of, 353–365; burial rite, absolution, 364; burial rite, at grave, 364; burial rite, extracts from, 361–365; burial rite, procession to church, 361; burial rite, Requiem Mass, 362, 363; Catacomb of St. Callistus (*illustr.*), 358; Christian epitaphs, 356; Christian burial places, 355; Church's attitude on cremation, 366; entrance into larger life, 359; funeral processions, 357; funerary flowers, 357; funerary rites Christianized, 356, 357; pagan attitude toward, 353, 355; pagan *columbarium* (*illustr.*), 354; papal crypt in catacombs (*illustr.*), 358; resurrection through Christ, 360; use of black for mourning, 357

de Grandmaison, L., *Lectures on the History of Religions*, 66

de la Taille, M., *The Mystery of Faith, an Outline*, 66, 193

de Puniet, J., *The Mass*, 92, 136, 193, 210

Dialogue Mass, 135; nature and scope of, 217; provided for in Missal rubrics, 225, 226; a restoration (Archbishop J. J. Glennon), 217; sanctioned by Bishop J. A. Duffy, 218; sanctioned by Holy See, 217,

218; urged by Bishop A. J. Muench, 218

Didache (*Teaching of Twelve Apostles*), 86, 87, 162, 230, 297

Didascalia Apostolorum, 57, 143, 305

Divine Office, 228–237; as joint prayer of Mystical Body (Pius XI), 234; as related to Mass (*illustr.*), 231; Christ praying for us, 236; compline, 229; compline for Sundays, 237–242; "Hours" Jewish, 229; how related to Mass, 228, 229; laity 'discovering' it, 237; Lauds, 229; league of, 245; Matins, 229; None, 229; Prime, 229; rapid spread in West, 230, 231; sext, social aspects of, 234–236; terce, 229; vespers, 229

Dix, G., *A Detection of Aumbries*, 152

Dominic, St., 387

Dominican Rite, 183

Dominicans, 146

Douglas, W., *Church Music in History and Practice*, 227

Doyle, F. X., *The Wonderful Sacraments*, 263, 278, 308, 322, 334, 351

Dread, cultual in East, 139, 140; cultual in West, 140, 141; cultual, spread by barbarian Arians, 141, 142

Duchesne, L., *Christian Worship*, 136

Duffy, J. A., 390; on dialogue Mass, 218

Duperray, J., *Christ in the Christian Life*, 26

Duquesne University, 222

Durandus, 342

Eckhoff, F. C. –(P. Parsch), *The Liturgy of the Mass*, 92, 172, 193, 210

Ellard, G., *Men at Work at Worship*, 54, 227, 245; *The Mystical Body and the American Bishops*, 227; *The Dialog Mass*, 227

Epistles (N.T.), 3

Etheria, 105

Eucharist, Holy, *see* Holy Eucharist, Mass, Communion

Eucharist, Holy, why instituted, 195

Eusebius, 233, 356, 357

Extreme Unction, administration of (*illustr.*), 338; and apparent death, 351; and major operation, 351; anointing with oil, 337; as complement of Penance, 341; compared with Confirmation, 338; doctrine, history, 336–342; effects on soul, and body (at times), 340; former names of sacrament, 342; former variety of rites, 339; "form" in Eastern Church, 347; for seriously sick only, 339; how remissive of sin, 341; place of, in Mystical Body, 73; preparation for immediate glory, 342;

promulgation of (St. James), 339; rites of, 343–350; special propriety of (St. Thomas), 337

Ferreres, J. B., *Death Real and Apparent*, 351; *The Decree on Daily Communion*, 152

Field, Christ's work a, 13

Fitzsimons, J. –(P. McGuire), *Restoring All Things*, 227

Florida, colony, 277

Fortescue, A., *The Mass*, 92, 136, 172; *Vespers for Sundays*, 245

Fortunatus, 234

Francis de Sales, St., 306

Francis of Assisi, St., 387; on priests, 324

Francis Xavier, St., 387

Fulgentius, St., 118

Furfey, P. H., *Fire on the Earth*, 386

Gasquet, A., *Sacramentals*, 378

Geddes, L. W. –(H. Thurston), *The Catholic Church and Confession*, 308

Gelasius, Pope, 164, 273, 274

Georgia, colony, 277

Glennon, J. J., on dialogue Mass, 217

Goodier, A., *The Inner Life of the Catholic*, 26, 209, 397

Gospels, Synoptic, 3

Grace, as super-soul, 36; bibliography on, 40; sanctifying, 28–38; super-faculties of, 36, 37; working of, chart, 34

Gratitude, element of worship, 58

Gregory I, Pope, St., Canon by, 184; Communion at Mass, 144; contributed to Divine Office, 234; father of Gregorian Chant, 221; High Mass of, 124–133; High Mass of, Communion for absent, 131; High Mass of, Communion for all, 132; High Mass of, entrance procession, 126; High Mass of, Offertory procession, 128; High Mass of, procession to altar, 127, 128; High Mass of, stational Church, 125; (*illustr.*), 69; introduced *Christe, eleison*, 164; *Mass Book* of, 317; on Mass and Mystical Body, 76, 77; Our Father, in Mass, 201

Gregory VII, Pope, St., 244

Gregory of Nyssa, St., 68, 331

Gregory the Wonder-worker, St., 68

Grimaud, C. –(J. F. Newcomb), "*My*" *Mass*, 209, 215; *One Only Christ*, 26, 54, 263, 366

Gruden, J. C., *The Mystical Christ*, 6, 21, 26

Guardini, R., *Sacred Signs*, 378; *The Church and the Catholic*, 11, 26, 378

Guilday, J., *Life and Times of John Carroll*, 278

Gurian, A., 381

Haering, O., *Living with the Church*, 108

Harrington, H., *The Sacrament of Penance*, 308

Hedley, J. C., *The Holy Eucharist*, 92, 152, 292

Heenan, J. C., *Priest and Penitent*, 308

Hellriegel, M. B., *Our High Mass*, 227

Hilary of Poitiers, St., 134, 141

Hippolytus, St., 138, 174, 274; *Apostolic Tradition*, 230; (*illustr.*), 175; Mass-Canon of, 186–188

Hoffman, R. J. S., *Restoration*, 390

Holy Eucharist, as font of other sacraments (*illustr.*), 281; as related to other sacraments, 280; as Sacrament, 280–288; celebrated at funerary banquets, 103; extra-sacrificial worship, 285; increases grace in soul, 287; in modern mentality, 395; "offering Communion for . . . ," how understood, 292; permanence of, 282; Real Presence originally not worshiped, 284; "Thing" and "Person," 283, 284; transubstantiation, 282; uses in sacrifice, Communion, 283; Viaticum, rite of, 288–290

Holy Orders, as described in Catechism of Trent, 323; conferring of (*illustr.*), 325; Council of Trent on institution of, 326; divine dignity of priesthood, 324; doctrine, 323–334; major, 327, 328; minor, 328; ordination by laying on of hands, 326; ordination ritual, 330–332; priesthood, episcopacy, 328; relations of priests to Mystical Body, 324; relation of various grades to Eucharist (St. Thomas), 329; ritual, anointing with oil, 331; ritual, concelebration of Mass, 332; ritual, imposing of hands, 331; ritual, investiture, 332; ritual, outline of whole, 330; ritual, peoples' veto, 330–331; social aspect of in Mystical Body, 73

Hoornaert, R., *The Breviary and the Laity*, 245

Horace, 355

Husslein, J., *The Mass of the Apostles*, 92, 152, 172

Hymn, Persian pagan, 65

Hypostatic Union, 31

Ignatius Loyola, St., *Book of the Spiritual Exercises*, 146; on frequent Communion, 146, 147

Ignatius of Antioch, St., 88–90

Ildephonse of Toledo, St., 91, 92

Incorporation, Christian, 9

Indulgences, 304

Indwelling of Christ, 33

Indwelling of God, 37, 38

Innocent III, Pope, 146, 190, 192, 202

Irenaeus, St., 50; *False Wisdom Unmasked*, 25, 26; on Mystical Body, 25, 26

Irreligion, modern, 56

Isaac Jogues, St., 105

Isidore of Seville, St., 118

Jansenism, deterrent from reception of Communion, 149

Jerome, St., 50, 68, 112, 122, 190, 201, 233, 302, 357; on abstaining from Communion, 140

John Berchmans, St., 292

John Chrysostom, St., 4, 50, 275, 317, 357; on *Agape*, 81; on 'dread' mysteries, 140; on mystery, 6; on priesthood in Mystical Body, 52, 53

John de Brebeuf, St., 105

John the Beloved, St., 102

John the Fuller, 169

Johner, D., *A New School of Gregorian Chant*, 227

Joyce, G. H., *Christian Marriage*, 322

Jungmann, J. A., *Liturgical Worship*, 54

Justin, St., 189; *Apology*, 156, 157; *Apology*, description of Mass, 84, 85

Karrer, O., *Religions of Mankind, The*, 66, 308, 367, 378

Kearney, J., *The Meaning of the Mass*, 227

Kearney, R. A., 389

Kelly, J. R. –(E. Mersch), *The Whole Christ*, 12

Kelly, P. A., *The Romance of a Priest*, 334

Kilker, A. J., *Extreme Unction*, 351

Kingdom, Christ's work a, 13

Kingship of Christ, in Divine Office, 108

Kolbe, F. C., *The Four Mysteries of the Faith*, 26, 78, 263, 334; *The Sacrament of Confirmation*, 278

Kramp, J., *Eucharistia*, 136, 152, 192, 209, 292; *The Liturgical Sacrifice*, 152, 192, 209

Lactantius, 78, 293

LaFarge, J., *Interracial Justice,* 390

Laros, M., *Confirmation in the Modern World,* 278

Lateran, Council of (1215), 144

Lattey, C., *Atonement, The,* 11, 54; *Man and Eternity,* 352, 366; *Six Sacraments,* 263, 279, 308, 322, 334, 352

Leaflet Missal, 216

Leaven, Christ's work a, 13

Leen, E., *The Holy Ghost,* 40; *The True Vine and Its Branches,* 192, 209, 292

Lefebvre, G., *Catholic Liturgy,* 192, 210, 378

Leo XIII, Pope, *Christian Marriage,* 322; Communion as union in Mystical Body, 149, 150; Encyclical on Labor, 211; *Mirae Caritatis,* 80; on frequent Communion (*Mirae Caritatis*), 149; on marriage as symbol of Incarnation, 309

Leo Great, Pope, St., 76; on Christmas and Mystical Body, 99, 100

Litanies, 107

Liturgical Arts, 123, 384

Liturgist, Christ as, 42, 43

Liturgy, corporate activity of Mystical Body, 384, 385; first rank in Catholic action (Villeneuve), 384; in New Testament, 42; meanings of, 41, 42; schematic definition, 47; to be studied for Catholic Action (Civardi), 266

Livy, 17

Loehr, A., *The Year of Our Lord,* 108

Lord, D. A., 385; *Our Part in the Mystical Body,* 27, 40, 54

Louisiana, colony, 277

Louisiana State University, 222

Lucas, H., *Holy Mass,* 123, 172, 192, 210

Lucian, St., 113

Maas, N., *The Treasure of the Liturgy,* 172, 192, 210, 378

MacMahon, M. S., *Liturgical Catechism,* 108, 172, 193, 210

Madison Square Garden, 388

Mahoney, E. J., *Christian Marriage,* 322

Manning, H. E., *The Eternal Priesthood,* 334

Maranget, P., *The Roman Mass,* 172, 193, 210

Marcus Aurelius, *Thoughts,* 61

Marmion, C., *Christ in His Mysteries,* 108; *Christ, the Life of the Soul,* 27, 172, 264, 292, 306–308, 366, 388; *Our Way and Our Life,* 108

Marriage (*illustr.*), 311; becomes Sacrament, 313; Christ's work a, 13; fountainhead of life, 310; God, third Partner, 312; "happy one prepared in youth" (Pius XI), 322; in and like the Mystical Body, 309–314; rites of, 315–320; rites of nuptial blessing, 318; title to grace by Sacrament, 313, 314

Martindale, C. C., 249; –(E. Przwara), *An Augustine Synthesis,* 65; *Compline for Sundays and Festivals,* 245; *The Faith of the Roman Church,* 37, 76; *The Last Sacraments,* 288; *Man and His Destiny,* 40, 66; *The Mind of the Missal,* 108; *Morning Prayers from the Liturgy,* 245; *The Prayers of the Missal: I, Collects,* 172; *The Sacramental System,* 78; *Wedlock,* 320–322

Maryland, colony, 277

Mass, Dialogue, *see* Dialogue Mass

Mass, holy, active participation in, 211–225; font of Christian spirit, 214, 215; as related to Calvary, 175, 176; as related to Pasch, 173, 175; Canon of, and nuptial blessing, 318; Canon of, Part I, 183; Canon of, Part II, 184–189; commemoration of the dead, 189; commemoration of living, 185; as communal oblation of service (*illustr.*), 212, 213; communal praying at (Pius XI), 211; *Communicantes* prayer, 185; Communion, crown of active participation, 223–225; Communion part of, 194–207; concelebration at ordinations, 332; Consecration, elevation, 186–187; dead, commemoration for, at, 357; description of, at Jocist Convention, 1937, 224; funeral, 362, 363; incensation at, 180–181; "incomplete without Communion" (Bishop K. J. Alter), 223; Innocent III on Mystical Body and, 190–192; *Nobis quoque* prayer, 189; offering extends through Canon, 188; offering of whole Church (*illustr.*), 177; Offertory anthem from St. Augustine, 192; Offertory prayers, 179–182; Ordinary of, Part III, 201–207; origin of Sunday obligation, 143; origin of word, 153; "Preface," 183, 184; "principal parts," how understood, 188; sacrifice of whole Mystical Body, 176; sequence and structure (*illustr.*), 160; silent participation in, deplored (Pius XI), 214; thank-offering

(*Eucharist*), 173–174; washing of hands, 181

Matrimony, social aspect of, in Mystical Body, 73

McCann, J., *The Resurrection of the Body*, 366

McFadden, J. A., 216

McGarry, W. J., *Paul and the Crucified*, 11, 27

McGuire –(J. Fitzsimons), *Restoring All Things*, 227

McLaughlin, J. B., *Purgatory*, 366

Mersch, E. –(J. Kelly), *The Whole Christ*, 11; –(D. F. Ryan), *Morality and the Mystical Body*, 12, 27

Michel, V., *Christian Social Reconstruction*, 386; *The Liturgy of the Church*, 172, 193, 210, 227, 245, 378

Minoretti, C. D., 227

Minutius, Felix, *Octavius*, 55, 79

Mishna, 174

Missal, lay use encouraged (Pius XI), 216; lay use urged by Bishop F. J. Tief, 217; use of, by laity, 215; use of, urged by Bishop J. A. McFadden, 216; Roman, on free-standing altar, 113; Roman, outline of Ante-Mass, 156, 157

Missal, Leaflet, see Leaflet Missal

Mississippi, colony, 277

Monica, St., 357

Mooney, E. A., 287

Moore, T. H., *Beyond the Altar Rail*, 172, 193, 210

Moses, 156

Muench, A. J., 218

Mundelein, G. W., 222

Murphy, J. P., *The Sacrament of Baptism*, 264

Murray, J. G., 216, 383

Myers, E., *The Mystical Body of Christ*, 27

Mystery (Sacrament), 5

Mystical Body, *Aesop's Fables* and, 16; Blessed Virgin Mary, 17; and resurrection from the dead, 360; Archbishop J. G. Murray on, 383; Archbishop J. F. Rummel on, 382; Archbishop S. A. Stritch on, 383, 384; as associated with sinner in Penance, 303; as basis of Catholic Action (Pius XI), 382; as foreshadowed by marriage, 309–314; as model of society (Pius XI), 381; Bartmann, B., on Purgatory and, 350, 351; bibliography of, 26, 27; *II Clement* on, 40; Bishop J. A.

Duffy on, 390; Bishop R. A. Kearney on, 388; Bourdaloue, L., on Baptism and, 262, 263; can prevent a Soviet America (O'Hara), 388; Christ on American sidewalks (*illustr.*), 396; Christopher Dawson on, 389; Christ's actions in, 22; Christ's headship of, 22; common prayer in Divine Office (Pius XI), 234; "concorporated" by Eucharist, 199; diagram of, 21; doctrine explained, 13–25; Encyclicals of Pius XI, and, 26; faithful figured by water in wine, 180; Holy Spirit in, 22, 23; in language of modern papacy, 381, 382; in St. Paul, 18–20; Innocent III on Mass and, 190–192; J. H. Newman on Eucharist and, 290, 291; how effected by priesthood, 324; Mediation of Christ in, 393; Msgr. F. J. Sheen on Communism and, 399–401; moral virtues and, 26; motivates *Catholic Worker* group (Day), 386; mysteriousness of, 23; offers sacrifice, 75; Peter Damian on Mass and, 151, 152; Pius XI on relations of priests to, 333–334; prays through Divine Office, 228; priesthood in, 48–51; providential doctrine of today, 287, 288; sacramental system of, 71–74; St. Athanasius on Baptism and, 249, 250; St. Augustine on, 8; St. Augustine on Confirmation and, 275, 276; St. Augustine on members at Mass, 183; St. Augustine writing on, 24; St. Catherine of Siena on Mass and, 208–209; St. Clement I, Pope, on, 10; St. Cyprian on, 38, 39; St. Ildephonse on Communion in, 91, 92; St. Irenaeus on, 25, 26; St. Robert Bellarmine on Divine Office in, 243, 244; Spanish Bishops on, 390; survey of, as in this book, 391–398; what my function is, 379, 280; worship through liturgy, 384, 385

New England, colonies, 277

New Jersey, colony, 277

New York, colony, 277; martyrs, 105

Newcomb, J. F. –(C. Grimaud), *"My" Mass*, 209, 215; *One Only Christ*, 26, 54, 263, 366

Newman, J. H., 40, 234, 240, 290, 291, 366, 398

Nicaea, Council of, 170

Oath, baptismal, 251; Roman, pagan, 66

O'Connell, W., 222

Office, Divine, *see* Divine Office

O'Hara, E. V., 227, 388
Omaha, Eucharistic Congress (1930), 214;
  Resolution of, 226
Operation, major, and Extreme Unction, 351
Optatus, St., 111
Opus Dei, see Divine Office
Order, Carthusian, 162; Dominican, 162
Orders, Holy, see Holy Orders
Origin, 201
Overproduction, 235
Ovid, 355

Pacian, St., 303
Pammachius, 357
Parsch, P. —(F. C. Eckhoff), The Liturgy
  of the Mass, 92, 172, 193, 210
Pasch and Eucharist, 173–174
Passover, see Pasch
Pater, Walter, 78
Paul, St., conversion of, 15
Paula, St., 233
Paulinus of Aquileia, St., 170
Penance, administered by Apostles, 296;
  ancient usage, 297–300; and indulgences,
  304; confession, dignity of (Pius XI),
  301, 302; doctrine, 293–304; element of
  sorrow for sin, 302, 303; gradual mitigation of strictness, 300, 301; institution of,
  296; judicial nature of, 301; medicinal, in
  Mystical Body, 72; nature of jurisdiction,
  301, 302; on exercise of whole Mystical
  Body, 303; path of jurisdiction (illustr.),
  294; public, classes of penitents, 298, 299;
  public, described (Tertullian), 297, 298;
  public, Roman system (Sozomen), 300;
  rite of, 305–306; sacrament needed, 295;
  satisfaction ("penance"), nature of, 303;
  self-accusation, 302
Pennsylvania, colony, 277
Perkins, M., At Your Ease in the Catholic
  Church, 245; Speaking of How to Pray,
  27, 40, 172, 193, 210, 264, 279, 308, 322,
  352, 378
Philip Neri, St., 146
Pius X, Pope, 17; banned paganized art
  (Cardinal O'Connell), 222; on frequent
  Communion as part of Mass, 155; on
  function of song in worship, 220; on purpose of frequent Communion, 286; pleads
  for understanding of reform aims, 219;
  revival of spirit behind chant reform, 221;
  School of liturgical music, 222
Pius XI, articulate participation in Mass
  urged by, 217; danger of relapse into
  barbarism, 287; deplores silent participation in Mass, 214; Divine Office as prayer

of Mystical Body, 234; Encyclical on the
  Catholic Priesthood, 334; Encyclical on
  Christian Marriage, 322; Encyclical on
  Christian Social Order, 211, 212; Encyclical on Priesthood, 43; Encyclicals of,
  and Mystical Body, 26; enjoins Gregorian
  chant on faithful, 218; grounds Catholic
  Action on Mystical Body, 382; (illustr.),
  383; Mystical Body, model of society,
  381; on active participation in Mass, 211;
  on active participation in worship, 92,
  135; On Atheistic Communism, 390; on
  Catholic Action in colleges, 389; on Confirmation and Catholic action, 265; on
  Feast of Christ the King, 101, 102; on
  function of feasts, 95; on lay priesthood,
  51; on permanent graces in matrimony,
  313; on prayer and economic ills, 235,
  236; on praying the Mass, 135; On the
  Reconstruction of the Social Order, 390;
  on relations of priests to Mystical Body,
  333–334; on sacrament of Penance, 302;
  on self-offering at Mass, 150, 151; on wife
  as heart of family, 314; Present Position
  of Catholic Church in German Empire,
  390; priest, "another Christ," 326; quoting Lactantius, 78; reaffirms objective of
  chant restoration, 221
Plato, Republic, 17
Pliny, 156
Plus, R., Baptism and Confirmation, 264,
  279; In Christ Jesus, 40; The Eucharist,
  292; God within Us, 27; The Ideal of
  Reparation, 308
Polycarp, St., 90, 102
Porphyrius, 111
Power, R. E., The Gift of Life, 253; God's
  Healing, 343; Marriage in Christ, 315;
  The Seal of the Spirit, 273
Prat, F., The Theology of St. Paul, 27,
  54
Pre-Mass, see Ante-Mass
Priesthood, and sacramental characters of,
  51; Christ's extension of, 50, 51; Christ's
  perpetuation of, 48, 49; lay, 50, 51; of
  Christ, 41–52; of Christ, stages in
  (illustr.), 49; of laity, and active partici-
  pation, 215; of laity, and Confirmation,
  270; of laity, Archbishop M. J. Curley
  on, 215; of laity, Archbishop J. G.
  Murray on, 216; of laity, Bishop J. H.
  Schlarmann on, 215; of laity, discussion
  topics on, 53, 54; of laity, Pius XI on,
  51

Prince, J. F. T., *Creative Revolution*, 390

Processions, Offertory, history of, 143–145; Offertory, last vestiges of, 145, 146; Rogation, 106, 107

Przwara, E. –(C. C. Martindale), *An Augustine Synthesis*, 65

Psalms, popularity of, 232–234

Purgatory, as related to Mystical Body, 350, 351

Putz, J., *My Mass,* 172, 193, 210

Relics, cult of, 105, 106

Religion, analysis of, 43, 44; natural, preserved, elevated by Christ, 394; social character of, 61

Remigius of Auxerre, description of Mass, 133–135

Rickaby, J., *The Ecclesiastical Year,* 108; *Readings from St. Augustine on the Psalms,* 245

Robert Bellarmine, St., 189; contributed to Divine Office, 234; *(Controv.),* on Divine Office in Mystical Body, 243, 244

Robertson, A., *The Interpretation of Plain Chant,* 227

Robison, W. F., *The Seven-fold Gift,* 264, 279, 308, 322, 335, 352

Ross, E. J., *Rudiments of Sociology,* 386

Roulin, A., *Vestments and Vesture,* 123

Rummel, J. F., 382

Ryan, D. F. –(E. Mersch), *Morality and the Mystical Body,* 12, 27

Sacrament (Mystery), 5

Sacramentals, blessing of aircraft, 374; blessing of automobile, 374; blessings for rural life, 375; blessing for urban life, 374; creation, irrational and sin, 367, 368; creation, irrational, emancipated, 368, 369; nature hallowed, elevated, 369, 370; nature, scope, use, 367–376; not superstitions, 370; of the home, 371, 373, 374; wide range of *(illustr.),* 372

Sacramentum, see oath, baptismal, 251

Sacrifice, 43; basically gift-giving, 75; bloody, for sin, 63; crown of worship, 61–64; defined, 61; ends in banquet, 63; oblation and immolation, 176, 178; of Christ, 46; perfection of Christian, 63; place and function of, in Mystical Body, 74–76; St. Thomas on, 74; self-dedication of, in, 75, 76

Sacrificial-mindedness, 137–151

St. Riquier, Abbey of, 106

Schlarmann, J. H., 215, 386

Schlüter-Hermkes, M. –(E. R. Smothers), *The Family,* 322

Schmidt, A. G., *The Ceremonies of Ordination,* 335

Scholastica, St., 387

Schrembs, J., 223

Scotus, Duns, 342

Sedulius, 234

Seligenstadt, Council of, 207

Sertillanges, A. D., *The Church,* 66, 78

Sheed, F. J., *A Map of Life,* 27, 40, 193, 366

Sheen, F. J., *The Life of All Living,* 40; on Mystical Body and Communism, 399–401

Smith, G. D., *The Sacrament of the Eucharist,* 292

Smothers, E. R. –(M. Schlüter-Hermkes), *The Family,* 322

Society, economic division of, 235

Sodality of Blessed Virgin, 385

Sozomen, 300

Stanbrook, Nuns of, *The Day Hours of the Church,* 245; *The Roman Breviary,* 245

Stephen, St., 105; Protomartyr, 327

Stephen I, Pope, St., 123

Steuart, R. H. J., *The Inward Vision,* 352, 392

Strabo, Walafrid, Mystical Body worshiping, 119, 122, 123

Stratmann, F., *The Church and War,* 390

Stritch, S. A., 383, 384

Super-sacrament (Church), 10

Sylvester, Pope, St., 122, 123

Symmachus, Pope, St., 165

Synagogue, building, service, 155; floor plan *(illustr.),* 154

Synesius, 378

Tanquerey, A., *The Spiritual Life,* 27, 40, 108

Taille, de la, *see* de la Taille

Teaching of Twelve Apostles (Didache), 156, 162, 230, 297

Terry, R. R., *The Music of the Roman Rite,* 227

Tertullian, 54, 67, 79, 85, 86, 138, 201, 252, 297, 298, 313, 314, 316, 317

Theatines, 146

Theophilus, St., 268

Theresa of Avila, St., 387

Thérèse of Lisieux, St., 387

Thomas, St., on characters of lay priesthood, 51

Thomas Aquinas, St., 30; contributed to Divine Office, 234; on chief effect of Extreme Unction, 341; on Church Year, 95; on Confirmation and lay priesthood, 270; on Confirmation as maturity, 266; on Easter and Mystical Body, 101; on effects of Christ's Sacrifice on the Mystical Body, 75; on effects of Communion, 286, 287; on effects of grace in marriage, 314; on equality of sacrificing priesthood, 329; on Extreme Unction and immediate glory, 342; on frequent Communion, 145; on gifts of union in Mass, 194, 195; on holiness of priesthood, 326; on internal self-oblation at Mass, 180; on need of sacrifice, 61; on propriety of Extreme Unction, 337; on relation of various orders to Eucharist, 329; on sacrifice, 74; unity of Mystical Body by Communion, 199

Thorold, A., *The Mass and the Life of Prayer*, 404

Thurston, H., *Lent and Holy Week*, 299; –(L. W. Geddes), *The Catholic Church and Confession*, 308

Tief, F. J., 217

Toner, P. J., *Extreme Unction*, 352

Towers, E., *Sanctifying Grace*, 40

Trajan, 156

Trent, Council of, effect of Communion, 80; Mass Book of, 200; on Canon of the Mass, 184, 185; on conditional healing effect of Extreme Unction, 341; on Extreme Unction as "complement of Penance," 341; on frequent, daily, Communion, 147, 148; on grace, 29, 32, 35; on institution of Holy Orders, 326; on judicial character of Penance, 301; on love as fruit of Communion, 203; on Mass as holiest work of faithful, 178; on need of ceremonial, 60; on nature and value of our satisfaction, 304; on Penance, 296; on sanctification by marriage, 313; on temptations of deathbed, 336; on water mixed with wine, 179, 180; on rationale of Eucharist, 195; quoting St. Jerome on Confession, 302

Unction, Extreme, *see* Extreme Unction

Underhill, E., *Worship*, 226

Undset, S., *Stages on the Road*, 322

Urban IV, Pope, 286

Urban VIII, Pope, 153

Valens, Emperor, 235

Vatican, Council of the (1869–70), 381

Vermeersch, A., *What is Marriage*, 322

Vestments, sacred, 116; alb, 117; amice, 116; chasuble, 118, 121; classical antecedents of (*illustr.*), 120, 121; dalmatic, 117; maniple, 117; maniple (*illustr.*), 126; ninth-century (*illustr.*), 127; sacred, *paenula*, 118; sacred, stole, 117, 118; sacred, tunic, 117

Vienne, Council of, 320

Villeneuve, R., Card., 384

Vincent de Paul, St., 387

Virgil, 355

Virginia, colony, 277

von le Fort, G., *Hymns to the Church*, 365

von Nell-Breuning, O., *Reorganization of the Social Order*, 390

Vonier, A., *Death and Judgment*, 366; *A Key to the Doctrine of the Eucharist*, 292

Walsh, M. E., *The Saints and Social Work*, 387

Walsh, P. J., 222

Ward, Justine B., 227

Ward, M., *Insurrection vs. Resurrection*, 390

Watkin, E. I., *The Catholic Centre*, 12, 245

Webb, G., *The Liturgical Altar*, 123

Weller, P. T., *Roman Ritual*, 378

"Wheat of God," St. Ignatius, M., 89

White, C. D., 196, 214

Wine (and bread), elements of sacrifice, 75

Worship, Choral, *see* choral worship

Worship, corporate, dictate of nature, 393

Wust, P., "The Crisis in the West," 56

Xenophon, 17

Year, liturgical, 93–106; chart (*illustr.*), 96, 97; Christmas cycle, 99; cycles of, 98; dominical cycle of, 102; feasts of martyrs, 102; funerary banquets, 102; kingship cycle of, 101; paschal cycle of, 100; pedagogy of, 94, 95; a prism of faith, 95, 96

Zeno of Verona, St., 141

Zundel, M., *The Splendour of the Liturgy*, 193, 210

PASSAGES OF HOLY WRIT

PAGE

Genesis
ii, 24   191, 310
iv, 4   188
xiv, 18   188
xxii   188

Exodus
xx, 2   58
xxv, 10   190
xxx, 10   163

Leviticus
xvi, 12   163

Deuteronomy
iv, 7   378

Ruth
ii, 4   163

II Esdras
viii, 5   168

Job
xii, 12   188

Psalms
i, 4   161
iv   238, 239
viii   59
viii, 6   30, 263
xv, 5   327
xviii, 3   231
xxi, 2   236
xxii, 5   187
xxv, 6–12   181–182
xlii, 1–6   161
xlix, 23   244
lxvii, 36   98
lxxxii, 19   165
lxxxiii, 5   243
lxxxiv, 7, 8   163
xc   239, 240
xciv   58

PAGE

ci, 2   163
cv, 1   58
cix, 1   164
cix, 4   164
cx, 1   179
cxiv   59
cxv   60
cxv, 12, 13   204
cxv, 13   188, 203
cxviii, 62   232
cxviii, 164   232
cxxix   60, 361
cxxxiii   240
cxxxv   174
cxl, 2–4   181
cl, 2   44

Wisdom
viii, 1   336

Ecclesiasticus
iii, 12, 15   53
xxii, 10, 11   359
xxxiii, 7–10   94
xxxiii, 10   93

Isaias
i, 6   337
vi, 3   184
vi, 6   168
xi, 23   273, 274
liii, 7, 8   202
lvi, 7   243

Jeremias
xiv, 9   241

Daniel
iii, 39, 40   180
vii, 9   29

Osee
xi, 4   370

PAGE

Malachy
i, 10   51
i, 11   86

I Machabees
xii, 11   185

Matthew
iii   308
iii, 13–17   247
iv, 23   153
v, 23   203
v, 44   388
vi, 9–13   201
vii, 16   379
viii, 6   141
viii, 8   204
ix   293, 295
ix, 15   13
x, 24   293
xi, 28, 29   100
xiii   13
xiii, 33   13
xvi, 18   13, 20, 203
xviii   293, 296
xviii, 20   13
xxiii, 19   110
xxiii, 23   122
xxv   122
xxv, 36   39
xxv, 40   13, 387
xxvi, 26   137, 195
xxvii, 20   134
xxviii, 18–20   249
xxviii, 20   13

Mark
i   308
vi, 12, 13   337
vii, 32–36   259
xi, 9, 10   184
xvii   295

	PAGE
Luke	
i, 23	42
i, 68–79	364
i, 78	113
ii, 4	164, 165
ii, 29–32	242
iii, 8	304
iv, 16	171
iv, 16–21	166, 167
iv, 18	167
vii	293
ix	293
ix, 23	307
x, 34	336, 337
xi, 2–4	201
xi, 3	280
xv, 4	293
xix, 6	141
xxii, 14–20	168, 169
xxiv, 49	269
xxxi, 19	133
John	
i, 3	31
i, 4–16	7
i, 5	102
i, 14	13, 31
i, 16	31
i, 29	165, 174, 202, 204
i, 51	52, 394
iii, 2	71
iii, 5	246
iii, 5–7	249
iii, 13	191
iii, 22–26	249
iv	293
iv, 1, 2	249
iv, 23	48
iv, 24	388
vi, 51	201
vi, 54–58	72
vi, 56	197
vi, 57	152, 191, 197
vi, 58	195
viii	293
viii, 36	25
viii, 46	45
x, 10	32, 197
x, 11–18	15
xi, 21–27	363
xi, 25	359
xiii, 35	79
xiv, 6	391

	PAGE
xiv, 16	269
xiv, 23	37
xiv, 26	13
xiv, 27	202
xv, 5	15, 29, 147, 391
xv, 16	9, 327
xvii, 4	50
xvii, 20, 21	192
xvii, 23–26	7
xix, 34	179
xx, 19	101, 203
xx, 21, 22	296
Acts of the Apostles	
ii, 15	230
ii, 37, 38	249
ii, 42	79, 80, 150
ii, 46	81
iii, 1	230
iv, 12	371
iv, 32	80, 150, 215
v	296
viii, 12–19	271
viii, 27	374
viii, 32, 33	202
ix, 4	65, 77
x, 9	230
xiii, 2	42, 331
xiii, 15	157, 158
xiii, 27	156
xv, 21	156
xvii, 26, 27	55
xvii, 27	393
xvii, 28	37, 304
xix, 2–7	272
xx, 7	81
xx, 11	81
xxvi, 14–18	15
Romans	
i, 19	58
ii, 14, 15	58
iii, 3–5	250
iv, 25	46, 296
v, 5	397
v, 10	304
vi, 4	51
vi, 8	23
vi, 9	77
vi, 11	23
vi, 23	62
viii, 11	360
viii, 16	270

	PAGE
viii, 17	304
viii, 19–22	368
viii, 20	376
viii, 21	367
viii, 23	23
viii, 26	37, 270
viii, 30, 31	190
ix, 4	391
xi, 17–24	36
xi, 24	16
xi, 26	51
xi, 33	32
xii, 1	150
xii, 4	18
xii, 4–11	26
xii, 5	88
xvi, 25, 26	5
I Corinthians	
i, 31	304
ii, 3	195
ii, 6	3
iii, 1	3
iii, 2	1
iii, 9	16
iii, 16	37, 38, 250, 270
iii, 18	23
iii, 23	8
iii, 32	367
iv, 1	166, 323, 333
iv, 2	166
v	296
v, 7	16
vi, 9	16
vi, 10	295
vi, 15	101
vi, 15–19	26
vi, 15–20	32
vi, 19	23
vi, 20	100, 101
vii, 7	219
x	196
x, 11	174
x, 12	190
x, 13	271
x, 14–16	80
x, 14–22	26
x, 17	92, 150, 151
	196, 223
x, 17 variant	199
x, 17, 18	194
x, 21	112
x, 31	371

PAGE

xi 196
xi, 2 173
xi, 3 148
xi, 17 88
xi, 17–34 81, 82, 84
xi, 20 286
xi, 24 195
xi, 24, 25 205
xi, 26 124, 195
xi, 33 218
xii, 4–11 26
xii, 12 18
xii, 13 270
xii, 12–27 18, 19, 251
xii, 13 9, 23
xii, 26 26, 38, 380
xii, 27 18, 91
xiii 88
xiii, 4–7 11
xiii, 11–12 2
xiv, 15 213
xiv, 16 211
xiv, 16, 17 214
xv, 19 365
xv, 20–24 360
xv, 24 176
xv, 31 306
xvi, 1 157

II Corinthians

i, 22 270
ii 296
iii, 5 304
iv, 10 51, 397
iv, 14 360
v, 14 381
v, 17–19 295
vi, 6 216
vi, 15 32
vi, 16 134
xi, 29 38
xiii, 3 23

Galatians

i, 11–12 16
ii, 20 38, 260, 392
iii, 20 18
iii, 27 39
iii, 28 20, 26
iii, 29 386
v, 24 32, 51
vi, 15 32

PAGE

Ephesians

i, 5 9
i, 6 31
i, 8–10 48
i, 10 381
i, 14 251
i, 22, 23 18, 263
i, 23 25, 398
ii, 10 380
ii, 13, 19 9
ii, 13 18
ii, 19 9, 26
ii, 20–22 22
ii, 22 23
iii, 6 23
iii, 8 32
iii, 12 138
iii, 16 265, 350
iii, 20 397
iv, 3 191
iv, 3–6 20
iv, 4 26, 101
iv, 4–6 10, 88
iv, 12 13, 48
iv, 12, 13 9
iv, 13 25, 380
iv, 14, 15 9
iv, 15 29
iv, 25 26
iv, 30 251
v, 2 45, 180
v, 5 37
v, 18, 19 220
v, 22–32 26, 309, 310
v, 23 16, 236
v, 25, 26 20
v, 27 379, 387
v, 32 6, 191

Philippians

i, 20–21 359
i, 21 18
ii, 7, 8 236
ii, 8, 9 48
ii, 12 397
iii, 9 32
iii, 9–14 398
iii, 10 32, 308
iii, 21 23
iv, 3 304
iv, 7 101

PAGE

Colossians

i, 9, 10 31
i, 9–14 34
i, 12 395
i, 15–19 22
i, 15–20 368
i, 17 394
i, 18 64
i, 24 77, 305, 306
i, 24–28 5
i, 28 324, 398
ii, 7 23
ii, 9 31
ii, 9, 10 28
ii, 13 23
ii, 18–19 22
iii, 1 165
iii, 9–11 26
iii, 10, 11 387
iii, 11 18, 20, 23, 393
iii, 15 26
iii, 16 156, 228
iii, 19 392

I Thessalonians

i, 9 179, 185
iv, 12–17 362
iv, 13 353

I Timothy

ii, 5 48, 64, 109, 183, 393
iii, 9 187
iv, 4 375
v 296
vi, 16 70

II Timothy

i, 12 351, 356
i, 14 285
ii, 1 157

Titus

ii, 13 351

Hebrews

i, 1 70
ii, 3 161
ii, 10–18 45
iv, 15 45
v 165
v, 1 46, 51, 326
v, 1–11 166, 167

	PAGE		PAGE		PAGE
v, 4–6	46	v, 14, 15	339	ii, 2	306
v, 10	45, 48			ii, 27	270
v, 11–14	2	*I Peter*		iii, 2	30
v, 12	3	i, 23	71	iii, 9	32
vi, 1	2	ii, 5, 6	52	v, 11, 12	67, 70
vii, 24	167	ii, 9	50, 51, 216		
vii, 24–28	42	ii, 10	355	*II John*	
vii, 25	52, 64	ii, 14	157	3	165
vii, 27	179	v, 8, 9	237		
viii, 1, 2	41			*Apocalypse*	
viii, 1–6	42	*II Peter*		i, 6	50
ix, 15	48	i, 4	30, 51	ii, 1	126
ix, 22	62	ii, 10	102	iv, 8	184
xii, 1	99	iii, 16	6	iv, 10	50
xii, 12, 14	179			v, 12	46
xiii, 10	109	*I John*		vi, 9	105
xiii, 17	326	i, 1	71	viii, 3	180, 188
		i, 1–3	7	xvii, 15	179
James		i, 8, 9	296	xxi, 6	397
iv	296	ii, 1	293		

30484

282
E14